THE MEDIEVAL ABBEYS AND PRIORIES OF ENGLAND AND WALES:

A RESOURCE GUIDE

Roland W. Morant

The picture shown on the cover is that of Snaith parish church, formerly a cell of Selby abbey.

Printed in Victoria, Canada

Note for Librarians: a cataloguing record for this book that includes Dewey Classification and US Library of Congress numbers is available from the National Library of Canada. The complete cataloguing record can be obtained from the National Library's online database at:
www.nlc-bnc.ca/amicus/index-e.html
ISBN 1-4120-2604-0

TRAFFORD

This book was published on-demand in cooperation with Trafford Publishing.
On-demand publishing is a unique process and service of making a book available for retail sale to the public taking advantage of on-demand manufacturing and Internet marketing. On-demand publishing includes promotions, retail sales, manufacturing, order fulfilment, accounting and collecting royalties on behalf of the author.

Suite 6E, 2333 Government St., Victoria, B.C. V8T 4P4, CANADA
Phone 250-383-6864   Toll-free 1-888-232-4444 (Canada & US)
Fax 250-383-6804   E-mail sales@trafford.com   Web site www.trafford.com
TRAFFORD PUBLISHING IS A DIVISION OF TRAFFORD HOLDINGS LTD.
Trafford Catalogue #04-0432   www.trafford.com/robots/04-0432.html

10   9   8   7   6   5   4   3   2

"O All ye Works of the Lord, bless ye the Lord: praise Him and magnify Him for ever"   *Benedicite Omnia Opera*

By the same author

Cheshire Churches
The Monastic Gatehouse
Monastic and Collegiate Cheshire
Owston and its Abbey

TYPICAL GROUND-PLAN OF A MEDIEVAL MONASTERY

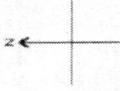

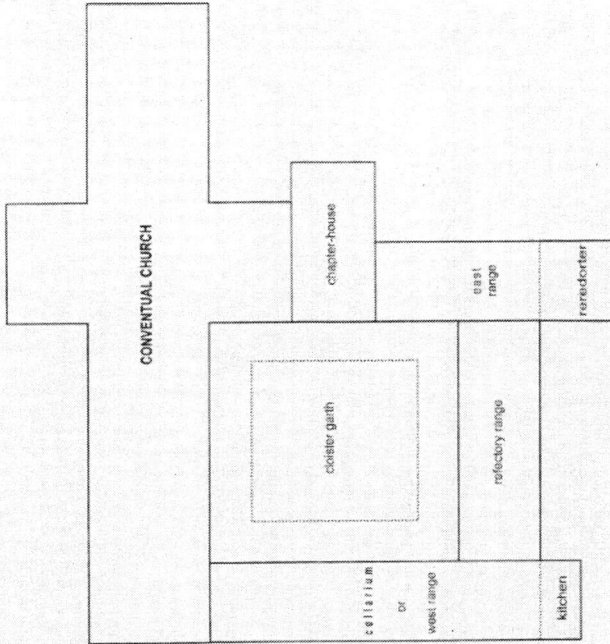

N

CONVENTUAL CHURCH

chapter-house

east range

reredorter

cloister garth

refectory range

collarium or west range

kitchen

THE CONVENTUAL CHURCH

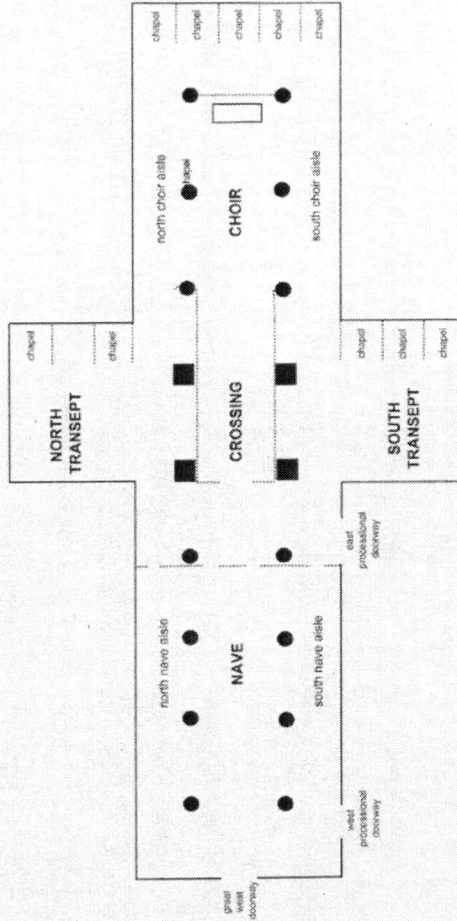

NORTH TRANSEPT

SOUTH TRANSEPT

CROSSING

CHOIR

north choir aisle

south choir aisle

chapel

NAVE

north nave aisle

south nave aisle

west processional doorway

great west doorway

east processional doorway

chapel

Foreword

Before the Dissolution of the monasteries, there were in round terms about one thousand abbeys and priories in England and Wales . By the end of the year 1540 all these houses had been closed and their occupants dispersed. It was not long afterwards that many of the buildings were dismantled and their contents destroyed or sold.

Notwithstanding this bleak picture, we are left with a residue of perhaps several hundred monastic sites which today display substantial remains of one kind or another. On some sites there are intact but isolated buildings (such as a refectory or chapter- house) or even groups of buildings that continue to envelop the original cloister-garth; while many other buildings are roofless but otherwise intact (for instance at Fountains abbey).

It is also true that although many of the contents of monastic houses were wantonly destroyed, some did survive for a variety of reasons - frequently because they were sold or given away, or because some items were required by local parishioners who had acquired the conventual church. Some such contents which included diverse items such as fonts, pulpits or screens were often dispersed over a wide area and are now not always easy to track down.

The aim of this Resource Guide is to assemble within one volume as much information as possible involving all these surviving buildings and smaller artefacts. The Guide is targeted both at researchers from a variety of disciplines (historical, archaeological, architectural etc.) as well as at enthusiasts who wish to locate items of particular personal interest. For practical reasons the distinction is made here between on the one hand items of all kinds that are intact or reasonably so, and on the other, those that are fragmentary or barely recognisable. The former are listed, and the latter apart from a few exceptions, are not. As far as the author is aware, no comprehensive guide bringing all this data together has been compiled.

The Introduction states this aim and summarises the existing sources of written information which are currently available to researchers. This is followed by a Directory of Monastic Sites which lists all the religious houses where significant remains are to be found. .It gives under each house named in the Directory its grid reference and brief details of site accessibility, and provides numerical references to the ensuing sections of the book, thus enabling the reader to find the locations of surviving physical remains and artefacts. To facilitate cross-referencing, the sites are listed by historic counties and religious orders as well as alphabetically.

The remainder of the Guide consists of twenty sections summarising these remains and artefacts. The first sixteen are ordered on the traditional precinct layout, these being:-

1. Chapels & churches provided for lay people
2. The precinct boundaries
3. Conventual churches
4. Choirs, chapels & crypts

5. Naves, transepts, porches, crossings & towers
6. Screens
7. Other fittings, fixtures & furnishings 1. (i.e. altars, fonts, lecterns & pulpits)
8. Other fittings, fixtures & furnishings 2. (i.e. piscinas, aumbries & sedilia)
9. Other fittings, fixtures & furnishings 3. (i.e. stalls, canopies, misericords, thrones & seats, pavements, stained glass, paintings, statuary & sculpture)
10. Chantries, shrines & tombs
11. Cloisters
12. Dormitory ranges 1. (mainly vestibules, chapter-houses, sacristries, slypes etc.)
13. Dormitory ranges 2. (mainly nightstairs, daystairs, reredorters, warming houses etc.)
14. Refectory ranges
15. Cellar ranges
16. Little cloisters & infirmary buildings.

Section 17 lists a number of monastic properties found chiefly outside the precinct (such as barns, manor-houses & granges). In Section 18, Miscellaneous, are included other rare, special or unusual items of interest, many of which do not logically fit into one of the earlier sections. Also placed here is a list of other monastic buildings which though conventual, are difficult to interpret within the normal claustral context.

Section 19 identifies the best surviving monastic sites, each considered as a whole and identified in terms of belonging to one or other named religious order. Lastly, Section 20 brings together in a summary those individual ranges which survive around the cloister, some in combination with a surviving conventual church

♦♦♦♦♦♦♦♦♦♦♦♦♦♦♦♦

Contents

Section 3:
CONVENTUAL CHURCHES

Section 4:
CHOIRS, CHAPELS & CRYPTS

♦♦♦♦♦♦♦♦♦♦♦♦♦♦♦

Photographic Illustrations

15/4 Battle abbey, west range (abbot's lodging) to west

16/2 Woodspring priory, infirmary to north

17/1 Hurley priory, monastic barn

18/1 Maplestead commandery, conventual church with round nave

19/4 Mount Grace charterhouse, view across great cloister garth to south west

20/9 St. Anthony-in-Roseland, view of Place House to south, with steeple of conventual church peeping over the top

◆◆◆◆◆◆◆◆◆◆◆◆◆◆◆◆

INTRODUCTION

EXISTING SOURCES OF INFORMATION

We now need to ask what work has been accomplished in recent years to identify and list those monastic sites which continue to retain and exhibit substantial observable artefacts. At the *lowest level of specificity* the number of writers who have addressed this need is small. **David Knowles & R. Neville Hadcock** in **'Medieval Religious Houses, England and Wales' (London: Longman, 1953)** provided the first comprehensive list of all the religious houses and hospitals. They also indicated against the names of individual monasteries and hospitals basic information on residual remains. This information was restricted to marking the houses in terms of the following categories:-

    * *In charge of the Commissioner of Works or on Crown Property*
       (e.g. Rievaulx abbey, Westminster abbey)
    ¶ *Scheduled as an Ancient Monument*
       (e.g. Kenilworth abbey, Winchelsea friary)
    † *Church or part(s) of Church in ecclesiastical use*
       (e.g. York Holy Trinity priory, Hamble priory)
    § *Remains of importance, sometimes private, or incorporated in mansions or farms, and not necessarily open to the public*
       (e.g. Horsham St. Faith priory, Woodspring priory)

1

The reader is therefore pointed in a given direction by one or more of these symbols. This information though does not indicate what may be found at a particular site.

This brings us to a gazetteer of monasteries entitled **'English Mediaeval Monasteries 1066-1540' (London: Heinemann, 1979) by Roy Midmer**. The work, we should note, excludes Welsh houses of all kinds, alien priories unless made denizen and almost every military establishment. We find that under each named house appears the heading *Remains* which briefly states what may (or may not) be found there. Although under the Remains of most houses Midmer tersely states 'None', in a number of others he does offer a brief description (often acknowledging his source to be Pevsner). His information is also helpful in affording a useful starting point for investigation. This example is typical of the amount of detail that Midmer gives: *Hereford Franciscan friary - Remains: Some parts of the w. range of the cloister are in Widemarsh Street. Also the beautiful 14th C. preaching cross, the only surviving example of a friars pulpit in England. Part of the ch. and S. walk of the cloister were excavated in 1958 in advance of new developments (p.163).*

The next writer to list the houses (in England, Scotland and Wales) was **Frank Bottomley** in **'The Abbey Explorer's Guide'(London: Kaye & Ward, 1981)**. His comprehensive Gazetteer (which follows a Glossary) indicates under each named house a brief description and account of remains, e.g. *Forde abbey: Church entirely destroyed; some domestic quarters survive in C17 mansion including chapter-house, frater, dorter, kitchen (p.211).*

Bottomley's Gazetteer is also useful in providing three additional pieces of information for each site: The first consists of a four-figure grid reference number (e.g. *Margam abbey 8086, Polesworth abbey 2602*). The second is availability of access utilising the following categories:

+ *(part of) church open to public*
  (e.g. Ewenny priory, Malton priory)
§ *in private ownership, not usually accessible*
  (e.g. Combe abbey, Syon abbey)
DE *in care of Department of Environment* (now English Heritage)
  (e.g. Buildwas abbey, Leiston abbey)
NT *owned by National Trust*
  (e.g. Hailes abbey, Lacock abbey)
AM *listed Ancient Monument (not necessarily implying free access)*
  (e.g. Prittlewell priory, Tupholme abbey).

The third piece of information provided by Bottomley is the classification of the site in terms of five grades, viz:-

A *First rate example, substantially complete*
  (e.g. Durham cathedral-priory, Gloucester abbey*)
B *Considerable and interesting remains*
  (e.g. Chester abbey*, Finchale priory)
C *Well worth a visit*
  (e.g. Shrewsbury abbey, Worksop priory)
D *Modest remains*
  (e.g. Monmouth priory, Strata Florida abbey)
E *Little surviving.*
  (e.g. Meaux abbey, Louth Park abbey).

* now cathedral

The problem of classifying monastic sites in this way is that the grades can be entirely misleading, not least because the criteria adopted by the author are highly subjective and do not appear to be reflected by equal increments on the 5-point alphabetic scale.   Having said this, the grid references are very useful, and information regarding accessibility may often prevent wasted journeys.

Another book which also summarises the main points of generalised interest to visitors of abbey sites only is **'A Guide to the Abbeys of England and Wales' (London: Constable, 1985)** by **Anthony New**. This information is given under six headings with appropriate categories for each abbey site, viz:-

architecture	**o** moderately important	
	oo of particular importance	
setting	I poor	
	o attractive	
	oo specially fine	
guide	**o** leaflet available	
	oo book available	
restrictions	I limited times of access	
	II no public access	
	III exterior not visible to public	
accessibility	I physically difficult	
extent	**o** considerable remains	
	oo unusually complete	
	ooo 'live' community	
	I little to be seen above ground	
	II exact site uncertain	

(Example: Cleeve abbey - architecture **o**, setting **o**, guide **oo**, restrictions nil, accessibility nil, extent **oo**)
In addition, National Grid 6-figure reference numbers are also given for each site.

What other sources of information are available to the observer? At *an intermediate level of specificity* there are five main sources of which all their publications are organised and issued on a geographical basis. These sources are:-

1. the **Victoria County History Series published by the Oxford University Press on behalf of the University of London Institute of Historical Research**,
2. the **Buildings of England and Buildings of Wales Series (Pevsner Architectural Guides) originally published by Penguin Books and now Yale University**,
3. the **Royal Commission on Ancient and Historical Monuments**,
4. the **Royal Commission on the Ancient and Historical Monuments of Wales**, and
3. the **Arthur Mee King's England and Queen's Wales Series published by Hodder and Stoughton.**

The Victoria County History which addresses each county in turn, places the history of religious houses in one of perhaps six or seven volumes and this makes the relevant data easier to find. However, the descriptions of surviving buildings of individual houses are brief and normally do not supply anything like the architectural or archaeological detail that may be wanted.

Pevsner's Architectural Guides are, of course, in a category of their own. Especially in their more recent editions, they provide a wealth of detail on most, if not all, the monastic houses. As Guides have not yet been published on some of the Welsh counties and a number of the earlier English Guides have not yet been republished, it is not yet possible to say that an architectural description of every monastery is available, although this gap will obviously be narrowed within the next few years.

The publications of the Royal Commissions both for England and Wales, though like those of the Victoria County History series normally reflect geographical interests, tend to be more selective in the types of buildings, archaeological sites etc. reported on.

Arthur Mee's volumes on individual counties are aimed at general readers with a taste for topography and local history. They do not purport to provide weighty historical material for the research scholar. They should however not be disregarded or written off. In following up a particular line of inquiry these county volumes are always worth referring to, not only because the reader may have his attention drawn to a topic about which he was ignorant, but also because he may come across that elusive piece of information missing from one of the more serious historical or architectural publications.

Perhaps at this level we should include a small number of books which track the architectural remains of houses of one or other monastic order. Two instances come to mind. One is **A.R.Martin's** 'Franciscan Architecture in England' (Manchester: The University Press, 1937); the other is the recently published 'Traces of the Templars' (Rotherham: The King's England Press, 2000) by George F. Tull.

At *the highest level of specificity* we may place the **learned historical, archaeological and architectural journals,** all containing articles written about individual houses, and which can usually be tracked down in public or educational libraries if not obtained through purchase. Though many such articles are recent, quite a number of the original investigations took place as long as a hundred or more years ago and their reports still afford valid starting points for present day researchers. Indeed these articles, old and new, are not infrequently the only detailed site descriptions that may be consulted today. It hardly needs saying that these journals contain a wealth of valid material.

Much the same may be said about the highly informative **booklets published by English Heritage, CADW and** (to a lesser extent) **the National Trust written about particular monastic houses..** Like the journals, many booklets published by these national bodies undoubtedly contain invaluable detailed archaeological and architectural descriptions of monastic sites. A bonus is that having to cater for the interests of a great visiting public to their historic sites, they regularly need to update such publications

Finally, there are a number of full-scale **books and monographs** written about individual houses, these being somewhat of a mixed bag. All of them tend to include full accounts of their histories, and most are informative of the development of their buildings. But some are far more detailed than others in their architectural or archaeological detail. So we must not assume that because a book has been written about a particular abbey or priory, it will contain the detail required by many readers. Two instances of publications meeting these architectural and/or archaeological requirements are **J. Patrick Greene**'s **'Norton Priory, the archaeology of a medieval religious house' (Cambridge: Cambridge University Press, 1989)** and a monograph listed under the general joint authorship of **The Royal Commission on the Ancient and Historical Monuments of Wales & the Dean and Chapter of Brecon Cathedral (ed. D. Walker)**, namely **'An architectural study of the Cathedral Church of St. John the Evangelist, Brecon' (Brecon: Friends of Brecon Cathedral, 1994).**

Apart from the fact that many of these publications are out of print, we should bear in mind that a great number of individual religious houses have not received specific authorship let alone detailed archaeological investigation.
It often happens that before such publications that are available or in print can be drawn on, it is necessary first to acquire some basic data on a given topic. It is within this context that this Guide has been assembled.

8

PURPOSE OF THIS RESOURCE GUIDE

Granted that these sources of information are diffuse, frequently inadequate in their detail, and often difficult to access or find, this Guide has been written for the purpose of bringing together in one volume much of this basic data.

To illustrate how the Guide may be used, we will take monastic refectories or fraters as an example. Suppose the reader wants to know how many buildings of this type have survived and in what condition they are, the basic information can be obtained from the appropriate Section in the Guide. It is of course true that the surviving identifiable refectories vary enormously in their present condition. Some consist of roofed buildings (as at Dover priory or Worcester cathedral-priory) that appear to look much as they did before the Dissolution. Others are high-standing roofless buildings (such as at Fountains abbey or Leiston abbey), ruins which convey almost as much of their original appearance to the observer as those that are intact. Apart from these, there are other remains of refectories varying from crags of masonry to low inarticulate ruins or a few tooled stones in the grass.

In this Resource Guide a line has been drawn between on the one hand those architectural artefacts which are intact or in good condition (the latter including high-standing ruins) or possess some other noteworthy quality, and on the other hand those other artefacts which do not meet these criteria of substantiveness or special interest.

The reasons for making this distinction resulting in inclusion or exclusion are twofold: Firstly it is a matter of practicality. Many of the monastic sites are privately owned and/or have not been (properly) excavated. It may therefore not be certain as to what may be found at a particular site. Yet there is a second and more important reason for including some artefacts and excluding others. The Guide seeks to highlight all those remains or remnants that are readily identifiable and are reasonably intact and which display features that were present before the Dissolution. If an observer wishes to see a refectory more or less as it was in the days of the monks or nuns, that building will be listed in the Resource Guide.

SOME TERMS USED IN THE GUIDE

Some of the well-known writers (e.g. Pevsner) in describing a particular building or other artefact do not always make it clear to the reader its condition. Is it intact? Is it a ruin? Or is its description what it was like before it was demolished?

The meaning of the term, 'intact'
This term is much used in the Guide. It indicates that a particular building is not ruined; it also means that a smaller artefact (such as a font) has not been destroyed and is recognisable as such (though it may be worn or weathered). To list an artefact as being intact does not preclude that it may have been remodelled or repaired (but not completely rebuilt or reconstructed) since the Dissolution.

The meaning of the term, 'high-standing ruin'

Many medieval buildings survive in a roofless but otherwise intact condition. They are described here as high-standing ruins. The term also applies to buildings where most (or many) of the walls stand to the eaves or gables.

Other terminology

Choir: This is taken here to mean the eastern wing of a conventual church, that is, the structure beyond the crossing or where there is no crossing, the structure immediately to the east of the nave. The term **quire** is used to mean that part of the choir, crossing or nave which accommodated the monks, canons or nuns while undertaking their religious services. Usually, the quire has to its east (also in the nave, crossing or choir) the presbytery (or open space) and sanctuary (in which is placed the high altar).

Nave and aisles: The nave is the western wing of a conventual church, that is, the structure beyond the crossing or where there is no crossing, the structure immediately to the west of the choir. Like the choir it may be aisleless; alternatively it may consist of two or more aisles (hence the terms: north nave aisle, south choir aisle, central or main nave aisle etc.).

Bay structure: The division of choir, nave and transepts is usually marked by arcade arches or windows. In the absence of such normally reliable evidence, occasionally the roof has to be examined in order to ascertain the number of bays. Individual bays of choir and nave are identified by numbering them from the east; thus the nave bay immediately to the west of the crossing is Bay 1. Transept bays are numbered from north or south; thus Bay

1 of a south transept is at its north end and adjacent to the crossing arch on the south side of the church.

ORGANISATION OF DATA

The information has been listed in Sections which correspond with the traditional layout of a monastic precinct, that is with the domestic buildings or living quarters of the monks or nuns arranged round a cloister on the south side of the conventual church, the whole area being surrounded and protected by a precinct-wall punctuated by gatehouses.

Of course many houses did not fit this standard plan. Thus where a refectory (using our earlier illustration) was placed less usually on the north side of a north cloister (as at Chester), this exception is noted. Or take warming houses as another example. In most houses they were usually placed in the east range and this arrangement is assumed to be the norm in this Guide. However in Cistercian and related houses they were placed next to the refectory in the south (or north) range and this exception is duly noted. Locations which are not normal are always indicated in the text.

NOMENCLATURE OF SITES

In the course of their long histories, individual precinct sites were sometimes successively occupied and owned by more than one monastic house. To avoid confusion, the final owner and status of a particular site is given. The only exception to this rule has been to identify the precinct sites or preceptories of the Knights Templar, although in every case after the final suppression of the order in 1314, they were transferred to the ownership of the Knights Hospitaller or some other body.

POST-DISSOLUTION TOTAL REBUILDS

In some of the great churches, important parts were completely destroyed or permitted to deteriorate to a state in which repair of the original fabric became impossible. In such few cases where total rebuilding took place after the Dissolution (and frequently as late as the nineteenth century), the information is given in italics to emphasise the lesser significance of the information.

In a number of cases (minor ones it is to be hoped) it has not been possible in this volume to corroborate the veracity of the information provided. In these instances, the items have been excluded from the lists.

DATA FROM EXTERNAL BIBLIOGRAPHICAL SOURCES

A small number of entries are placed in square brackets thus [....]. These comprise information obtained here from other written sources. These entries, though usually reliable, have not been verified within the context of this Resource Guide.

DATES AND ABBREVIATIONS

The following practices have been used throughout this resource guide:-

1. **C** = century & **M** = millennium: For example C13 stands for thirteenth century & M1 for first millennium.

2. Where a period is shown thus:-
   C12/C13 , 1250/1300 etc.
   it means that the structure or artefact referred to was built (or remodelled) *any time* within the two parameters.

   In contrast where a period is shown thus:-
   C12-C13 or **1250-1300**
   it means that the structure or artefact referred to was built or (remodelled) *over the whole of the time* indicated.

3. **c (*circa*)** followed by a date = approximate date

4. **lmp** = later medieval period

5. **pDp** = post-Dissolution period

6. **unknown date**: This means that either the appropriate information is unavailable (that is, to the author) or that the structure itself lacks sufficient detail to attempt to give it a date.

♦♦♦♦♦♦♦♦♦♦♦♦♦♦♦♦

DIRECTORY OF MONASTIC SITES

EXPLANATORY NOTES ON THE INDIVIDUAL ENTRIES

THE HISTORIC COUNTIES

The reorganisation of local government in 1974 resulted in the formation of a number of entirely new counties, the abolition of some ancient counties and the transfer of territory between others. More recently, a further bout of reorganisation of local government has changed the picture yet again with some of these post-1974 administrative counties (for such we must call them) being abolished, divided or renamed. **All our entries below show the monastic houses listed within their historic counties, these being the counties that existed for nearly a thousand years, apart from a few exceptions, until 1974.**

There are several reasons for listing them in this way. Firstly, all the literature written about them before 1974 (and quite a lot written subsequently) assumes a topographical and geographical context dependent on the historic county framework. Secondly, learned historic societies operating at county or local level continue to cover and work within those geographic areas with which they have been associated for many years. Thirdly, much library and local resource material continues to be used by

15

local historians who continue to focus on traditional modes of interest and organisation within shires. And fourthly, who knows whether the post-1974 administrative county set-up might change again in the future, even to the extent of all of the counties disappearing within a new structure of local government?

GRID REFERENCES

Four-figure references have been used throughout this Section. Within the standard 10 km. (6.21 mile) square superimposed on Ordnance Survey maps, these references will allow the user to find the co-ordinates of any location moderately well. However, allowance must be made for the fact that averaging up or down on a four-figure reference number may not always pinpoint the location precisely.

ACCESSIBILITY OF SITES

Public access to site
This means that the site of the monastic house referred to is open to people generally, either at all reasonable times (when admittance is usually free) or within published hours (when there may well be an admittance charge). The site normally includes the whole or most of the precinct area and the conventual church whether intact or ruined.

Public access to church
Where this is stated, it indicates that an intact church (*not necessarily the conventual church*) associated with the monastic house yet still public property, is available to be visited. However, the building in question may be locked and special arrangements entered into in order to gain access. It is most unlikely that an admittance charge would be made, except in the case of some of the cathedrals and one or two of the larger other churches.

Limited access to site
There are a number of sites, mostly privately owned, which may be visited as a result of getting special permission (for instance, from an estate office), or because they are opened to the public on a few set days in the year which are previously publicised. Alternatively, limited access means that in respect of some houses only part of the monastic precinct is available for visiting (sometimes in conjunction with having to ask for special permission).

Nil access to site
Nearly all the sites to which this entry refers are privately owned, comprising monastic buildings of one kind or another which have been converted into mansions or farmhouses. Quite clearly, their owners have the right not to open their homes or estates to visitors, and no one in a free society would wish to dissent from such a wish. Yet in a number of cases, it is possible for a visitor to obtain special permission from the owner, either by writing, telephoning or even knocking on the door. Access to many sites of course may be quite impossible when redevelopment has covered the area with new buildings.

LOCATION OF CLOISTERS

On many sites the position of the cloister is known and is indicated 'north' or 'south'. In a number of other houses no information is immediately available and where applicable, is noted 'nia'. In a few cases chiefly houses of the military orders, there was no cloister or at least, no cloister where it would be contiguous with the conventual church in the normal manner. Such omissions are recorded as 'nil'.

That the location of the cloister has been identified at a particular site does not indicate that there is necessarily anything to see. Many locations are the result of archaeological excavations of foundations of the cloister ranges or walks which have now been covered over.

THE SITES LISTED ALPHABETICALLY

Abbotsbury abbey, *Benedictine, Dorset, SY5885, public access to site, south*
1/3, 1/4, 2/1, 17/1, 17/6, 18/2

Abergavenny priory, *Benedictine, Monm., SO3115, public access to church, south*
3/1, 4/1, 4/4, 5/1, 5/2, 5/4, 7/2, 8/1, 9/1, 9/6, 12/1, 17/1, 18/1, 20/9

Abingdon abbey, *Benedictine,* Berks., *SU4997, public access to site, south*
1/1, 2/1, 2/5, 2/7, 17/1, 17/2, 17/5, 18/1

Aconbury priory, *Augustinian (canonesses), Heref., SO5233, public access to church, south*
3/1, 4/1, 5/1, 5/3, 8/1, 11/2, 18/1

Alberbury priory, *Grandmontine, Shrops., SJ3715, nil access to site, nia*
3/6, 8/1, 11/2

Aldeby priory, *Benedictine, Norf., TM4593, public access to church, nia*
4/1, 5/1, 5/2, 5/3, 5/4, 7/2, 8/1, 8/2, 17/1

Alkborough cell, *Benedictine, Lincs., SE8822, public access to church, nil*
3/1, 4/1 5/1, 5/5, 7/2, 11/4, 18/1

Allerton Mauleverer priory, *Benedictine, Yorks. WR, SE4258, public access to church, nia*
3/3

Alnesbourn (or Nacton) cell, *Augustinian, Suff., TM1940, nil access to site, nia*
17/1

Alnwick abbey, *Premonstratensian, Northumb., NU1814, limited access to site, south*
2/1, 13/8, 17/5

Alvecote priory, *Benedictine, Warws., SK2404, public access to church, nia*
1/3, 17/6

Alvingham priory, *Gilbertine (mixed), Lincs., TF3791, public access to church, nia*
1/3, 3/1, 4/1, 5/1, 5/5, 7/2, 18/1

Amesbury priory, *Benedictine (nuns), Wilts., SU1542, public access to church, north*
3/1, 4/1, 4/4, 5/1, 5/2, 5/4, 6/3, 7/2, 8/1, 11/2

Anglesey priory (now called abbey), *Augustinian, Cambs., TL5362, public access to site, north*
12/1, 12/4, 12/5, 12/7, 13/1, 13/9, 17/8

Ansty commandery, *Knights Hospitaller, Wilts., ST9526, nil access to site, nil*
2/5, 18/2

Arundel priory, *Benedictine, Ssx., TQ0107, public access to church, nia*
3/1, 7/1, 7/2, 7/4

Ashridge priory/college, *Bonhommes, Herts., SP9913, nil access to site, nia*
18/2

Astley priory, *Benedictine, Worcs., SO7967, public access to church, nia*
3/3

Atherstone friary, *Augustinian, Warws., SP3098, public access to church, north*
3/1, 4/1, 5/1, 5/4, 7/2, 18/1

Augustinian abbeys, *in collective ownership*
17/3

Axford 'priory', *unknown monastic house owning grange(?) at Axford (near Marlborough), Wilts., SU2370, nil access to site, nia*
17/2

Aylesford friary, *Carmelite, Kent, TQ7458, public access to site, south*
2/1, 11/1, 11/7, 14/4, 14/5, 14/6, 14/9, 15/1, 15/4, 20/6

Bamburgh cell, *Augustinian, Northumb., NU1835, public access to church, nia*
3/1, 4/1, 4/4, 4/5, 5/1, 5/2, 5/5, 8/1, 8/2, 9/2, 10/1, 10/2, 10/6

Bardney abbey, *Benedictine, Lincs., TF1169, public access to site, south*
1/3, 7/1

Barking abbey, *Benedictine (nuns), Essex., TO4584, public access to site, north*
1/2, 1/3, 2/1, 9/6

Barlings (or Oxeney) abbey, *Premonstratensian, Lincs., TF0973, public access to site, south*
17/8, 18/1

Barnwell priory, *Augustinian, Cambs., TL4658 (in Cambridge), public access to church, nia*
1/1

Barrow Gurney (or **Minchinbarrow**) **priory,** *Benedictine (nuns), Som., ST5268, public access to church, nia*
3/5, 5/1

Basingwerk abbey, *Cistercian, Flint., SJ1977, public access to site, south*
3/7, 13/4, 14/4, 14/5, 14/8

Baswich (St. Thomas by Stafford) priory, *Augustinian, Staffs., SJ9422, nil access to site, nia*
18/2

Bath cathedral-priory (now co-cathedral & called abbey), *Benedictine, Som., ST7464, public access to church, south*
3/1, 4/1, 4/4, 5/1, 5/2, 5/4, 10/1, 11/2, 17/1

Battle abbey, *Benedictine, Ssx., TQ7515, public access to site, south*
1/3, 2/1, 2/3, 2/5, 12/1, 12/7, 13/1, 13/9, 14/9, 15/1, 15/4, 17/4, 17/8, 20/8

Bayham abbey, *Premonstratensian, Ssx., TQ6536 (near Lamberhurst), public access to site, south*
2/1, 3/7, 4/4, 5/2, 8/1, 11/2, 11/3, 12/3, 14/9, 17/2, 19/4

Beauchief abbey, *Premonstratensian, Yorks. WR, SK3382, public access to site, south*
3/5, 5/5

Beaulieu abbey, *Cistercian, Hants., SU3802, public access to site, south*
1/2, 2/1, 3/7, 7/2, 9/3, 11/2, 11/3, 12/3, 12/6, 13/3, 13/4, 13/5, 13/8, 14/3, 14/4, 14/5, 14/9, 15/1, 15/5, 17/1, 17/2, 17/8, 18/1, 20/6

Beauvale charterhouse (called priory), *Carthusian, Notts., SK3949 (near Hucknall), south*
2/1, 2/3, 15/4

Beckford cell, *Augustinian, Glos., SO9836, public access to church, nia*
3/3

Beddgelert priory, *Augustinian, Carnarv., SH5948, public access to church, south*
3/5, 4/1, 5/1

Beeleigh abbey, *Premonstratensian, Essex, TL8408, nil access to site, south*
12/1, 12/3, 12/4, 12/7, 13/1, 13/6, 13/9

Beeston priory, *Augustinian, Norf., TG1742, public access to site, south*
3/7, 17/8

Bermondsey abbey , *Cluniac, Sry., TQ3379 (in London), nil access to site, south*
17/1, 17/2

Beverley friary, *Dominican, Yorks. ER, TA0440, limited access to site, nia*
2/1, 2/3, 18/2

Bicester priory, *Augustinian, Oxon., SP5822, limited access to site, nia*
1/3, 2/3, 10/2

Bilsington priory, *Augustinian, Kent, TR0434, nil access to site, nia*
16/2

Bindon abbey, *Cistercian, Dorset, SY8687, limited access to site, south*
17/8

Binham priory, *Benedictine, Norf., TF9840, public access to site, south*
2/1, 2/3, 3/1, 3/2, 5/1, 5/6, 6/4, 6/6, 7/1, 7/2, 8/1, 8/2, 9/1, 9/2, 9/3, 11/4, 18/1

Birkenhead priory, *Benedictine, Ches., SJ3389, public access to site, north*
12/3, 12/4, 13/2, 14/1, 14/3, 14/4, 15/1, 15/3, 15/4, 19/1, 20/2

Bisham abbey, *Benedictine, Berks., SU8585, nil access to site, nia*
11/1, 17/1, 17/6

Bishopsgate St. Helens priory, *Benedictine (nuns), Mdx., TQ3381 (in London), public access to church, north*
1/5, 3/1, 4/1, 4/4, 5/1, 5/2, 8/1, 9/1, 9/3, 10/6, 11/2, 13/3, 18/1

Blackmore priory, *Augustinian, Essex, TL6001, public access to church, south*
3/1, 5/1, 5/5, 7/2, 11/2, 18/1

Blakeney (or **Snitterley) friary**, *Carmelite, Norf., TG0343, public access to church, nil*
1/5, 2/1, 2/3, 3/1, 4/1, 4/2, 4/4, 5/1, 5/3, 5/5, 7/2, 8/1, 8/2, 9/1, 9/2, 10/3, 11/4, 18/1

Blanchland abbey, *Premonstratensian, Northumb., NY9750, public access to site, south*
2/1, 3/1, 4/1, 4/4, 5/2, 5/4, 5/5, 7/2, 8/1, 8/2, 9/4, 11/7, 14/4, 14/6, 15/1, 15/4, 17/8, 19/4, 20/5

Blyth priory, *Benedictine, Notts., SK6287, public access to church, north*
1/5, 3/1, 3/2, 5/1, 5/3, 5/5, 6/3, 6/4, 6/5, 8/1, 9/5, 11/2, 11/4, 18/1

Bodmin friary, *Franciscan, Corn., SX0767, nil access to site, nia*
2/1

Bodmin priory, *Augustinian, Corn., SX0767, public access to site, nia*
1/3, 2/3, 10/2, 17/2, 18/1

Bolton priory (now called abbey), *Augustinian, Yorks. WR, SE0754, public access to site, south*
1/5, 2/1, 2/3, 3/1, 3/2, 4/1, 4/6, 5/1, 5/2, 5/4, 5/5, 6/4, 7/1, 8/1, 8/2, 9/2, 9/4, 10/6, 11/2, 11/4, 16/2, 17/1, 18/1

Boston friary, *Dominican, Lincs., TF3344, public access to site, nia*
14/1, 14/4

Bourne abbey, *Augustinian, Lincs., TF1020, public access to church, north*
3/1, 4/4, 5/1, 5/2, 5/3, 5/5, 7/2, 8/1, 11/4, 18/1

Boxgrove priory, *Benedictine, Ssx., SU9108, public access to site, north*
1/5, 3/1, 3/2, 4/1, 4/4, 5/2, 5/3, 5/4, 6/4, 7/1, 7/2, 8/1, 10/1, 11/2, 11/3, 11/4, 12/3, 12/6, 15/4

Boxley abbey, *Cistercian, Kent, TQ7859, nil access to site, south*
2/1, 2/3, 7/3, 17/1

Bradenstoke priory, *Augustinian, Wilts., SU0079, nil access to site, nia*
14/4, 15/2, 15/4, 17/1, 20/6

Bradsole St. Radegund's abbey , *Premonstratensian, Kent, TR2742 (near Alkham), nil access to site, south*
3/6, 5/5, 14/4, 15/4, 17/8

Bradwell priory: *Benedictine, Bucks., SP8339 (in Milton Keynes), public access to site, nia*
3/5, 4/4, 9/3, 9/5, 17/1

Brecon friary, *Dominican, Breck., SO0429, nil access to site, south*
2/3, 3/1, 3/2, 4/1, 4/4, 5/1, 5/4, 8/1, 8/2, 9/1, 10/6, 11/2, 15/4, 16/2

Brecon priory (now cathedral), *Benedictine, Breck., SO0429, public access to site, south*
1/3, 2/1, 2/3, 2/5, 3/1, 4/1, 4/2, 4/4, 5/1, 5/2, 5/3, 5/4, 6/6, 7/2, 8/1, 8/2, 10/1, 11/2, 13/3, 15/1, 15/4, 17/1, 18/1, 20/9

Breedon priory, *Augustinian, Leics., SK4023, public access to church, north*
2/4, 3/1, 4/1, 4/4, 5/2, 5/3, 5/4, 7/2, 8/1, 9/6, 10/6, 11/2, 11/4

Brewood priory (also called Black Ladies), *Benedictine (nuns), Staffs.,SJ8808, nil access to site, nia*
18/2

Brewood St. Leonard's priory (commonly known as White Ladies at Boscobel), *Augustinian, (nuns sic), Shrops., SJ8308, public access to site, north*
3/7, 8/1, 11/2

Bridlington priory, *Augustinian, Yorks. ER, TA1767, public access to site, south*
2/1, 3/1, 5/1, 5/3, 5/5, 7/1, 7/2, 8/1, 9/6, 10/3, 11/1, 11/2, 11/3, 18/1

Brimpton preceptory, *Knights Templar, Berks., SU5564, nil access to site, nil*
3/6

Brinkburn priory , *Augustinian, Northumb., NZ1299 (north west of Longhorsley), public access to site, south*
1/5, 2/1, 3/1 4/1, 5/1, 5/2, 5/4, 7/1, 7/2, 8/1, 11/2, 11/3, 13/7, 14/2, 20/9

27

Bristol abbey (now cathedral), *Augustinian, Glos., ST5872, public access to site, south*
2/1, 3/1, 4/1, 4/2, 5/1, 5/2, 5/4, 5/5, 6/2, 6/6, 7/2, 8/1, 8/2, 9/1, 9/2, 9/4, 9/6, 10/1, 11/1, 12/1, 12/3, 12/4, 12/5, 12/6, 12/7, 13/2, 13/3, 13/4, 14/3, 14/4, 14/7, 16/1, 17/1, 17/2, 18/1, 19/3, 20/3

Bristol friary, *Carmelite, Glos., ST5872, nil access to site, nia*
6/6

Bristol friary, *Dominican, Glos., ST5872, public access to site, nia*
11/1, 12/1, 19/5, 20/2

Bristol St. James' priory, *Benedictine, Glos., ST5872, public access to church, nia*
1/5, 3/1, 5/1, 5/3, 5/5

Bristol Temple preceptory(?), *Knights Templar, Glos., ST5872, limited access to site*
3/4

Bromfield priory, *Benedictine, Shrops., SO4877, public access to site, south*
2/1, 3/1, 5/1, 5/4, 5/5, 7/2, 8/1, 11/4

Broomholm (or **Bacton**) **priory**, *Cluniac, Norf., TG3433, nil access to site, south*
2/1, 2/3, 3/7, 5/2

Bruern abbey, *Cistercian, Oxon., SP2620, nil access to site, nia*
18/2

Bruton abbey, *Augustinian, Som., ST6835, public access to church, nia*
1/3, 2/1, 17/5, 17/6

Buckfast abbey, *Cistercian, Devon, SX7467, public access to site, south*
1/3, 2/1, 2/2, 3/1, 15/1, 15/4, 17/2, 17/4

Buckland abbey, *Cistercian, Devon, SX4967, public access to site, north*
2/3, 2/7, 3/6, 8/1, 8/2, 15/4, 17/1, 18/2

Buildwas abbey, *Cistercian,. Shrops., SJ6404, public access to site, north*
3/7, 4/1, 4/4, 4/5, 5/1, 5/2, 5/4, 5/6, 8/2, 9/3, 12/2, 12/3, 12/4, 12/6, 12/7, 13/3, 15/4

Bungay priory, *Benedictine (nuns), Suff., TM3390, public access to site, south*
1/5, 2/3, 3/1, 3/2, 4/4, 5/1, 5/3, 5/5, 6/3, 7/2, 8/1, 11/4

Burnham abbey, *Augustinian (canonesses), Bucks., SU9382, limited access to site, north*
2/3, 12/1, 12/3, 12/4, 12/6, 12/7, 13/6, 13/9, 16/2, 17/1, 17/2, 17/6

Burnham Norton friary, *Carmelite, Norf., TF8442, public access to site, north*
2/1, 3/7, 5/6

Burton-on-Trent abbey, *Benedictine, Staffs., SK2423, limited access to site, south*
7/2, 16/2, 17/2

Bury St. Edmunds abbey, *Benedictine, Suff., TL8565, public access to site, north*
1/3, 2/1, 2/3, 3/7, 4/5, 5/6, 7/1, 10/4, 17/7, 18/1

Bury St. Edmunds (Babwell) friary, *Franciscan, Suff., TL8565, nil access to site, nia*
2/3

Bushmead priory, *Augustinian, Beds., TL1260, public access to site, north*
11/7, 14/4, 14/8, 17/8, 18/1

Butley priory, *Augustinian, Suff., TM3850, nil access to site, nia*
2/1, 17/8

Byland abbey, *Cistercian, Yorks. NR, SE5579, public access to site, south*
2/1, 5/6, 7/1, 7/3, 8/1, 9/2, 9/3, 13/4, 13/9, 18/1

Calder abbey, *Cistercian, Cumb., NY0506, nil access to site, south*
2/1, 3/7, 4/1, 4/4, 5/2, 5/4, 8/2, 12/1, 12/3, 12/4, 12/6, 12/7, 13/1, 14/2, 14/4, 20/4

Caldey cell, *Tironensian, Pembr., SS1496, public access to site, north*
2/1, 3/1, 4/1, 5/1, 5/5, 8/1, 9/6, 12/1, 13/1, 13/4, 13/9, 15/1, 15/3, 15/4, 17/8, 18/1, 19/4, 20/7

Cambridge Buckingham college (now part of Magdalene college), *Benedictine, Cambs.,TL4559, limited access to site, north*
18/2

Cambridge friary (now part of Emmanuel college), *Dominican, Cambs., TL4558, limited access to site, nia*
3/6

Cambridge St. Radegund's priory (now part of Jesus college), *Benedictine (nuns), Cambs., TL4558, limited access to site, north*
3/1, 4/1, 5/1, 5/2, 5/4, 8/1, 8/2, 9/2, 11/1, 11/4, 12/3, 14/4, 15/1, 15/4, 20/1

Cammeringham priory, *Premonstratensian, Lincs., SK9582, nil access to site, nia*
18/2

Canons Ashby priory, *Augustinian, Northants., SP5850, public access to church, south*
3/1, 5/1, 5/5

Canonsleigh abbey (near Burlescombe), *Augustinian (canonesses), Devon, ST0617, nil access to site, nia*
2/1

Canterbury cathedral-priory (now cathedral), *Benedictine, Kent, TR1558, public access to site, north*
2/1, 2/2, 2/3, 2/5, 2/7, 3/1, 4/1, 4/2, 4/3, 4/4, 4/5, 5/1, 5/2, 5/3, 5/4, 5/5, 6/2, 6/3, 6/4, 6/6, 8/1, 9/2, 9/3, 9/4, 9/5, 9/6, 10/1, 10/4, 10/6, 11/1, 11/2, 11/7, 12/3, 12/4,

12/7, 13/2, 13/8, 14/3, 14/8, 15/4, 16/1, 16/2, 17/1, 17/3, 18/1, 19/1, 20/9

Canterbury friary, *Dominican, Kent, TR1558, limited access to site, nia*
14/4, 14/5, 15/4

Canterbury friary, *Franciscan, Kent, TR1558, limited access to site, nia*
18/2

Canterbury St. Augustine's abbey, *Benedictine, Kent, TR1558, public access to site, north*
2/1, 2/3, 3/7, 4/3, 4/5, 7/1, 8/1, 10/3, 10/4, 14/9, 15/4, 17/1, 17/2

Cardigan cell, *Benedictine, Card., SN1846, public access to church, nil*
3/1, 4/1, 5/1, 5/5, 7/2, 8/1, 11/4

Carisbrooke priory, *Benedictine, IoW, SZ4888, public access to church, north*
3/1, 4/4, 5/1, 5/3, 5/5, 8/1

Carlisle cathedral-priory (now cathedral), *Augustinian, Cumb., NY4056, public access to site, south*
2/1, 3/1, 4/1, 4/4, 5/1, 5/2, 5/4, 6/3, 6/6, 8/1, 9/1, 9/4, 9/5, 9/6, 10/1, 11/1, 11/2, 12/3, 14/3, 14/4, 14/5, 14/8, 15/4, 17/1, 18/1, 19/3, 20/9

Carmarthen priory, *Augustinian, Carm., SN4120, nil access to site, nia*
1/3, 2/1

Carrow priory, *Benedictine (nuns), Norf., TG2308, nil access to site, nia*
15/4

Cartmel priory, *Augustinian, Lancs., SD3879, public access to church, south & later north*
1/5, 2/1, 3/1, 4/1, 4/4, 5/1, 5/2, 5/4, 8/1, 8/2, 9/1, 9/4, 11/2, 18/1

Castle Acre priory, *Cluniac, Norf., TF8115, public access to site, south*
1/3, 2/1, 2/2, 3/7, 5/5, 5/6, 7/1, 8/1, 8/2, 9/3, 12/1, 12/4, 13/5, 13/6, 13/7, 14/9, 15/1, 15/3, 15/4, 18/1, 19/4

Catesby priory, *Cistercian (nuns), Northants., SP5159, public access to church, nia*
8/1, 8/2

Cerne abbey, *Benedictine, Dorset, ST6701, public access to site, north*
1/3, 2/1, 2/2, 15/4, 17/1

Chacombe priory, *Augustinian, Northants., SP4844, nil public access to site, nia*
18/2

Chatteris abbey, *Benedictine (nuns), Cambs., TL3986, nil public access to site*
2/3

Chepstow priory, *Benedictine, Monm., ST5494, public access to church, south*
3/1, 4/1, 5/1, 7/2

Chertsey abbey, *Benedictine, Sry., TQ0566, limited access to site, north*
1/3, 2/1, 17/1, 17/8

Chester abbey (now cathedral), *Benedictine, Ches., SJ4166, public access to site, north*
1/3, 1/5, 2/1, 2/3, 3/1, 4/1, 4/2, 4/4, 5/1, 5/2, 5/3, 5/4, 5/5, 6/3, 8/1, 8/2, 9/1, 10/2, 11/1, 11/2, 11/3, 11/5, 11/7, 12/2, 12/3, 12/4, 12/5, 12/7, 13/3, 13/4, 13/8, 13/9, 14/1, 14/3, 14/4, 14/5, 15/2, 15/3, 15/4, 17/2, 18/1, 19/1, 20/1

Chetwode cell, *Augustinian, Bucks., SP6430, public access to church, south*
3/1, 4/1, 4/4, 5/5, 8/1, 8/2, 9/4, 9/5, 18/1

Chibburn commandery, *Knights Hospitaller, Northumb., NZ2798, nil access to site, nil*
3/7, 19/6

Chichester friary, *Franciscan, Ssx., SU8605, public access to site, north*
3/6, 4/1, 8/1, 8/2

Chicksands priory, *Gilbertine (mixed), Beds., TL1239, limited access to site, south & north*
11/1, 12/1, 14/1, 15/1, 19/4, 20/2

Chirbury priory, *Augustinian, Shrops., SO2699, public access to church, north* .
3/1, 4/1, 4/4, 5/1, 5/5, 6/3, 8/1, 9/1, 9/3, 11/4

Christchurch (or Twynham) priory, *Augustinian, Hants., SZ1692, public access to site, south*
1/5, 2/3, 2/5, 3/1, 4/1, 4/2, 4/3, 4/4, 4/5, 5/1, 5/2, 5/3, 5/4, 5/5, 6/1, 6/2, 6/3, 6/6, 7/1, 7/2, 8/1, 9/1, 9/2, 9/3, 9/5, 10/1, 11/2, 13/3, 18/1

Church Gresley priory, *Augustinian, Derbs., SK2918, public access to church, south*
3/1, 4/1, 5/1, 5/5, 11/2

Church Preen cell, *Cluniac, Shrops., SO5498, public access to church, south*
3/1, 4/1, 5/1, 7/2, 8/1, 8/2, 11/2

Cirencester abbey, *Augustinian, Glos., SP0102, public access to site, north*
1/3, 2/1, 2/3, 17/5

Cistercian abbeys, *in collective ownership/control*
17/3

Clare friary, *Augustinian, Suff., TL7745, limited access to site, south*
3/7, 7/2, 8/1, 8/2, 9/1, 10/4, 11/1, 11/2, 11/4, 11/7, 12/3, 13/6, 14/5, 15/1, 15/3, 15/4, 16/2, 18/1

Clattercote priory, *Gilbertine, Oxon., SP4549, nil access to site, nia*
18/2

Cleeve (or Vallis Florida) abbey , *Cistercian, Som., ST0440 (near Washford), public access to site, south*
2/1, 2/3, 8/1, 9/2, 9/3, 9/6, 11/1, 11/6, 11/7, 12/1, 12/3, 12/4, 12/6, 12/7, 13/1, 13/4, 13/9, 14/1, 14/3, 14/4, 14/5, 14/7, 17/2, 19/2, 20/2

Clerkenwell commandery (known as priory), *Knights Hospitaller, Mdx., TQ3282 (in London), public access to church, nil*
2/1, 3/1, 4/1, 4/4, 4/5, 7/2

Clifford priory, *Cluniac, Heref., SO2446, nil access to site, nia*
1/3, 18/2

Cockerham cell, *Augustinian, Lancs., SD4652, public access to church,nia*
3/5, 5/5

Cockersand abbey, *Premonstratensian, Lancs., SD4354, limited access to site, south*
12/3, 12/4

Cogges priory, *Benedictine, Oxon., SP3609, public access to church, nia*
3/3, 18/2

Coggeshall abbey, *Cistercian, Essex, TL8622, limited access to site, south*
1/1, 12/2, 13/6, 15/4, 16/2, 17/1

Colchester St. Botolph's priory, *Augustinian, Essex, TM0025, public access to site, south*
3/7, 5/1, 5/6, 18/1

Colchester St. John's abbey, *Benedictine, Essex, TM0024, limited access to site, nia*
2/1, 2/3

Combe abbey (near Coventry, *Cistercian, Warws., SP4080, limited access to site, north*
11/1, 12/3

Combermere abbey, *Cistercian, Ches., SJ5944, nil access to site, nia*
15/4

Conway abbey, *Cistercian, Carnarv., 7878, public access to church, nia*
3/5, 5/1

Cornworthy priory, *Augustinian (canonesses), Devon, SX8255, limited access to site, nia*
2/1

Coventry cathedral-priory, *Benedictine, Warws., SP3379, public access to site, north*
1/3, 3/7, 9/3

Coventry charterhouse (called priory), *Carthusian, Warws., SP3378 limited access to site, nia*
2/1, 18/2

Coventry friary, *Carmelite, Warws., SP3379, public access to site, south*
2/1, 11/1, 12/1, 12/3, 12/5, 12/7, 13/1, 13/9, 19/5

Coventry friary, *Franciscan, Warws., SP3379, limited access to site, nia*
3/7, 5/4

Coverham abbey, *Premonstratensian, Yorks. NR, SE1186, nil access to site, south*
1/3, 2/1, 3/7, 11/3, 15/4, 17/7, 18/1

Coxford priory, *Augustinian, Norf., TF8428, nil access to site, south*
3/7

Cranborne cell, *Benedictine, Dorset, SU0513, public access to church, south*
3/1, 4/1, 5/1, 5/3, 5/5, 7/2, 7/4, 9/5, 11/2, 11/4

Creake abbey, *Augustinian, Norf., TF8639, public access to site, south*
8/1, 11/2, 12/1

Croxden abbey, *Cistercian, Staffs., SK0640, public access to site, south*
2/3, 3/7, 5/2, 5/6, 8/1, 9/3, 11/1, 11/2, 12/3, 12/6, 12/7, 13/7, 13/9, 18/1

Croxton abbey, *Premonstratensian, Leics., SK8227, nil access to site, north*
15/4, 17/8

Croyland abbey, *Benedictine, Lincs., TF2410, public access to site, south*
1/4, 1/5, 3/1, 3/2, 4/4, 5/1, 5/3, 5/5, 6/4, 6/6, 7/1, 7/2, 9/6, 11/4, 17/3, 17/7

Cwmhyr abbey, *Cistercian, Radnor., SO0671, public access to site, south*
3/5, 5/1, 10/4

Cymmer abbey , *Cistercian, Merion., SH7220 (near Llanelltyd), public access to site, south*
3/7, 4/1, 4/6, 5/1, 5/5, 8/1, 8/2, 15/4

Dale (or **Depedale) abbey**, *Premonstratensian, Derbs., SK4439, public access to site, south*
2/1, 4/6, 7/2, 9/2, 9/4, 9/5, 16/2

Dartford priory, *Dominican (nuns), Kent, TQ5374, nil access to site, nia*
2/3

Davington priory, *Benedictine (nuns), Kent, TR0162, public access to church, south*
2/1, 2/3, 3/1, 4/4, 5/1, 5/5, 6/4, 8/1, 11/1, 11/2, 11/4, 11/7, 15/1, 20/9

Deeping St. James priory, *Benedictine, Lincs., TF1610, public access to church, north*
3/1, 4/1, 4/4, 5/1, 5/3, 5/5, 7/2, 8/1, 8/2, 10/6, 11/2, 18/1

Deerhurst priory, *Benedictine, Glos., SO8730, public access to church, south*
3/1, 4/4, 5/1, 5/2, 5/4, 5/5, 7/2, 8/1,9/2, 9/4, 9/6,10/6, 11/2, 12/1, 18/1, 20/9

Delapre (de Pratis) abbey, *Cluniac (nuns), Northants.,SP7659, limited access to site, south*
3/6, 11/1, 18/1, 19/4, 20/1

Denbigh friary, *Carmelite, Denbigh., SJ0666, public access to site, south*
3/7, 4/1, 8/1, 8/2, 11/2

Denney abbey, *Franciscan (nuns), Cambs., TL4968, public access to site, north*
3/6, 5/1, 5/2, 5/4, 14/4, 20/9

Dieulacres abbey (near Leek), *Cistercian, Staffs., SJ9858, nil access to site, south*
2/1

Dinmore commandery, *Knights Hospitaller, Heref., SO4850, public access to site, nil*
3/1, 4/1 5/1, 5/5, 8/1, 10/6, 11/4, 13/8, 17/8, 18/1, 18/2

Dorchester abbey, *Augustinian, Oxon., SU5894, public access to site, north*
1/5, 2/5, 3/1, 4/1, 4/2, 4/4, 4/5, 5/1, 5/2, 5/3, 5/4, 6/2, 7/2, 8/1, 8/2, 9/1, 9/4, 9/5, 10/2, 11/2, 15/4, 18/1

Dore abbey, *Cistercian, Heref., SO3930, public access to church, north*
3/1, 3/2, 4/1, 4/4, 5/2, 5/4, 7/1, 8/1, 9/3, 9/6, 10/3, 18/1

Dover priory (at Dover castle), *Augustinian, Kent, TR3241, public access to site, nia*
3/1, 4/1, 4/4, 5/1, 5/2, 5/4, 5/5, 8/1, 8/2, 10/6, 18/1

Dover priory (at Dover college), *Benedictine, Kent, TR3141, nil access to site, north*
2/1, 11/7, 14/3, 14/4, 15/4, 18/1

Dudley priory, *Cluniac, Worcs., SO9491, public access to site, north*
3/7, 4/2, 5/1, 9/3, 11/2, 13/3, 18/1

Dunkeswell abbey, *Cistercian, Devon, ST1407, limited public access to site, south*
2/1

Dunstable priory, *Augustinian, Beds., TL0222, public access to church, south*
1/5, 2/1, 2/5, 3/1, 5/1, 5/5, 6/4, 6/5, 7/2, 8/1, 18/1

Dunster priory, *Benedictine, Som., SS9944, public access to site, north*
1/5, 2/1, 2/3, 2/5, 3/1, 4/1, 4/4, 5/1, 5/2, 5/3, 5/4, 6/4, 6/5, 6/6, 7/1, 7/2, 8/1, 8/2, 9/2, 11/2, 12/6, 15/4, 17/1, 17/6, 20/9

Dunwich friary, *Franciscan, Suff., TM4770, public access to site, south*
2/1, 2/3, 11/1

Durham cathedral-priory (now cathedral), *Benedictine, Durh., NZ2842, public access to site, south*
1/2, 2/1, 3/1, 4/1, 4/2, 4/4, 5/1, 5/2, 5/3, 5/4, 5/5, 6/1, 8/1, 8/2, 9/2, 9/4, 9/5, 9/6, 10/1, 10/2, 11/1, 11/2, 11/5, 11/7, 12/1, 12/3, 12/4, 12/7, 13/1, 13/2, 13/3, 13/9, 14/1, 14/4, 14/6, 14/7, 15/1, 15/4, 17/3, 17/5, 18/1, 19/1, 20/1

Earls Colne priory, *Benedictine, Essex, TL8528, nil access to site, nia*
17/2, 18/1

Easby abbey, *Premonstratensian, Yorks. NR, NZ1900, public access to site, south*
1/3, 2/1, 3/7, 6/6, 7/1, 9/1, 9/2, 9/3, 12/4, 13/1, 13/5, 13/6, 13/9, 14/1, 14/3, 14/4, 14/5, 14/8, 14/9, 15/1, 15/4, 17/1, 18/1, 19/4

Easebourne priory, *Augustinian (canonesses), Ssx., SU9022, public access to church, south*
1/5, 3/1, 4/1, 5/1, 5/5, 7/2, 11/2, 12/1, 12/3, 12/4, 13/1, 13/9, 14/4, 20/3

Ecclesfield priory, *Benedictine, Yorks. WR, SK3593, public access to church, nil*
3/3, 3/6, 18/2

Edington priory, *Bonhommes, Wilts., ST9253, public access to church, north*
2/3, 3/1, 4/1, 4/2, 5/1, 5/2, 5/3, 5/4, 6/3, 7/2, 8/1, 8/2, 9/4, 10/1, 11/2, 13/8, 17/8

Egglestone abbey: *Premonstratensian, Yorks. NR, NZ0615, public access to site, north*
3/7, 4/6, 5/1, 5/6, 8/1, 11/2, 18/1

Ellerton priory, *Cistercian (nuns), Yorks. NR, SE0897 (near Grinton & south of R. Swale), nil access to site, north*
3/7, 5/5

Elstow abbey, *Benedictine (nuns), Beds., TL0547, public access to church, south*
3/1, 5/1, 5/5, 7/2, 7/4, 8/1, 9/6, 11/2, 11/4, 15/3, 18/1

Ely cathedral-priory (now cathedral), *Benedictine, Cambs., TL5480, public access to site, south*
1/3, 2/1, 2/5, 2/7, 3/1, 4/1, 4/2, 4/3, 4/4, 5/1, 5/2, 5/3, 5/4, 5/5, 6/2, 6/6, 8/1, 8/2, 9/1, 9/2, 9/5, 9/6, 10/1, 10/2, 11/1, 11/2, 15/4, 16/2, 17/1, 18/1, 19/1, 20/9

Esholt priory, *Cistercian (nuns), Yorks. WR, SE1840, nil access to site, nia*
18/1

Evesham abbey, *Benedictine, Worcs., SP0343, public access to site, south*
1/3, 2/1, 2/2, 2/5, 5/5, 7/3, 9/2, 12/3, 17/1, 17/5, 17/6, 17/8

Ewenny priory, *Benedictine, Glam., SS9178, public access to church, south*
2/1, 2/3, 3/1, 3/2, 4/1, 5/1, 5/2, 5/4, 6/3, 6/4, 7/1, 7/2, 8/1, 9/3, 10/3, 10/6, 11/2, 13/3, 17/6, 18/1

Ewyas Harold cell, *Benedictine, Heref., SO3929, public access to church, nia*
3/3, 5/5

Exeter Polsloe priory, *Benedictine (nuns), Devon, SX9293, nil access to site, nia*
2/1, 15/1, 15/3, 15/4

Exeter St. Nicholas' priory, *Benedictine, Devon SX9292, public access to site, north*
2/2, 14/4, 14/6, 15/1, 15/3, 15/4, 20/6

Farewell (or Fairwell) priory, *Benedictine (nuns), Staffs., SK0812, public access to church, nil(?)*
3/1, 4/1, 5/1, 9/1, 18/1

Farne Island cell, *Benedictine, Northumb., NU2236, limited access to site, nia*
3/1, 4/1, 5/1

Faversham abbey, *Independent Benedictine, Kent, TR0261, public access to site, north*
1/2, 2/1

Finchale priory, *Benedictine, Durh., NZ3047, public access to site, south*
3/7, 4/1, 5/1, 5/2, 5/6, 7/3, 8/1, 8/2, 9/2, 10/2, 11/2, 12/3, 13/3, 14/3, 14/4, 14/9, 15/4, 18/1, 19/1

Flanesford priory, *Augustinian, Heref., SO5821 (near Goodrich), nil access to site, nia*
14/1, 14/4

Flaxley (or **Dene) abbey**, *Cistercian, Glos., SO6915, nil access to site, south*
13/6, 15/1, 15/4, 15/5, 17/2

Folkestone priory, *Independent, Kent, TR2336, public access to church, nia*
3/3, 10/2

Forde abbey, *Cistercian, Dorset, ST3605, public access to site, north*
2/1, 9/6, 11/1, 11/7, 12/1, 12/4, 13/1, 13/6, 14/1, 14/4, 14/5, 14/6, 15/1, 15/4, 17/8, 20/2

Fordingbridge preceptory(?), *Knights Templar, Hants., SU1514, public access to church, nil*
3/4

Fountains abbey, *Cistercian, Yorks. WR, SE2769, public access to site, south*
1/3, 2/1, 2/3, 2/7, 3/7, 4/1, 4/4, 4/6, 5/1, 5/2, 5/3, 5/5, 5/6, 7/1, 8/1, 9/2, 9/3, 11/2, 11/3, 11/7, 12/3, 12/4, 12/6, 12/7, 13/2, 13/3, 13/4, 13/6, 13/7, 13/8, 13/9, 14/1, 14/3, 14/4, 14/5, 14/8, 14/9, 15/1, 15/4, 15/5, 17/2, 17/5, 17/7, 17/8, 18/1, 19/2

Freiston priory, *Benedictine, Lincs., TF3844, public access to church, south*
3/1, 5/1, 5/3, 5/5, 6/5, 6/6, 7/2, 11/2, 18/1

Frithelstock priory, *Augustinian, Devon, SS4619, public access to site, north*
1/3, 3/7, 5/6

Furness abbey, *Cistercian, Lancs., SD2271, public access to site, south*
1/1, 2/1, 2/2, 3/7, 4/1, 5/2, 5/5, 7/1, 8/1, 8/2, 9/2, 9/3, 10/5, 11/2, 11/3, 12/1, 12/3, 12/4, 12/5, 12/6, 12/7, 13/1, 13/3, 13/7, 16/2, 17/2, 17/5, 17/7, 17/8, 18/1, 19/2

Garway preceptory, *Knights Templar, Heref., SO4522, public access to church, nil*
3/1, 4/1, 4/4, 5/1, 5/5, 7/1, 8/1, 17/6, 18/1

Glastonbury abbey, *Benedictine, Som., ST5039, public access to site, south*
1/3, 1/4, 2/1, 2/3, 2/6, 3/7, 4/2, 4/5, 5/3, 8/1, 9/2, 9/3, 10/4, 11/2, 14/6, 17/1, 17/2, 17/4, 17/5, 18/1

Gloucester abbey (now cathedral), *Benedictine, Glos., SO8318, public access to site, north*
2/1, 2/5, 3/1, 4/1, 4/2, 4/3, 4/4, 4/5, 5/1, 5/2, 5/3, 5/4, 6/2, 6/6, 7/1, 7/3, 8/1, 8/2, 9/1, 9/2, 9/3, 9/4, 10/1, 10/3, 10/4, 10/6, 11/1, 11/2, 11/5, 11/7, 12/3, 12/4, 12/6, 12/7, 13/8, 14/3, 14/4, 14/7, 14/9, 15/3, 15/4, 16/1, 16/2, 17/1, 17/2, 17/4, 17/6, 18/1, 19/1, 20/9

Gloucester friary, *Dominican, Glos.,SO8318, public access to site, south*
2/1, 2/3, 3/6, 4/1, 5/2, 8/1, 11/7, 13/1, 14/1, 15/1, 18/1, 19/5, 20/1

Gloucester friary, *Franciscan, Glos., SO8318, public access to site, south*
3/7, 5/1, 19/5

Gloucester Lanthony priory, *Augustinian, Glos., SO8218, public access to site, nia*
2/1, 2/3, 17/1, 18/2

Gloucester St. Oswald's priory, *Augustinian, Glos., SO8418, public access to site, south*
3/7, 8/1

Godsfield commandery, *Knights Hospitaller, Hants., SU6237, nil access to site, nil*
3/1, 4/1

Godstow abbey (near Oxford), *Benedictine (nuns), Oxon., SP4809, public access to site, nia*
1/3, 2/1, 2/3, 17/6

Goring priory, *Augustinian (canonesses), Oxon., SU6080, public access to church, south*
1/5, 3/1, 4/1, 5/1, 5/3, 5/5, 7/2, 8/1, 11/2

Grace Dieu priory: *Augustinian (canonesses), Leics., SK4318, public access to site, nia*
18/2

Grantham friary, *Franciscan, Lincs., SK9136, nil access to site, nia*
13/8

Grantham Templars, *a precise identity of this house is unknown*
17/4

Great Bricett priory, *Augustinian, Suff., TM0451, public access to church, north*
1/5, 3/1, 4/1, 5/1, 5/4, 6/4, 7/2, 8/1, 9/4, 11/2, 15/1, 15/4, 20/9

Guisborough (or Gisburn) priory, *Augustinian, Yorks. NR, NZ6217, public access to site, south*
1/3, 2/1, 4/6, 15/3

Guyzance priory, *Premonstratensian (canonesses), Northumb., NU2103, public access to site, nia*
3/7

Hackness cell, *Benedictine. Yorks. NR, SE9790, public access to church, nia*
3/3

Hailes abbey, *Cistercian, Glos., SP0530, public access to site, south*
1/3, 9/3, 9/6, 10/2, 11/1, 11/2, 11/3, 11/7, 12/3, 13/4, 13/7, 14/3, 14/9, 17/1, 18/1

Halesowen abbey, *Premonstratensian, Worcs., SO9782, public access to site, south*
14/4, 16/2, 17/8

Hamble priory, *Tironensian, Hants., SU4806, public access to church, south*
3/1, 4/1, 5/1, 5/3, 5/5, 8/1, 11/2

Hardham priory, *Augustinian, Ssx., TQ0417, nil access to site, south*
12/3, 12/4, 14/4

Hartland abbey, *Augustinian, Devon, SS2424, nil access to site, south*
15/1, 15/4, 18/1

Hatfield Broad Oak (or **Regis**) **priory**, *Benedictine, Essex, TL5517, public access to church, north*
3/1, 4/4, 5/1, 5/3, 5/5, 6/6, 8/1, 11/4

Hatfield Peverel priory , *Benedictine, Essex, TL7911, public access to church, south*
3/1, 5/1, 6/6, 11/4

Haughmond abbey, *Augustinian, Shrops., SJ5415 (near Shrewsbury), public access* to site, south
7/2, 9/6, 11/2, 11/7, 12/3, 12/4, 13/7, 13/8, 14/6, 14/8, 14/9, 15/4, 16/2, 19/3

Haverfordwest priory, *Augustinian, Pembr., SM9515, public access to site, south*
3/7, 13/3

Hayling priory, *Benedictine, Hants., SU7200, public access to church, nia*
3/1, 4/1, 4/4, 5/1, 5/2, 5/3, 5/4, 7/2, 8/1, 17/6

Hereford friary, *Dominican, Heref., SO5141, public access to site, nia*
11/1, 18/1

Hexham priory (now called abbey), *Augustinian, Northumb., NY9464, public access to site, south*
2/1, 3/1, 4/1, 4/4, 4/5, 5/1, 5/2, 5/4, 6/2, 6/3, 6/6, 7/1, 7/2, 7/3, 8/1, 8/2, 9/1, 9/2, 9/5, 9/6, 10/1, 11/2, 11/6, 11/7, 12/3, 12/5, 12/7, 13/3, 15/1, 15/3, 18/1, 20/9

Heynings (or **Knaith) priory**, *Cistercian (nuns), Lincs., SK8384, public access to church, nia*
3/1, 5/1, 7/2, 18/1

Hickling priory, *Augustinian, Norf., TG4125, nil access to site, nia*
15/2, 15/3

Higham (or **Lillechurch) priory**, *Benedictine (nuns), Kent, TQ7174, public access to church, nia*
1/3

Hinton charterhouse (also known as priory), *Carthusian, Som., ST7859, nil access to site, nia*
2/1, 8/1, 12/3, 12/4, 12/6, 14/4, 17/4, 17/6, 18/2

Hitchin friary (known as priory), *Carmelite, Herts., TL1829, nil access to site, nia*
2/4, 11/1

Holme Cultram abbey, *Cistercian, Cumb., NY1851 (at Abbey Town), public access to church, south*
1/5, 3/1, 5/1

Holystone priory, *Augustinian (canonesses), Northumb., NT9603, public access to church, nia*
3/5, 4/1

Hood cell, *Augustinian, Yorks. NR, SE5182 (near Thirsk), nil access to site, nia*
17/1

Horsham St. Faith's priory, *Benedictine, Norf., TG2115 limited access to site, north*
1/3, 9/5, 11/7, 14/1, 14/4, 14/5, 14/7, 14/8

Horsley priory, *Augustinian, Glos., ST8398, public access to church, nia*
3/5, 5/5

Horton priory, *Benedictine, Dorset, SU0307, public access to church, nia*
3/5, 5/2

Hulne friary (near Alnwick), *Carmelite, Northumb., NU1716, limited access to site, south*
2/1, 2/3, 3/7, 5/6, 8/1, 8/2, 11/2, 12/4, 12/6, 16/2, 17/5, 18/1

Humberston abbey, *Tironensian, Lincs., TA3105, public access to site, south*
3/5, 5/5, 14/7

Hurley priory, *Benedictine, Berks., SU8384, public access to church, north*
2/1, 3/1, 4/1, 5/1, 7/2, 10/6, 11/2, 14/4, 17/1, 17/6, 17/8, 20/9

Hyde (or **New Minster) abbey** , *Benedictine, Hants., SU4829 (in Winchester), limited access to site, south*
1/3, 2/1

Ingham friary, *Trinitarian, Norf., TG3926, public access to church, north*
3/1, 4/1, 5/1, 5/3, 5/5, 6/3, 7/2, 8/1, 8/2, 9/1, 10/3, 11/1, 11/2

Isleham cell, *Benedictine, Cambs., TL6475, public access to site, nia*
1/3, 3/6

Ixworth priory, *Augustinian, Suff., TL9271, nil access to site, nia*
12/1, 12/7, 13/1, 13/9, 15/4

Jarrow priory, *Benedictine, Durh., NZ3265, public access to site, south*
3/1, 4/1, 5/1, 5/4, 8/1, 9/2, 9/4, 11/2, 18/1

Jervaulx abbey, *Cistercian, Yorks. NR, SE1786, public access to site, south*
2/1, 2/3, 3/7, 6/3, 7/1, 8/1, 9/1, 9/2, 11/2, 12/1, 12/3, 12/4, 13/1, 13/3, 13/4, 13/5, 13/6, 14/6, 14/8, 14/9, 15/3, 16/2, 17/2, 18/1, 18/2

Kenilworth abbey, *Augustinian, Warws., SP3271, public access to site, south*
1/3, 2/1, 15/4, 18/1

Kersey priory, *Augustinian, Suff., TM0044, nil access to site, nia*
3/7, 4/4, 15/1

Kerswell cell, *Cluniac, Devon, ST0806, nil access to site, nia*
18/2

Kidwelly cell, *Benedictine, Carm., SN4107, public access to church, north*
3/1, 4/1, 4/2, 5/1, 5/2, 5/3, 5/4, 5/5, 8/1, 8/2, 9/6, 10/6, 11/4, 12/6, 18/1

King's Langley friary. *Dominican, Herts., TL0702, nil access to site, nia*
10/4, 18/2

King's Lynn friary, *Augustinian, Norf., TF6219, limited access to site (part), nia*
2/1

King's Lynn friary, *Carmelite, Norf., TF6219, public access to site, nia*
2/1

King's Lynn friary, *Franciscan, Norf., TF6219, public access to site, south*
3/7, 5/4

King's Lynn priory, *Benedictine, Norf., TF6219, public access to church, south*
2/1, 3/1, 4/1, 4/4, 5/1, 5/2, 5/4, 5/5, 6/6, 7/3, 9/1, 12/1, 14/1, 14/4, 18/1, 20/3

Kingswood abbey, *Cistercian, Glos., ST7592, limited access to site (part), nia*
2/1, 17/1, 17/2

Kington St. Michael's priory, *Benedictine (nuns), Wilts., ST9077, nil access to site, nia*
15/1, 15/4

Kirby Bellars priory, *Augustinian, Leics., SK7218, public access to church, nia*
1/3

Kirkham priory, *Augustinian, Yorks. ER, SE7466, public access to site, south*
2/1, 3/7, 9/6, 11/7, 13/6, 13/7, 14/3, 14/4, 15/3

Kirklees priory, *Cistercian (nuns), WR, SE1723, nil access to site, nia*
2/1, 18/2

Kirkstall abbey, *Cistercian, Yorks. WR, SE2735, public access to site, south*
1/2, 2/1, 3/7, 4/1, 4/4, 5/1, 5/2, 5/4, 5/6, 8/1, 8/2, 11/2, 11/3, 11/7, 12/1, 12/3, 12/4, 12/5, 12/6, 12/7, 13/1, 13/2, 13/3, 13/4, 13/6, 14/3, 14/4, 14/9, 15/1, 15/4, 15/5, 18/1, 19/2

Kirkstead abbey, *Cistercian, Lincs., TF1961, public access to site, south*
1/1, 17/8

Kyme priory, *Augustinian, Lincs., TF1750, public access to church, north*
3/5, 5/1, 5/3, 9/2, 9/6, 11/4, 17/8

Lacock abbey, *Augustinian (canonesses), Wilts., ST9269, public access to site, north*
1/3, 2/1, 3/6, 4/4, 8/1, 9/2, 9/3, 9/5, 10/3, 10/6, 11/1, 11/2, 11/3, 11/7, 12/1, 12/3, 12/4, 12/6, 12/7, 13/1, 13/3, 13/6, 13/9, 14/1, 14/4, 14/6, 14/7, 15/1, 15/4, 17/1, 18/1, 19/3, 20/2

Lancaster priory, *Benedictine & for short time later Bridgittine cell, Lancs., SD4862, public access to church, north*
1/5, 3/1, 4/1, 4/4, 5/1, 5/5, 7/2, 8/1, 9/1, 18/1

Lanercost priory, *Augustinian, Cumb., NY5563, public access to site, south*
1/5, 2/1, 3/1, 3/2, 4/1, 4/2, 4/4, 5/1, 5/2, 5/4, 8/1, 9/6, 11/2, 11/3, 11/4, 11/7, 14/2, 14/9, 15/1, 15/3, 15/4, 20/5

Langdon abbey, *Premonstratensian, Kent, TR3247, nil access to site, south*
15/2, 15/3

Langley abbey, *Premonstratensian, Norf., TG3603, nil access to site, south*
2/1, 2/7, 11/7, 12/3, 12/4, 14/9, 15/1, 15/3, 15/5

Lapley priory, *Benedictine, Staffs., SJ8713, public access to church, north*
3/1, 4/1, 5/1, 5/4, 6/5, 8/1, 8/2, 9/3

Lastingham abbey, *Benedictine, Yorks. NR, SE7390, public access to church, nil*
3/1, 4/1, 4/5, 5/4, 9/6

Latton priory, *Augustinian, Essex, TL4709 (in Harlow), limited access to site, nia*
3/6, 8/1, 11/2

Launceston priory, *Augustinian, Corn., SX3384, public access to site, south*
1/3

Launde priory, *Augustinian, Leics., SK8004, limited access to site, south*
3/5, 4/1

Leez (or **Leighs) priory**, *Augustinian, Essex, TL7018, nil access to site, south*
2/1

Leicester (St. Mary de Pratis) abbey, *Augustinian, Leics., SK5905, public access* to site, south
2/1, 2/3, 10/4, 17/2

Leiston abbey, *Premonstratensian, Suff., TM4464, public access to site, south*
2/2, 3/5, 3/7, 4/1, 4/2, 13/4, 14/1, 14/4, 15/4, 19/4

Lenton priory, *Cluniac, Notts., SK5539, public access to site, south*
2/5, 7/2

Leominster priory, *Benedictine, Heref., SO4959, public access to church, north*
1/5, 3/1, 4/4, 5/1, 5/3, 5/5, 7/2, 8/1, 8/2, 13/6

Leonard Stanley priory, *Benedictine, Glos., SO8003, public access to church, south*
1/3,3/1, 4/1, 4/4, 5/1, 5/2, 5/3, 5/4, 8/1, 11/2, 17/1, 17/5, 17/6, 17/8

Letheringham priory, *Augustinian, Suff., TM2758, public access to site, north*
2/1, 2/3, 3/1, 5/1, 5/5, 11/2, 16/2, 18/1

Lewes friary, *Franciscan, Ssx., TQ4110, limited access to site (part), nia*
2/1

Lewes (or Southover) priory, *Cluniac, Ssx., TQ4110, public access to site, south*
2/1, 2/5, 10/3, 13/6, 17/2

Lilleshall abbey, *Augustinian, Shrops., SJ7315, public access to site, south*
3/7, 4/1, 11/2, 11/3, 12/6, 12/7, 18/1

Lincoln friary, *Carmelite, Lincs., SK9871, nil access to site, nia*
13/8

Lincoln friary, *Franciscan, Lincs., SK9871, public access to church, south*
3/6

Lincoln St. Mary Magdalene's cell (now called Monks Abbey**)**, *Benedictine, Lincs., SK9872, public access to site, nia*
3/7, 4/1

Lindisfarne (or Holy Island) priory, *Benedictine, Northumb., NU1342, public access to site, south*
1/3, 2/3, 2/7, 3/7, 4/1, 4/3, 4/6, 5/5, 5/6, 8/1, 10/5, 13/3

Little Dunmow priory, *Augustinian, Essex, TL6521, public access to church, south*
3/5, 4/1, 4/2, 6/2, 7/2, 8/1, 9/2, 15/4

Little Malvern priory, *Benedictine, Worcs., SO7740, public access to church, limited access to remainder of site, south*
3/1, 3/2, 4/1, 5/4, 6/4, 7/2, 8/1, 8/2, 9/1, 9/3, 9/4, 10/6, 11/2, 15/1, 15/4, 17/8, 20/9

Little Maplestead commandery, *Knights Hospitaller, Essex, TL8233, public access to church, nil*
3/1, 4/1, 5/1, 7/2, 18/1

Littlemore priory, *Benedictine (nuns), Oxon., SP5402, nil access to site, nia*
12/1

Llanbadarn-fawr priory, *Benedictine, Card., SN6081, public access to church, nia*
3/1, 4/1, 5/1, 5/2, 5/4, 7/2

Llangennith cell, *Benedictine, Glam., SS4391, public access to church, south*
3/1, 4/1, 5/1, 5/3, 5/5, 7/2, 8/1

Llanllugan priory, *Cistercian (nuns), Montg., SJ0602, public access to church, north*
3/1, 4/1, 5/1, 7/2, 9/4, 18/1

Llantarnam abbey, *Cistercian, Monm., ST3193, nil access to site, nia*
17/1

Llanthony priory, *Augustinian, Monm., SO2928, public access to site, south*
2/1, 3/7, 5/1, 5/2, 5/5, 5/6, 12/7, 15/1, 15/3, 15/4, 16/2, 19/3

Loders priory, *Benedictine, Dorset, SY4994, public access to church, nia*
3/3

London charterhouse, *Carthusian, Mdx., TQ3282, nil access to site, north*
2/1, 2/3, 2/7, 8/1, 10/3, 10/6, 12/4, 12/5, 13/2, 13/8, 14/8, 19/4

London friary, *Carmelite. Mdx., TQ3181, nil access to site, nia*
18/2

Louth Park abbey, *Cistercian, Lincs., TF3489 (at Keddington), limited access to site, south*
17/8

Ludlow friary, *Carmelite, Shrops., SO5175, limited access to site (part), nia*
2/3

Lyminster priory *Benedictine (nuns), Ssx., TQ0205, public access to church, nia*
3/3

Maiden Bradley priory, *Augustinian, Wilts., ST8039, nil access to site, nia*
18/2

Malling abbey, *Benedictine (nuns), Kent, TQ6958, limited access to site, south*
1/2, 1/3, 2/1, 3/6, 3/7, 5/6, 11/1, 11/4, 12/4, 15/4, 17/1

Malmesbury abbey, *Benedictine, Wilts., ST9387, public access to site, north*
1/3, 3/1, 3/2, 5/1, 5/3, 5/6, 6/3, 6/6, 9/6, 10/4, 10/6, 11/2, 13/6, 15/4, 18/1

Malpas cell (near Newport), *Cluniac, Monm., ST3090, public access to church, nia*
3/5, 4/1

Malton priory (in Old Malton), *Gilbertine, Yorks. NR, SE8072, public access to church, south*
3/1, 3/2, 5/1, 5/5, 9/1, 11/2, 14/2, 18/1, 19/4, 20/9

Malvern priory, *Benedictine, Worcs., SO7746, public access to church, south*
2/1, 3/1, 4/1, 4/4, 4/5, 5/1, 5/2, 5/4, 6/1, 6/6, 7/2, 8/1, 8/2, 9/1, 9/3, 9/4, 10/1, 11/2

Margam abbey, *Cistercian, Glam., SS8086, public access to site, south*
1/3, 2/3, 3/1, 3/2, 5/1, 8/1, 11/2, 11/3, 12/3, 12/4, 12/5, 13/6, 20/9

Marham abbey, *Cistercian (nuns), Norf., TF7110, public access to church, south*
1/3, 3/7, 15/3

Marrick priory, *Benedictine (nuns), Yorks. NR, SE0898, nil access to site, nia*
3/6, 5/5

Mattersey priory, *Gilbertine, Notts., SK7090, public access to site, south*
7/1, 14/8, 19/4

Maxstoke priory, *Augustinian, Warws., SP2386, nil access to site, north*
1/3, 2/1, 2/3, 7/2

Meaux (or Melsa) abbey , *Cistercian, Yorks. ER, TA0939 (east of Beverley), limited access to site, south*
18/2

Merevale abbey, *Cistercian, Warws., SP2798, public access to church, limited access to remainder of site, south*
1/1, 14/3, 14/4, 14/5

Merton priory, *Augustinian, Sry., TQ2669, nil access to site, nia*
2/3

Michelham priory, *Augustinian, Ssx., TQ5609, public access to site, south*
2/1, 2/4, 11/7, 14/1, 14/3, 14/4, 14/9, 15/3, 15/4, 17/1, 18/1, 20/6

Milton (or Milton Abbas) abbey, *Benedictine, Dorset, ST8102, public access to church, north*
1/4, 3/1, 4/1, 5/2, 5/4, 6/1, 6/3, 7/2, 7/4, 8/1, 8/2, 9/1, 9/2, 9/3, 9/5, 9/6, 10/1, 11/1, 11/2, 15/4, 18/1

Minster (or Talcarne) cell, *Benedictine, Corn., SS1191 (near Boscastle), public access to church, nia*
3/3

Minster-in-Sheppey priory (now called abbey), *Augustinian (canonesses), Kent, TR9673, public access to church, north*
1/5, 2/1, 3/1, 5/1, 5/5, 6/4, 6/5, 7/2, 8/1, 8/2, 11/4

Missenden abbey (at Great Missenden), *Augustinian, Bucks., SP8901, limited access to site, south*
12/1

Moatenden (or Mottenden) friary, *Trinitarian, Kent, TQ8346, nil access to site, nia*
18/2

Monk Bretton priory, *Benedictine, Yorks. WR, SE3807, public access to site, south*
2/1, 2/3, 8/1, 8/2, 9/3, 11/2, 11/3, 13/7, 14/4, 14/8, 14/9, 17/5, 18/1

Monkland (or Monkenlane) cell, *Benedictine, Heref., SO4757, public access to church, nil*
3/1, 4/1, 5/1, 5/5, 7/2, 8/1

Monks Horton priory, *Cluniac, Kent, TR1340 (near Postling), nil access to site, nia*
15/1

Monks Kirby priory, *Benedictine, Warws., SP4683, public access to church, nia*
3/1, 4/1, 4/4, 5/1, 5/3, 5/5, 8/1, 8/2

Monkton Farleigh priory, *Cluniac, Wilts., ST8066, nil access to site, nia*
13/8

Monkton (or **Pembroke**) **priory**, *Benedictine, Pembr., SM9801, public access to church, north*
2/3, 3/1, 4/1, 4/4, 5/1, 5/2, 5/3, 5/4, 5/5, 7/2, 8/1, 10/6, 11/4, 18/1

Monkwearmouth cell, *Benedictine, Durh., NZ4058, public access to church, south*
3/1, 4/1, 5/1, 5/5, 8/1

Monmouth priory, *Benedictine, Monm., SO5113, public access to church, north*
2/1, 3/5, 5/5, 9/3

Montacute priory, *Cluniac, Som., ST4917, public access to church, nia*
1/3, 2/1, 17/6, 17/8

Morville cell, *Benedictine, Shrops., SO6794, public access to church, nil*
3/1, 4/1, 5/1, 5/5, 7/2, 17/8, 18/1

Mottisfont priory (now called abbey), *Augustinian, Hants., SU3227, public access to site, south*
1/3, 3/6, 6/3, 15/2, 15/3, 20/9

Mount Grace charterhouse (called priory), *Carthusian, Yorks. NR, SE4598, public access to site, north*
1/3, 2/1, 2/3, 3/7, 4/4, 5/1, 5/2, 5/4, 5/6, 11/7, 13/8, 14/8, 15/4, 18/1, 19/4

Muchelney abbey, *Benedictine, Som., ST4224, public access to site, south*
1/3, 9/3, 11/1, 13/6, 14/6, 14/8, 15/4, 17/5

Neath abbey, *Cistercian, Glam., SS7398, public access to site, south*
2/1, 2/2, 3/7, 7/1, 8/1, 9/2, 11/2, 12/2, 13/3, 13/4, 13/6, 13/7, 15/1, 15/3, 15/5, 17/2, 20/8

Netley abbey, *Cistercian, Hants., SU4509, public access to site, south*
3/7 4/4, 4/6, 5/2, 5/6, 8/1, 9/3, 11/2, 11/7, 12/3, 12/4, 12/6, 13/6, 13/7, 13/9, 14/8, 15/4, 19/2

Newark (or Aldbury) priory (near Ripley), *Augustinian, Sry., TQ0557, nil access to site, nia*
1/4, 3/7, 6/4

Newcastle-upon-Tyne friary, *Augustinian, Northumb., NZ2564, nil access to site, nia*
3/6, 5/4

Newcastle-upon-Tyne friary, *Carmelite, Northumb., NZ2564, public access to site*
2/1, 2/3

Newcastle-upon-Tyne friary, *Dominican, Northumb., NZ2564, public access to site, south*
11/7, 12/1, 12/3, 12/5, 13/1, 13/9, 14/1, 14/4, 15/1, 15/4, 19/5, 20/2

Newminster abbey, *Cistercian, Northumb., NZ1986, limited access to site, south*
11/1

Newstead priory (now called abbey), *Augustinian, Notts., SK5454, public access to site, south*
3/6, 3/7, 5/6, 7/3, 11/1, 11/2, 11/7, 12/1, 12/3, 12/4, 12/7, 13/1, 13/9, 14/1, 14/3, 14/4, 14/7, 15/3, 15/4, 18/1, 19/3, 20/2

Newstead priory, *Gilbertine, Lincs., TA0105 (at Cadney near R.Ancholme), nia*
18/2

Newton Longville cell, *Cluniac, Bucks., SP8431, public access to church, nia*
3/3

Norton abbey , *Augustinian, Ches., SJ5582 (at Runcorn), public access to site, south*
9/2, 9/3, 9/6, 15/2, 15/3, 18/1

Norwich cathedral-priory (now cathedral), *Benedictine, Norf., TG2309, public access to site, south*
1/2, 1/3, 2/1, 2/2, 2/3, 2/7, 3/1, 4/1, 4/2, 4/3, 4/4, 5/1, 5/2, 5/4, 6/2, 6/3, 6/6, 7/1, 7/2, 7/3, 8/1, 9/1, 9/2, 9/3, 9/4, 9/5, 9/6, 10/1, 10/2, 10/3, 11/1, 11/2, 11/3, 11/7, 12/3, 14/3, 14/4, 14/7, 15/3, 15/4, 18/1, 19/1, 20/1

Norwich friary, *Carmelite, Norf., TG2309, public access to site, nia*
2/1, 18/2

Norwich friary, *Dominican, Norf., TG2309, public access to site, north*
3/6, 4/1, 5/1, 5/4, 11/1, 11/2, 12/1, 12/2, 13/1, 14/4, 19/5, 20/7

Nostell priory , *Augustinian, Yorks. WR, SE4117 (near Sharlston), nil access to site, nia*
2/5

Notley (or **Nutley) abbey** , *Augustinian, Bucks., SP7109 (near Thame), nil access to site, south*
14/3, 15/4, 17/6

Nuneaton priory, *Benedictine (nuns), Warws., SP3692, public access to church, south*
3/5, 5/2, 5/4

Nun Monkton priory, *Benedictine (nuns), Yorks. WR, SE5158, public access to church, south*
3/1, 5/1, 5/5, 7/1, 7/2, 8/1, 8/2, 11/2, 11/6

Osney abbey, *Augustinian, Oxon., SP5005, limited access to site (part), nia*
2/1, 2/5

Otterton priory, *Benedictine, Devon., SY0885, public access to church, nia*
3/3

Ovingham cell, *Augustinian, Northumb., NZ0964, public access to church, nil*
3/1, 4/1, 5/1, 5/2, 5/3, 5/5, 7/1, 7/2, 8/1, 8/2, 9/2, 18/2

Owston abbey, *Augustinian, Leics., SK7708, public access to church, south*
2/3, 3/1, 5/1, 5/5, 7/2, 8/1, 11/2, 17/8, 18/1

Oxford Durham college (now part of Trinity college), *Benedictine, Oxon., SP5106, limited access to site, north*
12/1

Oxford friary, *Franciscan, Oxon, SP5106, nil access to site, nia*
2/3

Oxford Gloucester college (now part of Worcester college), *Benedictine, Oxon., SP5106, limited access to site, south*
14/1

Oxford St. Bernard's college (now part of St. John's college), *Cistercian, Oxon., SP5106, limited access to site, south*
2/2, 3/1

Oxford St. Frideswide's priory (now cathedral & part of Christ Church college), *Augustinian, Oxon., SP5106, public access to site, south*
3/1, 4/1, 4/2, 4/4, 5/1, 5/2, 5/4, 8/1, 9/1, 9/4, 10/2, 10/6, 11/1, 11/2, 12/1, 12/3, 12/4, 12/7, 14/1, 14/3, 14/4, 14/5, 18/1, 19/3, 20/3

Oxford St. Mary's college (now part of Frewen hall owned by Brazenose college), *Augustinian, Oxon., SP5106, limited access to site, nia*
2/1

Pamber (or Monk Sherborne) priory, *Benedictine, Hants., SU6158 (at Pamber End), public access to church, south*
3/1, 4/1, 5/4, 6/3, 7/2, 8/1, 18/1

Patrixbourne cell, *Augustinian, Kent, TR1955, public access to church, nia*
3/3

Penmon priory, *Augustinian, Angls., SH6381, public access to site, south*
2/3, 3/1, 4/1, 5/1, 5/2, 5/4, 7/2, 8/1, 13/1, 13/8, 13/9, 14/1, 14/3, 14/4, 14/5, 14/6, 15/1, 15/4, 17/6, 18/1, 19/3, 20/5

Pentney priory, *Augustinian, Norf., TF7012, nil access to site, nia*
2/1

Pershore abbey, *Benedictine, Worcs., SO9546, public access to church, south*
1/3, 1/5, 2/5, 3/1, 3/2, 4/1, 4/2, 4/4, 5/2, 5/4, 6/6, 7/2, 7/3, 8/1, 8/2, 9/3, 9/6, 11/2, 11/3, 13/3, 17/2, 18/1

Peterborough abbey (now cathedral), *Benedictine, Northants., SP1998, public access to site, south*
1/1, 1/2, 1/3, 2/1, 2/3, 3/1, 4/1, 4/4, 5/1, 5/2, 5/3, 5/4, 5/5, 6/6, 7/1, 7/2, 7/3, 8/1, 9/1, 9/2, 9/5, 9/6, 10/2, 10/4, 10/6, 11/2, 11/7, 12/6, 14/3, 14/7, 14/9, 15/4, 16/2, 18/1, 19/1

Pill priory, *Tironensian, Pembr., SM8809 (near Milford Haven), nil access to site, south*
3/7, 12/3, 12/4, 12/7, 13/6

Pilton priory, *Benedictine, Devon, SS5534 (in Barnstaple), public access to church, north*
1/5, 3/1, 5/1, 5/2, 5/3, 5/4, 6/5, 6/6, 7/2, 7/4, 8/1, 10/1, 10/6, 11/2, 11/4, 15/4

Pinley priory, *Cistercian (nuns), Warws., SP2166 (near Claverdon), nil access to site, nia*
15/4

Plymouth friary, *Franciscan, Devon, SX4855, public access to site, nia*
2/1

Plympton priory, *Augustinian, Devon., SX5356, public access to church, nia*
1/4, 2/2

Polesworth abbey, *Benedictine (nuns), Warws., SK2602, public access to church, south*
1/5, 2/1, 3/1, 4/1, 5/1, 5/5, 6/6, 7/2, 8/1, 11/2, 15/1, 18/1, 20/9

Poling commandery, *Knights Hospitaller, Ssx., TQ0404, nil access to site, nil*
18/2

Portchester priory, *Augustinian, Hants., SU6204, public access to site, south*
3/1, 4/1, 5/1, 5/2, 5/4, 7/2, 8/1, 9/2, 10/6, 11/2, 18/1

Poughley priory, *Augustinian, Berks., SU4175 (near Chaddleworth), nil access to site, nia*
15/1

Priestholme (or Puffin Island) cell, *Augustinian, Angls., SH6582, limited access to site, nia*
3/7, 5/4

Prittlewell priory, *Cluniac, Essex, TQ8687 (in Southend-on-Sea), public access to site, south*
14/3, 14/4, 15/4, 20/6

Quarr abbey, *Cistercian, IoW, SZ5692, limited access to site, north*
1/3, 2/3, 10/3, 15/1

Quenington commandery, *Knights Hospitaller, Glos., SP1404, public access to church, limited access to site (part), nia*
1/3, 2/1, 17/6

Ramsey abbey, *Benedictine, Hunts., TL2985, public access to present church, limited access to remainder of site, nia*
1/4, 2/1, 2/3, 2/5, 3/6, 4/2, 7/3, 17/7

Ranton priory, *Augustinian, Staffs., SJ8624, nil access to site, nia*
3/7, 5/5, 11/2

Reading abbey, *Benedictine, Berks., SU7273, public access to site, south*
1/1, 2/1, 2/5, 10/3, 12/3, 12/4, 12/7

Reading friary, *Franciscan, Berks., SU7173, public access to church, north*
3/1, 5/1, 5/2, 11/2

Redlingfield priory, *Benedictine (nuns), Suff., TM1971, public access to church, north(?)*
2/5, 3/1, 4/1, 5/1, 5/3, 5/5, 7/2, 8/1, 11/2, 17/1, 17/8

Repton (Anglo-Saxon) **abbey**, *Benedictine, Derbs., SK3027, public access to church, nia*
3/5, 4/1, 4/5

Repton priory, *Augustinian, Derbs., SK3027, limited access to site, north*
1/3, 2/1, 2/3, 2/7, 15/1, 15/3, 15/4, 18/1

Rewley abbey, *Cistercian, Oxon., SP5006, public access to site (part), nia*
2/1, 2/3

Ribstone (or **Ribston**) **preceptory**, *Knights Templar, Yorks. WR, SE3954, nil access to site, nil*
3/3

Richmond friary, *Franciscan, Yorks. NR, NZ1701, limited access to site, nia*
2/1, 5/4

Richmond St. Martin's priory, *Benedictine, Yorks. NR, NZ1801, nil access to site, nia*
3/7, 5/5

Rievaulx abbey, *Cistercian, Yorks. NR, SE5885, public access to site, south*
1/1, 3/7, 4/1, 4/4, 5/2, 5/3, 7/1, 8/1, 9/2, 9/3, 10/2, 11/1, 11/3, 11/7, 12/7, 14/1, 14/3, 14/4, 14/5, 14/8, 16/1, 19/2

Robertsbridge abbey, *Cistercian, Ssx., TQ7323, nil access to site, south*
15/4

Rocester abbey, *Augustinian, Staffs., SK1139, public access to church, nia*
1/3

Roche abbey, *Cistercian, Yorks. WR, SK5490 (near Maltby), public access to site, south*
2/1, 2/3, 3/7, 4/4, 5/2, 8/1, 9/3, 13/7

Rochester cathedral-priory (now cathedral), *Benedictine, Kent, TQ7468, public access to site, south*
1/3, 2/1, 2/2, 2/3, 3/1, 4/1, 4/2, 4/4, 4/5, 5/1, 5/2, 5/4, 5/5, 6/3, 6/6, 8/1, 8/2, 9/1, 9/3, 9/5, 9/6, 10/1, 10/2, 11/2, 11/7, 12/3, 12/6, 13/4, 14/3, 14/9, 18/1

Romsey abbey, *Benedictine (nuns), Hants., SU3521, public access to church, south*
1/5, 3/1, 4/1, 4/3, 5/1, 5/2, 5/4, 6/2, 8/1, 9/3, 9/5, 9/6, 11/2, 11/3, 14/4, 20/9

Rothley Temple preceptory, *Knights Templar, Leics., SK5813, limited access to church, nil*
3/1, 4/1, 5/1, 5/3, 8/1

Royston priory, *Augustinian, Herts., TL3641, public access to church, south*
2/3, 3/1, 4/1, 5/4, 7/2, 8/1

Rufford abbey, *Cistercian, Notts., SK6464, public access to site, south*
13/3, 15/1, 15/3, 15/5

Rumburgh cell, *Benedictine, Suff., TM3582, public access to church, north*
2/4, 3/1, 4/1, 5/1, 5/3, 5/5, 6/4, 6/5, 7/2, 8/1, 10/6, 11/2, 11/4

Ruthin priory: *Bonhommes, Denbigh, SJ1258, public access to church, north*
2/3, 3/1, 5/1, 5/4, 8/1, 18/1, 18/2

Rye friary, *Augustinian, Ssx., TQ9220, nil access to site, nia*
3/6

Rye friary, *Sack friars, Ssx., TQ9220, nil access to site, nia*
18/1, 18/2

St. Albans abbey (now cathedral), *Benedictine, Herts., TL1407, public access to site, south*
2/1, 3/1, 4/1, 4/2, 4/4, 5/1, 5/2, 5/4, 6/1, 6/4, 6/6, 8/1, 8/2, 9/3, 9/5, 10/1, 10/2, 10/6, 11/2, 11/4, 12/7, 17/8, 18/1

St. Anthony-in-Roseland cell, *Augustinian, Corn., SW8532, public access to church, nil*
3/1, 4/1, 5/1, 5/2, 5/4, 8/1, 14/4, 20/9

St. Bees priory, *Benedictine, Cumb., NX9712, public access to church, south*
2/3, 3/1, 3/2, 4/1, 4/4, 5/1, 5/2, 5/4, 8/1, 9/6, 18/1

St. Benet of Holme's (or Holme) abbey, *Benedictine, Norf., TG3815 (near Thurne), public access to site, south*
2/1, 17/8, 18/1

St. Clear's cell, *Cluniac, Carm., SN2816, public access to church, nia*
3/1, 4/1, 5/1, 5/5, 7/2, 8/1, 18/1

St. Dogmael's abbey, *Tironensian, Pembr., SN1646, public access to site, south*
1/3, 3/7, 4/5, 5/2, 16/2, 18/1, 19/4

St. Germans priory, *Augustinian, Corn., SX3757, public access to church, south*
1/5, 3/1, 4/4, 5/1, 5/3, 5/5, 7/2, 8/1, 9/1, 11/4, 13/8, 14/4, 20/9

St. Michael's Mount priory, *Benedictine, Corn., SW5230, public access to site, nil*
2/1, 3/1, 4/1, 4/2, 5/1, 5/4, 14/4

St. Olave's (or **Herringfleet) priory**, *Augustinian, Suff., TM4699, public access to site, north*
14/2

St. Osyth abbey, *Augustinian, Essex, TM1215, public access to site, north*
1/3, 2/1, 2/2, 2/3, 2/5, 2/7, 12/2, 14/7, 15/2, 17/1, 18/1, 20/8

Salisbury friary, *Franciscan, Wilts., SU1529, nil access to site, nia*
18/2

Salley (or **Sawley) abbey**, *Cistercian, Yorks. WR, SD7847, public access to site, south*
2/1, 3/7, 7/1, 8/1, 9/3, 13/3, 13/6, 13/7, 15/5

Sandford preceptory, *Knights Templar, Oxon., SP5302, nil access to site, nil*
3/6, 9/6, 18/1

Scarborough cell, *Cistercian, Yorks. NR, TA0488, public access to church, south*
3/3

Seaton priory, *Benedictine (nuns), Cumb., NY0131, public access to site, nia*
4/6

Seez abbey, *mother house in Normandy, n/a*
17/2

Selby abbey, *Benedictine, Yorks. WR, SE6232, public access to church, south*
3/1, 4/1, 5/1, 5/2, 5/3, 5/4, 5/5, 6/1, 7/2, 8/1, 8/2, 10/1, 11/2, 12/6

Sele (or **Beeding) friary**, *Carmelite, Ssx., TQ1910, public access to church, nia*
1/5, 3/1, 4/1, 5/1, 5/5, 7/2, 8/1, 18/2

Sempringham priory, *Gilbertine (mixed), Lincs., TF1132 (near Billingborough), public access to church, north (canons) & south (nuns)*
1/3

Shaftesbury abbey, *Benedictine (nuns), Dorset, ST8623, public access to site, south*
4/5, 10/2, 17/1, 17/2, 17/6

Shap (or **Hepp) abbey**, *Premonstratensian, Westmld., NY5515, public access to site, south*
3/7, 5/5, 13/7, 15/2

Sheen charterhouse (called priory), *Carthusian, Sry., TQ1775 (in Richmond), nil access to site, nia*
17/2, 17/6

Sherborne abbey, *Benedictine, Dorset, ST6417, public access to church, limited access to remainder of site, north*
1/5, 2/1, 3/1, 3/2, 4/1, 4/2, 4/4, 5/1, 5/2, 5/3, 5/4, 6/6, 7/2, 8/1, 9/1, 9/2, 9/3, 9/4, 9/6, 10/4, 11/2, 11/7, 12/7, 14/6, 15/1, 15/3, 15/4, 17/1, 17/2, 18/1, 20/9

Sheringham cell, *Augustinian, Norf., TG1441, public access to church, nia*
3/3

Shipley preceptory, *Knights Templar, Ssx., TQ1422, public access to church, nil*
3/1, 4/1, 5/1, 5/3, 5/4, 7/2, 8/1, 8/2

Shrewsbury abbey, *Benedictine, Shrops., SJ4912, public access to site, south*
3/1, 4/1, 5/1, 5/3, 5/5, 7/2, 8/1, 10/2, 11/2, 14/5, 16/2

Shrewsbury friary, *Franciscan, Shrops., SJ4912, nil access to site, nia*
18/2

Shulbrede priory, *Augustinian, Ssx., SU8729, nil access to site, south*
9/5, 11/7, 14/4, 15/1, 15/4, 17/8, 20/6

Sibton abbey, *Cistercian, Suff., TM3670, limited access to site, south*
14/4

Slebech commandery, *Knights Hospitaller, Pembr., SN0315 (east of Haverford-west), nil access to site, nil*
17/6

Smithfield St. Bartholomew's priory, *Augustinian, Mdx., TQ3282 (in London), public access to site, south*
3/1, 4/1, 4/2, 4/5, 5/2, 5/4, 6/3, 6/6, 7/2, 8/2, 10/3, 10/6, 11/1, 11/2, 12/3, 18/1

Snainton preceptory, *Knights Templar, Yorks. ER, SE9282, nil access to site, nil*
18/2

Snaith cell, *Benedictine, Yorks. WR, SE6422, public access to church, nil*
3/1, 4/1, 4/4, 5/1, 5/2, 5/3, 5/5, 8/1, 10/1, 10/2, 12/6, 18/1

Sompting preceptory(?), *Knights Templar, Ssx., TQ1605, public access to church, nil*
3/4

Southwark priory (or **St. Mary Overie)** (now cathedral), *Augustinian, Sry., TQ3280, public access to church, north*
3/1, 4/1, 4/4, 5/1, 5/2, 5/4, 6/1, 8/1, 10/1, 11/2, 11/4, 18/1

Southwick priory, *Augustinian, Hants., SU6308, nil access to site, nia*
1/3

Spalding priory, *Benedictine, Lincs., TF2522, nil access to site, nia*
17/2, 17/5, 18/2

Sporle cell, *Benedictine, Norf., TF8411, public access to church, nia*
3/3

Stamford friary, *Carmelite, Lincs., TF0307, nil access to site, nia*
2/3

Stamford friary, *Franciscan, Lincs., TF0307, nil access to site, nia*
2/1

Stamford St. Leonard's priory, *Benedictine, Lincs., TF0407, public access to site, south*
3/7, 5/6

Stavordale priory, *Augustinian, Som., ST7532, nil access to site, nia*
3/6

Steventon priory, *Benedictine, Berks., SU4691, nil access to site, nia*
3/3, 15/4

Stidd commandery, *Knights Hospitaller, Lancs., SD6536, public access to church*
3/4

Stixwould priory, *Premonstratensian (canonesses), Lincs., TF1866, nil access to site, nia*
17/8

Stogursey (or Stoke Courcy) priory, *Benedictine, Som., ST2142, public access to church, nia*
3/1, 4/1, 4/4, 5/1, 5/2, 5/3, 5/4, 7/2, 8/1, 9/2, 17/6, 18/1

Stoneleigh abbey, *Cistercian, Warws., SP3271, limited access to site, south*
2/1, 2/5, 3/6, 12/2, 12/3, 12/4, 12/6, 12/7, 17/7

Stonely priory, *Augustinian, Hunts., TL1167, nil access to site, nia*
18/2

Stone priory, *Augustinian, Staffs., SJ9034, partial public access to site, south*
15/2

Stow abbey, *Benedictine, Lincs., SK8882, public access to church, north(?)*
3/1, 4/1, 4/4, 5/1, 5/2, 5/4, 7/2, 8/1, 9/2, 9/5, 11/2

Strata Florida abbey, *Cistercian, Card., SN7565, public access to site, south*
3/7, 4/4, 5/6, 9/3, 10/5, 11/6, 13/3, 18/1

Strood preceptory, *Knights Templar, Kent, TQ7369, public access to site, nil*
17/2, 18/2

Sudbury friary, *Dominican, Suff., TL8841, nil access to site, nia*
2/1

Sudbury St. Bartholomew's cell, *Benedictine, Suff.,* *TL8842, limited access to site, nia*
3/6, 8/1

Sutton-at-Hone St. John's Jerusalem commandery, *Knights Hospitaller, Kent, TQ5670, public access to site, nil*
2/4, 3/6, 8/1

Swaffham Bulbeck priory, *Benedictine (nuns), Cambs.,* *TL5562, nil access to site, nia*
18/2

Swavesey priory, *Benedictine, Cambs., TL3669, public access to church, nia*
3/3

Swine priory, *Cistercian (nuns), Yorks. ER, TA1336, public access to church, nia*
1/5, 3/1, 4/1, 4/4, 5/5, 6/6, 8/1, 8/2, 9/1, 10/1, 10/6

Swingfield commandery, *Knights Hospitaller, Kent, TR2343, public access to site, nil*
3/6

Syningthwaite (or **Sinningthwaite) priory**, *Cistercian (nuns), Yorks. WR, SE4649, nil access to site, nia*
11/7, 14/4

Syon abbey, *Bridgettine (nuns), Mdx., TQ1675 (in Hounslow), public access to site, nia*
15/2

Takeley priory, *Benedictine, Essex, TL5620, nil access to site, nia*
17/1, 17/2

Talley abbey, *Premonstratensian, Carm., SN6332, public access to site, south*
3/7

Tarrant (or Tarrant Kaines) abbey, *Cistercian (nuns), Dorset, ST9203 (at Tarrant Crawford), public access to church, nia*
3/3, 17/1, 18/2

Taunton priory, *Augustinian, Som., ST2324, nil access to site, nia*
17/1

Tavistock abbey, *Benedictine, Devon, SX4874, public access to site, south*
1/3, 2/1, 2/3, 16/2, 17/2

Temple Balsall preceptory, *Knights Templar, Warws., SP2076, public access to site, nil*
3/1, 4/1, 5/1, 8/1, 8/2, 14/4, 18/2, 19/6

Temple Bruer preceptory, *Knights Templar, Lincs., TF0054, public access to site, nil*
3/7, 5/5, 7/1, 8/1, 8/2, 9/2

Temple Combe preceptory, *Knights Templar, Som., ST7022, nil access to site, nil*
18/2

Temple Cressing (& Witham) preceptory, *Knights Templar, Essex, TL8019, public access to site, nil*
17/1

Temple Ewell preceptory, *Knights Templar, Kent, TR2944, public access to church, nil*
3/1, 4/1, 4/2, 5/1, 5/5, 8/1, 8/2

Temple Guiting preceptory, *Knights Templar, Glos., SP0928, public access to church, nil*
3/1, 4/1, 4/4, 5/1, 5/3, 7/2, 8/1, 9/4

Temple preceptory (known as The Temple), *Knights Templar, Mdx., TQ3181 (in London), public access to church, nil*
3/1, 4/1, 4/4, 4/5, 5/1, 5/3, 8/1, 10/6, 18/1

Tewkesbury abbey, *Benedictine, Glos., SO8932, public access to site, south*
1/5, 2/1, 2/5, 3/1, 4/1, 4/3, 4/4, 5/1, 5/2, 5/3, 5/4, 6/6, 7/1, 7/2, 8/1, 8/2, 9/1, 9/3, 9/4, 10/1, 10/3, 10/4, 11/2, 12/6, 13/3, 15/4, 17/1, 17/2, 17/4, 17/5, 17/6, 18/1

Thame abbey, *Cistercian, Oxon, SP7005, nil access to site, south*
1/1, 14/6, 15/4

Thetford friary, *Dominican, Norf., TL8683, nil access to site, nia*
3/7

Thetford priory, *Cluniac, Norf., TL8683, public access to site, south*
2/1, 3/7, 4/2, 7/1, 9/3, 10/4, 13/5, 14/9, 15/4, 16/1, 17/1, 17/5, 18/1

Thetford St. George's priory, *Benedictine (nuns), Norf., TL8882, limited access to site, south*
3/6, 12/4, 16/2, 18/2

Thetford St Sepulchre's priory, *Independent, Norf., TL8782, public access to site, north*
3/6, 5/1, 11/2

Thorney abbey, *Benedictine, Cambs., TF2804, public access to church, south*
3/1, 4/1, 5/1, 5/5, 9/6, 18/1

Thornton abbey, *Augustinian, Lincs., TA1219, public access to site, south*
1/2, 2/1, 2/3, 8/1, 9/6, 12/4, 12/7, 13/2, 17/8, 18/1

Throwley priory, *Benedictine, Kent, TQ9955, public access to church, nia*
3/3

Thurgarton priory, *Augustinian, Notts., SK6949, public access to church, south*
3/1, 5/1, 5/3, 5/5, 7/1, 9/1, 15/2, 20/9

Tilty abbey, *Cistercian, Essex, TL6026, public access to site, north*
1/1

Tintern abbey, *Cistercian, Monm., SO5300, public access to site, north*
1/1, 2/1, 3/7, 4/1, 4/4, 5/1, 5/2, 5/4, 5/6, 8/1, 8/2, 9/2, 11/2, 11/3, 11/6, 12/6, 13/3, 13/7, 13/9, 14/4, 14/5, 14/7, 14/8, 14/9, 15/1, 16/1, 18/1, 19/2

Titchfield abbey, *Premonstratensian, Hants., SU5406, public access to site, north*
2/3, 3/6, 9/3, 17/1, 18/1

Torre abbey, *Premonstratensian, Devon, SX9164, public access to site, south*
2/1, 2/2, 8/1, 12/3, 14/1, 14/4, 15/1, 15/4, 17/1, 19/4, 20/6

Tortington priory, *Augustinian, Ssx., TQ0005, nil access to site, nia*
3/6

Totnes priory, *Benedictine, Devon, SX8060, public access to site, north*
1/5, 3/1, 4/1, 4/4, 5/1, 5/3, 5/5, 6/4, 6/6, 7/2, 7/4, 8/1, 8/2, 10/6, 11/4, 14/1, 14/4, 20/9

Trentham priory, *Augustinian, Staffs., SJ8741, public access to church, south*
3/1, 4/1, 5/1, 5/3, 11/2

Tresco (or Trescaw) cell, *Benedictine, Scilly, SV8914, public access to site, nia*
3/7

Tupholme abbey, *Premonstratensian, Lincs., TF1467 (near Bardney), public access to site, south*
14/4, 14/5

Tutbury priory, *Benedictine, Staffs., SK2129, public access to church, north*
1/5, 3/1, 4/1, 5/1, 5/5, 18/1

Tynemouth priory, *Benedictine, Northumb., NZ3869, public access to site, south*
2/1, 2/3, 3/5, 3/7, 4/6, 5/6, 6/4, 8/1, 8/2, 9/2, 9/3, 10/1, 11/2, 15/4, 18/1

Ulverscroft priory, *Augustinian, Leics., SK5013 (near Copt Oak), nil access to site, south*
2/4, 3/7, 5/5, 9/3, 12/7, 15/4

Upholland priory, *Benedictine, Lancs., SD5206, public access to church, south*
3/1, 4/1, 4/4, 5/1, 5/5, 8/1, 18/1

Usk priory, *Benedictine (nuns), Monm., SO3801, public access to church, south*
1/5, 2/1, 3/1, 5/1, 5/3, 5/4, 6/5, 7/2, 18/1

Vale Royal abbey, *Cistercian, Ches., SJ6369 (near Winsford), public access to church, limited access to site of abbey, south*
1/1, 14/1, 14/4, 14/6, 15/1, 20/6

Valle Crucis abbey, *Cistercian, Denbigh., SJ2044, public access to site, south*
4/1, 4/4, 4/6, 5/2, 5/6, 6/3, 7/1, 8/1, 11/2, 11/7, 12/1, 12/3, 12/4, 12/6, 12/7, 13/1, 13/4, 13/8, 17/8, 18/1

Walsingham friary, *Franciscan, Norf., TF9336, nil access to site, south*
2/3, 16/1, 19/5

Walsingham priory, *Augustinian, Norf., TF9336, public access to site, south*
1/3, 1/4, 2/1, 2/3, 3/7, 4/6, 8/1, 10/6, 12/2, 13/9, 14/3, 14/4, 14/5, 14/9, 18/1

Waltham abbey, *Augustinian, Essex, TL3801, public access to site, north*
1/5, 2/1, 2/3, 3/1, 4/2, 4/5, 5/1, 6/1, 6/6, 7/2, 8/1, 8/2, 9/2, 9/5, 10/4, 14/7, 17/7, 18/1

Wangford priory, *Cluniac, Suff., TM4679 (near Southwold), public access to church, nia*
3/3

Warburton cell, *Premonstratensian, Ches., SJ7090, public access to church, nia*
3/5, 5/1

Ware friary, *Franciscan, Herts., TL3614, public access to site, nia*
11/1, 14/1, 14/4, 15/1, 15/4, 19/5, 20/6

Wareham cell, *Benedictine, Dorset, SY9288, public access to church, nia*
3/3

Watton priory, *Gilbertine (mixed), Yorks. ER, TA0250, public access to site (part), north (nuns), north (canons) adjacent churches*
1/3, 15/4

Waverley abbey, *Cistercian, Sry., SU8745 (near Farnham), public access to site, south*
12/7, 15/5

Welbeck abbey, *Premonstratensian, Notts., SK5674, nil access to site, south*
15/2

Welnetham friary, *Crutched friars, Suff., TL8860 (at Little Welnetham), nil access*
18/2

Welsh Newton preceptory(?), *Knights Templar, Heref., SO5018, public access to church*
3/4

Wendling abbey, *Premonstratensian, Norf., TF9313, nil access to site, south*
17/8

Wenlock priory, *Cluniac, Shrops., SJ6201, public access to site, south*
1/3, 3/7, 4/4 4/5, 5/2, 7/1, 7/3, 8/1, 9/3, 9/6, 11/2, 11/7, 12/3, 12/4, 12/6, 15/4, 16/1, 16/2, 19/4

West Acre priory, *Augustinian, Norf., TF7815, public access to church, south*
1/3, 2/1, 3/7, 5/5, 15/2, 15/3, 17/1

West Dereham abbey, *Premonstratensian, Norf., TF6500, nil access to site, nia*
2/1

West Mersea priory, *Benedictine, Essex, TM0113, public access to church, nia*
to site, nia
3/3

Westminster abbey, *Benedictine, Mdx., TQ3079, public access to site, south*
1/3, 2/2, 2/3, 3/1, 4/1, 4/2, 4/3, 4/4, 5/1, 5/2, 5/3, 5/4, 5/5, 6/1, 6/2, 6/3, 6/5, 6/6, 7/1, 7/4, 8/1, 8/2, 9/1, 9/2, 9/3, 9/4, 9/5, 9/6, 10/1, 10/2, 10/3, 10/4, 10/6, 11/1, 11/2, 11/5, 11/6, 11/7, 12/1, 12/3, 12/4, 12/5, 12/6, 12/7, 13/1, 13/2, 13/3, 13/4, 13/9, 14/3, 14/6, 14/7, 14/8, 14/9, 15/3, 15/4, 16/1, 16/2, 18/1, 19/1, 20/7

Wetheral priory, *Benedictine, Cumb., NY4754, public access to site (part), nia*
2/1

Weybourne priory, *Augustinian, Norf., TG1143, public access to church, north*
1/5, 3/1, 3/2, 5/1, 5/3, 5/4, 5/5, 6/3, 8/1, 8/2, 9/2, 10/6

Whalley abbey, *Cistercian, Lancs., SD7336, public access to site, south*
1/2, 1/3, 2/1, 2/3, 3/7, 8/1, 9/1, 11/3, 11/7, 12/1, 12/3, 12/5, 13/6, 13/7, 14/6, 14/8, 14/9, 15/1, 15/4, 15/5, 18/1

Whitby abbey, *Benedictine, Yorks. NR, NZ9011, public access to site, south*
1/3, 3/7, 4/4, 4/6, 5/2, 5/6, 8/1

Widmere commandery, *Knights Hospitaller, Bucks., SU8891 (near Marlow), nil access to site, nil*
3/6

Wigmore abbey, *Augustinian, Heref., SO4171, nil access to site, south*
1/3, 2/1, 2.3, 3/7, 9/3, 15/4, 18/1

Wilberfoss priory, *Benedictine (nuns), Yorks. ER, SE7351, public access to church, nia*
3/3

Wilmington priory, *Benedictine, Ssx., TQ5404, public access to site, nil*
1/5, 2/2, 3/1, 4/1, 4/4, 5/1, 5/3, 7/2, 8/1, 18/2

Wilton abbey, *Benedictine (nuns), Wilts., SU0931, nil access to site, nia*
2/5

Winchcombe abbey, *Benedictine, Glos., SP0228, public access to church, nia*
1/3, 2/7, 15/4, 17/1, 17/4

Winchelsea friary, *Franciscan, Ssx., TQ9017, nil access to site, south*
3/7, 4/1, 18/1

Winchester cathedral-priory (now cathedral), *Benedictine, Hants., SU4829, public access to site, south*
2/1, 2/2, 2/3, 2/7, 3/1, 4/1, 4/2, 4/4, 4/5, 5/1, 5/2, 5/4, 6/1, 6/2, 6/6, 7/2, 7/4, 8/1, 9/1, 9/2, 9/3, 9/4, 9/5, 9/6, 10/1, 10/2, 10/4, 11/2, 12/3, 12/6, 12/7, 15/4, 18/1, 20/9

Witham (or **Selwood) charterhouse** (also called friary), *Carthusian, Som., ST7441, public access to church, nia*
1/1,17/6, 17/8

Wix (or **Sopwick) priory** (now called abbey), *Benedictine (nuns), Essex, TM1628, public access to church, nia*
3/5, 5/1

Wolston cell, *Benedictine, Warws., SP4175, nil access to site, nia*
18/2

Woodhouse friary, *Augustinian, Shrops., SO6678 (north west of Cleobury Mortimer), nil access to site, nia*
2/4

Woodkirk cell, *Augustinian, Yorks. WR, SE2725, public access to church, nia*
3/5, 5/5

Woodspring priory, *Augustinian, Som., 3363, public access to site, south*
2/1, 3/6, 9/1, 11/2, 16/2, 17/1

Worcester cathedral-priory (now cathedral), *Benedictine, Worcs., SO8554, public access to site, south*
2/1, 2/3, 3/1, 4/1, 4/2, 4/4, 4/5, 5/1, 5/2, 5/3, 5/4, 6/2, 6/6, 8/1, 8/2, 9/1, 9/5, 9/6, 10/1, 10/4, 10/6, 11/1, 11/2, 11/3, 11/7, 12/1, 12/3, 12/4, 12/6, 12/7, 13/6, 14/1, 14/3, 14/4, 14/5, 14/7, 15/3, 15/4, 16/2, 18/1, 19/1, 20/3

Worcester friary, *Franciscan, Worcs., SO8554, public access to site, nia*
15/4

Worcester St. Wulstan's hospital, *Augustinian, Worcs., SO8554, public access to site, nia*
9/1, 9/4, 9/5, 18/2

Worksop (Radford) priory, *Augustinian, Notts., SK5979, public access to site, north*
1/2, 2/1, 3/1, 4/1, 4/2, 4/4, 5/1, 5/2, 5/3, 5/4, 5/5, 6/2, 8/1, 8/2, 11/2, 15/3

Wroxall priory (now called abbey), *Benedictine (nuns), Warws., SP2270, nil access to site, south*
3/5, 5/1, 9/4

Wykeham priory, *Cistercian (nuns), Yorks. NR, SE9684, nil access to site, nia*
3/7

Wymondham abbey, *Benedictine, Norf., TG1001, public access to site, south*
1/4, 1/5,2/3, 3/1, 3/2, 4/2, 4/4, 5/1, 5/3, 5/4, 5/5, 6/1, 7/2, 8/1, 8/2, 10/6, 17/4, 18/1

Wymondley priory, *Augustinian, Herts., TL2128, nil access to site, nia*
3/6, 13/8

Yarmouth friary, *Franciscan, Norf., TG5208, public access to site, south*
11/1

Yarmouth priory, *Benedictine, Norf., TG5208, public access to church, nil*
3/5, 4/1, 4/2, 5/1, 5/2, 5/3, 5/4, 6/3, 8/1, 11/2, 14/3, 14/4, 18/1

Yeaveley (& Barrow) preceptory, *Knights Templar, Derbs., SK1840, nil access to site, nil*
3/7

Yedingham priory, *Benedictine (nuns), Yorks. NR, SE8979, nil access to site, nia*
3/6, 11/2, 11/4, 17/2

York Holy Trinity priory, *Benedictine, Yorks., SE6052, public access to church, south*
1/5, 3/1, 4/1, 5/1, 5/5, 7/1, 7/2, 17/5

York St. Mary's abbey, *Benedictine, Yorks., SE6052, public access to site, south*
1/3, 2/1, 2/3, 2/5, 3/7, 5/6, 9/6, 12/3, 12/5, 15/4

THE SITES LISTED BY HISTORIC COUNTIES

ENGLAND

Bedfordshire
Bushmead priory
Chicksands priory
Dunstable priory
Elstow abbey

Berkshire
Abingdon abbey
Bisham abbey
Brimpton preceptory
Hurley priory
Poughley priory
Reading abbey
Reading friary
Steventon priory

Buckinghamshire
Bradwell priory
Burnham abbey
Chetwode cell
Missenden abbey
Newton Longville cell
Notley abbey
Widmere commandery

Cambridgeshire
Anglesey priory
Barnwell priory
Cambridge Buckingham college
Cambridge friary
Cambridge St. Radegund's priory
Chatteris abbey

Denney abbey
Ely cathedral-priory
Isleham cell
Swaffham Bulbeck priory
Swavesey priory
Thorney abbey

Cheshire
Birkenhead priory
Chester abbey
Combermere abbey
Norton abbey
Vale Royal abbey
Warburton cell

Cornwall (including Scilly)
Bodmin friary
Bodmin priory
Launceston priory
Minster cell
St. Anthony-in-Roseland cell
St. Germans priory
St. Michael's Mount priory
Tresco cell

Cumberland
Calder abbey
Carlisle cathedral-priory
Holme Cultram abbey
Lanercost priory
St. Bees priory
Seaton priory
Wetheral priory

Derbyshire
Church Gresley priory
Dale abbey
Repton (Anglo-Saxon) abbey

Repton priory
Yeaveley preceptory

Devonshire
Buckfast abbey
Buckland abbey
Canonsleigh abbey
Cornworthy priory
Dunkeswell abbey
Exeter Polsloe priory
Exeter St. Nicholas' priory
Frithelstock priory
Hartland abbey
Kerswell cell
Otterton priory
Pilton priory
Plymouth friary
Plympton priory
Tavistock abbey
Torre abbey
Totnes priory

Dorset
Abbotsbury abbey
Bindon abbey
Cerne abbey
Cranborne cell
Forde abbey
Horton priory
Loders priory
Milton abbey
Shaftesbury abbey
Sherborne abbey
Tarrant abbey
Wareham cell

Durham
Durham cathedral-priory

Finchale priory
Jarrow priory
Monkwearmouth cell

Essex
Barking abbey
Beeleigh abbey
Blackmore priory
Coggeshall abbey
Colchester St. Botolph's priory
Colchester St. John's abbey
Earls Colne priory
Hatfield Broad Oak priory
Hatfield Peverel priory
Latton priory
Leez priory
Little Dunmow priory
Little Maplestead commandery
Prittlewell priory
St. Osyth abbey
Takeley priory
Temple Cressing preceptory
Tilty abbey
Waltham abbey
West Mersea priory
Wix priory

Gloucestershire
Beckford cell
Bristol abbey
Bristol Carmelite friary
Bristol Dominican friary
Bristol St. James' priory
Bristol Temple preceptory
Cirencester abbey
Deerhurst priory
Flaxley abbey
Gloucester abbey
Gloucester Dominican friary

Gloucester Franciscan friary
Gloucester Lanthony priory
Gloucester St. Oswald's priory
Hailes abbey
Horsley priory
Kingswood abbey
Leonard Stanley priory
Quenington commandery
Temple Guiting preceptory
Tewkesbury abbey
Winchcombe abbey

Hampshire
Beaulieu abbey
Christchurch priory
Fordingbridge preceptory
Godsfield commandery
Hamble priory
Hayling priory
Hyde abbey
Mottisfont priory
Netley abbey
Pamber priory
Portchester priory
Romsey abbey
Southwick priory
Titchfield abbey
Winchester cathedral-priory

Herefordshire
Aconbury priory
Clifford priory
Dinmore commandery
Dore abbey
Ewyas Harold cell
Flanesford priory
Garway preceptory
Hereford friary
Leominster priory

Monkland cell
Welsh Newton preceptory
Wigmore abbey

Hertfordshire
Ashridge priory/college
Hitchen friary
King's Langley friary
Royston priory
St. Albans abbey
Ware friary
Wymondley priory

Huntingdonshire
Ramsey abbey
Stonely priory

Isle of Wight
Carisbrooke priory
Quarr abbey

Kent
Aylesford friary
Bilsington priory
Boxley abbey
Bradsole St. Radegund's abbey
Canterbury cathedral-priory
Canterbury Dominican friary
Canterbury Franciscan friary
Canterbury St. Augustine's abbey
Dartford priory
Davington priory
Dover Augustinian priory
Dover Benedictine priory
Faversham abbey
Folkestone priory
Higham priory
Langdon abbey

Malling abbey
Minster-in-Sheppey priory
Moatenden friary
Monks Horton priory
Patrixbourne cell
Rochester cathedral-priory
Strood preceptory
Sutton-at-Hone St. John's Jerusalem commandery
Swingfield commandery
Temple Ewell preceptory
Throwley priory

Lancashire
Cartmel priory
Cockerham cell
Cockersand abbey
Furness abbey
Lancaster priory
Stidd commandery
Upholland priory
Whalley abbey

Leicestershire
Breedon priory
Croxton abbey
Grace Dieu priory
Kirby Bellars priory
Launde priory
Leicester abbey
Owston abbey
Rothley Temple preceptory
Ulverscroft priory

Lincolnshire
Alkborough cell
Alvingham priory
Bardney abbey
Barlings abbey

Boston friary
Bourne abbey
Cammeringham priory
Croyland abbey
Deeping St. James priory
Freiston priory
Grantham friary
Grantham Templars(?)
Heynings priory
Humberston abbey
Kirkstead abbey
Kyme priory
Lincoln Carmelite friary
Lincoln Franciscan friary
Lincoln St. Mary Magdalene's cell
Louth Park abbey
Newstead Gilbertine priory
Sempringham priory
Spalding priory
Stamford Carmelite friary
Stamford Franciscan friary
Stamford St. Leonard's priory
Stixwould priory
Stow abbey
Temple Bruer preceptory
Thornton abbey
Tupholme abbey

Middlesex
Bishopsgate St. Helens priory
Clerkenwell commandery
London charterhouse
London friary
Smithfield St. Bartholomew's priory
Syon abbey
Temple preceptory
Westminster abbey

Norfolk

Aldeby priory
Beeston priory
Binham priory
Blakeney friary
Broomholm priory
Burnham Norton friary
Carrow priory
Castle Acre priory
Coxford priory
Creake abbey
Hickling priory
Horsham St. Faith's priory
Ingham friary
King's Lynn Augustinian friary
King's Lynn Carmelite friary
King's Lynn Franciscan friary
King's Lynn priory
Langley abbey
Marham abbey
Norwich cathedral-priory
Norwich Carmelite friary
Norwich Dominican friary
Pentney priory
St. Benet of Holme's abbey
Sheringham cell
Sporle cell
Thetford friary
Thetford Cluniac priory
Thetford St. George's priory
Thetford St. Sepulchre's priory
Walsingham friary
Walsingham priory
Wendling abbey
West Acre priory
West Dereham abbey
Weybourne priory
Wymondham abbey
Yarmouth friary

Yarmouth priory

Northamptonshire
Canons Ashby priory
Catesby priory
Chacombe priory
Delapre abbey
Peterborough abbey

Northumberland
Alnwick abbey
Bamburgh cell
Blanchland abbey
Brinkburn priory
Chibburn commandery
Farne Island cell
Guyzance priory
Hexham priory
Holystone priory
Hulne friary
Lindisfarne priory
Newcastle-upon-Tyne Augustinian friary
Newcastle-upon-Tyne Carmelite friary
Newcastle-upon-Tyne Dominican friary
Newminster abbey
Ovingham cell
Tynemouth priory

Nottinghamshire
Beauvale charterhouse
Blyth priory
Lenton priory
Mattersey priory
Newstead Augustinian priory
Rufford abbey
Thurgarton priory
Welbeck abbey
Worksop priory

Oxfordshire
Bicester priory
Bruern abbey
Clattercote priory
Cogges priory
Dorchester abbey
Godstow abbey
Goring priory
Littlemore priory
Osney abbey
Oxford Durham college
Oxford friary
Oxford Gloucester college
Oxford St. Bernard's college
Oxford St. Frideswide's priory
Oxford St. Mary's college
Rewley abbey
Sandford preceptory
Thame abbey

Shropshire
Alberbury priory
Brewood St. Leonard's Augustinian priory
Bromfield priory
Buildwas abbey
Chirbury priory
Church Preen cell
Haughmond abbey
Lilleshall abbey
Ludlow friary
Morville cell
Shrewsbury abbey
Shrewsbury friary
Wenlock priory
Woodhouse friary

Somerset
Barrow Gurney priory

Bath cathedral-priory
Bruton abbey
Cleeve abbey
Dunster priory
Glastonbury abbey
Hinton charterhouse
Montacute priory
Muchelney abbey
Stavordale priory
Stogursey priory
Taunton priory
Temple Combe preceptory
Witham charterhouse
Woodspring priory

Staffordshire
Baswich priory
Brewood Benedictine priory
Burton-on-Trent abbey
Croxden abbey
Dieulacres abbey
Farewell priory
Lapley priory
Ranton priory
Rocester abbey
Stone priory
Trentham priory
Tutbury priory

Suffolk
Alnesbourn cell
Bungay priory
Bury St. Edmunds abbey
Bury St. Edmunds friary
Butley priory
Clare friary
Dunwich friary
Great Bricett priory
Ixworth priory

Kersey priory
Leiston abbey
Letheringham priory
Redlingfield priory
Rumburgh cell
St. Olave's priory
Sibton abbey
Sudbury friary
Sudbury St. Bartholomew's cell
Wangford priory
Welnetham friary

Surrey
Bermondsey abbey
Chertsey abbey
Merton priory
Newark priory
Sheen charterhouse
Southwark priory
Waverley abbey

Sussex
Arundel priory
Battle abbey
Bayham abbey
Boxgrove priory
Chichester friary
Easebourne priory
Hardham priory
Lewes friary
Lewes priory
Lyminster priory
Michelham priory
Poling commandery
Robertsbridge abbey
Rye Augustinian friary
Rye Sack friary
Sele friary
Shipley preceptory

Shulbrede priory
Sompting preceptory
Tortington priory
Wilmington priory
Winchelsea friary

Warwickshire

Alvecote priory
Atherstone friary
Combe abbey
Coventry cathedral-priory
Coventry charterhouse
Coventry Carmelite friary
Coventry Franciscan friary
Kenilworth abbey
Maxstoke priory
Merevale abbey
Monks Kirby priory
Nuneaton priory
Pinley priory
Polesworth abbey
Stoneleigh abbey
Temple Balsall preceptory
Wolston cell
Wroxall priory

Westmorland

Shap abbey

Wiltshire

Amesbury priory
Ansty commandery
Axford "priory"
Bradenstoke priory
Edington priory
Kington St. Michael's priory
Lacock abbey
Maiden Bradley priory

Malmesbury abbey
Monkton Farleigh priory
Salisbury friary
Wilton abbey

Worcestershire
Astley priory
Dudley priory
Evesham abbey
Halesowen abbey
Little Malvern priory
Malvern priory
Pershore abbey
Worcester cathedral-priory
Worcester friary
Worcester St. Wulstan's hospital

Yorkshire_East Riding (including city of_York)
Beverley friary
Bridington priory
Kirkham priory
Meaux abbey
Snainton preceptory
Swine priory
Watton priory
Wilberfoss priory
York Holy Trinity priory
York St. Mary's abbey

Yorkshire North Riding
Byland abbey
Coverham abbey
Easby abbey
Egglestone abbey
Ellerton priory
Guisborough priory
Hackness cell
Hood cell

Jervaulx abbey
Lastingham abbey
Malton priory
Marrick priory
Mount Grace charterhouse
Richmond friary
Richmond St. Martin's priory
Rievaulx abbey
Scarborough cell
Whitby abbey
Wykeham priory
Yedingham priory

Yorkshire West Riding

Allerton Mauleverer priory
Beauchief abbey
Bolton priory
Ecclesfield priory
Esholt priory
Fountains abbey
Kirkstall abbey
Monk Bretton priory
Nostell priory
Nun Monkton priory
Ribstone preceptory
Roche abbey
Salley abbey
Selby abbey
Snaith cell
Syningthwaite priory
Woodkirk cell

WALES

Anglesey

Penmon priory
Priestholme cell

Brecknock (Breconshire)
Brecon friary
Brecon priory

Cardiganshire
Cardigan cell
Llanbadarn-fawr priory
Strata Florida abbey

Carmarthenshire
Carmarthen priory
Kidwelly cell
St. Clear's cell
Talley abbey

Carnarvonshire
Beddgelert priory
Conway abbey

Denbighshire
Denbigh friary
Ruthin priory
Valle Crucis abbey

Flintshire
Basingwerk abbey

Glamorganshire
Ewenny priory
Llangennith cell
Margam abbey
Neath abbey

Merionethshire
Cymmer abbey

Monmouthshire
Abergavenny priory
Chepstow priory
Llantarnam abbey
Llanthony priory
Malpas cell
Monmouth priory
Tintern abbey
Usk priory

Montgomeryshire
Llanllugan priory

Pembrokeshire
Caldey cell
Haverfordwest priory
Monkton priory
Pill priory
St. Dogmael's abbey
Slebech commandery

Radnorshire
Cwmhyr abbey

THE SITES LISTED BY RELIGIOUS ORDERS

N.B. Sites of houses of nuns or canonesses and mixed houses are noted accordingly.

CONTEMPLATIVE ORDERS

Benedictine
Abbotsbury abbey
Abergavenny priory
Abingdon abbey

Aldeby priory
Alkborough cell
Allerton Mauleverer priory
Alvecote priory
Amesbury priory (nuns)
Arundel priory
Astley priory
Bardney abbey
Barking abbey (nuns)
Barrow Gurney priory
Bath cathedral-priory
Battle abbey
Binham priory
Birkenhead priory
Bisham abbey
Bishopsgate St. Helens priory (nuns)
Blyth priory
Boxgrove priory
Bradwell priory
Brecon priory
Brewood priory (nuns)
Bristol St. James' priory
Bromfield priory
Bungay priory (nuns)
Burton-on-Trent abbey
Bury St. Edmunds abbey
Cambridge Buckingham college
Cambridge St. Radegund's priory
Canterbury cathedral-priory
Canterbury St. Augustine's abbey
Cardigan cell
Carisbrooke priory
Carrow priory (nuns)
Cerne abbey
Chatteris abbey (nuns)
Chepstow priory
Chertsey abbey
Chester abbey
Cogges priory

Colchester St. John's abbey
Coventry cathedral-priory
Cranborne cell
Croyland abbey
Davington priory (nuns)
Deeping St. James priory
Deerhurst priory
Dover priory
Dunster priory
Durham cathedral-priory
Earls Colne priory
Ecclesfield priory
Elstow abbey (nuns)
Ely cathedral-priory
Evesham abbey
Ewenny priory
Ewyas Harold cell
Exeter Polsloe priory (nuns)
Exeter St. Nicholas' priory
Farewell priory (nuns)
Farne Island cell
Faversham abbey (Independent)
Finchale priory
Freiston priory
Glastonbury abbey
Gloucester abbey
Godstow abbey (nuns)
Hackness cell
Hatfield Broad Oak priory
Hatfield Peverel priory
Hayling priory
Higham priory
Horsham St. Faith's priory
Horton priory
Hurley priory
Hyde abbey
Isleham cell
Jarrow priory
Kidwelly cell

King's Lynn priory
Kington St. Michael's priory (nuns)
Lancaster priory
Lapley priory
Lastingham abbey
Leominster priory
Leonard Stanley priory
Lincoln St. Mary Magdalene's cell
Lindisfarne priory
Little Malvern priory
Littlemore priory (nuns)
Llanbadarn-fawr priory
Llangennith cell
Loders priory
Lyminster priory (nuns)
Malling abbey (nuns)
Malmesbury abbey
Malvern priory
Marrick priory (nuns)
Milton abbey
Minster cell
Monk Bretton priory
Monkland cell
Monks Kirby priory
Monkton priory
Monkwearmouth cell
Monmouth priory
Morville cell
Muchelney abbey
Norwich cathedral-priory
Nuneaton priory (nuns)
Nun Monkton priory (nuns)
Otterton priory
Oxford Durham college
Oxford Gloucester college
Pamber priory
Pershore abbey
Peterborough abbey
Pilton priory

Polesworth abbey (nuns)
Ramsey abbey
Reading abbey
Redlingfield priory (nuns)
Repton Anglo-Saxon abbey
Richmond St. Martin's priory
Rochester cathedral-priory
Romsey abbey (nuns)
Rumburgh cell
St. Albans abbey
St. Bees priory
St. Benet of Holme's abbey
St. Michael's Mount priory
Seaton priory (nuns)
Selby abbey
Shaftesbury abbey (nuns)
Sherborne abbey
Shrewsbury abbey
Snaith cell
Spalding priory
Sporle cell
Stamford St. Leonard's priory
Steventon priory
Stogursey priory
Stow abbey
Sudbury St. Bartholomew's cell
Swaffham Bulbeck priory (nuns)
Swavesey priory
Takeley priory
Tavistock abbey
Tewkesbury abbey
Thetford St. George's priory (nuns)
Thorney abbey
Throwley priory
Totnes priory
Tresco cell
Tutbury priory
Tynemouth priory
Upholland priory

Usk priory (nuns)
Wareham cell
West Mersea priory
Westminster abbey
Wetheral priory
Whitby abbey
Wilberfoss priory (nuns)
Wilmington priory
Wilton abbey (nuns)
Winchcombe abbey
Winchester cathedral-priory
Wix priory (nuns)
Wolston cell
Worcester cathedral-priory
Wroxall priory (nuns)
Wymondham abbey
Yarmouth priory
Yedingham priory (nuns)
York Holy Trinity priory (nuns)
York St. Mary's abbey

Cluniac

Bermondsey abbey
Broomholm priory
Castle Acre priory
Church Preen cell
Clifford priory
Delapre abbey (nuns)
Dudley priory
Kerswell cell
Lenton priory
Lewes priory
Malpas cell
Monks Horton priory
Monkton Farleigh priory
Montacute priory
Newton Longville cell
Prittlewell priory
St. Clear's cell

Thetford priory
Wangford priory
Wenlock priory

Cistercian

Basingwerk abbey
Beaulieu abbey
Bindon abbey
Boxley abbey
Bruern abbey
Buckfast abbey
Buckland abbey
Buildwas abbey
Byland abbey
Calder abbey
Catesby priory (nuns)
Cleeve abbey
Coggeshall abbey
Combe abbey
Combermere abbey
Conway abbey
Croxden abbey
Cwmhyr abbey
Cymmer abbey
Dieulacres abbey
Dore abbey
Dunkeswell abbey
Ellerton priory (nuns)
Esholt priory (nuns)
Flaxley abbey
Forde abbey
Fountains abbey
Furness abbey
Hailes abbey
Heynings priory (nuns)
Holme Cultram abbey
Jervaulx abbey
Kingswood abbey
Kirklees priory (nuns)

Kirkstall abbey
Kirkstead abbey
Llanllugan priory (nuns)
Llantarnam abbey
Louth Park abbey
Margam abbey
Marham abbey (nuns)
Meaux abbey
Merevale abbey
Neath abbey
Netley abbey
Newminster abbey
Oxford St. Bernard's college
Pinley priory (nuns)
Quarr abbey
Rewley abbey
Rievaulx abbey
Robertsbridge abbey
Roche abbey
Rufford abbey
Salley abbey
Scarborough cell
Sibton abbey
Stoneleigh abbey
Strata Florida abbey
Swine priory (nuns)
Syningthwaite priory (nuns)
Tarrant abbey (nuns)
Thame abbey
Tilty abbey
Tintern abbey
Vale Royal abbey
Valle Crucis abbey
Waverley abbey
Whalley abbey
Wykeham priory (nuns)

Carthusian
Beauvale charterhouse

Coventry charterhouse
Hinton charterhouse
London charterhouse
Mount Grace charterhouse
Sheen charterhouse
Witham charterhouse

Grandmontine
Alberbury priory

Tironensian
Caldey cell
Hamble priory
Humberston abbey
Pill priory
St. Dogmael's abbey

Bridgettine
Syon abbey

Augustinian
Aconbury priory (canonesses)
Alnesbourn cell
Anglesey priory
Bamburgh cell
Barnwell priory
Baswich priory
Beckford cell
Beddgelert priory
Beeston priory
Bicester priory
Bilsington priory
Blackmore priory
Bodmin priory
Bolton priory
Bourne abbey
Bradenstoke priory
Breedon priory
Brewood St. Leonard's priory (nuns)

Bridlington priory
Brinkburn priory
Bristol abbey
Bruton abbey
Burnham abbey (canonesses)
Bushmead priory
Butley priory
Canons Ashby priory
Canonsleigh abbey (canonesses)
Carlisle cathedral-priory
Carmarthen priory
Cartmel priory
Chacombe priory
Chetwode cell
Chirbury priory
Christchurch priory
Church Gresley priory
Cirencester abbey
Cockerham cell
Colchester St. Botolph's priory
Cornworthy priory (canonesses)
Coxford priory
Creake abbey
Dorchester abbey
Dover priory
Dunstable priory
Easebourne priory (canonesses)
Flanesford priory
Frithelstock priory
Gloucester Lanthony priory
Gloucester St. Oswald's priory
Goring priory (canonesses)
Grace Dieu priory (canonesses)
Great Bricett priory
Guisborough priory
Hardham priory
Hartland abbey
Haughmond abbey
Haverfordwest priory

Hexham priory
Hickling priory
Holystone priory (canonesses)
Hood cell
Horsley priory
Ixworth priory
Kenilworth abbey
Kersey priory
Kirby Bellars priory
Kirkham priory
Kyme priory
Lacock abbey (canonesses)
Lanercost priory
Latton priory
Launceston priory
Launde priory
Leez priory
Leicester abbey
Letheringham priory
Lilleshall abbey
Little Dunmow priory
Llanthony priory
Maiden Bradley priory
Maxstoke priory
Merton priory
Michelham priory
Minster-in-Sheppey priory (canonesses)
Missenden abbey
Mottisfont priory
Newark priory
Newstead priory
Norton abbey
Nostell priory
Notley abbey
Osney abbey
Ovingham cell
Owston abbey
Oxford St. Frideswide's priory
Oxford St. Mary's college

Patrixbourne cell
Penmon priory
Pentney priory
Plympton priory
Portchester priory
Poughley priory
Priestholme cell
Ranton priory
Repton priory
Rocester abbey
Royston priory
St. Anthony-in-Roseland cell
St. Germans priory
St. Olave's priory
St. Osyth abbey
Sheringham cell
Shulbrede priory
Smithfield St. Bartholomew's priory
Southwark priory
Southwick priory
Stavordale priory
Stonely priory
Stone priory
Taunton priory
Thornton abbey
Thurgarton priory
Tortington priory
Trentham priory
Ulverscroft priory
Walsingham priory
Waltham abbey
West Acre priory
Weybourne priory
Wigmore abbey
Woodkirk cell
Woodspring priory
Worcester St. Wulstan's hospital
Worksop priory
Wymondley priory

Premonstratensian

Alnwick abbey
Barlings abbey
Bayham abbey
Beauchief abbey
Beeleigh abbey
Blanchland abbey
Bradsole St. Radegund's abbey
Cammeringham priory
Cockersand abbey
Coverham abbey
Croxton abbey
Dale abbey
Easby abbey
Egglestone abbey
Guyzance priory (canonesses)
Halesowen abbey
Langdon abbey
Langley abbey
Leiston abbey
Shap abbey
Stixwould priory (canonesses)
Talley abbey
Titchfield abbey
Torre abbey
Tupholme abbey
Warburton cell
Welbeck abbey
Wendling abbey
West Dereham abbey

Bonhommes

Ashridge priory/college
Edington priory
Ruthin priory

Gilbertine

Alvingham priory (mixed canons & nuns)
Chicksands priory (mixed canons & nuns)

Clattercote priory
Malton priory
Mattersey priory
Newstead priory
Sempringham priory (mixed canons & nuns)
Watton priory (mixed canons & nuns)

Independent contemplative
Folkestone priory
Thetford St. Sepulchre's priory

MENDICANT ORDERS

Franciscan
Bodmin friary
Bury St. Edmunds friary
Canterbury friary
Chichester friary
Coventry friary
Denney abbey (nuns)
Dunwich friary
Gloucester friary
Grantham friary
King's Lynn friary
Lewes friary
Lincoln friary
Oxford friary
Plymouth friary
Reading friary
Richmond friary
Salisbury friary
Shrewsbury friary
Stamford friary
Walsingham friary
Ware friary
Winchelsea friary
Worcester friary

Yarmouth friary

Carmelite
Aylesford friary
Blakeney friary
Bristol friary
Burnham Norton friary
Coventry friary
Denbigh friary
Hitchin friary
Hulne friary
King's Lynn friary
Lincoln friary
London friary
Ludlow friary
Newcastle-upon-Tyne friary
Norwich friary
Sele friary
Stamford friary

Dominican
Beverley friary
Boston friary
Brecon friary
Bristol friary
Cambridge friary
Canterbury friary
Dartford priory (nuns)
Gloucester friary
Hereford friary
King's Lynn friary
Newcastle-upon-Tyne friary
Norwich friary
Sudbury friary
Thetford friary

Augustinian
Atherstone friary
Clare friary

King's Lynn friary
Newcastle-upon-Tyne friary
Rye friary
Woodhouse friary

Sack
Rye

Trinitarian
Ingham friary
Moatenden friary

Crutched or Crossed
Welnetham friary

MILITARY ORDERS

Knights Templar
Brimpton preceptory
Bristol Temple preceptory
Fordingbridge preceptory
Garway preceptory
Grantham Templars
Ribstone preceptory
Rothley Temple preceptory
Sandford preceptory
Shipley preceptory
Snainton preceptory
Sompting preceptory
Strood preceptory
Temple Balsall preceptory
Temple Bruer preceptory
Temple Combe preceptory
Temple Cressing preceptory
Temple Ewell preceptory
Temple Guiting preceptory
Temple (London) preceptory

Welsh Newton preceptory
Yeaveley preceptory

Knights Hospitaller
Ansty commandery
Chibburn commandery
Clerkenwell commandery
Dinmore commandery
Godsfield commandery
Little Maplestead commandery
Poling commandery
Quenington commandery
Slebech commandery
Stidd commandery
Sutton-at-Hone commandery
Swingfield commandery
Widmere commandery

Unknown order
Axford 'priory'

♦♦♦♦♦♦♦♦♦♦♦♦♦♦♦♦

Section 1:
CHAPELS & CHURCHES PROVIDED FOR LAY PEOPLE

1/1   **CHAPELS AT THE GATE**

Abingdon abbey: intact chapel contiguous with gatehouse, now parish church of St. Nicholas; mainly C15

Barnwell priory: intact chapel, now church of St. Andrew the Less, Cambridge; mainly of early C13 date

Coggeshall abbey: intact chapel, became barn after Dissolution & after full restoration is now church dedicated to St. Nicholas; early C13

Furness abbey: high-standing ruined chapel adjacent to outer gate; c.1300

Kirkstead abbey: intact chapel standing in isolated location, now church of St. Leonard; C13

Merevale abbey: intact chapel, now parish church of Our Lady; late C13, C14 & late C15

Peterborough abbey: intact chancel only survives of chapel of St. Thomas contiguous with main gatehouse, now refectory & shop of present cathedral; c.1300

Reading abbey: intact chapel contiguous with now destroyed outer gate, now parish church of St. Laurence; C12, C15

Rievaulx abbey: intact chapel adjacent to inner gate, now parish church of St. Mary; C13, severe restoration C19

Thame abbey: intact chapel, located to north of post-Dissolution mansion; early C14, remodelled 1836

Tilty abbey: intact chapel, now parish church of St. Mary the Virgin; C13 & C14

Tintern abbey: house called St. Ann's incorporates some remnants of chapel; unknown date

1/1 Kirkstead abbey, chapel at the gate to north east

Vale Royal abbey: intact & restored chapel, now the parish church of St. Mary, Whitegate; main surviving part of the original chapel are the C15 timber piers of nave;

Witham charterhouse: intact lay brothers' chapel, now parish church of St. Mary, St. John the Baptist & All Saints; late C12 date

Barking abbey: chapel of Holy Rood in upper storey, has stone rood fitted to wall interior (See entry under Statuary & Sculpture); 1370, c.1460

Beaulieu abbey: intact twin-chapels over gate-hall of inner gatehouse (Palace House), now adapted to domestic use; C14, C19

Durham cathedral priory: intact chapel of St. Helen over gate-hall; c.1500

Faversham abbey: intact part of chapel of outer gatehouse, adapted to domestic use; unknown date

Kirkstall abbey: intact chapel over gate-hall of inner gatehouse, now adapted to domestic use; C13, 1893

Malling abbey: intact chapel now known as Pilgrims' Chapel, attached at ground floor level to gatehouse, owned by Anglican community of nuns; C14

Norwich cathedral-priory: intact chapel over gate-hall of St. Ethelbert's Gate; 1316+

Peterborough abbey: intact chapel of St. Nicholas over gate-hall of outer gatehouse; C12, 1302-07

Thornton abbey: intact small chapel or oratory at first floor level over gate-hall; early C15

Whalley abbey: intact over gate-hall of outer gatehouse, latter a high-standing ruin; early C14

Worksop priory: intact chapel within gatehouse at ground floor level; C14

Abbotsbury abbey: intact parish church of St. Nicholas adjacent to site of abbey church; C14, C15 & C16

Alvecote priory: small parish church of St. Matthew, Shuttington; dates from C12

Alvingham priory: intact small parish church of St. Adelwold, adjacent to priory church of St. Mary; late C13, C14/C15, 1806, 1933

Bardney abbey: intact parish church of St. Lawrence built when old church near abbey collapsed; constructed 1434+ in one campaign

Barking abbey: intact parish church of St. Margaret adjacent to site of abbey church; several construction periods including early C13, late C14 & C17

Battle abbey: intact parish church of St. Mary, close to precinct wall; late C12 & several construction periods afterwards

Bicester priory: intact parish church of St. Eadburgha adjacent to precinct wall, formerly cruciform; C12, mainly C13, C15

Bodmin priory: intact great parish church of St. Petroc, with north tower at junction of chancel & nave; C12, 1469-72, later C19

Brecon priory: intact building originally chapel-of-ease to priory, since 1923 parish church of St. Mary; earliest remnant C12, with later work of C14, C15 & C16

Bruton abbey: intact parish church of St. Mary close to site of abbey; late C14, C15 & 1743

Buckfast abbey: recently fired parish church of Holy Trinity, Buckfastleigh; C13, C15

Bury St. Edmunds abbey: 1. intact building, formerly church of St. James within precinct & now cathedral of Anglican diocese; c.1510 - mid C16, with new work at east end C20

2. intact church of St. Mary within precinct; mainly dating from 1430+

Carmarthen priory: intact parish church of St. Peter; much work of C14

Castle Acre priory: intact parish church of St. James, sited between castle & precinct of priory; C13, C15/C16

Cerne abbey: intact parish church of St. Mary, close to site of abbey; late C13, C15/C16

Chertsey abbey: intact parish church of St. Peter; variety of construction dates from C15 onwards

Chester abbey: intact but considerably altered chapel of St. Nicholas, has had a number of ecclesiastical & secular uses & now a china store; 1488 & C19

Cirencester abbey: intact parish church of St. John the Baptist, adjacent to abbey precinct; many construction dates from late C12

Clifford priory: intact parish church of St. Mary outside immediate area of precinct; C13, C19

Coventry cathedral-priory: intact parish church of Holy Trinity for prior's tenants & servants; C13, but mainly C14 & C15

Coverham abbey: intact church of Holy Trinity now redundant, antedates founding of abbey on this site; C13, mainly C14 & 1854

Easby abbey: intact small parish church of St. Agatha within precinct probably antedates founding of abbey; dates from C12, also C13 & C15

Ely cathedral-priory: intact parish church of St. Mary; mainly constructed 1198 - 1215

Evesham abbey: 1. intact parish church of All Saints, within precinct; earliest work comes from late C12

2. intact parish church of St. Lawrence, within precinct, now redundant; C16 & C19

Fountains abbey: restored chapel of St. Michael, How Hill, ¾ mile from precinct; C12, 1778, C20

Frithelstock priory: intact parish church of St. Mary & St. Gregory, located within a few feet of priory church; mostly C15

Glastonbury abbey: 1. intact parish church of St. John outside precinct; C12, rebuilt 1403-1495

2. intact parish church of St. Benignus (Benedict) outside precinct; c.1520

Godstow abbey: high-standing ruined chapel (dedication unknown) just within precinct wall; C15

Guisborough priory: intact parish church of St. Nicholas, adjacent to precinct; several construction dates from c.1500

Hailes abbey: intact small parish church of unknown dedication, antedates founding of abbey; c.1130, also C14

Higham priory: intact parish church of St. Mary, basically of 2 aisles & spirelet over present north aisle; C12, C13, C14, 1863

Horsham St. Faith's priory: intact large parish church of St. Mary & St. Andrew to south of precinct; c.1290+, C15

Hyde abbey: intact parish church of St. Bartholomew; C12, C19

Isleham cell: intact parish church of St. Andrew, 100 yds. from conventual church; all medieval centuries from C12, also pDp

Kenilworth abbey: intact parish church of St. Nicholas, adjacent to site of abbey church; C12, C14 & C15

Kirby Bellars priory: intact parish church of St. Peter, almost certainly not conventual; mainly C13 & C14

Lacock abbey: intact parish church of St. Cyriac; transepts c.1300, remainder C15

Launceston priory: intact church of St. Thomas immediately north of scanty ruins of priory, originally chapel of ease to mother church of Launceston; mainly C15

Leonard Stanley priory: intact church of St. Swithun, later used as priory chapel & post-Dissolution farm building; mid C11, C14

Lindisfarne priory: intact parish church of St. Mary, adjacent to precinct of priory; dates from late C13

Malling abbey: intact parish church of St. Mary, West Malling; C12, C13 plus later periods of construction

Malmesbury abbey: intact west tower only survives of parish church of St. Paul demolished soon after Dissolution, close to abbey church; C14

Margam abbey: roofless high-standing ruined Cryke chapel (Hen Eglwys), on hillside overlooking site of abbey; C15

Marham priory: intact parish church of Holy Trinity with west tower; C12, C14, C15

Maxstoke priory: intact parish church, possibly originally antedating the founding of the priory, adjacent to precinct wall; mainly late C14

Montacute priory: intact parish church of St. Catherine, close to precinct of priory; earliest portion C12, also C15

Mottisfont priory: intact parish church of St. Andrew; of C12 & later

Mount Grace charterhouse: intact small rectangular church (Lady's Chapel) at Osmotherley; early C16

Muchelney abbey: intact parish church of St. Peter & St. Paul, adjacent to site of abbey church; C15

Norwich cathedral-priory: intact chapel of   Carnary College (now Norwich School) just west of cathedral church; c.1316+

Pershore abbey: intact church of St. Andrew, now redundant; C12, C15

Peterborough abbey: intact parish church of St. John Baptist in market square; whole structure dates from 1402-07

Quarr abbey: intact parish church of Binstead Holy Cross; chancel late C13, remainder C19

Quenington commandery: intact parish church of St. Swithin; C12, C13, C15

Repton priory: intact parish church of St. Wystan, adjacent to precinct wall of priory; earliest portions including crypt are pre-Conquest in date & formed part of original Anglo-Saxon abbey

Rocester abbey: intact parish church of St. Michael, close to site of abbey precinct; remnants of C13 plus major rebuild of C19

Rochester cathedral-priory: intact church of St. Nicholas now disused as church, adjacent to cathedral church; 1423, C17

St. Dogmael's abbey: intact parish church of St. Thomas, close to site of abbey precinct; C13

St. Osyth abbey: intact parish church of St. Peter & St. Paul, near site of abbey precinct; C13, C16

Sempringham priory: intact parish church of St. Andrew; C12 & severe restoration C19

Southwick priory: 1. intact chapel-of-ease (& later parish church) of St. Thomas Becket at Portsea, now Portsmouth cathedral; c.1188, c.1196

2. [chapel of Domus Dei at Portsmouth (now Royal Garrison church), with intact chancel & roofless shell of nave; probably c.1212-20, 1827, 1866]

Tavistock abbey: intact parish church of St. Eustace, adjacent to site of abbey church; mainly C15

Walsingham priory: intact parish church of St. Mary; C14 tower & modern restoration of remainder after 1961 fire

Watton priory: intact parish church of St. Mary, close to site of priory; mainly C16

Wenlock priory: intact parish church of Holy Trinity; mainly C12, C13 & C14

West Acre priory: intact parish church of All Saints, close to gatehouse of priory; mainly C14 & C15

Westminster abbey: intact parish church of St. Margaret, adjacent to abbey church; C15

Whalley abbey: intact parish church of St. Mary antedates founding of abbey; most of structure C13, with west tower C15

Whitby abbey: intact parish church of St. Mary; portions belong to C12 & C13, but most dates from c.1764

Wigmore abbey: intact parish church of St. James the Less antedates founding of abbey; C11, C14, C15, C19

Winchcombe abbey: intact parish church of St. Peter, close to site of abbey; most of building c.1460

York St. Mary's abbey: intact parish church of St. Olave Marygate, adjacent to main gatehouse of abbey; earliest part dates from C15, with rebuilding in C18 & 1908

Abbotsbury abbey: intact St. Catherine's chapel, may also have been chantry chapel; whole building late C14

Croyland abbey: intact chapel (The Hermitage) at Peakirk (successor of St. Pega's cell); c.1300, C15

Glastonbury abbey: 1. intact but adapted slipper chapel now private house; C14/C15(?)

2. intact small chapel of St. Dunstan within precinct, containing stone altar & plain squarish aumbry; c.1500

Milton abbey: intact St. Catherine's chapel, restored in recent years; C12, C20

Newark priory: intact chapel of St. Martha (or Martyrs) at Chilworth near Guildford; C12, extensively restored C19

Plympton priory: intact large chapel & dormitory for pilgrims embarking for Santiago de Compostela, now parish church of St. Mary; C14, C15

Ramsey abbey: intact bridge chapel of St. Leger, at town of St. Ives for pilgrims to shrine of St. Ivo; c.1426, finally restored 1930

Walsingham priory:1.   intact wayside chapel of Red Mount at King's Lynn on route to Walsingham; constructed c.1485

2.   intact Houghton St. Giles' slipper chapel; whole structure of mid C14, restored 1879

Wymondham abbey: intact redundant chapel of St. Thomas Becket, now local library; c.1400

1/5   SURVIVING PARTS OF CONVENTUAL CHURCHES ALLOCATED TO LAY PEOPLE

Bishopsgate St. Helens priory: south nave aisle

Blakeney friary: nave
Blyth priory: south nave aisle
Bolton priory: nave
Boxgrove priory: nave (exchanged for east end at Dissolution)
Brinkburn priory: nave(?)
Bristol St. James' priory: nave made parochial in 1374
Bungay priory: nave
Cartmel priory: south choir aisle
Chester abbey: enlarged south transept
Christchurch priory: nave
Croyland abbey: north nave aisle (only?)
Dorchester abbey: south west nave aisle
Dunstable priory: north nave aisle , & after 1392 whole nave
Dunster priory: nave
Easebourne priory: probably all except south nave aisle & present south chancel chapel
Goring priory: original (present) nave
Great Bricett priory: nave
Holme Cultram abbey: nave
Lancaster priory: whole church (dual role)
Lanercost priory: north nave aisle
Leominster priory: outer south nave aisle & south choir aisle or chapel
Minster-in-Sheppey priory: whole of south church (now main nave aisle)
Pershore abbey: nave (exchanged for east end at Dissolution)
Pilton priory: south nave aisle & outer south nave aisle
Polesworth abbey: north nave aisle
Romsey abbey: north nave aisle & outer north nave aisle
St. Germans priory: south nave aisle

Sele friary: nave
Sherborne abbey: nave
Swine priory: choir
Tewkesbury abbey: nave & north porch
Totnes priory: whole church except for north nave aisle & choir
Tutbury priory: west 6 bays of nave
Usk priory: west part of nave & porches
Waltham abbey: west nave
Weybourne priory: former nave (now north nave aisle) and latterly present nave & chancel
Wilmington priory: nave
Wymondham abbey: central & north aisles of nave
York Holy Trinity priory: nave (after demolition of nearby St. Nicholas' church)

◆◆◆◆◆◆◆◆◆◆◆◆◆◆◆◆

Section 2
THE PRECINCT BOUNDARIES

2/1   GATEHOUSES & GATEWAYS

Abbotsbury abbey: 1. intact inner gatehouse, converted into private house; C15, adapted pDp
2. intact plain gateway with segmental arch, almost certainly resited; C15

Abingdon abbey: intact gatehouse (Abbey Gate); dates from late C15, restored C19

Alnwick abbey: intact gatehouse, equipped with battlements etc.; mid C14

Aylesford friary: 1.intact inner gatehouse, converted into domestic accommodation; C15, adapted c.1590
2. intact outer gatehouse of plain appearance; C15, c.1590
3. intact gatehouse (watergate); C15, restored c.1590

Barking abbey: intact gatehouse (cemetery gate, Curfew Gatehouse or Tower, Fire Bell Gate); 1370, c.1460

Battle abbey: 1. intact gatehouse of 3 storeys; C12, major rebuild 1338, C15
2. intact postern opposite parish church; late C13/early C14
3. intact postern next to gatehouse, now infilled; C12

Bayham abbey: high-standing ruined gatehouse (Kentish Gate), converted into summerhouse; early C14, C18

Beaulieu abbey: 1. intact inner gatehouse, now core of Palace House; C14, major adaptation 1872
2. intact small outer gatehouse lacking external ornamentation; late C13, 1885, c.1900

Beauvale charterhouse: intact gatehouse drastically modified into post-Dissolution granary; C14/C15

Beverley Dominican friary: 1. intact brick gateway reset in Eastgate; early C16, 1964

2. intact brick gateway in Friary Walk, now blocked; early C16

Binham priory: ruined gatehouse, standing to first storey level; C15

Blakeney friary: intact gateway with segmental arch in precinct wall facing sea, C15, restored with brick C19

Blanchland abbey: intact gatehouse of plain appearance; c.1500

Bodmin friary: gateway of former gatehouse concealed within shop; probably C14/C15

Bolton priory: intact gatehouse, converted into mansion; early C14, with adaptations 1806 & mid C19

Boxley abbey: ruined gatehouse with side walls surviving to top of ground-floor; C14/C15

Brecon priory: 2 intact gateways, each with vehicular & pedestrians' entrances; C15/C16

Bridlington priory: intact gatehouse (Bayle Gate), with priory arms still prominently displayed; 1388

Brinkburn priory: severely reduced but otherwise intact gatehouse, now storage facility; unknown date

Bristol abbey: 1. intact gatehouse (Abbey Gatehouse); first constructed c.1165, with major reconstruction c.1500

2. intact gatehouse, probably abbot's gatehouse; c.1165, with major reconstruction pDp

Bromfield priory: intact gatehouse, stone below & half-timbering above; C14

Broomholm priory: high-standing rear archway of gatehouse; C15

Bruton abbey: intact archway, now blocked, in precinct wall; C15

Buckfast abbey: 1. intact south gatehouse, drastically reconstructed in recent years; unknown medieval date, C20
2. ruined north gatehouse, now consisting only of one arch & part of one wall; C12

Burnham Norton friary: intact gatehouse; of early C14 date

Bury St. Edmunds abbey: 1. intact gatehouse (Great Gate); two building campaigns: 1327/46 & 1353-c.1384
2. intact gatehouse (St. James Tower or Gate); 1120-48
3. high-standing ruined & mutilated postern;C15

Butley priory: intact gatehouse, converted into private house; 1320-25

Byland abbey: 1. high-standing ruined rear archway of gatehouse; late C12
2. intact plain archway with semicircular head, almost certainly relocated; C12

Calder abbey: intact gatehouse adapted as post-Dissolution barn; C14

Caldey cell: intact gatehouse, comprises west range; C13

Canonsleigh abbey: intact gatehouse, converted into private house; C15

Canterbury cathedral-priory: 1. intact gatehouse (Christ Church Gate); 1507-17
2. intact gatehouse (Forrens Gate); C15
3. intact gatehouse (Larder Gate), largely rebuilt after bomb damage in last War; C15, c.1953
4. intact gateway (Mint Yard Gate); C15
5. intact gatehouse (North, Court or Latter Gate); c.1153+, major reconstruction C15
6. intact gatehouse (Pentise Gate); C12, c.1400, & reconstructed pDp

7. intact relocated cemetery gateway (at entrance to Kent War Memorial Garden); C12

2/1 Bromfield priory, gatehouse to front

8. intact blocked gateway in The Borough; late C14
9. intact gatehouse (Palace Gatehouse) now partly blocked & reordered; early C16
Canterbury St. Augustine's abbey: 1. intact gatehouse (Cemetery Gate), converted into hall of residence; c.1390
2. intact gatehouse (Fyndon or Great Gate); 1300-09, with restoration 1942+
3. intact gateway of brick; early/mid C16
Carlisle cathedral-priory: intact gatehouse of unadorned appearance; dated 1527
Carmarthen priory: intact rendered gatehouse, now part of row of terraced houses; unknown date

Cartmel priory: intact gatehouse, enroached on by neighbouring buildings; c.1330

Castle Acre priory: high standing ruined gatehouse; probably constructed late C15 or early C16

Cerne abbey: intact blocked gatehouse, now built into post-Dissolution house; C15, pDp

Chertsey abbey: intact blocked archway with pointed top in walling; unknown date

Chester abbey: 1. intact gatehouse (Abbey Gateway); dates from C14, but extensively restored C19

2. intact gateway (Kaleyards Gate); of uncertain date, possibly C13

3. intact gateway (Little Abbey Gateway); C15

Cirencester abbey: intact gatehouse (Saxon Arch, Spital Gate); c.1180

Cleeve abbey: high-standing ruin, inner gatehouse; originally dates from C13, reconstructed C14 & C15

Clerkenwell priory: intact gatehouse (St. John's Gate); 1504, extensively restored C19

Colchester St. John's abbey: intact gatehouse; C15, restored C19

Cornworthy priory: high-standing ruined gatehouse; early C15

Coventry Carmelite friary: intact outer gatehouse; C15, considerably altered pDp

Coventry charterhouse: intact but damaged gateway in long run of precinct wall; C15

Coverham abbey: ruined gatehouse reduced to ground floor storey; early C16

Dale abbey: intact small stone building, believed to be remnant of gatehouse; unknown date

Davington priory: intact but battered gateway in length of walling; C13/C14

Dieulacres abbey: intact half-timbered gatehouse or gateway incorporated into post-Dissolution farmhouse; late C15/early C16, c.1612

Dover Benedictine priory: intact gatehouse; 1320, restored C19

Dunkeswell abbey: part ruined (gate-hall) & part intact porter's lodge or almonry (converted into cottage); C15

Dunstable priory: gatehouse reduced to lower storey of front wall; c.1450

Dunster priory: 2 intact gateways of plain appearance; unknown date

Dunwich friary: largely intact double gateway in run of walling; late C14/early C15

Durham cathedral-priory: intact gatehouse; c.1500, restored mid C19

Easby abbey: high standing ruined gatehouse; c.1300

Ely cathedral-priory: 1. intact gatehouse (Palace gatehouse), converted into part of post-Dissolution house & now Sue Ryder Home; late C15, C16, C17

2. intact gatehouse (Porta or Walpole's Gate, South Gatehouse); 1396-97

3. intact gatehouse (Sacrist's or Sextry Gate); 1325-26

4. intact gatehouse (Steeple Gate); C14, c.1500

5. reduced great gatehouse (Porta Monachorum), now wayside memorial; C14

Evesham abbey: 1. intact gatehouse (North, Norman or Cemetery Gate, Abbot Reginald's Gateway); c.1139/43; remodelled C15

2. intact blocked gatehouse (Great Gatehouse), now built into post-Dissolution mansion; c.1316/1332, c.1711

Ewenny priory: 1. high-standing ruined north or main gatehouse; C13

2. intact south gatehouse; originally C13, but additional work C15

Exeter Polsloe priory: intact gateway in surviving run of precinct wall; C15

Faversham abbey: intact timbered house incorporating part of gatehouse & chapel; unknown date

Forde abbey: intact small west gatehouse; C15

Fountains abbey: 1. ruined inner gatehouse, mostly standing one storey high; early C13

2. two intact gateways in precinct wall to south of abbey; C14

Furness abbey: 1. intact outer double gateway next to chapel-at-the-gate; c.1300

2. high-standing ruined west gatehouse; C14

3. high-standing ruined cemetery gatehouse, one storey high; early C14

Glastonbury abbey: intact gatehouse, with array of transomed windows; C15/C16

Gloucester abbey: 1. intact inner gatehouse (Inner Gate); C15

2. intact outer gatehouse (St. Mary's or Great Gate); C13

3. intact gatehouse (St. Michael's or Cemetery Gate); C15, upper storey pDp

4. intact but severely reduced main gatehouse (King Edward's Gate), surviving portion incorporated into front of later house; C14

Gloucester Dominican friary: intact gateway at north west corner of precinct; C14/C15

Gloucester Lanthony priory: high-standing ruined front part of gatehouse; late C14

Godstow abbey: intact but blocked gateway in precinct wall, has 4-centred arch; C15

Guisborough priory: reduced & ruined gatehouse front; late C12

Hexham priory: ruined gatehouse, now reduced to single storey; c.1160

Hinton charterhouse: [gatehouse incorporated into later house; C15(?)]

Hulne friary: 1. almost intact gatehouse; C15 2. intact south west gateway, probably postern; mid C13

Hurley priory: intact gateway possibly repositioned; C12(?), reconstructed 1970

Hyde abbey: intact gatehouse of one storey; C15

Jervaulx abbey: (See entry under Other Buildings or Undercrofts etc.)

Kenilworth abbey: ruined gatehouse reduced to one storey; C14

King's Lynn Augustinian friary: 1. intact blocked gateway (North East Gate), with 4-centred arch; C15 2. intact blocked smaller gateway (North West Gate), with 2-centred arch, C14

King's Lynn Carmelite friary: intact gateway; late C14

King's Lynn priory: intact gatehouse of south range; C15, with alterations pDp

Kingswood abbey: intact part gatehouse; late C14, C16, rear portion dismantled pDp

Kirkham priory: high-standing ruined gatehouse; late C13

Kirklees priory: (See entry under Other Buildings or Undercrofts etc.)

Kirkstall abbey: 1. intact inner gatehouse, adapted as house now museum; C12, C13, chief alterations C19 2. high-standing ruined gatehouse at entrance to lay-brothers' lane; late C12, C13

Lacock abbey: intact blocked gateway at north end of west range; C15

Lanercost priory: ruined rear main arch, retained to mark entrance to church; C13

Langley abbey: intact gatehouse with main archway blocked off, much of building replaced by post-Dissolution work; C14, pDp

Leez priory: 1. intact inner gatehouse of 3 storeys; C16
2. intact outer gatehouse of 2 storeys; C16

Leicester St. Mary's abbey: high-standing ruined wall connected to ruins of post-Dissolution house; unknown date

Letheringham priory: intact gatehouse adapted as stable, made of brick; late C15

Lewes friary: intact gateway; late C15/early C16

Lewes priory: intact but rebuilt & repositioned gateway near Southover church; C13

Llanthony priory: intact gatehouse, adapted as cowbyre; C13

London charterhouse: 1. intact reconstructed inner gateway; early C16
2. intact outer gatehouse; dates from C15, upper part rebuilt 1716

Malling abbey: intact gatehouse with projecting chapel; mid C14, C15

Malvern priory: intact gatehouse (Abbey Gateway); C15, restored 1891

Maxstoke priory: 1. intact inner gatehouse (Inner or Middle Gatehouse), now core of mansion; C14, adapted pDp
2. high-standing ruined gatehouse (Outer Gatehouse); C14

Michelham priory: intact gatehouse (watergate, Gateway Tower); c.1395

Minster-in-Sheppey priory: intact gatehouse of 3 storeys; C13, C15

Monk Bretton priory: high-standing ruined gatehouse; C14, early C15

Monmouth priory: intact gatehouse probably extensively rebuilt, retains famous oriel (Geoffrey's Window) over blocked front archway; C15, pDp

Montacute priory: intact gatehouse, adapted as house; C15

Mount Grace charterhouse: ruined gatehouse reduced to lower storey; C15

Neath abbey: ruined portion of gatehouse survives by roadway; C13

Newcastle-upon-Tyne Carmelite friary: intact blocked gateway in surviving length of city wall; C14/C15

Norwich Carmelite friary: intact gateway within short length of walling, has 2 centred arch & deeply cut mouldings; c.1400

Norwich cathedral-priory: 1. intact gatehouse (Bishop's Gate or Bishop Alnwick's Gateway); c.1436
2. intact gatehouse (Erpingham Gate); 1420
3. intact gatehouse (watergate, Pull's Ferry); C15, with major restoration 1949
4. intact gatehouse (St. Ethelbert's or Great Gate); 1316+, restored C19

Osney abbey: intact watergate with segmental arch & straight parapet; C15

Oxford St. Mary's college: intact but reduced front part of gatehouse now leading to Frewen hall of Brazenose college; C15

Pentney priory: 1. high-standing ruined gatehouse; late C14/early C15
2. intact gateway hidden within farmhouse; C15

Peterborough abbey: 1. intact main or outer gatehouse; C12, reconstructed 1302-07

2. intact gatehouse (Abbot's Gatehouse); late C13

3. intact gateway (Prior's Gateway); 1510

4. intact cemetery gateway; C14/C15

Plymouth friary: intact rendered gatehouse, now leading into public house; C15

Polesworth abbey: intact gatehouse, has timber-framed upper floor with brick infilling; C14

Quenington commandery: intact gatehouse (Knights' Gate); early C15

Ramsey abbey: 1. high-standing ruined part of gatehouse at entrance to abbey site; c.1500

2. intact portion of same gatehouse at Hinchinbrooke house; c.1500, C17

Reading abbey: intact inner gatehouse (Abbey or Inner Gate); C13, drastic restoration 1869

Repton priory: 1. intact gateway, probably front arch of former gatehouse; late C13

2. intact small postern in precinct wall; C15/C16

Rewley abbey: intact gateway in length of precinct wall; C15

Richmond friary: intact gateway with modern embattled parapet; C15/C16, C19

Roche abbey: ruined gatehouse taken down to one storey; late C13/early C14

Rochester cathedral-priory: 1. intact gatehouse (Cemetery, College or Chertsey's Gate); C15, pDp

2. intact gatehouse (Sextry or Deanery Gate); C14/C15, pDp

3. intact gatehouse (Prior's Gate); C15

St. Albans abbey: 1. intact gatehouse (Great Gateway), of heavy solid appearance & with embattled parapet; 1360+, C19

2. intact & drastically remodelled gatehouse (Waxhouse Gate); unknown medieval date, C18

St. Benet of Holme's abbey: high-standing ruined gatehouse with brick windmill; early C14, C18

St. Michael's Mount priory: intact gateway with post-Dissolution refacing; C15, 1879

St. Osyth abbey: 1. intact gatehouse (Great Gatehouse); c.1475

2. intact gateway or front arch of gatehouse; C14

3. intact blocked gateway in precinct wall; C14/C15

Salley abbey: intact relocated gateway on west side of abbey site; C14/C15

Sherborne abbey: intact gateway (Cemetery Gate); C15

Stamford Franciscan friary: intact gatehouse; mid C14

Stoneleigh abbey: intact gatehouse; C14

Sudbury friary: intact timber double gateway or façade of gatehouse; C15/C16

Tavistock abbey: 1. high-standing ruined gatehouse (Betsy Grimbal's Tower); C15

2. intact gatehouse (Town, Court or Higher Abbey Gate); C12, C15, C19

3. gatehouse now heightened as tower of parish church (cemetery gate); early C14, followed by major alteration C15, C19

Tewkesbury abbey: intact gatehouse (Abbot's Gatehouse); C15/C16, restored 1849

Thetford Cluniac priory: 1. high-standing ruined main gatehouse; C14

2. high-standing ruined gatehouse forming part of prior's lodging; C12, C14

Thornton abbey: intact massive gatehouse with barbican; 1382, C16

Tintern abbey: 1. much modified & adapted main gatehouse, now private residence; C13 & pDp

2. intact gateway (Watergate) in incomplete section of walling; C14

Torre abbey: intact inner gatehouse (Mohun Gate or Gatehouse); c.1320

Tynemouth priory: intact military gatehouse with barbican, but part-dismantled; late C14, C18, C19

Usk priory: intact gatehouse; C16

Walsingham priory: 1. intact gatehouse; c.1440

2. intact gateway (Knight's Gate) drastically restored after Dissolution; C14, C19

Waltham abbey: intact & reduced gateway (Watergate), probably façade of gatehouse; c.1370

West Acre priory: intact gatehouse, but part-dismantled; C14

West Dereham: part-dismantled gatehouse or gateway, converted into post-Dissolution farm building; C15(?)

Wetheral priory: intact gatehouse of 3 storeys; C15

Whalley abbey: 1. intact inner gatehouse (North East Gateway); 1480

2. high-standing ruined outer gatehouse (North West Gateway); early C14

Wigmore abbey: 1. intact inner gatehouse; C14

2. ruined & divided building said to be outer gatehouse; C14

Winchester cathedral-priory: intact gateway (Prior's or St. Swithun's Gate); C15

Woodspring priory: intact & reduced gatehouse to one storey gateway; C14

Worcester cathedral-priory: 1. intact main gatehouse (Edgar Tower, Great Gate); early C14, C19
2. intact gatehouse (watergate, Ferry Gate); C15 & pDp
Worksop priory: intact gatehouse, incorporates ground-floor chapel; early C14, mid C14, restored C19
York St. Mary's abbey: 1. high-standing ruined main gatehouse (Marygate, Great Gate); C12, C15
2. intact gateway (Postern Gate); c.1503
3. high-standing ruined & reduced rear wall of gatehouse (Watergate); C15

2/2 OTHER PORTALS

Buckfast abbey: 1. intact porch-tower (Abbot's Tower), fronting rebuilt west range; C14
2. intact but largely rebuilt gatehouse-range at front of former town-house of abbot, in Close of Exeter cathedral, early C16, mid C20
Canterbury cathedral priory: 1. intact porch-tower (Prior Selling's Porch); 1472/1494
2. intact porch of North Hall, with entrance of 3 archways; C12
Castle Acre priory: intact porch-tower (Prior's House Porch), leading into inner porch; C12, early C16
Cerne abbey: intact porch-tower (Abbot's Hall Porch), originally fronting west range; c.1500
Evesham abbey: intact detached gate-tower (inner cemetery gate, Abbot Lichfield's Bell Tower, New Tower); 1529-39
Exeter St. Nicholas' priory: intact porch-tower at front of west range, 3 storeys; late C15/early C16

Forde abbey: intact porch-tower (Abbot Chard's Tower), 3 storeys & with oriel running through top 2 storeys; inscription dated 1528

Furness abbey: intact gate-tower (Hawkshead Old Hall Courthouse); C15

Leiston abbey: high-standing ruined portion of porch-tower leading into west range; late C15

Neath abbey: high-standing ruined porch-tower at front of west range, with intact rib vault in one bay; C14

Norwich cathedral-priory: intact porch-tower fronting Bishop Salmon's former hall; 1318+

Oxford St. Bernard's college: intact gate-tower now fronting St. John's college; mid C15

Plympton priory: intact façade of porch-tower leading into post-Dissolution house; C12

Rochester cathedral-priory: intact porch-tower (Cloister Gate) to west range, with modern parapet; C14, C15, C19

St. Osyth abbey: intact front façade of abbot's lodging hall porch; dated 1527, 1865

Torre abbey: intact porch-tower (Abbot's Tower) fronting west range; C15

Westminster abbey: 1. intact porch-tower (Entrance Tower) at corner of abbot's accommodation & cellarium; c.1388-91
2. intact gate-tower (Blackstole Tower) one third along cellarium; c.1388-91

Wilmington priory: intact porch-tower, adapted to domestic use; C13, C14/C15

Winchester cathedral-priory: intact porch-tower of prior's lodging (now deanery); c.1230, early C16

Battle abbey: walling on north side of precinct
Beauvale charterhouse: lengths of wall
Beverley Dominican friary: substantial section of brick wall
Bicester priory: long length of stone wall adjacent to Priory Lane to south east of parish church, much standing to original height
Binham priory: long lengths of wall mostly in good condition especially to south east & east
Blakeney friary: length of tall flint walling on north side of site & another long length facing sea; C15 or earlier
Bodmin priory: length of precinct wall survives in grounds of Priory House on west side of site
Bolton priory: tall length of wall fronting road to west & south west of precinct
Boxley abbey: considerable lengths of wall, some broken down
Brecon friary: long portions of wall to east & north
Brecon priory: long run of wall on south side
Broomholm priory: longish run of wall towards east
Buckland abbey: length of wall to north east of site
Bungay priory: two short lengths of flint walling standing to full height in St. Mary's St. & Trinity St.
Burnham abbey: long stretch of wall with tiled top, to east of precinct along Huntercombe Lane
Bury St. Edmunds abbey: considerable lengths of wall around site
Bury St. Edmunds friary: much of boundary wall surviving

Canterbury cathedral-priory: considerable lengths of wall, especially to north west, also sharing city wall to east & north east

Canterbury St. Augustine's abbey: some lengths of walling notably to south & west, with flint & stone checkerboard patterning

Carlisle cathedral-priory: continuous length of wall on south side of precinct

Chatteris abbey: disconnected sections of walling along East Park St., South Park St. & Victoria St.

Chester abbey: length of city wall doubling as precinct boundary

Christchurch priory: considerable lengths of wall on south side

Cirencester abbey: lengths of wall towards Gosditch & Dollar Streets

Cleeve abbey: length of wall fronting river

Colchester St. John's abbey: long lengths of wall, next to St. Giles church (masonic hall) & along Mersea Road

Croxden abbey: several short sections of walling to north & west

Dartford priory: [length of wall survives in Kingsfield Terrace]

Davington priory: long high length of walling to north east of church, heavily buttressed towards west end

Dunster priory: lengths of walling connected to 2 gateways

Dunwich Franciscan friary: perimeter wall largely complete

Edington priory: high wall on 4 sides to north east of church; C14

Ewenny priory: two thirds or more of perimeter wall; C13 or earlier

Fountains abbey: considerable lengths of wall along south & east sides; C14

Glastonbury abbey: considerable length of wall on north & west sides of precinct

Gloucester Dominican friary: length of stone wall at north west corner of precinct; probably C14

Godstow abbey: considerable portions of wall survive round more than one side

Hulne friary: complete wall round precinct with sentry walk, less parapet

Jervaulx abbey: section of intact wall with coping on east side of precinct

Gloucester Lanthony priory: good stretch of wall to south of gatehouse, rebuilt in brick; early C16

Leicester abbey: considerable lengths of wall around precinct

Letheringham priory: sections of wall to east & west of site

Lindisfarne priory: 1. portion of precinct wall on south side of site

2. high-standing defensive wall constructed immediately to east of east range in later medieval period; C14/C15

London charterhouse: length of wall connecting to outer gatehouse, consisting of flint checkers

Ludlow Carmelite friary: considerable lengths of wall standing to full height, mainly around modern churchyard

Margam abbey: considerable portion of high wall to west of church; unknown date

Maxstoke priory: considerable lengths of wall, much of it intact

Merton priory: [two disconnected runs of wall along Station Road & behind Windsor Avenue]

Monk Bretton priory: some intact walling to south east of precinct site

Monkton priory: sections of high-standing wall, especially on north side

Mount Grace charterhouse: some intact curtain wall, especially on east side of outer court; early C15

Newcastle-upon-Tyne Carmelite friary: length of city wall forming precinct boundary

Norwich cathedral-priory: some lengths of wall in good order; earliest sections late C11 & C12

Owston abbey: length of wall to south of church along village street

Oxford Franciscan friary: short length of rubble walling on west side & south end of Littlegate Street

Penmon priory: considerable lengths of wall on north & west sides

Peterborough abbey: walling especially to west & east

Quarr abbey: [much walling survives, details unidentified]

Ramsey abbey: walling especially to west & north

Repton priory: considerable lengths of still functional wall

Rewley abbey: lengths of wall on both sides of intact gateway

Roche abbey: fairly long length of wall on side of valley north of precinct

Rochester cathedral-priory: sections of wall survive, some in good order especially to south & east

Royston priory: sections of knapped flint walling survive to south west, including some portions to maximum height

Ruthin priory: section of wall to north west of church skirting west side of precinct area; unknown date but probably C14

St. Bees priory: short section of high-standing wall on west side of church beyond vicarage garden; unknown date

St. Osyth abbey: much walling survives on south side of site

Stamford Carmelite friary: lengths of walling on both sides of gateway

Tavistock abbey: good length of wall along River Walk

Tewkesbury abbey: lengths of wall on each side of abbot's lodging

Thornton abbey: sections of wall adjacent to gatehouse

Titchfield abbey: section of existing high-standing walling on east side of site, consisting of stone (& not post-Dissolution adjacent Tudor brick); unknown date

Tynemouth priory: sections of common wall of priory & castle to north & south; C12/C13

Walsingham friary: considerable lengths of wall

Walsingham priory: long length of wall on north side

Waltham abbey: short sections of wall north of church

Westminster abbey: wall on south side; c.1374

Whalley abbey: intact section of wall on north side of precinct, complete with mural turrets; C14

Wigmore abbey: intact section of wall between outer & inner gatehouse, also another section further north near stables

Winchester cathedral-priory: portions of close wall to south & west

Worcester cathedral-priory: section of wall on south east side

Wymondham abbey: section of wall along south side of Church Street bordering churchyard, includes brick & flint; C16 & later

York St. Mary's abbey: considerable lengths of wall; 1266+, 1318+, c.1354

2/4   OTHER PRECINCT BARRIERS

Breedon priory: remnants of bank & ditch (Bulwarks) on north west & south west sides of precinct; original Iron Age fort pre C1, with reconstruction in medieval times
Hitchin friary: [site retains moat; unknown date]
Michelham priory: intact wide system of moats surrounding site; c.1400
Rumburgh cell: series of moats & ponds around site
Sutton-at-Hone St. John's Jerusalem commandery: intact 4-sided moated precinct; unknown date
Thornton abbey: portions of moat now mostly dry fronting precinct wall; unknown date
Ulverscroft priory: moat & ditch serving as precinct wall, marked out by line of trees on 3 sides; probably C13
Woodhouse friary: [considerable portion of rectangular moat; unknown date]

2/5   ALMONRIES & HOSPITIA

Abingdon abbey: intact hospitium of St. John Baptist attached to gatehouse, now used as Municipal Buildings; C15, C18 & C19
Ansty commandery: intact hospitium, became post-Dissolution barn; early C16, pDp
Battle abbey: almonry, wing of gatehouse, became post-Dissolution courtroom & now high-standing ruin; probably of C13 & C14 date

Brecon priory: intact almonry adapted as private house; unknown construction date(s)

Canterbury cathedral-priory: intact hospitium (North Hall) but heavily restored; C12+, C19

Christchurch priory: intact cottage west of church believed to have been almonry; unknown date

Dorchester abbey: almonry combined with guesthouse, intact & adapted first as village school & now museum; C14, C15

Dunstable priory: intact detached much-altered building known as The Priory believed to be hospitium, has long rib vaulted undercroft; C14, pDp

Dunster priory: almonry known as The Nunnery, intact but adapted as row of three cottages; c.1346, C15

Ely cathedral priory: intact almonry, adjoining reduced Porta Monachorum; c.1200, C13

Evesham abbey: intact almonry, considerably altered & extended for domestic use, now museum; originally dates from C14/C15, also C17

Gloucester abbey: intact almoner's lodging, recently restored & used for storage of ecclesiastical records; C16 & earlier

Lenton priory: intact chancel of chapel of hospitium or hospital of St. Anthony; C12, pDp

Lewes priory: intact hospitium, now in use as Southover parish church; late C12, C14, C16

Nostell priory: [intact & restored hospice (Barley Hall) in York, timber-framed building; c.1360, mid C15, 1990-92]

Osney abbey: small intact barn shaped building (hospitium?), with roof truss inside; C15

Pershore abbey: intact black-&-white cottages, said to have been almonry; unknown date

Ramsey abbey: intact hospitium with crypt, now used as Ramsey parish church; dates from early C12

Reading abbey: intact dormitory of hospitium of St. John Baptist, has had many uses such as school, barracks & college; 1486

Redlingfield priory: intact & recently restored 2-storeyed building, probably hospitium or almonry & latterly barn; unknown date

St. Osyth abbey: intact buildings flanking great gatehouse probably hospitium & almonry; C15

Stoneleigh abbey: intact hospitium, wing of gatehouse, used after the Dissolution for domestic purposes; C14, late C16

Tewkesbury abbey: intact L-shaped domestic block (Monastery Cottage) to south west of gatehouse, probably represents almonry; C15/C16 & later

Wilton abbey: [intact low & detached building, originally 2-storeyed, believed to be almonry; late C13]

York St. Mary's abbey: intact hospitium adjacent to watergate, drastically restored; c.1300, C19

2/6   MONASTIC ALMSHOUSES

Glastonbury abbey: 1. intact chapel (St. Patrick's chapel), of Abbot Beere's almshouses in Glastonbury; 1512
2. intact chapel (St. Mary Magdalene's chapel), of almshouses of St. Mary Magdalene (known as Royal hospital after Dissolution); 1264+, C15

2/7 SERVICE BUILDINGS IN OR NEAR GREAT COURT

Abingdon abbey: intact granary barn, now divided into rooms; C13(?)

Buckland abbey: intact stabling block (detached), sometimes called guest-house; early C14, C15, c.1570

Canterbury cathedral-priory: intact brewhouse, bakehouse & granary (now converted into classrooms) on north side of Green Court; 1303, pDp

Ely cathedral-priory: intact granary, now used as gymnasium etc. of school; late C14

Fountains abbey: intact mill; C12, but mainly C13, alterations & additions; pDp

Langley abbey: intact thatched stable block, continuing use after Dissolution; early C16

Lindisfarne priory: high-standing west & south walls of brewhouse & bakehouse to west of south range, with remains of ovens; C14/C15

London charterhouse: [intact outbuildings & lay-brothers' quarters adapted as service court (Washhouse Court) of post-Dissolution mansion; 1531-35, pDp]

Norwich cathedral-priory: 1. intact granary to east of Bishop's Gate; C13, C15

2. granary & brewhouse converted into post-Dissolution houses in area of Lower Close; C13, C15, C18

Repton priory: intact barn adjacent to gatehouse with 5-bay tie beam & queen post roof, now teaching area of school; C15/C16

St. Osyth abbey: intact large barn near great gatehouse, one side stone & others timber framed; C16

Winchcombe abbey: intact building (called Winchcombe Abbey) claimed as malthouse of abbey, has Cotswold stone roof; C15/C16

Winchester cathedral-priory: intact range of stables, probable continuing use after Dissolution; early C16

◆◆◆◆◆◆◆◆◆◆◆◆◆◆◆◆

Section 3:
CONVENTUAL CHURCHES

3/1 CHURCHES SUBSTANTIALLY SURVIVING & IN USE TODAY AS RELIGIOUS BUILDINGS

N.B. This list includes a few churches that have recently been made redundant.

Abergavenny priory: intact cruciform church; mainly early C14, also some C15 & C19

Aconbury priory: intact small single aisled church with no architectural distinction between choir & nave (very recently made redundant); c.1260+

Alkborough cell: intact church with Anglo-Saxon tower, but choir rebuilt as chancel after Dissolution; 1052+, mainly C13, 1887

Alvingham priory: intact small church of St. Mary with south west tower, became parish church of North Cockerington & now redundant; late C12, c.1300, 1841

Amesbury priory: intact cruciform church; C12, mainly C13, also C14, 1853

Arundel priory: *intact cruciform church rebuilt immediately after suppression of priory in 1380; hence whole building late C14*

Atherstone friary: intact cruciform church, with nave rebuilt after Dissolution; choir with walking place & central tower 1357, C15, & remainder 1849

Bamburgh cell: intact pseudo-cruciform church; mainly early C13

Bath cathedral-priory: intact cruciform church; whole church rebuilt c.1499-1539, nave vaulting 1860-73

Binham priory: intact part nave, remainder destroyed; mainly C12, also C13

Bishopsgate St. Helens priory: intact 2-aisled church; much of building late C13, recently restored 1993-95

Blackmore priory: intact nave & timbered west tower, but crossing & choir destroyed; C12 & later centuries

Blakeney friary: intact church with west tower, preceding coming of friars; C13, mainly 1435, 1880+

Blanchland abbey: intact east and north portions of church, nave destroyed; choir c.1200, north tower & north transept c.1300, mid C18, 1854, 1881

Blyth priory: intact nave, but crossing, transepts & choir destroyed; mainly c.1090

Bolton priory: intact nave, eastern parts of church are high-standing ruins; crossing & choir date from late C12 & C14, nave late C12, mid C13 & early C14

Bourne abbey: intact nave & south west tower, remainder of church destroyed; nave mainly C12, tower c.1200, C15

Boxgrove priory: intact eastern portion of church, western part of nave destroyed; crossing & transepts C12, choir early C13

Brecon friary: intact choir & walking space, now school chapel, ruined nave; c.1250+, also early C14

Brecon priory: intact cruciform church, now cathedral; eastern parts of church C13, nave early C14

Breedon priory: intact eastern section of church, nave demolished; central tower C12, choir mainly C13

Bridlington priory: intact nave with west front & portions of west towers, remainder destroyed; nave dates mainly from mid C13

Brinkburn priory: intact cruciform church; building mainly c.1190/1210, restored 1858-59

Bristol abbey: intact cruciform church; choir c.1298-1330, transepts & crossing C12 & mid C15-early C16, nave rebuilt 1868/88

Bristol St. James' priory: intact nave & part of west front, eastern section destroyed after Dissolution; C12, C19

Bromfield priory: intact nave & crossing, choir & transepts destroyed; C12, mainly c.1300

Buckfast abbey: *cruciform church totally rebuilt over site of medieval church; 1907-32*

Bungay priory: intact nave & south west tower, building now redundant, eastern (conventual) parts stand fairly high as ruin; early C14, mid C15

Caldey cell: intact small church of choir, nave & west tower; mainly C13, also C14

Cambridge St. Radegund's priory: intact central part of church, now chapel of Jesus College; earliest work C12, choir mainly mid C13

Canons Ashby priory: intact west portion of nave & north west tower, remainder of nave & everything to east destroyed; C13, C14

Canterbury cathedral-priory: intact cruciform church; eastern limb & east transepts late C11 & late C12, nave 1391-1405, main transepts C15

Cardigan cell: intact choir & substantially restored nave, western tower rebuilt after Dissolution; C14, C15/C16, C18

Carisbrooke priory: intact church with south nave aisle & tall west tower, choir gone; C12, C13, C15, 1870

Carlisle cathedral-priory: intact cruciform church, but western part of nave destroyed; every century represented C12-C15

Cartmel priory: intact cruciform church; crossing & choir c.1190-1220, nave mainly 1420

Chepstow priory: intact central aisle of nave & west front, remainder of church substantially rebuilt after Dissolution; nave early C12, choir & transepts 1840 & 1904

Chester abbey: intact cruciform church; chief periods represented C12, C14, C15, C16

Chetwode cell: intact medieval choir & choir chapel now parish church, with added post-Dissolution west tower; c.1245, early C14+, c.1600

Chirbury priory: intact nave & west tower, remainder demolished after Dissolution, & shallow chancel built; nave C13, sanctuary 1733

Christchurch priory: intact cruciform church; all medieval centuries represented from late C11

Church Gresley priory: intact church , but choir destroyed & rebuilt as chancel after Dissolution; mainly C13/C14, C15 & new chancel 1872

Church Preen cell: intact little church of choir & nave forming one long body; early/mid C13

Clerkenwell priory: intact choir & crypt, round nave demolished; crypt C12, choir C16 & later

Cranborne cell: intact nave, choir destroyed at Dissolution but rebuilt afterwards; late C12, c.1300, 1875

Croyland abbey: intact north aisle & north west tower serving as present church, remainder destroyed; C13, C15, C19

Davington priory: intact nave, east part destroyed; mainly C12, with major restoration 1845+

Deeping St. James priory: intact 2-aisled church, west tower rebuilt after Dissolution; mainly late C12

Deerhurst priory: intact church much altered, less eastern apse; core of building 804 or earlier & C10, c.1200, later work mainly C14

Dinmore commandery: intact small church probably reduced at west end from being axial building; C12, mainly C14

Dorchester abbey: intact church; C12, C13, early C14

Dore abbey: intact crossing & choir, remainder destroyed; mainly c.1180 & early C13

Dover Augustinian priory: intact small cruciform church of St. Mary-in-Castro, now garrison church; earliest work c.1000, C12, C13, 1860-62

Dunstable priory: intact nave & much of west front, crossing & choir destroyed; surviving portions mid/late C12, mid C13 & late C15

Dunster priory: intact cruciform church; C12, C13 & mostly mid C15

Durham cathedral-priory: intact great cruciform church; choir c.1093-1100, nave c.1100-33

Easebourne priory: intact church though heavily restored in recent years; earliest work comes from C11 & C12, much 1876

Edington priory: intact cruciform church; whole building dates from 1352-1361

Elstow abbey: most of nave intact, remainder of church to east destroyed; earliest part of nave c.1100, detached tower C13 & mainly c.1500

Ely cathedral-priory: intact cruciform church except for demolished north west tower; nave & transepts late C11/early C12, choir c.1322-35, octagon mid C14

Ewenny priory: intact cruciform church except for demolished north transept; mid C12, C19

Farewell priory: intact small church much rebuilt after Dissolution; choir late C13, remainder 1740 & 1747

Farne Island cell: intact small 2-cell church with no structural division between choir & nave; c.1370, restored 1844-48

Freiston priory: intact nave, crossing & choir destroyed; C12, C13, mid C15, restoration C19

Garway preceptory: intact church with rebuilt medieval nave; C12, mainly C13

Gloucester abbey: intact cruciform church; several building periods mainly from late C11 to late C14, also c.1430 & later C15

Godsfield commandery: intact small chapel-like church, attached to priest's lodging; C14

Goring priory: intact nave & west tower, nuns' choir destroyed but apsed chancel rebuilt in recent years; late C11/early C12, early C13; 1886, 1937

Great Bricett priory: intact nave & choir, transepts destroyed; mainly C12, also c.1300

Hamble priory: intact small church with west tower, confusing pattern of development; C12, C13, C14

Hatfield Broad Oak priory: intact nave & west tower, but crossing & choir destroyed; mainly C15

Hatfield Peverel priory: intact nave, but crossing & choir destroyed; C12, C13, C15

Hayling priory: intact cruciform church of St. Mary (South Hayling), built as replacement for earlier church swept away by sea; mainly C13, 1869, 1892-93

Hexham priory: intact cruciform church but nave rebuilt recently; c.1180-1250, early C13, east end 1858+, nave 1907-09

Heynings priory: intact church of curious design considerably remodelled after Dissolution, retaining old nave; C11, early C14, C17, C18, 1894

Holme Cultram abbey: intact portion of nave, remainder of church destroyed; late C12

Hurley priory: intact nave, remainder of church destroyed & partly rebuilt after Dissolution; C12, C14, 1852

Ingham friary: intact church; most building periods from C14

Jarrow priory: intact church, nave rebuilt after Dissolution; choir 681 & c.1300, central tower c.1075, nave 1866

Kidwelly cell: intact church with pseudo-cruciform crossing; c.1320, 1884

King's Lynn priory: intact church, with much of nave rebuilt after Dissolution because of storm; C12, C13, C15, c.1746

Lancaster priory: intact church with west tower; nearly all building 1420+

Lanercost priory: intact nave, high-standing ruins of crossing, transepts & choir; c.1190+, mainly C13

Lapley priory: intact cruciform church though transepts have disappeared; mainly C12, also late C13, C15

Lastingham abbey: intact church, but original design never fully carried out; earliest date late c.1078

Leominster priory: intact nave & added medieval outer south aisle, crossing & choir demolished; nave mid C12, outer south aisle 1320

Leonard Stanley priory: intact small cruciform church; mostly c.1129

Letheringham priory: intact small nave, east end of church destroyed; C12, c.1300, C15, 1789+

Little Malvern priory: intact choir & crossing, remainder of building destroyed leaving high-standing walls of choir chapels etc.; C14, c.1480

Little Maplestead commandery: intact church including round nave; c.1335, restored 1851-57

Llanbadarn-fawr priory: intact big & severe-looking cruciform building; c.1200, C15, 1868

Llangennith cell: intact single aisled church with north saddleback tower; earliest dates C13, C14, 1882-84

Llanllugan priory: intact small single aisled church of choir & nave forming one entity; C14/C15

Malmesbury abbey: intact 6 eastern bays of nave, remainder of building to east & west partially demolished; c.1160, early C14

Malton priory: intact west section of part of nave & south west tower, remainder of building destroyed; mainly late C12/early C13, 1636

Malvern priory: intact cruciform church, save for demolished south transept & lady chapel; nave c.1120, remainder nearly all mid C15

Margam abbey: intact west portion of nave, remainder of building demolished or ruined; c.1150-80, C13, 1805-10, 1873

Milton abbey: intact choir & crossing, non-existent nave probably never constructed; c.1310-25, C15

Minster-in-Sheppey priory: intact nave & west tower, eastern portions of building destroyed; conventual nave dates: C8/C9, C12, C13, 1879-81

Monkland cell: intact nave & west tower but choir rebuilt in recent times; earliest work of late C11 & later C13

Monks Kirby priory: intact church substantially unaltered since Dissolution; almost all C14 & C15

Monkton priory: intact nave & south tower, much of east end of church rebuilt since Dissolution; nave C12 & C13/C14, tower C15, choir early C14 & 1882/1907

Monkwearmouth cell: intact church; nave & west tower C7+ & C13, choir mainly C14, restored 1875-76

Morville cell: intact small church with west tower; nearly all building C12

Norwich cathedral-priory: intact cruciform church; mostly early C12, also C14 & C15

Nun Monkton priory: intact nave, demolished choir; nearly all surviving building dates from late C12 to early C13, 1873

Ovingham cell: intact pseudo-cruciform church with some modern rebuilding; west tower late C10/early C11, main portions of church C13, 1855+

Owston abbey: intact nave & north west tower, destroyed choir; c.1300, C15, C19

Oxford St. Bernard's college: intact chapel on north side of Front Quadrangle of St. John's college, heavily remodelled after Dissolution; late C15, 1843

Oxford St. Frideswide's priory: intact cruciform church though shorn of west bays of nave; mostly late C12, central tower & spire c.1200+

Pamber priory: intact choir & crossing, destroyed nave & transepts; C12, C13

Penmon priory: intact small cruciform church, much of choir rebuilt in recent times; c.1140+, C19

Pershore abbey: intact choir & crossing, nave destroyed; crossing etc. c.1100 & early C14, choir early C13

Peterborough abbey: intact cruciform church; most of building mid C12, retrochoir late C15+

Pilton priory: intact church considerably restored after Dissolution, choir demolished; much of building late C14/early C15, also 1696

Polesworth abbey: intact west portion of nave & north tower, remainder of building to east destroyed; C12, C14, 1869

Portchester priory: most of small cruciform church intact, south transept & east part of choir destroyed; all c.1133+, restored 1888

Reading friary: intact nave, choir & crossing destroyed but north & south transepts off nave rebuilt in recent times; c.1311, 1863

Redlingfield priory: intact small church, heavily restored after Dissolution; mainly C14 & pDp

Rochester cathedral-priory: intact cruciform church; earliest parts north tower c.1077 & west portion of nave C11+, most of remainder C13

Romsey abbey: intact cruciform church; east limb c.1120-50, nave c.1150-90 & early C13

Rothley Temple preceptory: intact small church preserved as domestic chapel of adjacent post-Dissolution mansion to which it is attached; mainly c.1280, C15

Royston priory: most of monastic choir survives as nave of present parish church; early C13, C14, C15, 1872-75, 1891

Rumburgh cell: intact church without aisles or chapels; earliest date of fabric C13

Ruthin priory: intact & much restored axial church with additional south nave aisle, but with choir gone; 1310-15, later C14, 1854-59

St. Albans abbey: intact cruciform church; most of building C11, also C12 & C13

St. Anthony-in-Roseland cell: intact cruciform church now redundant; devoid of aisles, porches & west towers; C12, C13, 1850

St. Bees priory: intact cruciform church, with considerable restoration after Dissolution; earliest parts include crossing & transepts C12, choir & nave c.1200

St. Clear's cell: intact & much restored small church of choir, nave & west tower, with Norman archway to choir the chief architectural feature; C12, C14, 1854-55

St. Germans priory: intact nave & west front, eastern portions of building demolished; oldest work c.1180

St. Michael's Mount priory: intact small axial church, now in care of National Trust; C12, late C14, C15

Selby abbey: intact cruciform church, though central tower & south transept rebuilt in recent years; nave early C12, choir c.1280-1340

Sele friary: intact small church with west tower, severely restored in recent times; oldest work mostly of c.1308, also C16, C19

Sherborne abbey: intact cruciform church; west front & crossing pre-1066, choir c.1425+, nave & central tower c.1475+

Shipley preceptory: intact axial church with modern north aisle & vestry; c.1125, 1893

Shrewsbury abbey: intact nave & part of crossing, choir destroyed & rebuilt as small chancel in recent times; nave mainly late C12, west tower 1360-70, choir 1886-88

Smithfield St. Bartholomew's priory: intact choir & crossing, nearly all nave destroyed; mainly C12, C14, C19

Snaith cell: intact pseudo-cruciform church with west tower, much altered & added to over the centuries; C12, C13, C14, C15, 1868

Southwark priory: intact choir & crossing, nave destroyed but rebuilt in recent times; most of medieval work dates from C13, nave 1890-97

Stogursey priory: intact small cruciform church; c.1100, C12, C15, 1865

Stow abbey: intact cruciform church; crossing & transepts pre-1066, nave late C11, choir early C12

Swine priory: intact choir, remainder of building destroyed but tower rebuilt; c.1190, C15

Temple Balsall preceptory: intact church of choir & nave (architecturally one); c.1290, 1849

Temple Ewell preceptory: intact small church with west tower; mainly C12, C13, 1874

Temple Guiting preceptory intact small church with modern west tower; C12, early C14, C15, C17, 1740-42, C19

Temple preceptory: intact church with round nave; nave c.1160-85, choir c.1220-40, 1825-30, 1841-43, 1862, 1947-57

Tewkesbury abbey: intact cruciform church except for destroyed lady chapel; chief construction period for church late C11-earlier C12

Thorney abbey: intact nave though shorn of aisles, everything to east destroyed, modest east end rebuilt in recent times; 1085-1108, C15, 1638, 1840

Thurgarton priory: intact west three bays of nave & part of west front, remainder of medieval building destroyed, some recent reconstruction; c.1230, 1853

Totnes priory: intact building representing almost whole of medieval church, except for monks' destroyed north west choir; largely mid C15

Trentham priory: intact nave, choir destroyed & now replaced by shallow chancel; c.1180-90, restored 1844

Tutbury priory: intact nave, remainder of church destroyed but choir replaced by apsed chancel in recent times; 1100/50, 1866-68

Upholland priory: intact choir & nave forming one architectural   entity (now all nave of parish church); remainder possibly never built or completed, modern chancel constructed to east; early C14, chancel added 1883

Usk priory: intact nave & crossing, choir & transepts destroyed; c.1135+, C13, C15, C19

Waltham abbey: intact nave of original collegiate church (with post-Dissolution west tower), whole of crossing & canons' church to east destroyed; mainly late C11-mid C12, south nave chapel c.1320, tower 1556-58

Westminster abbey: intact cruciform church; choir & transepts 1245-55, nave 1272 & 1376+

Weybourne priory: intact nave (now rebuilt north nave aisle) & later parochial nave & chancel, high-standing ruined choir & central tower; mainly C13, C15, 1866

Wilmington priory: intact small church of choir, nave & north nave chapel; C12, C14, C19

Winchester cathedral-priory: intact cruciform church; construction periods range mainly from late C11 to late C14

Worcester cathedral-priory: intact cruciform church; two west bays of nave c.1180, remainder of nave c.1320+, choir 1224+

Worksop priory: intact nave & west towers, east end reconstructed in recent times; c.1140-70+, C19, C20

Wymondham abbey: intact nave & west tower, east tower now high-standing ruin, remainder of conventual church to east destroyed; main construction period c.1107-30

3/1 Worksop priory, conventual church to north

York Holy Trinity priory: intact north west tower & portion of nave, remainder destroyed but modern chancel erected over site of crossing; late C12/early C13, C19

3/2 SUMMARY OF ABOVE CHURCHES RETAINING RUINED PARTS

Binham priory: tall fragments of crossing piers
Blyth priory: empty shell of crossing
Bolton priory: crossing , choir & transepts
Boxgrove priory: part of north side of nave
Brecon friary: nave
Bungay priory: north wall of nuns' choir

Croyland abbey: west front & 3 arches of nave south arcade, also west crossing arch & rood screen
Dore abbey: small part of east end of nave
Ewenny priory: small portions of north transept
Lanercost priory: crossing, choir & transepts
Little Malvern priory: choir chapels
Malmesbury abbey: parts of crossing & south transept
Malton priory: small part of south nave aisle
Margam abbey: high-standing portions of south wall of choir & east wall of south transept chapels, also small part of south nave aisle
Pershore abbey: small part of east end of nave
St. Bees priory: length of outer wall & blocked inner arcading of south choir aisle; late C13/early C14
Sherborne abbey: north wall of contiguous parish church of All Hallows
Weybourne priory: crossing & choir
Wymondham abbey: central tower

3/3 OTHER PRE-DISSOLUTION CHURCHES ON OR NEAR SITES OF ALIEN OR INDIGENOUS MONASTIC HOUSES WHICH MAY HAVE BEEN CONVENTUAL

Allerton Mauleverer priory: intact cruciform church of St. Martin, curiously remodelled in Norman Revival style; C12, C14, c.1745
Astley priory; [intact church of St. Peter with west tower, built to quality standard; c.1160, C15, c.1838]
Beckford cell: [intact cruciform church of St. John Baptist; C12, C13]

Cogges priory: intact church, with tower placed diagonally across west end of north aisle; C12, C13, C14

Ecclesfield priory: intact large cruciform church, with embattled roofs; c.1200, early C14, C15

Ewyas Harold priory: intact small church with west tower originally detached; tower & chancel C13, nave rebuilt 1868

Folkestone priory: [intact cruciform church of St. Mary & St. Eanswythe, much rebuilt in recent times; C13, C15, 1856-59]

Hackness cell: [intact church of St. Mary The Virgin, possesses medieval stalls & misericords; early C13, C15]

Loders priory: [intact church of St. Mary Magdalene of all medieval periods, with west tower; mainly C14, C15]

Lyminster priory: [intact church of St. Mary Magdalene of Anglo-Saxon origin; c.1040, c.1160, C13, C15]

Minster cell: intact church of St. Merteriana or Merthiana, with unbuttressed & saddleback west tower, nave & south aisle of 5 bays; C12/13, early C16, 1869-71

Newton Longville cell: [intact church of St. Faith, with 2-bay arcades; late C12, early C14]

Otterton priory: [intact church of St. Michael, tower medieval & remainder rebuilt in recent times; C15, 1869-71]

Patrixbourne priory: intact church of St. Mary of special architectural interest; C12, C15, c.1824, 1857

Ribstone preceptory: intact small & much restored church attached to house (Ribston Hall); late C13

Scarborough cell: intact though reduced cruciform church of St. Mary, with choir & north transept gone; late C12, C13, C14, C15, C17, 1848-52

Sheringham cell: intact church of All Saints with west tower, also possesses medieval rood screen & loft; C14, C15, 1849, 1872

Sporle cell: intact church of St. Mary with west tower; C13, mainly C15

Steventon priory: [intact church of St. Michael, with tower over south porch; mainly early C14]

Swavesey priory: [intact large church of St. Andrew with imposing tower; early C14, C15]

Tarrant abbey: intact parish church of St. Mary at Tarrant Crawford, adjacent to site of abbey & may have been conventual; C12, c.1300

Throwley priory: [intact church of St. Michael & All Angels, containing carved choir stalls & misericords; C12, C13, C14, C15, 1866]

Wangford priory: [intact church of St. Peter & St. Paul, much rebuilt in recent times; c.1370, 1865, 1875]

Wareham cell: [intact church of St. Mary, nave rebuilt in recent times; c.1100, C13, C15, 1841-42]

West Mersea priory: [intact church of St. Peter & St. Paul with west tower; C12, C14, 1833]

Wilberfoss priory: [intact parish church of St. John Baptist, may have been conventual church; mainly C15]

3/4 PARISH CHURCHES OWNED OR OCCUPIED BY KNIGHTS TEMPLAR WHOSE PRECEPTORIES HAVE NOT BEEN CONVINCINGLY IDENTIFIED

Fordingbridge (Hants.): [intact north chapel of church of St. Mary was non-parochial & belonged to Templars; c.1270]

Sompting (Ssx.): intact south transept (originally detached) of church of St. Mary served as Templar chapel; c.1180

Stidd (Lancs.) intact small church of St. Saviour near Ribchester, possibly a hospital church & later becoming property of Knights Hospitaller; C12, C13

Temple (Bristol): ruined church of Holy Cross of Templars (gutted during last war); c.1300, lateC14/early C15, C18, C19

Welsh Newton (Heref.): intact church of St. Mary built by Templars, contains official seat of preceptor (Seat of Freedom) on north side of chancel; C13

3/5   SMALL PORTIONS OF CONVENTUAL CHURCHES SURVIVING IN THEIR ORIGINAL FORM & USED FOR WORSHIP OR AS PART OF OTHERWISE ENTIRELY POST-DISSOLUTION CHURCH BUILDINGS

N.B. The dates (including those of later restorations) given below are those of the surviving medieval portions only.

Barrow Gurney priory: intact south nave aisle of church, remainder rebuilt after Dissolution; unknown date

Beauchief abbey: intact but shortened west tower of otherwise post-Dissolution church; C14, 1671

Beddgelert priory: east wall of choir & 2-bay north arcade of nave; early C13

Bradwell priory: [intact pilgrimage west chapel forming contiguous part of now destroyed conventual church & now free-standing, built to protect miraculous image of Our Lady; C14]

Cockerham cell: intact west tower of now parish church, remainder rebuilt in recent times; C15/C16

Conway abbey: west wall of nave of Cistercian church stands within later medieval parochial church; early C13

Cwmhyr abbey: 4 piers & 5 arches of north east side of nave form arcade in Llanidloes church; originally constructed c.1200-30, relocated c.1542

Holystone priory: [south wall & lower part of north wall of choir, now nave of parish church; C12/C13]

Horsley priory: intact ashlar tower of parish church otherwise totally rebuilt in recent times, with diagonal buttresses & embattled parapet with crocketed pinnacles; C15/C16

Horton priory: intact north transept of church, remainder totally rebuilt after Dissolution; probably c.1401+

Humberston abbey: intact tower of present post-Dissolution parish church, built of grey & amber stone; C15

Kyme priory: intact west part of south nave aisle, small section of central aisle & south porch; but north part of nave & whole of east end of church demolished; C12, mainly C14 & C15

Launde priory: intact south choir chapel incorporated as domestic chapel within post-Dissolution mansion; early C12, mid C13, C15

Leiston abbey: intact & reroofed north choir aisle (probably lady chapel), remainder destroyed; C14

Little Dunmow priory: intact south choir aisle (probably lady chapel), now parish church, remainder destroyed; c.1200, mid C14

Malpas cell: [intact fine choir (now chancel) arch in small building otherwise completely rebuilt in neo-Norman style; C12, 1849-50]

Monmouth priory: intact Norman respond at west end of nave & west tower of otherwise post-Dissolution church; C12, C14

Nuneaton priory: crossing piers & part of south transept wall only of post-Dissolution church; C12, virtually rebuilt C19 & C20

Repton (Anglo-Saxon) **abbey**: walls of sanctuary of choir (now chancel of parish church), also crypt; C8, C9

Tynemouth priory: intact east chapel (Percy chantry), remainder of church largely destroyed; C15

Warburton cell: half-timbered north wall of nave of intact small redundant church; possibly late C13

Wix priory: [blocked north nave arcade with octagonal piers in post-Dissolution reduced parish church; C13]

Woodkirk cell: intact west tower of otherwise entirely post-Dissolution church; C13

Wroxall priory: intact north aisle forming core of present redundant church; C14, C15

Yarmouth priory: intact large cruciform church rebuilt after being gutted in last War, only walls of central tower are original including Norman work; C12, C13, C19, but mainly 1957-1961

3/6 CONVENTUAL CHURCHES CONVERTED TO OR USED FOR POST-DISSOLUTION SECULAR PURPOSES

Alberbury priory: parts of church notably chapel of St. Stephen & south wall of nave incorporated into farmhouse; c.1226, 1578/90, 1857-58

Bradsole St. Radegund's abbey: high-standing ruined tower north of former nave, converted after Dissolution into gatehouse; probably pre c.1220, pDp

Brimpton preceptory: [intact small chapel of St. Leonard converted into farm storehouse, rectangular building with tympanum over north doorway; C12, C14]

Buckland abbey: intact nave, crossing, north transept chapel and choir; converted into private mansion, transepts destroyed; C13, extensive alterations 1576, 1772

Cambridge friary: intact church converted into hall of Emmanuel college; possibly C15, extensively remodelled 1764

Chichester friary: intact choir, now civic meeting hall, remainder of church destroyed if never built; 1282

Delapre abbey: intact north, west & south walls of nave form part of post-Dissolution house, choir destroyed; C12/C13

Denney abbey: largely intact nave & crossing converted into post-Dissolution house, choir destroyed; mainly C12

Ecclesfield priory: [intact small church standing on undercroft in non-typical monastic layout, now part of private house (The Priory); c.1300]

Gloucester Dominican friary: church intact but reduced & converted into town house (Bell's Place), nave especially shortened; c.1239/c.1270, C14, mid C16, also C18 & C19

Isleham cell: intact 3-celled church used as barn after Dissolution; C12

Lacock abbey: sacristy & 2 chapels north of former choir converted into service accommodation of post-Dissolution mansion; C13

Latton priory: intact crossing (tower demolished) converted into barn; C14

Lincoln Franciscan friary: intact church including undercroft (possibly infirmary building) now museum; c.1230 & late C13

Malling abbey: [intact south transept , first used as chapel & now as chapter-house by modern community of nuns; probably late C11]

Marrick priory: intact nave & west tower, now part of diocesan youth centre, high-standing ruined choir; mainly C14

Mottisfont priory: most of single aisled nave, crossing & south transept converted into private mansion; late C12, C13, pDp

Newcastle-upon-Tyne Augustinian friary: [restored & intact tower (See entry under Crossings & Central Towers); C13, C18]

Newstead Augustinian priory: south transept converted into orangery of private post-Dissolution mansion; C13, C19

Norwich Dominican friary: intact church except for dismantled central tower, now used as civic meeting halls; main periods of construction 1327+ & 1413-70

Ramsey abbey: almost intact lady chapel in angle between former north transept & former choir, converted into basement of mansion, now comprehensive school; C13

Rye Augustinian friary: intact nave with windows displaying flowing tracery & divided horizontally into 2 floors, now pottery; 1378+

Sandford preceptory: [much of church converted into barn; C13, C15]

Stavordale priory: most of church converted into private house; mainly c.1443

Stoneleigh abbey: [south transept incorporated into post-Dissolution mansion; probably c.1200]

Sudbury St. Bartholomew's cell: intact church used as barn after Dissolution; C13

Sutton-at-Hone St. John's Jerusalem commandery: east part of church converted after Dissolution into domestic chapel & latterly billiard room, 2/3 bays now divided horizontally; c.1234, mid C18

Swingfield commandery: chapel with undercroft & double storeyed north porch converted into farmhouse after Dissolution, later abandoned & now restored; mainly C13

Thetford St. George's priory: single aisled church with one surviving transept, converted into barn & now remodelled as resource centre; C12

Thetford St. Sepulchre's priory: nearly whole high-standing ruined nave, converted into post-Dissolution barn; lack of architectural detail makes dating difficult but probably C14

Titchfield abbey : high-standing nave, converted into gatehouse of post-Dissolution private mansion (gatehouse subsequently ruined), crossing & eastern end of church destroyed; 1232+, 1537-42

Tortington priory: [part of nave of conventual church converted into post-Dissolution barn; C13, pDp]

Widmere commandery: [church or chapel converted into part of post-Dissolution farmhouse, has undercroft of 2 x 4 bays; C13, also early C14 & later]

Woodspring priory: intact nave, north transept & crossing converted into farmhouse, choir destroyed; mainly mid C15

Wymondley priory: [intact nave with original roof converted into farmhouse, remainder of building demolished; C13]

Yedingham priory: [intact south wall of single aisled church forms part of shed of Abbey Farm; late C12]

3/7   RUINED HIGH-STANDING CONVENTUAL CHURCHES OR SUBSTANTIAL RUINED PORTIONS OF SUCH CHURCHES

Basingwerk abbey: high-standing fragment consisting of west wall of south transept; early C13

Bayham abbey: some portions of building stand to great height, especially nave south wall & new transepts; C13, C15

Beaulieu abbey: south wall of nave stands to about 25 ft. high, i.e. just above upper line of corbels of roof of north cloister-walk, also some of south transept to similar height; early C13

Beeston priory: considerable portions of single aisled nave & choir; C13, C14

Brewood St. Leonard's priory: high-standing nave & north wall of choir, transepts gone; late C12

Broomholm priory: some high-standing walls of north transept (more) & south transept (less), but not much else; late C12, early C13

Buildwas abbey: nave has lost its north & south aisles, otherwise building largely survives; church built c.1135- c.1200

Burnham Norton friary: (See entry under High-Standing West Fronts of Conventual Churches)

Bury St. Edmunds abbey: formless crags of high-standing masonry, chiefly north east & south west piers of crossing; c.1090+

Calder abbey: considerable high-standing portions exist including nave north arcade, 4 crossing arches, much of north transept, all south transept & choir (less east end); late C12, C13, C14

Canterbury St. Augustine's abbey: high-standing west part of nave north wall now topped with brick, also some of north west tower; C11, brick pDp

Castle Acre priory: high-standing portions of nave west front & south west tower, also some transept walling; mainly early C12

Chibburn commandery: [high-standing south & east walls of small church; with evidence of 2-storeyed west end; C14]

Clare friary: high-standing south wall of choir & nave (now capped with tiling); early C14

Colchester St. Botolph's priory: considerable high-standing portions of nave including north arcade & west front, eastern parts gone; 1093/1100, also mid C12

Coventry cathedral-priory: high-standing surviving portion of north west tower attached to post-dissolution secular building, also medium/low-standing west front; C13

Coventry Franciscan friary: (See entry under Crossings & Central Towers)

Coverham abbey: high-standing fragments including 2 nave arches , west wall of north nave aisle & west wall of north transept; C13, C14

Coxford priory: high-standing fragment embodying mainly intact archway from crossing to north transept; C14/C15

Croxden abbey: high-standing fragments of church include west front & gable end of south transept; late C12/early C13

Cymmer abbey: high-standing portions of choir & north nave arcade, also west tower of medium height; mainly early C13, also C14 (See also entries under Naves & Non-Central Towers)

Denbigh friary: choir standing up to top of gable end, also short length of nave walls plus intervening walking space; mainly C13, C15

Dudley priory: high-standing ruined walls of nearly all nave, lower portions of south transept & south nave chapel; later C12, c.1200, C13, c.1400

Easby abbey: high-standing fragments including parts of transepts & north nave chapel; late C12, early C14

Egglestone abbey: high-standing ruined walls of most of nave, also west wall of south transept & mainly east end of choir; c.1200, c.1250/75, c.1300

Ellerton priory: west tower & much of north & south walls of aisleless nave; C15

Finchale priory: high-standing cruciform building standing mainly to above window arches & blocked nave arcades; c.1237-c.1300, reduced mid C14

Fountains abbey: very large cruciform building; nave mainly mid & late C12, choir arcades destroyed but eastward extensions survive c.1210-40, north tower early C16

Frithelstock priory: considerable portions of building especially nave stand high; mid C13

Furness abbey: high-standing choir & transepts & west tower, nave & crossing largely gone; late C12, late C15

Glastonbury abbey: high-standing ruined lady chapel & galilee, also fragments of crossing & transepts; 1184+, also early & mid C13

Gloucester Franciscan friary: high-standing 2-aisled & 7-bay nave of conventual church; late C15/early C16)

Gloucester St. Oswald's priory: much modified north nave arcade stands to above arches; mid C12, C13

Guyzance priory: [much high-standing of north & south walls of nave; possible late C11/early C12]

Haverfordwest priory: high-standing fragments include some walling of transepts & some of west end of nave; C13

Hulne friary: long single aisled choir & nave, of which south & west walls stand to maximum height; mid C13

Jervaulx abbey: high-standing fragment at south west corner of nave, containing extant doorway; c.1200

Kersey priory: (See entry under Other Chapels)

King's Lynn Franciscan friary: hexagonal central tower & walking space with doorway at each end; C13, C14

Kirkham priory: high-standing fragments of part of east wall of choir & south west tower; later C12, C13

Kirkstall abbey: large cruciform building with all major portions surviving; constructed within dates 1152-75

Leiston abbey: considerable high portions survive, especially at east end (with intact & reroofed north lady chapel); C13, C14

Lilleshall abbey: considerable high portions survive, especially of choir & west end of nave; mainly C12 & C13

Lincoln St. Mary Magdalene's cell: (See entry under Choirs)

Lindisfarne priory: high portions of church survive, especially choir, west front, nave north wall & parts of transepts; mainly C12

Llanthony priory: high-standing west front & north nave arcade as well portions of south transept & choir; late C12, early C13

Malling abbey: high-standing west front incorporating stump of tower, with intact lateral turrets (See also entry under High-Standing Ruined West Fronts), also south transept survives largely intact; mid C12, C14

Marham abbey: high-standing fragment consisting of south wall of nave, including 2 large round windows quatrefoiled & sexfoiled respectively; late C13

Mount Grace charterhouse: high-standing ruined cruciform church, choir almost all gone; early C15

Neath abbey: high-standing sections include some walling of nave, choir & north transept east chapels; early C14

Netley abbey: high-standing ruined church except for north transept, internal arcading removed to make way for post-Dissolution mansion now destroyed; C13, c.1290-1320

Newark priory: high-standing flint walling devoid of detail of south transept & choir; C13

Newstead Augustinian priory: (See entry under High-Standing Ruined West Fronts of Conventual Churches)

Pill priory: high-standing fragments consisting of one side of crossing & end wall of south transept; C13

Priestholm cell: (See entry under Crossings & Central Towers)

Ranton priory: (See entry under Non-Central Towers)

Richmond friary: (See entry under Crossings & Central Towers)

Richmond St. Martin's priory: tower & another building to its north east; C12, C15

Rievaulx abbey: surviving building now consisting of choir & transepts, nave & crossing largely destroyed; c.1225+

Roche abbey: some walls of north & south transepts (& small parts of walls of choir) stand to fullest height; c.1170+

St. Dogmael's abbey: high-standing walls of north transept & some of nave; C13, early C16

Salley abbey: high-standing fragments in area of crossing; late C12/early C13

Shap abbey: high west tower almost intact plus low other walls of church; early C16

Stamford St. Leonard's priory: derelict roofed building now consisting of part of nave especially north arcade & west front; c.1100, late C12, pDp

Strata Florida abbey: nearly all building displays low standing walls, except for higher west wall of nave & parts of transept chapels; mostly c.1200

Talley abbey: high-standing fragment of 2 walls of crossing; early C13

Temple Bruer preceptory: (See entry under Non-Central Towers)

Thetford friary: high-standing south crossing arch of church dividing present library in two, also some walling of nave; mid C14

Thetford Cluniac priory: high-standing finger of masonry of south east pier at entrance to original central apse, displays some Norman detail; C12

Tintern abbey: cruciform church largely survives, except for north nave aisle & arcade; c.1270-1301

Tresco cell: [intact 2 arches within high-standing fragment of wall of church, arches are 2-centred; C13]

Tynemouth priory: 1. high-standing east & part of south walls of choir; c.1195/1220

2. medium high parts of crossing & adjacent walling; c.1090/1140

3. lower portion of west end of nave: c.1220/1250

(See also entry under Chantries & Chantry Chapels)

Ulverscroft priory: high-standing west tower & high-standing south wall of nave; C13, mainly C15

Valle Crucis abbey: high-standing choir, south transept & west front; C13

Walsingham priory: (See entry under High-Standing East Ends of Conventual Churches etc.)

Wenlock priory: 1. high-standing westerly 3 bays of south nave aisle in 3 stages, intact to roof of middle stage; C13

2. high-standing ruined south transept; C13

West Acre priory: (See entry under Non-Central Towers)

Whalley abbey: south wall of nave at west end stands to full height & some of south transept to medium height; C14

Whitby abbey: most of choir & north transept exists with north & west wall of nave, remainder destroyed; mainly C13 & C14

Wigmore abbey: high-standing gable end of south transept & lower long length of south wall of nave; C12

Winchelsea friary: apsidal choir with intact chancel arch & intact south bell turret; early C14

Wykeham priory: [much of north wall of nave, displaying 2 blocked arches to north transept; C12, C13]

Yeaveley preceptory: [part of side wall of church near Stydd Hall, displaying 3 lancet windows; early C13, reconstructed 1915]

York St. Mary's abbey: nave north wall & adjacent walling stand almost to full height; later C13

◆◆◆◆◆◆◆◆◆◆◆◆◆◆◆

Section 4:
CHOIRS, CHAPELS & CRYPTS

4/1   **CHOIRS**

Abergavenny priory: intact single aisled & 4-bay choir (excluding chapels to north & south); C14, C15, C19, C20

Aconbury priory: intact single aisled choir & nave of 4 bays architecturally one; c.1260+

Aldeby priory: intact choir of 2 aisles & 3 bays; mainly c.1300

Alkborough cell: *choir totally rebuilt as chancel in recent times; 1887*

Alvingham priory: intact single aisled choir of one bay; late C12

Amesbury priory: intact single-aisled choir of 6 bays measured by lancets; C13

Atherstone friary: intact single aisled choir of 3 bays; 1357, C15

Bamburgh cell: intact single aisled choir of 5 bays; early C13

Bath cathedral-priory: intact choir of 3 aisles & 3½ bays; 1499-1539

Beddgelert priory: (See entry under Small Portions of Conventual Churches etc.)

Bishopsgate St. Helens priory: 1. intact single aisled nuns' choir of 2 bays to north of parochial chancel; C13, C16, 1993-95

2. intact single aisled parochial chancel of 2 bays to south of nuns' choir; C13, late C15, 1993-95

Blakeney friary: intact single aisled choir of 3+ bays (windowing) or 2 bays (rib vaulting), with upper storey; C13, 1880+

Blanchland abbey: intact single aisled choir of 2 bays; c.1200, rebuilt 1881

Bolton priory: high-standing ruined single aisled choir of 5 bays; late C12, C14

Boxgrove priory: intact choir of 3 aisles & 4 bays; early C13

Brecon friary: intact single aisled choir of 5½ bays; c.1250+

Brecon priory: intact single aisled choir of 4 bays; early C13

Breedon priory: intact choir of 3 aisles & 4 bays; mainly C13, also C14, C18

Brinkburn priory: intact single aisled choir of 3 bays; c.1190-1200, restored 1858-59

Bristol abbey: intact choir of 3 aisles & 5 bays (excluding lady chapel to east); c.1298-1330

Buildwas abbey: high-standing ruined single aisled choir of 2 bays; mid C12

Calder abbey: high-standing ruined west end of single aisled choir of 2(?) bays, east end gone; early C13

Caldey cell: intact single aisled choir of 2 bays; mainly C13

Cambridge St. Radegund's priory: intact single aisled choir of 8 bays (5 short bays east & 3 long bays west) mid C13, c.1500, 1849-53

Canterbury cathedral-priory: intact choir of 3 aisles & 11 bays (excluding Trinity chapel to east); c.1096-1130, c.1175-84

Cardigan cell: intact single aisled choir of 3 bays; C14

Carlisle cathedral-priory: intact choir of 3 aisles & 8 bays; c.1220-50, C14

Cartmel priory: intact choir of 3 aisles (including Piper Choir to north & Town Choir to south) & 3 bays; c.1190-1220, c.1340, C15

Chepstow abbey: *east end of church totally rebuilt as chancel with crossing & transepts; mainly 1890-1913*

Chester abbey: intact choir of 3 aisles & 6 bays (excluding easterly 2 bays of lady chapel), south choir aisle now shortened by one possibly 2 bays; late C13, mainly early C14, early C16, restored 1868-72

Chetwode cell: intact long single aisled choir of 6 bays, now chancel & nave of parish church; c.1245

Chichester friary: intact single aisled choir of 5½ bays; built c.1282

Chirbury priory: *choir totally rebuilt as shallow chancel; 1733*

Christchurch priory: intact choir of 3 aisles & 5+ bays (excluding east extension of lady chapel); late C15/early C16

Church Gresley priory: *choir totally rebuilt as chancel; 1872*

Church Preen cell: intact single aisled choir of 2 bays architecturally one with single aisled nave of 3 bays, 13 ft. wide & 72 ft. long; early/mid C13, 1860

Clerkenwell priory: intact heavily restored & now single aisled choir of 4 bays; C16, 1721-23, 1955-58

Cranborne cell: *choir totally rebuilt as chancel; 1875*

Cymmer abbey: high-standing ruined choir of one aisle (excluding extended nave aisles) & 2 (or 3) bays; early C13

Deeping St. James priory: intact long single aisled choir of 4 bays (as indicated by windowing); late C12, C13

Denbigh friary: high-standing ruined single aisled choir of 2 or 3 bays, with bricked up 5-light window in east wall, C13, C15

Dinmore commandery: intact small choir & nave (architecturally one) of one aisle & 3 bays (?); C12, mainly C14

Dorchester abbey: intact choir of 4 aisles (including lady chapel aisles) & 4 bays (including east sanctuary bay); late C13, early C14, C19

Dore abbey: intact choir of 3 aisles & 5 bays, with east ambulatory; c.1180, early C13

Dover Augustinian priory: intact choir of church of St. Mary-in-Castro of one aisle & one bay; c.1000, C12/C13, 1860-62

Dunster priory: intact choir of 3 aisles (including north & south chapels) & 5+ bays (i.e. 2 large west & 3+ small east); mid C13, mid C15, 1875-77

Durham cathedral-priory: intact choir of 3 aisles & 5 bays (excluding east transept); c.1093-1100

Easebourne priory: intact choir (now south chancel chapel) of one aisle & 2 bays; C11, mainly 1876

Edington priory: intact single aisled choir of 3 bays; 1352-61

Ely cathedral-priory: intact choir of 3 aisles & 9 bays (reduced by one bay due to remodelled crossing); c.1322-35

Ewenny priory: intact single aisled choir of 3 bays; mid C12

Farewell priory: intact single aisled small choir of one bay; late C13, C15, 1689, C19, C20

Farne Island cell: [intact small church of choir & nave (architecturally one); c.1370, 1844-48]

Finchale priory: high-standing ruined choir of (now) one aisle & 5 bays; early C13, mid C14

Fountains abbey: moderately high-standing ruined choir less arcades; mid C12

Furness abbey: high-standing ruined choir of one aisle & 3 bays; late C15

Garway preceptory: intact choir of one aisle (excluding south choir chapel) & 2 bays; C12, C13, C16

Gloucester abbey: intact choir of 3 aisles & 5 bays (including east ambulatory); 1089-1100, remodelled c.1337-57

Gloucester Dominican friary: truncated intact single aisled choir, 2/3rds of original length in 2 west bays; C13, mid C16

Godsfield commandery: intact single aisled choir of 3(?) bays; C14

Goring priory: *choir rebuilt in modern times as short apse to east of medieval nave; 1886*

Great Bricett: intact single aisled choir of 3 (roof) bays which may include former crossing; mainly C12, also c.1300

Hamble priory: intact single aisled choir (notwithstanding modern south choir aisle) of 4 bays; C13, also c.1300

Hayling priory: intact single aisled choir of 4 bays; early C13, 1892-93

Hexham priory: intact choir of 3 aisles & now 6 bays; late C12-early C13, 1858+

Holystone priory: (See entry under Small Portions of Conventual Churches etc.)

Hurley priory: *east end of surviving post-Dissolution church rebuilt in recent times as chancel; 1852*

Ingham friary: intact single aisled high choir of 3 bays; mid C14

Jarrow priory: intact single aisled choir (former Anglo-Saxon church) of 4 bays (roof); 681, c.1300

Kidwelly cell: intact single aisled choir of 3 bays; c.1320

King's Lynn priory: intact choir of 3 aisles & 5 bays, north aisle now reduced; C13, C15

Kirkstall abbey: high-standing ruined but rib vaulted choir of one aisle & 3 bays; mainly 1152-75, C15

Lancaster priory: intact choir of three aisles & 4 bays; 1420+

Lanercost priory: high-standing ruined choir of one aisle (excluding north & south chapels) & 4 bays; early C13

Lapley priory: intact single aisled choir of 3 bays; C12, late C13

Lastingham abbey: intact choir of one bay (later divided into 2 bays) plus apse; c.1078+, C13, 1879

Launde priory: (See entry under Small Portions of Conventual Churches etc.)

Leiston abbey: (See entry under Small Portions of Conventual Churches etc.)

Leonard Stanley priory: intact single aisled choir of 2 bays; mainly c.1129, C14

Lilleshall abbey: high-standing ruined choir of one aisle & 4 bays; later C12

Lincoln St. Mary Magdalene's cell: high-standing ruined 3 walls of choir of one aisle & 3 bays; C13, late C14/early C15

Lindisfarne priory: high-standing ruined choir of one aisle & 4 bays; C12

Little Dunmow priory: (See entry under Small Portions of Conventual Churches etc.)

Little Malvern priory: intact choir of one aisle (excluding former north & south choir chapels) & 3 bays; C14, c.1480

Little Maplestead commandery: intact single aisled choir of 3½ bays, including semicircular apse; c.1335, 1851-57

Llanbadarn-fawr priory: intact single aisled choir of 3 bays; c.1200, C15, 1868

Llangennith cell: intact choir of one aisle & 2½ bays; late C13, 1882-84

Llanllugan priory: intact small single aisled choir of 2 bays architecturally one with single aisled nave of 4 bays; C14,C15

Malpas cell: (See entry under Small Portions of Conventual Churches etc.)

Malvern priory: intact choir of 3 aisles & 3 bays (east lady chapel demolished); mid C15

Milton abbey: intact choir of 3 aisles & 7 bays (shortened after Dissolution through destruction of retrochoir etc.); c.1310-25

Monkland cell: *choir completely rebuilt as chancel in recent times; 1866*

Monks Kirby priory: intact choir of one aisle & 3 bays (excluding north & south chapels); mid C14, C15

Monkton priory: intact single aisled choir of 4 bays drastically restored in recent times; early C14, 1882-1907

Monkwearmouth cell: intact single aisled choir of 3 bays; mainly C14

Morville cell: intact single aisled choir of 3 bays; C12

Norwich cathedral-priory: intact choir of 3 aisles & 7 bays (including east ambulatory); early C12, c.1360-70, late C15

Norwich Dominican friary: intact choir of one aisle & 5 bays; 1327+, 1413-70

Ovingham cell: intact single aisled choir of 3 bays; early C13

Oxford St. Frideswide's priory: intact choir of 3 aisles (excluding 2 outer chapel-aisles) & 5 bays (including bay of sanctuary); late C12, C13, c.1480-1503, 1870-76

Pamber priory: intact single aisled choir of 6 bays; C12, C13

Penmon priory: intact & heavily restored single-aisled choir of 3 bays, with new windows & doorway also roof; later C12, C19

Pershore abbey: intact choir of 3 aisles & 6 bays (including east choir aisle chapels); mainly early C13, also c.1288+, C19

Peterborough abbey: intact choir of 3 aisles & 6 bays (excluding New Building extension at east end); mid C12

Polesworth abbey: *choir rebuilt in recent times as chancel of parish church; 1869*

Portchester priory: intact but reduced single aisled choir of one bay; c.1133+, shortened c.1600+, 1888

Redlingfield priory: *choir rebuilt in recent times as chancel of parish church*, but retaining medieval windows; latter c.1300 & C14, *brick rebuild c.1817-27,*

Repton (Anglo-Saxon)**abbey**: (See entry under Small Portions of Conventual Churches etc.)

Rievaulx abbey: high-standing ruined choir of 3 aisles & 7 bays; c.1225+

Rochester cathedral-priory: intact choir of one central aisle (excluding north & south choir transepts, & 2 dissimilar choir aisles) & 10 bays; early C13

Romsey abbey: intact choir of 3 aisles & 4 bays; mainly c.1120-50, late C13

Rothley Temple preceptory: intact single aisled choir of one bay architecturally one with single aisled nave of 3 bays; mainly c.1280, C15

Royston priory: intact choir (now nave of parish church) of 3 aisles & 4½ bays; early C13, C14, C15

Rumburgh cell: intact single aisled choir of 2 bays, as wide as nave; possibly C13, also C15

St. Albans abbey: intact choir of 3 aisles & 7 bays (excluding east lady chapel & including 2-bay retrochoir), with original main timber vault; c.1257+, later C19

St. Anthony-in-Roseland cell: *choir rebuilt in recent times as chancel of restored church; 1850*

St. Bees priory: intact choir of one aisle (south choir aisle now ruined) & 6 bays, now divided by crosswall into west chancel (one bay) & east school hall (5 bays); C12, mainly c.1200, 1855-58

St. Clear's cell: intact single aisled choir of 2(?) bays; C12, 1854-55

St. Michael's Mount priory: intact single aisled choir of 2 bays; C12, late C14, C15

Selby abbey: intact choir of 3 aisles & 7 bays; 1280-1340, C19, 1908

Sele friary: intact choir of one aisle & one bay, possibly reduced in size after Dissolution; c.1308, C16, 1870

Sherborne abbey: intact choir of 3 aisles & 5 bays (including west portion of lady chapel but excluding latter's east bay); C13, c.1425+, 1849-58

Shipley preceptory: intact single aisled choir of one bay; c.1125

Shrewsbury abbey: *east end totally rebuilt as chancel with crossing & short transepts; 1886-88*

Smithfield St. Bartholomew's priory: intact choir of 3 aisles & 7 bays (excluding east lady chapel); 1123+, late C14

Snaith cell: intact choir of 3 aisles (including north & south chapel aisles) & 3 bays; early C14, C15, 1868

Southwark priory: intact choir of 3 aisles & 5 bays (excluding east retrochoir of 4 aisles & 3 bays); C13, 1818-23, retrochoir restored 1833

Stogursey priory: intact choir of 3 aisles (including side chapels) & 2½ bays; c.1100, c.1180, C15, 1865

Stow abbey: intact single aisled vaulted choir of 3 bays; earlier C12, 1853-64

Swine priory: intact choir of 3 aisles & 5 bays (including one large bay leading to north choir chapel), now divided into modern chancel & nave; c.1190, C15

Temple Balsall preceptory: intact single aisled choir & nave (architecturally one) of 4 bays; c.1290, 1849

Temple Ewell preceptory: intact choir of one aisle (not including north choir chapel) & 1½(?) bays; C13, C14, 1874

Temple Guiting preceptory: intact choir of one aisle & one extended bay; mid C12, C13, C14, C15

Temple preceptory: intact choir of 3 aisles & 5 bays; c.1220-40, 1825-30, 1841-43, 1947-57

Tewkesbury abbey: intact choir of 3 aisles & 4 bays (including eastern ambulatory); late C11-early C12, C13, early C14, 1603

Thorney abbey: *east end totally rebuilt as short chancel with crossing & transepts; 1840*

Tintern abbey: high-standing ruined choir of 3 aisles & 4 bays; late C13

Totnes priory: 1. intact parochial & present chancel of conventual church; C15

2. intact chapel north of parochial chancel, probably formed west end of monks' choir; C15

Trentham priory: *choir totally rebuilt as shallow chancel; 1844*

Tutbury priory: *choir totally rebuilt as apsed chancel; 1866-68*

Upholland priory: intact choir of 3 aisles & single bay architecturally one with nave of 3 aisles & 3 bays(all now nave of parish church); mainly early C14

Valle Crucis abbey: high-standing ruined choir of one aisle & 2 bays; C13

Westminster abbey: intact choir of 3 aisles & 6 bays (not including side chapels or Henry VII's chapel); 1245-55

Wilmington priory: intact choir of one aisle & 3 bays; C12, C15

Winchelsea Franciscan friary: high-standing ruined single aisled choir of 5 bays, with polygonal apse; c.1310-20

Winchester cathedral-priory: intact choir of 3 aisles & 7 bays (including retrochoir but not including east chapels); mainly early C14, c.1505, C19

Worcester cathedral-priory: intact choir of 3 aisles (not including 2-bay chapel to south) & 8 bays (including 3 west bays of retrochoir & lady chapel to east); 1224+, 1855-74

Worksop priory: *choir totally rebuilt as chancel & offices; 1966-74*

Yarmouth priory: *choir almost totally rebuilt after being firebombed in last war; 1957-61*

York Holy Trinity priory: *choir rebuilt as chancel in recent times within area of crossing; 1886-87*

N.B.   All these chapels are architecturally distinct from contiguous neighbouring buildings unless stated otherwise. Also, their identities are all medieval in origin.

Blakeney friary: intact chapel within & part of east end of south nave aisle; C15

Brecon priory: intact chapel (now Havard chapel) north of choir; c.1300 with some C19 windows

Bristol abbey: 1. intact Elder Lady Chapel north of choir; c.1215

2. intact Eastern Lady Chapel east of choir; 1298+

Canterbury cathedral-priory: 1. intact chapel (Our Lady of Undercroft chapel) occupying axial position in western crypt, with semicircular arcaded apse; c.1095, refitted c.1360+

2. intact chapel (now Dean's chapel) east of north transept; 1449-1455

Chester abbey: intact chapel east of choir; c.1270

Christchurch priory: intact chapel east of choir; 1450

Dorchester abbey: intact chapel south of choir & crossing, housing shrine of St. Birinus; c.1320

Dudley priory: high-standing ruined portions of south choir chapel (almost certainly lady chapel), fitted with niches in east wall;c.1400, c.1500

Durham cathedral-priory: intact 'Galilee' chapel west of nave in narthex position; c.1170-75

Edington priory: intact lady chapel fully occupies north transept; 1352-61

Ely cathedral-priory: intact chapel north of choir, semi-detached from main building; 1321-53

Glastonbury abbey: high-standing ruined chapel west of galilee; 1184-86

Gloucester abbey: intact chapel east of choir; 1470-83, c.1500

Kidwelly cell: intact chapel comprising south transept; c.1320

Lanercost priory: intact rib vaulted chapel in angle between choir & south east bay of north transept; early C13, C15

Leiston abbey: (See entry under Small Portions of Conventual Churches etc.)

Little Dunmow priory: (See entry under Small Portions of Conventual Churches etc.)

Norwich cathedral-priory: *regimental chapel of St. Saviour on site of lady chapel to east of choir constructed in modern times; 1930-32*

Oxford St. Frideswide's priory: intact chapel, in aisle north of choir; c.1220+

Pershore abbey: intact west bay only at east of choir (*remainder replaced by modern shallow apse*); early C13

Ramsey abbey: high-standing structure north of site of former choir, now part of mansion constructed over it; C13

Rochester cathedral-priory: intact body of chapel south of nave, with south transept serving as chancel; C14 and late C15

St. Albans abbey: intact chapel east of choir; early C14

St. Michael's Mount priory: intact detached chapel north west of choir converted into domestic accommodation (Blue Drawing Rooms); late C14, C15, conversion C18

Sherborne abbey: intact chapel east of choir ambulatory, restored & part rebuilt in recent times; C13, east bay 1921

Smithfield St. Bartholomew's priory: intact chapel east of choir; 1335, restored C19

Temple Ewell preceptory: intact chapel within east end of north choir aisle; C14, 1874

Thetford Cluniac priory: low ruin north of choir, with some high-standing remnants; C13

Waltham abbey: intact south nave chapel, stands over vaulted crypt; c.1320

Westminster abbey: intact chapel (usually called Henry VII's chapel) east of choir, of 3 aisles & 8 bays; 1504-12

Winchester cathedral-priory: intact chapel east of choir; west end 1202, east end c.1490+

Worcester cathedral-priory: intact chapel east of choir (with chancel of one bay architecturally distinct from retrochoir); 1224+

Worksop priory: intact chapel south of choir comprehensively restored recently, displays Early English lancet windows; c.1240, 1929

Wymondham abbey: (See entry below under Other Chapels)

Yarmouth priory: *intact chapel north of choir; of uncertain medieval date, plus major restoration C19*

4/3   APSIDAL CHAPELS

N.B. In those cases where there is firm evidence of a chapel being built or reconstructed as a chantry chapel, the entries are listed under Chantries & Chantry Chapels.

Canterbury cathedral-priory: 1. intact twin chapels to east of north east transept (inner chapel of St. Stephen &

outer chapel of St. Martin), with semicircular apses; early C12, late C12

2. intact twin chapels (inner chapel of St. Nicholas & outer chapel of St. Mary Magdalene) in crypt below north east transept, with semicircular apses & groin vaults; c.1095

3. intact twin chapels to east of south east transept (inner chapel of St. John Evangelist & outer chapel of St. Gregory), with semicircular apses; early C12, late C12

4. intact chapel of St. Andrew now vestry north of north choir ambulatory, with semicircular apse & rib vault; early C12, late C12

5. intact chapel of Holy Innocents in crypt below chapel of St. Andrew, with semicircular apse & groin vault; c.1095

6. intact chapel of St. Anselm south of south choir ambulatory, with semicircular apse & rib vault; early C12, late C12, 1336

7. intact chapel of St. Gabriel in crypt below chapel of St. Anselm, with semicircular apse & groin vault; c.1095

8. intact chapel of Our Lady Undercroft (See entry above under Lady Chapels & additional entry under Chantries & Chantry Chapels); c.1095, c.1396

9. intact Corona chapel (now chapel of Saints & Martyrs of Our Own Time) at extreme east end of church; c.1184

10. intact Jesus chapel occupying axial position in crypt below Corona chapel at east end, with semicircular apse & radiating rib vault with floral boss; c.1184

Canterbury St. Augustine's abbey: 1. ruined presbytery crypt north east chapel of St. Richard of Chichester; c.1073+

2. partly restored presbytery crypt axial chapel of St. Mary & the Angels, with east end squared off later (now new roof & floor); c.1073+, 1325, 1937

3. ruined presbytery crypt south east chapel of St. Thomas Apostle; c.1073+

Christchurch priory: intact chapel of St. Stephen east of south transept, with semicircular apse; C12, C13

Ely cathedral-priory: *chapel of St. Catherine east of south west transept entirely rebuilt; 1848*

Gloucester abbey: 1. intact chapel of St. Paul east of north transept, with irregular shaped semicircular or 3-sided apse & radiating groin vault; early C12

2. intact chapel of St. Andrew east of south transept, with irregularly shaped semicircular or 3-sided apse; early C12

3. intact chapel of St. Edmund & St. Edward (now known as County War Memorial chapel) north east of north choir ambulatory, with polygonal apse; early C12

4. intact chapel in crypt below chapel of St. Edmund & St. Edward, with semicircular apse; c.1089

5. intact chapel of St. Stephen south east of south choir ambulatory, with polygonal apse; early C12

6. intact chapel in crypt below St. Stephen's chapel, with semicircular apse; c.1089

7. intact chapel in crypt in axial position below lady chapel bridge, with semicircular apse; c.1089

8. intact central chapel of crypt below high altar, possesses hagioscope to east; c.1089

Lindisfarne priory: 1. ruined semicircular apsidal part of south transept chapel, with domed vaulting nearly intact; C12

2. footings only of high altar semicircular apse in excavation; C12

3. ruined semicircular apsidal wall of north transept chapel, stand about 8 ft. high; C12

Norwich cathedral-priory: 1. intact chapel of St. Andrew east of north transept now devoid of upper storey, with semicircular apse; early C12

2. intact Jesus chapel north east of north choir aisle, with semicircular apse; early C12

3. intact chapel of St. Luke (formerly chapel of St. John the Baptist) south east of south choir aisle, with semicircular apse; early C12

Romsey abbey: 1. intact chapel (now choir vestry) east of north transept, with semicircular apse & quadripartite rib vault; C12

2. intact chapel (now vestry) east of south transept, with semicircular apse & quadripartite rib vault; C12

3. intact chapel of St. George at east end of north choir aisle, with semicircular apse & broad unmoulded rib vault; C12

4. intact chapel of St. Anne at east end of south choir aisle, with semicircular apse & broad unmoulded rib vault; C12

Tewkesbury abbey: 1. intact chapel (now modern lady chapel) east of south transept, semicircular apse & rib vault; C12

2. intact chapel of St. Margaret north of north choir ambulatory, polygonal apse, C14

3. intact twin chapels (St. Edmund the Martyr & St. Dunstans' chapels) north east of north choir ambulatory, polygonal apses; C14

4. intact St. Faith's chapel south east of south choir ambulatory, polygonal apse; C14

5. intact chapel of St. Catharine south of south choir ambulatory, polygonal apse; C14

6. intact two-storeyed chapel (now sacristy) south west of south choir ambulatory, polygonal apse; C14

Westminster abbey: 1. intact chapel of St. John the Baptist north of north choir ambulatory, with polygonal apse & vault with 7 radiating ribs (See also entry under Chantries & Chantry Chapels); 1245/55

2. intact chapel of St. Paul north east of north choir ambulatory, with polygonal apse & vault with 7 radiating ribs; 1245/55

3. intact chapel of St. Nicholas south east of south choir ambulatory, with polygonal apse & vault with 7 radiating ribs; 1245/55

4. intact chapel of St. Edmund & St. Thomas the Martyr south of south choir ambulatory, with polygonal apse & vault with 7 radiating ribs; 1245/55

5. five intact sub-chapels forming east end of Henry VII's chapel, individually polygonal & collectively radiating outward; 1504+

4/4 OTHER CHAPELS

N.B. In those cases where there is firm evidence of a chapel being built or reconstructed as a chantry chapel, the entries are listed under Chantries & Chantry Chapels.

Abergavenny priory: 1. intact chapel (now called Lewis chapel) east of north transept & contiguous with choir; early C14, C15

2. intact chapel (now called Herbert chapel) east of south transept & contiguous with choir; early C14, C15

Amesbury priory: intact small chapel (now Jesus chapel) to east of north transept, possible chantry origin; C13

Bamburgh cell: 1. intact chapel in south transept or Shoreston Porch; C13/C14

2. intact chapel in north transept or Fowberry Porch; C13/C14

Bath cathedral-priory: 1. intact chapel (known as Norman chapel & now called Gethsemane chapel) within east end of south choir aisle; C12, c.1499+

2. intact chapel (now called chapel of St. Alphege) within east end of north choir aisle; C12, c.1499+

Bayham abbey: intact 2 chapels on east side of new north transept, both have intact rib vaults; later C13

Bishopsgate St. Helens priory: intact 2 chapels on east side of south transept (lately known as chapel of Holy Ghost & lady chapel); C14, 1993-95

Blakeney friary: intact chapel of St. Thomas of Canterbury within east end of north nave aisle; C15

Blanchland abbey: intact 2 chapels on east side of north transept, now combined into modern single chapel; c.1300, 1854

Bourne abbey: intact chapel (now lady chapel) within south transept; C13

Boxgrove priory: 1. intact chapel of St. John within east end of south choir aisle; early C13

2. intact chapel of St. Catherine within east end of north choir aisle; early C13

3. intact chapel of St. Blaise within east side of south transept; early C12

Bradwell priory: (See entry under Small Portions of Conventual Churches etc.)

Brecon friary: intact chapel (vestry) north of walking place; c.1250+, early C14

Brecon priory: 1. intact chapel of St. Lawrence to south of choir & east of south transept; late C14, restored from ruin 1929-30

2 intact chapel of St. Keyne (Corvisor's chapel) at east end of north nave aisle; early C14

Breedon priory: intact chapel (now lady chapel) within east end of south choir aisle; C13

Buildwas abbey: 2 intact chapels within east side of north & south transepts respectively, with groin vaulting; late C12

Bungay priory: 1. intact chapel of St. Eligius (now largely filled by church organ) within east end of south nave aisle; mid C15

2. intact chapel (now War Memorial chapel) within east end of north nave aisle; C15

Calder abbey: 2 roofless chapels on east side of south transept; early C13

Canterbury cathedral-priory: 1. intact axial Saints or Trinity chapel located within choir to east of presbytery & incorporating shrine area of St. Thomas Becket; c.1174/1184

2. intact chapel of St. Michael (sometimes known as Holland chapel, now Warriors' or The Buffs chapel), located to east of south transept; C15

3. intact chapel of All Saints over St. Michael's chapel; C15

Carisbrooke priory: intact chapel (now lady chapel) comprising widened portion of south nave aisle; late C12, C15

Carlisle cathedral-priory: . intact chapel of St. Michael within east end of north choir aisle; C13

Cartmel priory: 1. intact chapel within east end of south choir aisle (Town or Harrington Choir); c.1190-1220, c.1340

2. intact chapel (now redundant as such) within east end of north choir aisle (Piper Choir); c.1190-1220

Chester abbey: 1. intact chapel (now St. Werburgh's chapel) within east end of north choir aisle; late C13/early C14

2. intact chapel (now sacristry) to east of north transept; c.1100, c.1200

3. intact chapel of St. Anselm (originally abbot's private chapel) over outer parlour in west range; C12, C17, C19

4. intact chapel of St.Erasmus with modern east wall at east end of south choir aisle; mid C13, C19

5. intact set of 4 chapels in east aisle of south transept; mid C14

Chetwode cell: intact north choir chapel, converted into post-Dissolution mortuary & squire's chapel; C13, early C14, c.1822, 1998

Chirbury priory: intact chapel within east end of south nave aisle, now used as lady chapel; early C13

Christchurch priory: 1. intact chapel of instruction (St. Michael's Loft) for novices above lady chapel (& now museum); 1450

2. intact chapel within east end of north choir aisle, now filled with Chidiok tomb; early C16

Clerkenwell priory: 1. intact 3 crypt chapels occupying east end of north, middle & south aisles (south chapel called Almoner chapel); c.1185, restored 1900-07

2. intact crypt chapel now vestry occupying Bay 2 of north crypt aisle; mid C12

Croyland abbey: 1. 3 small intact chapels on north side of north nave aisle; dedicated respectively to St. Katherine, St. John Baptist & Holy Trinity (2 converted to other use); C12, C15

2. parvise chapel over west porch, room cruciform in shape; C15

Davington priory: intact chapel within east end of north nave aisle (now sometimes called chapel of Good Shepherd or St. Mary Magdalene); C12, C13

Deeping St. James priory: 1. intact inner chapel (now Children's Altar) within east end of south nave aisle; late C12, C13

2. intact outer chapel (now Corpus Christi chapel) within east end of south nave aisle; C13

Deerhurst priory: intact location of chapel or altar at east end of south nave aisle, indicated by position of piscina (See entry under Piscinas); C10/C11(?)

Dorchester abbey: 1. intact chapel (People's chapel) within east end of south west nave aisle; c.1325

2. intact chapel of St. Birinus occupying north choir aisle & surviving part of north transept; 1225/1293

Dore abbey: 1. intact 5 small altars within east ambulatory of choir; c.1280

2. intact chapel (Hoskyns chapel) forming part of east aisle of south transept; C12

3. intact chapel (now vestry) forming part of east aisle of north transept; C12

Dover Augustinian priory: intact small chapel within south side at east end of nave (possibly originally a rood or pulpitum chapel); C13, 1860+

Dunster priory: intact chapel comprising south transept; C13, mid C15

Durham cathedral-priory: 1. intact The Chapel of The Nine Altars, attached to east of choir; 1242-1279+ (See also entry under Transepts)

2. intact chapel of St. Benedict (now Gregory chapel) forming east aisle of north transept; c.1104

3. intact chapel (now of Durham Light Infantry) forming inner 2 bays of east aisle of south transept; c.1104

Ely cathedral-priory: 1. intact transeptal chapel of St. Edmund within south end of east side of north transept; C12

2. intact transeptal chapel of St. George within middle of east side of north transept; C12

3. intact transeptal chapel of St. Dunstan within south end of east side of south transept; C12

Fountains abbey: 1. high-standing ruined The Chapel of The Nine Altars, attached to east end of choir: c.1210-40, 1483 (See also entry under Transepts)

2. intact 2 chapels east of south transept, retain their pointed barrel vaults; C13

3. high-standing chapel east of north transept at south end, lacking vaulting; C13

Garway preceptory: intact chapel to south of choir (Templars Chapel), divided from latter by 2-bay arcade; C13, partly rebuilt C16

Gloucester abbey: 1. 2 intact small chapels on either side of lady chapel, almost certainly built as chantry chapels; late C15

2. intact chapel over western bridge above entry to lady chapel, designed for small responsory choir; late C15

3. intact chapel (Abbot's Chapel) in crypt below chapel of St. Paul; c.1089

4. intact chapel in crypt below chapel of St. Andrew, now housing switchgear; c.1089

5. intact chamber (former chapel of abbot & now office) over slype of west range; c.1120/35, C15, C19

Hatfield Broad Oak priory: intact chapel of St. John Baptist within east end of south nave aisle; C15

Hayling priory: intact chapel (now lady chapel) forming south transept; C13, 1869

Hexham priory: 1. intact 2 chapels to east of south transept; c.1200+

2. intact 3 chapels (now lady chapel) to east of north transept; early C13

Kersey priory: [high-standing ruined walls of south choir chapel; C13, C15]

King's Lynn priory: 1. intact Trinity chapel within east end of north choir aisle, now shortened by 2 bays; hallowed 1472

2. intact Benedict chapel within east end of south choir aisle; c.1433

Kirkstall abbey: intact 6 chapels with pointed tunnel vaults, comprising 3 to east of north & south transepts respectively; C12

Lacock abbey: intact 2 chapels immediately to north of former choir & immediately east of sacristy, vaulted with single chamfered ribs; mid C13

Lancaster priory: 1. intact chapel of St. Thomas of Canterbury within east end of south choir aisle; 1420+

2. intact chapel of St. Patrick (now of St. Nicholas) within east end of north choir aisle; 1420+

Lanercost priory: 1. high-standing ruined chapel of St. Catherine in angle between choir & north east bay of south transept; later C13

2. intact rib vaulted chapel to east of north bay of north transept; early C13, C15

Leominster priory: intact chapel within east end of outer south nave aisle; 1320

Leonard Stanley priory: intact chapel or altar within south transept (now vestry), indicated by piscina (See entry under Piscinas); C13

Malvern priory: 1. intact chapel of St. Anne within east end of south choir aisle; mid C15

2. intact chapel (unknown dedication) within east end of north choir aisle, mid C15

Monks Kirby priory: 1. intact Skipwith chapel (now lady chapel) of 2 bays south of choir; mid C14, C15

2. intact North chapel of 2 bays north of choir; mid C14, C15

Monkton priory: intact chapel north of choir rebuilt in Victorian times, said to have been prior's chapel & now lady chapel; c.1300, C19

Mount Grace charterhouse: 2 ruined mostly high-standing transeptal chapels to north & south of nave; later C15

Netley abbey: 2 ruined chapels forming east aisle of south transept, with vaulting intact; early C13

Norwich cathedral-priory: 1. intact & reduced Bauchun chapel of Our Lady of Pity south of south choir aisle; c.1330, C15, C19, 1968

2. intact chapel of St. Catherine of Alexandra (recently dean's vestry) east of south transept; c.1250-75

3. intact small chapel within choir area immediately to east of pupitum on south side; unknown date

Oxford St. Frideswide's priory: 1. intact Latin chapel north of lady chapel; early C14

2. intact chapel of St. Lucy in angle between south transept & choir; c.1330

Pershore abbey: 1. intact chapel of St. Michael & All Angels within east end of south choir aisle; early C13, c.1288+, C19

2. intact chapel within easy end of north choir aisle; early C13, late C13

3. intact chapel within north east transept; early C13

Peterborough abbey: 1. intact chapel of Holy Trinity above west porch, now new treasury & former library of cathedral; c.1375

2. intact chapel within north end of east aisle of north transept; C12

3. intact chapel within south end of east aisle of north transept, together with middle bay (which used to lead to now-demolished lady chapel) now present treasury; C12

4. intact chapel of St. Oswald within north end of east aisle of south transept; C12

5. intact chapel of St. Benedict within middle of east aisle of south transept; C12

6. intact chapel of St. Kyneburgha, St. Kyneswitha & St. Tibba within south end of east aisle of south transept; C12

7. intact chapel of St. Sprite within south west transept; C13, renewed 1920, restored 1965-67

8. 2 other chapels indicated (See entries under Piscinas) within east ends of north & south choir aisles; C13

Rievaulx abbey: intact rib vaulted chapel within north end of east aisle of north transept; early C13

Roche abbey: 1. partly intact vaulted 2 chapels within east aisle of south transept; c.1170

2. partly vaulted chapel within south end of east aisle of north transept; c.1170

Rochester cathedral-priory: 1. intact shallow Jesus chapel opening off east side of north transept; c.1240/1255

2. intact chapel of St. John Baptist to east of north east transept, now occupying 2 bays; C13

3. intact chapel of St. Peter in north bay to east of south east transept; C13

4. intact 2 crypt chapels (including that of St. Michael in north bay) under south east transept; C13

5. intact 2 crypt chapels (including that of St. Ithamar in south bay) under north east transept; C13

6. intact 3 crypt chapels (now collectively chapel of Holy Trinity) in crypt presbytery; C13

St. Albans abbey: 1. intact chapel of St. Michael comprising easterly 2 bays within north choir aisle; C13

2. intact chapel of Our Lady of the Four Tapers comprising easterly 2 bays within south choir aisle; C13

3. intact small chapel of Transfiguration leading off lady chapel at south east corner; C15, substantially rebuilt late C19

4. intact Saints' chapel within choir between high altar & retrochoir; C13

St. Bees priory: intact chapel (now of St. Bega) within north transept; C12

St. Germans priory: intact reliquary chapel at east end of south nave aisle; early C14

Sherborne abbey: 1. intact chapel (Bishop Roger's) north of north choir aisle (may have been chantry chapel), now choir vestry; C13

2. intact Wykeham chapel to east of north transept, fan vaulted; C12, early C15

3. intact chapel to east of north choir aisle, now used as clergy vestry; C15, C16 & later

4. intact chapel of St. Mary le Bow to east of south choir aisle, now shortened in length & used as baptistry, fan vaulted; c.1450, 1560, 1921

5. intact chapel of Holy Sepulchre (or Holy Spirit) to east of south transept, lierne vaulted; C12, C14

6. intact chapel of St. Katherine to south of south nave aisle, fan vaulted with liernes; C14, C15

Snaith cell: 1. intact chapel of Holy Trinity south of 'crossing' & forming south transept (also site of shrine to St. Etheldreda); C15

2. also 2 intact chapels (now Stapleton & Dawney chapels respectively) within north & south choir aisles; C15

Southwark priory: 1. intact & restored 4 chapels within east end of retrochoir (from north to south respectively: chapels of St. Andrew, St. Christopher, Our Lady & St. Francis); C13, 1833

2. intact chapel of St. John the Evangelist (now Harvard chapel) on east side of north transept; C12, mainly 1907

Stogursey priory: 1. intact Verney chapel comprising south choir aisle; c.1180, C15

2. intact chapel of St. Erasmus (now lady chapel) comprising north choir aisle; c.1180, C15

Stow abbey: intact chapel within north transept, indicated by partly surviving wall painting on east wall which served as reredos; pre-1066

Strata Florida abbey: ruined 3 chapels leading off east side of south transept & now roofed over for protection (equivalent chapels on north side more ruined & not protected); c.1200

Swine priory: intact chapel within east end of south choir aisle, now houses organ; C15

Temple Guiting preceptory: intact chapel leading off north side of nave; early C14, C15, C18

Temple preceptory: intact 2 former chapels at east end of north & south choir aisles, now providing general seated accommodation for choir congregation; c.1220-40

Tewkesbury abbey: 1. intact chapel (later of St. James & now abbey shop) east of north transept; C12, C13

2. intact 'chancel' of St. Nicholas chapel (former chapel of St. Eustace & before that, lady chapel) to north east of north transept, now choir vestry; C13

3. intact location of chapel or altar at junction of south transept & south nave aisle, indicated by piscina (See entry under Piscinas); C13/C14

Tintern abbey: high-standing 2 chapels within east side of each of north & south transepts, with vaulting gone; late C13

Totnes priory: intact chapel (now of St. George) south of parochial & present chancel; C15

Upholland priory: 1. intact chapel (now Gethsemane Millennium chapel) within east end of south choir aisle; early C14

2. intact chapel (now lady chapel) within east end of north choir aisle; early C14

Valle Crucis abbey: 1. almost intact 2 chapels within east side of south transept, with most of vaulting; C13

2. ruined 2 chapels within east side of north transept with vaulting gone, standing to above level of east lancet windows; C13

Wenlock priory: intact chapel of St. Michael over westerly 3 bays of south nave aisle of conventual church, probably was prior's private chapel; C13

Westminster abbey: 1. intact chapel of St. Edward the Confessor (Chapel of the Kings) within 3 easterly bays of choir behind high altar; 1245/55

2. intact bridge chapel of Annunciation (Henry V's chantry) over east ambulatory of choir; 1422+

3. intact reduced chapel of St. John Evangelist now within south bay of east aisle of north transept; 1245/55

4. intact chapel of St. Michael, St. Martin & All Saints within middle bay of east aisle of north transept; 1245/55

5. intact chapel of St. Andrew within north bay of east aisle of north transept; 1245/55

6. intact diminutive chapel of Our Lady of the Pew (erroneously sometimes called chapel of St. Erasmus) now lobby to chapel of St. John Baptist, in north wall pier of north choir ambulatory; 1245/55, late C14

7. intact chapel of St. Benedict south of south choir ambulatory at west end; 1245/55

8. intact east wall & space of chapel of St. Blase within south end of south transept; unknown date

9. intact chapel of St. Faith within east end of revestry between south transept & chapter-house; mid C13

10. intact chapel of Pyx in sub-dorter at north end of east range (See also under Treasuries); late C11, mid C13

11. intact sub-chapel (now of Queen Elizabeth I) occupying north aisle of Henry VII's chapel; 1504+

Whitby abbey: intact chapel within east end of north choir aisle, complete with rib vault; C13

Wilmington priory: intact chapel to north of nave, now vestry; C13

Winchester cathedral-priory: 1. intact Epiphany chapel occupying middle bay within west side of north transept; late C11

2. intact chapel of Holy Sepulchre within south end of north transept; c.1200

3. intact Venerable chapel occupying north bay within east side of south transept; late C11

Worcester cathedral-priory: 1. intact chapel (now Jesus chapel) north of north nave aisle; mid C14

2. intact chapel of St. John in angle between south transept & south choir aisle; C13

3. intact chapel of St. George forming interior of north choir transept; c.1224+

4. intact chapel (now Dean's chapel) forming interior of south choir transept; c.1224

Worksop priory: 1. intact chapel of St. Cuthbert forming interior of reconstructed north transept; pDp, 1929

2. chapel of St. Leonard in Bay 2 of south nave aisle, marked by piscina in wall; 1300

Wymondham abbey: intact chapel (parochial lady chapel) within east end of north nave aisle; C12, 1440-45

4/5   CRYPTS

Bamburgh cell: intact crypt below south part of choir; C13

Buildwas abbey: intact crypt of 3 bays below north end of north transept; C12

Bury St. Edmunds abbey: low-standing ruined crypt at east end of church, gives full picture of layout; c.1090+

Canterbury cathedral-priory: intact series of crypts below east wing of church; west part c.1095, east part c.1184

Canterbury St. Augustine's abbey: ruined series of crypts below middle & east end of church; west rotunda crypt c.1050+, presbytery crypt c.1073+, lady chapel crypt C16

Christchurch priory: intact set of 3 crypts below choir & transepts; early C12

Clerkenwell priory: intact crypt below choir (See also section above on Other Chapels); west part mid C12, east part c.1185

Dorchester abbey: intact small crypt (charnel house) below south nave aisle; C14

Glastonbury abbey: roofless crypt below lady chapel & galilee; C13, C15

Gloucester abbey: intact crypt below Norman choir; c.1089

Hexham priory: intact crypt below nave; c.675-80

Lastingham abbey: intact crypt below east end of present nave (& former choir); c.1078+

Malvern priory: remnant of crypt immediately to east of choir & below position of former lady chapel, displays some Transitional style vaulting; c.1200

Repton (Anglo-Saxon) **abbey**: (See entry under Small Portions of Conventual Churches etc.)

Rochester cathedral-priory: intact crypt below east end of choir; two west bays 1077, remainder early C13

St. Dogmael's abbey: ruined crypt below floor of choir; C13

Shaftesbury abbey: ruined crypt below former chapel of St. Edward, king & martyr, both possibly built to house the saint's shrine; late C13

Smithfield St. Bartholomew's priory: intact crypt below lady chapel; C14

Temple preceptory: 1. intact undercroft or basement below west end of south choir aisle, may have been treasury; c.1170

2. crypt below former chapel of St. Anne south east of nave, possesses short strong vaulting shafts; C13

Waltham abbey: intact crypt below lady chapel; unknown date

Wenlock priory: crypt now devoid of vaulting in angle between nave & north transept, probably used as charnel house; C13

Winchester cathedral-priory: intact crypt below choir; 1079+

Worcester cathedral-priory: intact crypt below choir, claimed to be largest Norman crypt in England; 1084+

4/6   HIGH-STANDING RUINED EAST ENDS OF CONVENTUAL CHURCHES STANDING MAINLY OR PARTLY ON THEIR OWN

Bolton priory: high-standing wall to full height, with great window devoid of tracery, contiguous with high-standing side walls; C14

Cymmer abbey: ruined wall contiguous with high side walls, stands to above 3 intact lancets; early C13

Dale abbey: isolated east wall stands to above great window, latter devoid of tracery; c.1270

Egglestone abbey: east wall stands high over 5-light window intact with 4 straight mullions, contiguous with high side walls especially to north; c.1250/75

Fountains abbey: east face of The Chapel of The Nine Altars stands almost to maximum height & is contiguous with high-standing north & south walls; c.1210-40, 1483

Guisborough priory: isolated east wall stands to height of ridged gable (97 ft.), tracery in upper window & gone in lower window; late C13/early C14

Lindisfarne priory: east wall intact almost to gable point enclosing great window devoid of tracery, contiguous with some of north & south walls; mid C12, also C14

Netley abbey: east wall largely intact to above east window, contiguous with some of north & south walls; later C13

Seaton priory: isolated east wall of small conventual church stands to apex of gable, 3 lancet windows; c13

4/6 Walsingham priory, east end of choir
to east

Tynemouth priory: east & south wall of presbytery stand almost to full height, with 3 great lancets below & 4 smaller windows over in east wall; c.1195/1220

Valle Crucis abbey: east wall almost intact to maximum gable height & contiguous with some of north & south walls, with 3 great lancets below & 2 above; early C13

Walsingham priory: isolated east wall stands to apex of gable above great window which is devoid of tracery, ornamented with flushwork; C14

Whitby abbey: east wall stands to maximum height contiguous with considerable portions of adjacent walls, has 3 tiers of lancets; C13

♦♦♦♦♦♦♦♦♦♦♦♦♦♦♦

Section 5:
NAVES, TRANSEPTS, PORCHES, CROSSINGS & TOWERS

5/1   **NAVES**

Abergavenny priory: intact nave of 2 aisles & 4 bays (by windows) or 5 bays (by arcade), much restored with with modern arcade; early C14, 1881-82

Aconbury priory: (See entry under Choirs)

Aldeby priory: intact single aisled nave of 4 bays; basically late C12, also c.1300 & C15

Alkborough cell: intact nave of 3 aisles & 3 bays; early C13, C14, C15, C18

Alvingham priory: intact nave of 2 aisles & 3 bays; late C12, c.1300

Amesbury priory: intact nave of 2 aisles & 5 bays (estimated by roof partitions); C12, early C15

Atherstone friary: *nave totally rebuilt in recent times; 1849*

Bamburgh cell: intact nave of 3 aisles & 6 bays including engaged tower & 'crossing'; c.1200, C14

Barrow Gurney priory: (See entry under Small Portions of Conventual Churches etc.)

Bath cathedral-priory: intact nave of 3 aisles & 5 bays; 1499-1539, vaulting 1860-73

Beddgelert priory: (See entry under Small Portions of Conventual Churches etc.)

Binham priory: intact central aisle of nave (north & south aisles destroyed) of 7 bays (shortened by 2 bays from crossing after Dissolution), surviving west front; mid/late C12, c.1240, 1812, 1933

Bishopsgate St. Helens priory: intact parallel twin naves (nuns' & parochial) each of one aisle & 4½ bays; C12, mainly C13, c.1475, c.1632-33, 1993-95

Blackmore priory: intact nave of 3 aisles & 6 unequal bays; C12-C14, C16

Blakeney friary: intact nave of 3 aisles & 6 bays (including east chapels); hammerbeam roof with 26 angels; 1435, 1880+

Blyth priory: intact nave of 3 aisles & 7 bays including engaged tower bay (central nave aisle shortened by one bay after Dissolution); c.1090, c.1290

Bolton priory: intact nave of 2 aisles & 4 bays; late C12, mid C13, early C14

Bourne abbey: intact nave of 3 aisles & 4 bays, with west front; mainly C12, also C15, C19

Brecon friary: fairly high-standing ruined nave of 2 aisles & 4 bays; c.1250+, early C14

Brecon priory: intact nave of 3 aisles & 5 bays; early C14

Bridlington priory: intact nave of 3 aisles & 10 bays (including west towers-bay), with west front; mid C13, later C15

Brinkburn priory: intact nave of 2 aisles & 6 bays; c.1190-1210, restored 1858-59

Bristol abbey: *nave totally rebuilt in modern times; 1868-88*

Bristol St. James' priory: intact nave of 3 aisles & 5 bays, west front displaying interlace wall-arcading & outer aisles largely rebuilt after Dissolution; C12, 1698, C19

Bromfield priory: intact nave of 2 aisles & 4 bays (including north west tower-bay); C12, c.1300, 1577

Buildwas abbey: high-standing ruined central double arcaded aisle of nave of 7 bays, north & south aisles destroyed; mid C12

Bungay priory: intact nave of 3 aisles & 6 bays (south aisle 4 bays); early C14, mid C15, 1688+, C19

Caldey cell: intact single aisled nave of 5 (roof) bays; C13/C14

Cambridge St. Radegund's priory: intact reduced nave now of one aisle & 2 bays; C12, c.1500, 1849-53

Canons Ashby priory: intact reduced nave of 2 aisles & 2 bays; C13, early C14

Canterbury cathedral-priory: intact nave of 3 aisles & 9 bays (including west towers-bay, but excluding west portal); 1391-1405

Cardigan cell: intact nave though heavily restored of one aisle & 4 bays; late C15/early C16, early C18

Carisbrooke priory: intact nave of 2 aisles & 5 bays (3 bays of south aisle widened at east end); early C12, late C12, C15

Carlisle cathedral-priory: intact truncated nave of easterly 2 bays (3 aisles) only, remaining 6 bays destroyed in Civil War; early/mid C12

Cartmel priory: intact nave of 3 aisles & 3 bays; c.1190-1220, mainly 1420

Chepstow priory: intact central double arcaded aisle of nave of 5 bays (reduced by one bay at east end after Dissolution), west front incorporated into post-Dissolution west tower; early C12

Chester abbey: intact nave of 3 aisles & 7 bays (including west towers-bay), with facade of west front symbolising Assumption; mid C12, C13, mainly mid C14 & late C15

Chirbury priory: intact nave of 3 aisles & 5 bays; early C13, 1871

Christchurch priory: intact nave of 3 aisles & 8 bays (including engaged west tower); mainly c.1090-1120, early C13, 1819

Church Gresley priory: intact drastically restored nave of 2 aisles & 3 bays, older work in north arcade & north nave aisle; C13/C14, c.1820

Church Preen cell: (See entry under Choirs)

Colchester St. Botolph's priory: high-standing ruined portions of nave & west front, largely constructed of Roman brick; c.1093/1100, also mid C12

Conway abbey: (See entry under Small Portions of Conventual Churches etc.)

Cranborne cell: intact nave of 3 aisles & 5½ bays; late C12, c.1300

Croyland abbey: intact north nave aisle of 7 bays (excluding west tower-bay) serving as post-Dissolution parish church: 1114-1195, C15

Cwmhyr abbey: (See entry under Small Parts of Conventual Churches etc.)

Cymmer abbey: much of north & south walling stands to full height including 3 bays of arcading on north side; early C13

Davington priory: intact nave of 2 aisles & 5 bays (including west towers-bay); C12, C13, restored 1845+

Deeping St. James priory: intact 2-aisled nave of 7 bays; late C12, C13, C14, C15/C16

Deerhurst priory: intact nave of 3 aisles & 4 bays (including engaged tower to west, but excluding subsumed transepts & crossing to east); C7, C8, c.1200, C14, early C16

Denney abbey: intact nave embedded within complex later building, length extended & south nave aisle demolished in medieval period; late C12, C13, mid C14, also pDp

Dinmore commandery: (See entry under Choirs)

Dorchester abbey: intact nave of 2 aisles & 4 bays; late C12, c.1270-1300, C19

Dover Augustinian priory: intact nave of church of St. Mary-in-Castro of one aisle & 5 bays (roof plan); c.1000, C12/C13, 1860-62

Dudley priory: high-standing ruined nave of one aisle & 4 bays; c.1200, C13

Dunstable priory: intact nave of 3 aisles & 7 bays (including bay of north west tower & remnant of west front); mid/late C12, mid C13, late C15, 1852

Dunster priory: intact nave of 3 aisles & 6 bays (shorter by 2+ bays in north nave aisle); C12, mid C15, c.1498-1530

Durham cathedral-priory: intact nave of 3 aisles & 8 bays (excluding west galilee, but including bay of west towers); c.1100-33, C18, C19

Easebourne priory: intact nave of 2 aisles & 3½ bays; C11, C12, mid C13, 1876

Edington priory: intact nave of 3 aisles & 6 bays; 1352-61

Egglestone abbey: high-standing ruined nave of one aisle & 4 bays; c.1200, c.1300

Elstow abbey: intact nave of 3 aisles & 5 bays (now shortened by 2 bays from crossing); c.1100+, early C13, 1580, 1880

Ely cathedral-priory: intact nave of 3 aisles & 12 bays (reduced by one bay at east end due to remodelled crossing; & excluding west tower-bay); late C11/early C12

Ewenny priory: intact nave of 2 aisles & 4 bays (now shortened by single bay at west end), north nave aisle rebuilt in modern times; mid C12, C19

Farewell priory: *nave totally rebuilt after Dissolution in brick with tower added later; 1740, tower 1747*

Farne Island cell: (See entry under Choirs)

Finchale priory: high-standing ruined nave of (now) one aisle & 5 bays; early C13, mid C14

Fountains abbey: high-standing ruined nave of 3 aisles & 11 bays (excluding galilee to west); mid & late C12, 1484

Freiston priory: intact nave of 3 aisles & 9 bays; C12, C13, mid C15, C19

Garway preceptory: intact single aisled nave of 2 bays; C13

Gloucester abbey: intact nave of 3 aisles & 9 bays; c.1100-21, c.1242, c.1318, c.1430

Gloucester Franciscan friary: high-standing ruined major portion of nave of 2 aisles & 7 bays; late C15/early C16

Goring priory: intact nave of 2 aisles & 4 bays (3 bay arcade); late C11/early C12, early C13

Great Bricett priory: intact single aisled nave of 6 (roof) bays; C12, c.1300

Hamble priory: intact single aisled nave of 4(?) bays; C12

Hatfield Broad Oak priory: intact nave of 3 aisles & 6 bays; C12, C14, mainly C15, 1843

Hatfield Peverel priory: intact nave of 3 aisles & 7 bays, with some of south aisle rebuilt in Victorian period; C12, C13, C15, 1873

Hayling priory: intact nave of 3 aisles & 3 bays; later C13, 1892-93

Hexham priory: *nave rebuilt in modern times; 1907-09*

Heynings priory: intact nave now divided by post-Dissolution north-south arcade; C11, early C14, C17, C18, 1894

Holme Cultram abbey: intact central aisle of nave of 6 bays (reduced from 9 bays at east end after Dissolution); late C12, 1727/39, 1883

Hurley priory: intact single aisled nave of 6 bays; mainly C12, C14, 1852

Ingham friary: intact nave of 3 aisles & 5 bays; mid C14, restored 1876

Jarrow priory: *nave rebuilt in modern times; 1866*

Kidwelly cell: intact nave with single wide aisle of 3 bays (excluding pseudo-cruciform crossing area); c.1320

King's Lynn priory: intact nave of 3 aisles (reduced from 4) & 6 bays (including west towers-bay), drastically reconstructed after storm of 1741 with renewed upper parts of arcades; C13, C15, c.1746, 1875

Kirkstall abbey: high-standing ruined nave of 3 aisles & 8 bays; 1152-75

Kyme priory: (See entry under Small Portions of Conventual Churches etc.)

Lancaster priory: intact nave of 3 aisles (excluding modern north outer aisle) & 4 bays; mainly 1420+

Lanercost priory: intact nave of 2 aisles & 5 bays; c.1190, early C13, c.1740

Lapley priory: intact single aisled nave of 5 bays (as indicated by roof), reduced (chapels) south side; C12, C15

Leominster priory: intact nave of 4 aisles & 7 bays (including bay of engaged west tower); mid C12, 1239, 1320, C15, C19

Leonard Stanley priory: intact single aisled nave of 5 or possibly 4 bays; mainly c.1129, C14, C15

Letheringham priory: intact single aisled nave of 3 bays; late C12, c.1300

Little Maplestead commandery: intact round nave consisting of 6-arched central area surrounded by circular aisle, capped by timber turret; c.1335, 1851-57

Llanbadarn-fawr priory: intact single aisled nave of 4 bays; c.1200, 1868

Llangennith cell: intact nave of single aisle & 4 bays; C13/C14, 1882-84

Llanllugan priory: (See entry under Choirs)

Llanthony priory: high-standing ruined north arcade & crossing arch of 3-aisled nave, 8 bays including bay of west towers' area; late C12

Malmesbury abbey: intact nave of 3 aisles & 6 bays (now shortened at west end except for south nave aisle by 3 bays); c.1160, early C14

Malton priory: intact six west bays of central aisle of nave (including west tower-bay), 2 easterly central bays & outer nave aisles demolished after Dissolution; late C12/early C13, 1636

Malvern priory: intact nave of 3 aisles & 6 bays; c.1120, mid C15

Margam abbey: intact nave of 3 aisles (outer two largely rebuilt after Dissolution) & 6 bays (reduced at east end by 2 bays also after Dissolution); c.1150-80, 1805-10, 1873

Minster-in-Sheppey priory: intact nave of 2 aisles & 3 bays (as estimated by windows & buttressing on north side of north nave aisle); C8/C9, C12, mainly C13, 1879-81

Monkland cell: intact nave of one aisle & 4 bays; late C11, later C13

Monks Kirby priory: intact nave of 3 aisles & 5 bays (excluding east chapels); mid C14, C15

Monkton priory: intact single aisled nave of 4 bays (excluding crossing bay); C12, C13/C14

Monkwearmouth cell: intact nave of 2 aisles & 4 bays; C7, C13, 1875-76

Morville cell: intact nave of 3 aisles & 3 bays; mid & late C12, C19

Mount Grace charterhouse: high-standing ruined nave of one aisle (not including north & south transeptal chapels) & 2 bays; early C15

Norwich cathedral-priory: intact nave of 3 aisles & 14 bays; mainly early C12, C14, C15

Norwich Dominican friary: intact nave of 3 aisles & 7 bays; 1327+, 1413-70

Nun Monkton priory: intact single aisled nave of 7 bays (including bay of small engaged tower at west end); late C12-early C13, 1873

Ovingham cell: intact nave of 3 aisles (excluding outer short nave aisles or transepts on either side) & 4 bays (including pseudo-crossing area); C13, C14/C15, north aisle rebuilt 1857

Owston abbey: intact nave of 2 aisles & 3 bays (as indicated by windowing on south side, or as 2 bays as indicated by north nave arcade); c.1300, C15, C19

Oxford St. Frideswide's priory: intact nave of 3 aisles & 4 bays (shortened c.1525 by 3 or 4 bays); late C12, c.1500, 1816

Penmon priory: intact single aisled nave of 2 bays; c.1140

Peterborough abbey: intact nave of 3 aisles & 11 bays (including bay of western transepts but excluding porch & turret bay); mainly late C12, mid-late C13, C14

Pilton priory: intact nave of 3 aisles & 3 & 4 bays; C13, late C14/early C15

Polesworth abbey: intact nave of 2 aisles & 8 bays, considerably restored; C12, C14, 1869

Portchester priory: intact single aisled nave of 5 bays, with Romanesque west front; c.1133+, 1888

Reading friary: intact nave of 3 aisles & 5 bays (4 wide, one narrow); c.1311, drastically restored 1863

Redlingfield priory: intact single aisled nave of 5 (roof) bays; C14, heightened C15/C16

Rochester cathedral-priory: intact nave of 3 aisles & 8 bays, with Romanesque west front (excluding outer south nave aisle or lady chapel); C11+, mainly mid C12, late C13, c.1470, C17, C19

Romsey abbey: intact nave of 3 aisles & 7 bays; c.1150-90, early C13

Rothley Temple preceptory: (See entry under Choirs)

Rumburgh cell: intact single aisled nave of 3 bays, as wide as west tower & choir; C13, C15

Ruthin priory: intact nave of 2 aisles & 5 bays, 1310-15, later C14, 1854-59

St. Albans abbey: intact nave of 3 aisles & 13 bays (excluding western portico); c.1077-89, late C12-early C13, 1323+, 1879-85

St. Anthony-in-Roseland cell: intact single aisled nave of 3 long bays; C12/C13

St. Bees priory: intact nave of 3 aisles & 6 bays; late C12, c.1200, C15/C16, 1855-58

St. Clear's cell: intact single aisled nave of 4 bays; C12, 1854-55

St. Germans priory: intact nave of 2 aisles & 7 bays (including west towers-bay; nave shortened & north nave aisle destroyed since Dissolution); c.1180+, 1420/1455, C16, c.1802, 1888+

St. Michael's Mount priory: intact single aisled nave of 2 bays; C12, mainly late C14, C15

Selby abbey: intact nave of 3 aisles & 8 bays (including bay of twin-towered west front); mainly early C12, early C13, c.1300, 1908

Sele friary: intact single aisled nave (south nave aisle & porch constructed after Dissolution) of 3 bays; c.1308, much of C19

Sherborne abbey: intact nave of 3 aisles & 5½ bays; c.1000, C12, mainly c.1475-1500, 1849-58

Shipley preceptory: intact nave of one aisle (excluding modern north aisle) & 5 bays; c.1125, also late C12, c.1300

Shrewsbury abbey: intact nave of 3 aisles & 6 bays (including engaged west tower); late C12, c.1361-70, 1862, 1886-88

Snaith cell: intact nave of 3 aisles & 7 bays (including engaged west tower, but excluding easterly transepts); C12, C13, C15

Southwark priory: *nave almost totally rebuilt in recent times; 1890-97*

Stogursey priory: intact nave of single aisle & 7 (roof) bays; late C14, early C15, C19

Stow abbey: intact single aisled nave of 3 bays (windowing) or 6 bays (roofing); mainly c.1070, also mid C12, 1853-64

Temple Balsall preceptory: (See entry under Choirs)

Temple Ewell preceptory: intact single aisled nave of 3 long bays (6 roof bays); C12, C14, 1874

Temple Guiting preceptory: intact single aisled nave of 4 bays (5-bay roof); C12, C15, C18, C19

Temple preceptory: intact round nave consisting of 6-arched central area surrounded by circular aisle of 12 outer bay-divisions; c.1160-85, 1825-30, 1841-43, 1947-57

Tewkesbury abbey: intact nave of 3 aisles & 9 bays; late C11-earlier C12, mid C14, 1686

Thetford St. Sepulchre's priory: high-standing ruined nave of one aisle & 5 bays; C14

Thorney abbey: intact central aisle only of nave (3 aisles before Dissolution) with 5 west bays (7 or 8 before Dissolution), surviving west front with high turrets; 1085-1108, C15, 1638, 1840

Thurgarton priory: intact nave of 3 aisles & 3 bays (including west tower-bay & west front), considerably reduced in length at east end & breadth (south nave aisle narrowed); c.1230, 1853

Tintern abbey: high-standing ruined nave of 3 aisles (north nave aisle & arcade largely demolished) & 6 bays, intact south nave aisle vaulting; late C13-early C14

Totnes priory: intact nave (excluding modern outer north nave aisle) of 3 aisles & 4 bays; mid C15

Trentham priory: intact & heavily restored nave of 3 aisles & 4 bays (not including west gallery bay); c.1180-90, 1844

Tutbury priory: intact nave of 3 aisles & 6 bays (reduced after Dissolution from 8 bays); 1100/1150, c.1375, 1829, 1866-68

Upholland priory: (See entry under Choirs)

Usk priory: intact nave of 2 aisles & 4 bays (not including modern extension of nave to west); c.1135+, C13, late C15, 1844

Waltham abbey: intact nave of 3 aisles & 7 bays (not including south nave chapel); late C11-mid C12, early C14, 1860

Warburton cell: (See entry under Small Parts of Conventional Churches etc.)

Westminster abbey: intact nave of 3 aisles & 11 bays (excluding west towers-bay); 1272, c.1376-1471, 1498+

Weybourne priory: intact nave of 2 aisles & 3 bays (including chancel of present parish church), present north nave aisle rebuilt in modern times; C13, C15, 1866

Wilmington priory: intact nave of one aisle & 4 bays (excluding north nave chapel & modern south aisle), with spire-topped turret at west end; C12, C14, C19

Winchester cathedral-priory: intact nave of 3 aisles & 12 bays, with pinnacled & turretted west front; 1079-c.1100, mainly c.1367-1404, C19

Wix priory: (See entry under Small Portions of Conventional Churches etc.)

Worcester cathedral-priory: intact nave of 3 aisles & 9 bays; c.1180, mainly c.1320+, 1855-74

Worksop priory: intact nave of 3 aisles & 10 bays (including west towers-bay), displays severe west front; c.1140-70+

Wroxall priory: (See entry under Small Portions of Conventional Churches etc.)

Wymondham priory: intact nave of 3 aisles & 9 bays, (reduced by 3 bays before Dissolution from original length); c.1107-30, 1440-45, 1901-05

Yarmouth priory: *nave almost completely rebuilt after being firebombed in last war; 1957-61*

York Holy Trinity priory: intact nave of 2 aisles (formerly 3, of which south is part rebuild & north has been destroyed) & 5 bays; c.1180, late C12/early C13, 1850, 1902-03

Abergavenny priory: intact north & south transepts, each of one aisle & one bay; early C14

Aldeby priory: 1. intact single aisled north transept of 3 bays; mainly C13

2. intact shortened single aisled south transept of 1 bay; c.1300

Amesbury priory: intact north & south transepts, each of one aisle & 2 bays; C13

Bamburgh cell: 1. intact single aisled north transept (Fowberry Porch) of 2 bays in present pseudo-cruciform building; C12, C13/C14

2. intact single aisled south transept (Shoreston Porch) of 2 bays in present pseudo-cruciform building; C12, C13/C14

Bath cathedral-priory: intact north & south transepts, each of one aisle & 2 bays; c.1499-1539

Bayham abbey: much of ruined new north transept of one aisle & 2 bays (excluding east chapels) stands nearly to tops of walls; late C13

Bishopsgate St. Helens priory: intact south transept of 2 aisles & 2 bays (including east chapels); C13, C14, c.1475, early C17, 1993-95

Blanchland abbey: intact north transept of 2 aisles & 2 bays; c.1300, 1854

Bolton priory: high-standing ruined north & south transepts (south more ruined than north), each of 2 aisles & 2 bays (including east chapels); late C12, early C14

Bourne abbey: intact south transept (now shortened) of one aisle & one bay; C13, C20

Boxgrove priory: intact north & south transepts, each of one aisle & 2 bays; early C12

Brecon priory: 1. intact south transept (Capel-y-Cochiaid) of one aisle & 2 bays; mid C13
2. intact north transept (Battle chapel) of one aisle & 2 bays; mid C13

Breedon priory: intact south transept now reduced & divided horizontally into 2 storeys (porch & vestry); c.1300

Brinkburn priory: intact north & south transepts, each of 2 aisles & 2 bays (including east chapels); c.1190/1200, restored 1858-59

Bristol abbey: intact north & south transepts, each of one aisle & 2 bays (excluding east chapels); C12, c.1470-1515

Broomholm priory: high-standing ruined north transept, possesses flat buttresses & semicircular arched upper windows; late C12, also C13

Buildwas abbey: high-standing ruined north & south transepts, each of 2 aisles & 2 bays (including east chapels); mid C12

Calder abbey: high-standing ruined north & south transepts of 2 aisles & 2 bays (including east chapels), with south complete less its roof; C13, C14

Cambridge St. Radegund's priory: 1. intact north transept of one aisle & 2 bays; c.1150/1175, early C13, 1849-53
2. intact south transept of one aisle & 2 bays; C15, 1849-53

Canterbury cathedral-priory: 1. intact north transept of one aisle & 2 bays (excluding east chapel); 1448-68
2. intact south transept of one aisle & 2 bays (excluding east chapel); c.1414
3. intact north east & south east transepts each of one aisle & 2 bays (excluding choir ambulatories); c.1096-1130, c.1175-78

Carlisle cathedral-priory: 1. intact north transept of one aisle & 2 bays; early/mid C12, early C15

2. intact south transept of one aisle & 2 bays (excluding east chapel); early/mid C12, mid C19

Cartmel priory: intact north & south transepts of one aisle & 2 bays; c.1190-1220, C15

Chester abbey: 1. intact north transept of one aisle & 2 bays (excluding east chapel); mainly early C12, late C15/early C16, C19

2. intact south transept (St. Oswald's parochial church) of 3 aisles & 5 bays (including 4 east chapels), probably largest transept in country; mid C14, late C15, C19

Christchurch priory: intact north & south transepts of one aisle & 2 bays, Norman stair-turret on north side of north transept; c.1090-1120

Croxden abbey: considerable portions of high-standing ruined south & west walls of south transept; early C13

Deerhurst priory: intact north & south transepts (subsumed into later medieval nave), originally each was porticus of Anglo-Saxon church; c.715 & mainly C14

Denney abbey: north & south transepts largely intact within complex post-Dissolution house, each of one aisle & 2 bays; mainly late C12, also mid C14 & pDp

Dorchester abbey: 1. intact north transept (now reduced by one bay) of single aisle & bay; late C12, C13, 1633

2. intact south transept of one aisle & 2 bays; late C12, early C14, 1633

Dore abbey: intact north & south transepts, each of 2 aisles & 2 bays; c.1180

Dover Augustinian priory: intact north & south transepts, each of one aisle & one bay; c.1000, C12/C13, 1860-62

Dunster priory: intact north & south transepts, each of one aisle & 2 bays; C13, mid C15

Durham cathedral-priory: 1. intact north & south transepts, each of 2 aisles (including east chapels) & 4 bays; mainly c.1093-1100, C18, C19

2. intact east double transept (Chapel of The Nine Altars) of 2 aisles & 9 bays; 1242-1279+ (See also under Other Chapels)

Edington priory: intact north & south transepts, each of one aisle & 2 bays; 1352-61

Ely cathedral-priory: 1. intact north & south transepts, each of 3 aisles (including chapels & vestries) & 3 bays (not including bay eliminated by remodelled crossing); C12

2. intact north west transept of one aisle & one bay, probably never completed; late C12, early C13

3. intact south west transept of one aisle & 3 bays (including Victorian-rebuilt St. Catherine's chapel to east); late C12, early C13, 1848

Ewenny priory: intact south transept of one aisle & 2 bays; mid C12

Finchale priory: 1. high-standing ruined north transept (minus north wall) of one aisle & 2 bays; early C13, mid C14

2. high-standing ruined south transept of one aisle & 2 bays; early C13, mid C14

Fountains abbey: 1. high-standing ruined east double transept (The Chapel of The Nine Altars) of 2 aisles & 9 bays; c.1210-40, 1483 (See also under Other Chapels)

2. high-standing ruined north & south transepts, each of one aisle (excluding east chapel etc.) & 3 bays; mid & later C12

Furness abbey: high-standing ruined north & south transepts, each of 2 aisles (including east chapels & vestry accommodation) & 3 bays; late C12, late C15

Gloucester abbey: 1. intact north transept of one aisle (excluding east chapel) & 2 bays; c.1089-1100, late C14

2. intact south transept of one aisle (excluding east chapel) & 2 bays; c.1089-1100, earliest Perp. work in country c.1331-37

Gloucester Dominican friary: intact north transept of one aisle & one bay; C14, mid C16

Hayling priory: intact north & south transepts each of one aisle & one bay (effectively extended nave aisles); C13, 1869

Hexham priory: 1. intact north transept of 2 aisles & 4 bays; early C13

2.   intact south transept of 2 aisles & 3 bays (excluding slype); c.1200+

Horton priory: (See entry under Small Portions of Conventual Churches etc.)

Kidwelly cell: intact north & south transepts each of one aisle; divided by space formerly occupied by crossing dismantled at time of their construction; c.1320

King's Lynn priory: intact north & south transepts, each of one aisle & 2 bays, both transepts now shortened; C13, C15

Kirkstall abbey: high-standing ruined north & south transepts of 2 aisles (including east chapels) & 3 bays; 1152-75

Lanercost priory: high-standing ruined north & south transepts of 2 aisles & 2 bays; c.1190, C13, C15

Leonard Stanley priory: intact north & south transepts, each of one aisle & one bay; mainly c.1129, C15

Llanbadarn-fawr priory: intact north & south transepts, each of one aisle & one bay; c.1200, 1868

Llanthony priory: high-standing ruined south transept of one aisle (excluding east chapel) & 3 bays; early C13

Malvern priory: 1. intact north transept of one aisle & 2 bays; mid C15

2. intact south transept reduced to one bay, serving as vestry; mid C15

Milton abbey: 1. intact north transept of one aisle & 2 bays; 1309, C15

2. intact south transept of one aisle & 3 bays; c.1310-25

Monkton priory: (See entry under Non-Central Towers, as instance of transeptal tower)

Mount Grace charterhouse: (See entry under Crossings & Central Towers)

Netley abbey: high-standing ruined south transept of 2 aisles & 3 bays (including 2 partly intact vaulted east chapels); C13

Norwich cathedral-priory: intact north & south transepts, each of 2 aisles & 4 bays (excluding east chapels); mainly C12, C13, 1830+

Nuneaton priory: (See entry under Small Portions of Conventual Churches etc.)

Ovingham cell: intact north & south double aisled transepts of 2 bays in pseudo-cruciform building; C13, C14/C15

Oxford St. Frideswide's priory: 1. intact north transept of 2 aisles (including west aisle) & 3 bays; late C12, 1872

2. intact south transept of one aisle & 2 bays (excluding east chapel); c.1100, late C12, C13, early C16

Penmon priory: intact north & south transepts, each of one aisle & one bay, partly rebuilt after Dissolution; c.1170, C19

Pershore abbey: 1. intact south transept of one aisle & 3 bays; c.1100

2. intact north east transept of one aisle & one bay; early C13

3. north transept rebuilt as vestry in modern times; 1936

4. south east transept rebuilt in modern times; 1862-64

Peterborough abbey: 1. intact north & south transepts, each of 2 aisles (excluding west sacristry on south side) & 4 bays; mid C12, C13, C14

2. intact north west & south west transepts at west end of nave, each of one aisle & 2 bays (including west turret bay), east bay of north west transept with tower above; C13

Pilton priory: intact transeptal (parochial) chancel of 2 aisles & 2 bays; C15/C16

Portchester priory: intact north transept of one aisle & one bay; c.1133+, 1888

Reading friary: *north & south transepts rebuilt (or built) in recent times; 1863*

Rievaulx abbey: high-standing ruined north & south transepts, each of 2 aisles (including east chapels) & 3 bays; c.1225+

Roche abbey: high-standing ruined north & south transepts devoid of west walls, 2 aisles (including east chapels) & 2 bays c.1170+

Rochester cathedral-priory: 1. intact north transept of one aisle & 3 bays; mid C13

2. intact south transept of one aisle & 3 bays; late C13

3. intact north east & south east transepts, each of 2 aisles (including east chapels) & 2 bays; early C13

Romsey abbey: intact north & south transepts, each of one aisle & 2 bays; mainly mid C12

St. Albans abbey: intact north & south transepts, each of one aisle & 3 bays; c.1077-89, 1879-85

St. Anthony-in-Roseland cell: intact north & south transepts, each of one aisle & one bay; C12/C13

St. Bees priory: intact north & south transepts, each of one aisle & 2 bays; C12, 1855-58

St. Dogmael's abbey: high-standing ruined north transept; early C16

Selby abbey: 1. intact north transept of one aisle (excluding east chapel) & 2 bays; early C12, C14, C15, 1908

2. south transept totally rebuilt in recent times; 1912

Sherborne abbey: intact north & south transepts, each of one aisle (excluding east chapels) & 2 bays; mainly C12, also c.1475-1500

Smithfield St. Bartholomew's priory: *transepts largely rebuilt in modern times; 1891*

Snaith cell: intact north & south transepts in pseudo-cruciform building, each of one aisle & one bay; C14, C15

Southwark priory: 1. intact north transept of one aisle (excluding east chapel) & 3 bays; C12, late C13, 1830

2. intact south transept of one aisle (excluding eastern organ chamber) & 3 bays; late C13, 1830

Stogursey priory: intact north & south transepts, each of one aisle & one bay; c.1100, C15

Stow abbey: intact north & south transepts, each of one aisle & one bay; c.975, mid C12, C13, 1853-64

Tewkesbury abbey: 1. intact north transept of one aisle & 2 bays (excluding double east chapel); 1087-c.1121, C13, early C14

2. intact south transept of one aisle & 2 bays (excluding east chapel); 1087-c.1121, early C14

Tintern abbey: high-standing ruined north & south transepts, each of 2 aisles (including east transeptal chapels) & 3 bays; c.1270-1301

Valle Crucis abbey: high-standing ruined south transept of 2 aisles & 2 bays (including east chapels); C13

Wenlock priory: high-standing ruined south transept of 2 aisles & 4 bays; C13

Westminster abbey: 1. intact north transept of 3 aisles & 4 bays; 1245-55, 1875-90

2. intact south transept of 2 aisles & 4 bays; 1245-55, 1875/90

Whitby abbey: high-standing ruined north transept of 2 aisles (including east transeptal chapels) & 3 bays, roofless but otherwise mostly complete; C13

Winchester cathedral-priory: intact north & south transepts, each of 3 aisles & 4 bays (including east & west transeptal chapels); 1079-c.1100, c.1107+, C19

Worcester cathedral-priory: 1. intact north & south transepts, each of one aisle & 2 bays; late C12, 1224+, late C14, 1865-66

2. intact north choir & south choir transepts, each of one aisle & one bay (not including choir aisle); 1224+, 1855-74 (See also under Other Chapels)

Worksop priory: *1. south transept totally rebuilt; 1929*
2. north transept totally rebuilt; 1935

Yarmouth priory: *north & south transepts almost totally rebuilt after being firebombed in last war; 1957-61*

5/3   PORCHES & GALILEES

Aconbury priory: intact timber west porch, single storeyed & of 2 bays; C14/C15

Aldeby priory: intact small north porch, single storeyed; C15

Blakeney friary: intact small north porch with holy water stoup, single storeyed; 1435, 1896

Blyth priory: intact south porch, single storeyed; c.1290

Bourne priory: intact south porch, single storeyed; C14/C15

Boxgrove priory: intact porch of one storey (formerly chapel in angle between south transept & nave); c.1300

Brecon priory: intact porch north of nave, double storeyed; C14

Breedon priory: (See entry under Transepts)

Bridlington priory: intact porch north of nave, double storeyed; C13, C19

Bristol St. James' priory: intact porch south of nave of 2 storeys, appears to have been heavily restored after Dissolution; unknown dates

Bungay priory: intact porch north of nave, double storeyed; mid C15, restored 1865

Canterbury cathedral-priory: 1. intact porch (Chicheley porch) to south of south west tower, double storeyed; 1424-27, restored 1862

2. intact porch comprising part of west front of nave, single storeyed; 1380+, c.1460

Carisbrooke priory: intact south porch of one storey; C13, pDp

Chester abbey: intact porch to south west of nave, double storeyed; late C15/early C16, restored 1868-72

5/3 Aconbury priory, west porch to north east

Christchurch priory: intact double storeyed porch of 2 bays north of nave, longest in England; early C13

Cranborne cell: intact single storeyed porch on north side of nave; c.1200, C19

Croyland abbey: intact porch west of north west tower, double storeyed; 1460-69

Deeping St. James priory: intact south porch, single storeyed; C13

Dorchester abbey: intact porch south of nave, single storeyed & with original roof & timber arcading; C15

Dunster priory: intact porch south of nave, single storeyed; C15

Durham cathedral-priory: (See entry under Lady Chapels)

Edington priory: intact porch of 3 storeys south of nave; 1352-61 or a little later

Ely cathedral-priory: intact west porch or galilee of 2 bays & 2 storeys; c.1210-50, C19

Fountains abbey: part reassembled galilee west of nave; C12

Freiston priory: intact porch north of nave, single storeyed; C13, C15

Glastonbury abbey: high-standing galilee west of nave & east of lady chapel; 1184-86

Gloucester abbey: intact double storeyed porch south of nave; c.1420-30, C19

Goring priory: intact north porch, single storeyed; C14

Hamble priory: intact small north porch of one storey; probably C13

Hatfield Broad Oak priory: intact porch south of nave, single storeyed; C15

Hayling priory: intact single storeyed mainly timbered porch, of medieval construction but heavily restored lately; Imp(?), 1569, C19

Ingham friary: intact porch south of nave, triple storeyed; C15

Kidwelly cell: intact porch south of nave at west end, single storeyed with stoup & 2 aumbries in its walls; c.1320

Kyme priory: intact south porch, single storeyed; C14

Leominster priory: intact porch south of nave, single storeyed; 1320 (incorporating some C13 work)

Leonard Stanley priory: intact porch north of nave, single storeyed; c.1300

Llangennith cell: intact porch north of nave, single storeyed; C13/C14

Malmesbury abbey: intact porch south of nave, double storeyed, displays profuse array of carvings; c.1160, early C14

Monks Kirby priory: intact double storeyed porch south of nave, with tierceron star vault; mid C14

Monkton priory: intact porch south of nave, formerly double storeyed, dividing floor now gone; c.1200

Ovingham cell: intact porch south of nave, single storeyed; late C12, C13

Peterborough abbey: intact galilee west of nave, double storeyed; c.1375

Pilton priory: intact single storeyed porch south of nave; C15/C16

Redlingfield priory: intact single storeyed porch south of nave; early C14

Rievaulx abbey: ruined galilee west of nave standing to several feet, containing 6 grave stones; late C12

Rothley Temple preceptory: intact rib vaulted porch south of nave, double storeyed & connecting with manor house; c.1280

Rumburgh cell: intact porch south of nave, single storeyed; C15

St. Germans priory: intact porch south of nave, with depressed tunnel vault & 2 open arches to west & south; late C15

Selby abbey: intact porch north of nave, double storeyed; C12, C13, C15

Sherborne abbey: intact porch south of nave, double storeyed; c.1180

Shipley preceptory: intact small timber south porch, single storeyed; C16

Shrewsbury abbey: intact porch north of nave, triple storeyed; early C13, C15

Snaith cell: intact porch south of nave, originally double storeyed & now single; C15, 1868

Stogursey priory: intact porch north of nave, single storeyed(?); C15

Temple Guiting preceptory: intact & largely recently rebuilt north porch of one storey; C12, C19

Temple preceptory: intact west porch of one storey, with 3 outer doorways; c.1200

Tewkesbury abbey: intact porch north of nave, double storeyed; late C11/early C12, C15

Thurgarton priory: intact porch north of nave, single storeyed; C13

Totnes priory: intact porch south of nave, double storeyed; mid C15

Trentham priory: intact porch north of nave, single storeyed; c.1200, C19

Usk priory: 1. intact porch north of nave, single storeyed; c.1460
2. intact porch west of nave, single storeyed; c.1460

Westminster abbey: intact west porch between north west & south west towers; early C16

Weybourne priory: intact porch south of nave, double storeyed but intermediate floor gone; mid C15

Wilmington priory: intact single storeyed porch north of nave, with repositioned outer Norman doorway; C15

Worcester cathedral-priory: intact porch north of nave, double storeyed; c.1386, C19

Worksop priory: intact porch south of nave, single storeyed; C13/C14

Wymondham abbey: intact porch north of nave, double storeyed; c.1445

Yarmouth priory: *south porch almost totally rebuilt after being firebombed in last war; 1957-61*

Abergavenny priory: intact crossing & embattled tower; early C14

Aldeby priory: intact crossing & embattled tower; C13, 1633

Amesbury priory: intact crossing & low tower, with lancets & plain parapet; C13

Atherstone friary: intact crossing with walking place & pinnacled octagonal tower; C14, 1782, 1849

Bath cathedral-priory: intact crossing & embattled tower; c.1499-1539

Blanchland abbey: crossing in vestigial state, one crossing arch survives; c.1200, 1752-53, rebuilt 1884

Bolton priory: high-standing ruined crossing; late C12, late C13/early C14

Boxgrove priory: intact crossing & embattled tower; late C12, rebuilt pDp

Brecon friary: intact walking place (modified as ante-chapel); c.1250+, C19

Brecon priory: intact crossing & embattled tower; C13

Breedon priory: intact crossing & embattled tower; C12, C14/C15

Brinkburn priory: intact crossing & low tower; c.1190/1200, restored 1858-59

Bristol abbey: intact crossing & embattled tower; C12, c.1470-1515

Bromfield priory: crossing largely intact (now chancel), but no tower; C12, domestic conversion mid C16, reversion to church 1658

Buildwas abbey: high-standing ruined crossing & tower; late C12

Calder abbey: high-standing ruined crossing, with 4 tall pointed arches; C13

Cambridge St. Radegund's priory: intact crossing & embattled tower; 1150/75, C13, c.1500

Canterbury cathedral-priory: intact crossing & tower (Bell Harry), with multi-pinnacled parapet; c.1496-1503

Carlisle cathedral-priory: intact crossing & embattled tower; early/mid C12, early C15

Cartmel priory: intact crossing & embattled tower, with unusual diagonal top stage; c.1190-1220, early C16, C19

Chester abbey: intact crossing, & turreted & embattled tower; early C14, late C15

Christchurch priory: intact crossing now roofed but minus tower; early C12

Coventry Franciscan friary: intact octagonal central tower & spire, 230 ft. & standing on its own; c.1350

Deerhurst priory: crossing (but no tower) subsumed into body of church, serves as modern chancel; mainly C14

Denney abbey: intact crossing (but no tower) embedded in post-Dissolution house; late C12, mid C14, pDp

Dorchester abbey: intact crossing but no tower; late C12, 1633

Dore abbey: intact crossing & cap; c.1180, major restoration 1632-4

Dover Augustinian priory: intact crossing & parapeted tower; c.1000, C12/C13, 1860-62

Dunster priory: intact crossing & embattled tower; C12, mainly 1443

Durham cathedral-priory: intact crossing & embattled tower; 1093-1100, 1464-1488, C19

Edington priory: intact crossing & embattled tower; 1352-61

Ely cathedral-priory: intact replacement for crossing & tower in form of octagon & lantern; 1322-42

Ewenny priory: intact crossing & embattled tower; mid C12

Gloucester abbey: intact crossing, & turretted & embattled tower; c.1450+

Great Bricett priory: intact vestigial crossing comprising north & south arches, but no east & west arches or tower; c.1300

Hayling priory: intact crossing (effectively Bay 1 of nave) with low tower surmounted by shingled broach spire; early C13

Hexham priory: intact crossing & embattled tower with cap; late C12-early C13, c.1300

Jarrow priory: intact crossing & axial tower with plain parapet, built over Anglo-Saxon west porch; 681, c.1074-83

Kidwelly cell: intact crossing of pseudo-cruciform church, with no tower structure above 4 crossing arches; c.1320

King's Lynn Franciscan friary: intact hexagonal central tower, standing on its own; late C14

King's Lynn priory: intact crossing with modern low tower; C13, c.1746

Kirkstall abbey: crossing largely intact, but with south wall only of tower standing to full height; 1152-75, belfry c.1509-27

Lanercost priory: intact crossing & high-standing ruined tower; early C13

Lapley priory: intact crossing & great tower, with embattled parapet & pinnacles also frieze; C12, C15, C17

Lastingham abbey: intact crossing (later divided into 2 bays) but no tower; 1078+, C13, 1879

Leonard Stanley priory: intact crossing & embattled tower with cap & high external stair-turret; mainly c.1129, C14

Little Malvern priory: intact crossing & capped tower; c.1480

Llanbadarn-fawr priory: intact crossing, parapet tower & short spire; C13, C15, 1868

Malvern priory: intact crossing, & embattled & turretted tower; c.1120, mainly mid C15

Milton abbey: intact crossing, & pinnacled tower with pierced parapet; c.1310-25, 1789

Monkton priory: intact towerless crossing, flanked by transeptal tower to south; C13/C14

Mount Grace charterhouse: high-standing ruined central tower with mini-transepts superimposed on original plan, still possesses embattled parapet; early/mid C15

Newcastle-upon-Tyne Augustinian friary: intact tower (probably originally central) with Georgian top; C13, C18

Norwich cathedral-priory: intact crossing & tower with spire & corner-spirelets; mainly C12, C15

Norwich Dominican friary: intact crossing (walking place), tower collapsed after Dissolution; 1327+, 1413-70

Nuneaton priory: (See entry under Small Portions of Conventual Churches etc.)

Oxford St. Frideswide's priory: intact crossing & tower, crowned with recessed spire; late C12, early C13

Pamber priory: intact crossing & stumpy capped tower, with external square turret for stairs; C12

Penmon priory: intact crossing & low tower, with stone cap; c.1170

Pershore abbey: intact crossing & tower, with corner-spirelets & plain parapet; c.1100, mainly early C14

Peterborough abbey: *crossing & tower totally rebuilt in recent times; 1882-86*

Pilton priory: intact crossing & tower occupying position north of present chancel (tower possibly originally axial), embattled & pinnacled; late C13, much rebuilt 1696 & 1845-50

Portchester priory: intact crossing & low capped tower; c.1133+, 1888

Priestholme cell: high-standing ruined tower of conventual church; C12

Richmond friary: intact central tower, standing on its own; C15

Rochester cathedral-priory: *crossing & tower with short spire rebuilt twice; 1825, 1904-05*

Romsey abbey: intact crossing & low tower capped with cupola; mid C12

Royston priory: *crossing tower rebuilt after Dissolution as west tower; pDp, c.1872*

Ruthin priory: intact crossing & tower, with modern broach spire, 1310-15, C18, 1854-59

St. Albans abbey: intact crossing & high tower of Roman brick, with embattled parapet; c.1077-89

St. Anthony-in-Roseland cell: intact crossing & tower with broach spire of timber & lead; C13, 1850

St. Bees priory: intact crossing & rebuilt tower, with cap inside plain parapet; C12, 1855-58

St. Michael's Mount priory: intact crossing & embattled axial tower; late C14

Selby abbey: intact crossing with pinnacled high tower, much rebuilt in its upper stage in recent times; early C12, 1908

Sherborne abbey: intact crossing & high tower, embattled & pinnacled; c.1000, C12, c.1425

Shipley preceptory: intact axial tower of 3 storeys, with shallow cap inside plain parapet & unusual west crossing arch; c.1125

Smithfield St. Bartholomew's priory: intact crossing, now devoid of tower; mainly c.1150, C15

Southwark priory: intact crossing & high tower, with corner spirelets & battlements; late C14, 1818-23

Stogursey priory: intact crossing & tower with recessed spire behind plain parapet; c.1100, C19

Stow abbey: intact crossing & tower, embattled & pinnacled & now with external stair-turret; c.975, mid C11, c.1400, 1853-64

Tewkesbury abbey: intact crossing & high tower, pinnacled & embattled; early & mid C12, mid C14

Tintern abbey: intact crossing, but tower now dismantled; late C13

Usk priory: intact crossing & tower, with embattled parapet & external stair-turret at north west corner; c.1135+, C19

Westminster abbey: intact crossing & low capped tower; 1245-55

Weybourne priory: high-standing ruined crossing & much of tower; early C11(?), C15

Winchester cathedral-priory: intact crossing & high central tower, with plain parapet; mainly c.1107-20, 1635, C19

Worcester cathedral-priory: intact crossing & high tower, with corner-spirelets & pierced parapet; 1374+

Worksop priory: part of crossing original, *but squat tower with fleche rebuilt at same time as new chancel & offices;* C12, *1966-74*

Wymondham abbey: (See entry below on Non-Central Towers)

Yarmouth priory: (See entry under Small Portions of Conventual Churches etc.)

5/5   NON-CENTRAL TOWERS

Alkborough cell: intact west tower, unbuttressed & possessing great gargoyles; c.1052+, C13

Alvingham priory: *intact south west tower rebuilt in stuccoed brick in post-Dissolution period; 1841*

Bamburgh cell: intact west tower engaged within nave, unbuttressed & with embattled parapet; early C13, C19

Beauchief abbey: (See entry under Small Portions of Conventual Churches etc.)

Blackmore priory: intact west tower with broach spire, timber framed & timber clad; c.1480

Blakeney friary: intact west tower of 3 stages, 104 ft. high & embattled top with 4 pinnacles; 1435, 1880+

Blanchland abbey: intact tower north of north transept, plain parapeted top; c.1300, belfry stage C14

Blyth priory: intact engaged west tower with unusually pinnacled parapet; c.1400

Bolton priory: west tower unfinished at Dissolution, roofed in recent times; 1520, 1984

Bourne abbey: intact south west tower with embattled top; c.1200, early C15, C19

Bradsole St. Radegund's abbey: high-standing ruined north tower, converted into post-Dissolution gateway; c.1220 & pDp

Bridlington priory: 1. intact tower north west of nave, modern flat parapet at top; C13, C14, C19
2. intact tower south west of nave, modern pinnacled & embattled parapet; C15, C19

Bristol abbey: *west towers rebuilt in modern times; 1868-88*

Bristol St. James' priory: intact tower at east end of south nave aisle, with pinnacled & embattled top; unknown medieval date, pDp

Bromfield priory: intact tower north west of nave serving as porch, with embattled parapet; c.1300, C15

Bungay priory: intact engaged south west tower, with high pinnacled parapet & octagonal buttresses; mid C15, 1688+, 1879

Caldey cell: intact west tower, embattled parapet & quaint spire; C14

Canons Ashby priory: intact north west tower, with 4 spirelets on corners of parapet; C14

Canterbury cathedral-priory: 1. intact south west tower, with pinnacled & embattled parapet; c.1424-59
2. *north west tower totally rebuilt in recent times; 1832-41*

Cardigan cell: *west tower rebuilt after collapse in post-Dissolution period; C18*

Carisbrooke priory: *intact high west tower of 5 stages, with pinnacled parapet; c.1470*

Castle Acre priory: high-standing ruined south west tower of 4 storeys; early C12

Chester abbey: 1. intact north west tower built to 2 stages (ground floor as baptistry), hidden by secular building to west; mid C12
2. intact south west tower consisting of ground floor stage only (now consistory court), probably originally had timber campanile as upper stage; early C16 & later

Chetwode cell: *west tower constructed in place of crossing tower after Dissolution; c.1600*

Chirbury priory: intact west tower, with diagonal buttresses & low cap surrounded by pierced & pinnacled parapet; early C14, early C15

Christchurch priory: intact engaged west tower, with embattled parapet; late C15

Church Gresley priory: intact tower north of former choir & new chancel, with renewed embattled parapet; C15, c.1820

Cockerham cell: (See entry under Small Parts of Conventual Churches etc.)

Cranborne cell: intact west tower part engaged into westerly bay of nave, with embattled parapet; C15

Croyland abbey: intact north west tower, recessed blunt spire inside flat parapet; c.1460-69

Cymmer abbey: west tower stands to nearly half height, with narrow lancets in ground floor stage; C14

Davington priory: 1. intact south west capped tower; C12, top restored 1845+

2. intact ground floor stage only of north west tower; C12

Deeping St. James priory: *west tower rebuilt in post-Dissolution period; 1717*

Deerhurst priory: intact west tower engaged within nave; C8, C10, C14

Dinmore commandery: intact west tower (See also entry under Churches Substantially Surviving etc.), with recessed spire; C12, mainly C14

Dover Augustinian priory: high-standing ruined detached Roman pharos, adapted as bell tower in medieval period; C2/C3(?), C13

Dunstable priory: intact embattled north west tower; lower portion 1223-40, mainly C15

Durham cathedral-priory: intact north west & south west embattled towers; c.1093-1133, early C13, c.1801

Easebourne priory: intact west tower, with single bell openings & small parapet-spire; late C12

Ellerton priory: high-standing ruined west tower, complete to parapet; C15

Elstow abbey: intact detached tower (campanile) with embattled parapet & spirelet north west of nave; C13, mainly C15

Ely cathedral-priory: intact west tower crowned with octagon & corner pinnacles; late C12, late C14, pDp

Evesham abbey: intact detached tower (campanile) (Abbot Lichfield's Belltower) north of former conventual church, with embattled & pinnacled parapet; c.1529-39

Ewyas Harold cell: (See entry under Small Portions of Conventual Churches etc.)

Fountains abbey: high-standing ruined tower (Abbot Huby's tower) north of north transept, some battlements still in place; early C16

Freiston priory: intact west tower, with embattled parapet; c.1500

Furness abbey: high-standing ruined west tower, probably never finished; c.1500

Garway preceptory: intact tower north west of nave & originally detached, with low cap; C13

Goring priory: intact west tower, with external circular vice; late C11/early C12

Hamble priory: intact thin west tower, unbuttressed & with plain parapet; C12

Hatfield Broad Oak priory: intact west tower of 81 ft. with stepped battlements; C15

Horsley priory: (See entry under Small Portions of Conventual Churches etc.)

Humberston abbey: (See entry under Small Portions of Conventual Churches etc.)

Ingham friary: intact west tower of 4 stages, with double stepped battlements & pinnacles; mid C14

Kidwelly cell: intact north west tower of 5 storeys with tall spire inside flat parapet; c.1320, spire rebuilt 1884+

King's Lynn priory: 1. intact north west tower, with pinnacled & embattled parapet; C12, mainly 1453+

2. intact south west tower, also with pinnacled & embattled parapet, much renewed after storm of 1741; C12, c.1260-70, C14, c.1746

Lancaster priory: *west tower totally rebuilt in post-Dissolution period; 1753*

Leominster priory: intact west tower, with embattled & pinnacled parapet; mid C12, C15

Letheringham priory: intact west tower with diagonal buttresses & nicely panelled; C15

Lindisfarne priory: ruined but almost intact south west tower stands almost to full height; mid C12

Llangennith cell: intact tower north of nave, unbuttressed & with saddleback roof; C13

Llanthony priory: intact roofed south west tower at west end of ruined nave; mainly late C12

Malton priory: intact south west tower, with plain parapet; c.1200

Marrick priory: intact though considerable altered west tower, C13, C15, pDp

Minster-in-Sheppey priory: intact broad west tower with modern cap, probably never constructed to full height in medieval period; C15, C19

Monkland cell: intact west tower, with broach spire & timber shingles; later C13

Monks Kirby priory: intact large west tower with tierceron star vault & Gothick parapet; mid C14, C15, C18

Monkton priory: intact tall tower in transeptal position south of present nave, of 4 stages with embattled parapet & external stairway turret; C15

Monkwearmouth cell: intact slender & tall west tower, built over Anglo-Saxon porch; C7, late C10

Monmouth priory: (See entry under Small Portions of Conventual Churches etc.)

Morville cell: intact west tower, with embattled parapet; C12, C15/C16

Nun Monkton priory: intact small engaged tower at west end of nave, with recessed cap inside plain parapet; early C13

Ovingham cell: intact west tower of thin & tall appearance, with plain parapet; late C10/early C11

Owston abbey: intact tower north west of north nave aisle serving as porch, possesses short recessed spire inside embattled parapet; c.1300

Peterborough abbey: 1. intact north west tower (over north west transept), with pinnacled parapet; mid C13
2. intact outer north west & south west flanking turrets, each with pinnacles & recessed spire; mid C13

Polesworth abbey: intact tower north of present chancel; C14, C17(?)

Ranton priory: intact west tower, standing on its own; C15

Redlingfield priory: intact stumpy west tower with saddleback roof, lower part of Tudor brick & upper of lath and plaster; late C15/early C16, also C17

Richmond St. Martin's priory: high-standing ruined low west tower standing almost on its own; C14(?)

Rochester cathedral-priory: 1. intact low originally detached tower (Gundulph's tower) north of choir, probably defensive in character; c.1077-80

2. intact outer (2) & inner (2) turrets of west front, upper sections largely rebuilt in recent times; mid C12, 1888

Rumburgh cell: intact rectangular west tower, with timber upper storey & hipped roof; C13

St. Clear's cell: intact west tower, unbuttressed with embattled parapet; C14

St. Germans priory: 1. intact north west tower, with embattled octagonal upper stage; c.1180+, C13, 1888+

2. intact south west tower, with square embattled upper stage; c.1180+, C15

Selby abbey: intact north west & south west towers, with modern top stages; late C12, mid C13, 1935

Sele friary: intact west tower, with plain parapet & cap; C12, C13

Shap abbey: high-standing ruined west tower now standing almost on its own; early C16

Shrewsbury abbey: intact west tower, embattled parapet in brick; c.1360-70, 1646-47, 1908

Snaith cell: intact engaged west tower, with triple lancets in top storey & embattled pinnacled top; C13, C15

Swine priory: *central tower destroyed & replaced after Dissolution by west tower of Gothic appearance; 1787*

Temple Bruer preceptory: intact south east tower, 54 ft. high & now standing on its own; late C12

Temple Ewell preceptory: intact small west tower devoid of buttresses, with short cap inside plain parapet; mid C15

Thorney abbey: intact north west & south west octagonal turrets flanking central aisle of nave; early C12, C15

Thurgarton priory: intact north west tower over west bay of north nave aisle, with embattled parapet; c.1230, C15

Totnes priory: intact west tower with main facade to south, pinnacled & embattled parapet; c.1450

Tutbury priory: intact south west tower, with embattled & pinnacled parapet; C14/C15

Ulverscroft priory: high-standing ruined west tower; C15

Upholland priory: intact tower west of choir probably built in lieu of aborted T-crossing, with pinnacled & embattled parapet; late C15/early C16

West Acre priory: high-standing ruined portion of south west tower; C12, C13

Westminster abbey: intact north west & south west towers, each with post-Dissolution upper stages & corner spirelets & battlements; 1260+, 1375+, 1734-45

Weybourne priory: intact west tower, with embattled parapet; mid C15

Woodkirk cell: (See entry under Small Portions of Conventual Churches etc.)

Worksop priory: intact north west & south west towers, of similar appearance with embattled & pinnacled parapets; late C12, C15

Wymondham abbey: 1. intact west tower, with plain parapet; c.1448
2. high-standing ruined axial tower east of nave (but not central), square below & octagonal above; c.1390/1400

York Holy Trinity priory: intact north west tower, built over north nave aisle for former contiguous parish church of St. Nicholas, with embattled parapet; C13, 1463

5/6 HIGH-STANDING RUINED WEST FRONTS OF CONVENTUAL CHURCHES

Binham priory: intact central portion of front except for lost window tracery, ruined high-standing north & south nave aisle end-walls; 1226/1244

Buildwas abbey: largely intact front, with 2 equal lancets, connected to intact nave arcading; later C12

Burnham Norton friary: intact simple small gabled front, with 2-centred doorway & niches left & right; early C14

Bury St. Edmunds abbey: though drastically modified by later building, mutilated front is characterised by Abbot Anselm's 3 tall arches; 1120/1148, 1182/1211

Byland abbey: partly intact front displays major portion of great rose window; early C13

Castle Acre priory: well preserved front embellished & characterised by lines of wall arcading at every level comprising intersecting arches; mainly early C12, also C15

Colchester St. Botolph's priory: considerable part of front up to maximum height, displays much external wall-arcading & intact west doorway; 1093/1100

Croxden abbey: front stands to maximum height except for gable top, with 3 excessively long lancets (middle one stepped over doorway); late C12/early C13

Egglestone abbey: high-standing front to above west window of plain appearance, contiguous with largely surviving north & south walls of nave; c.1200, c.1300

Finchale priory: fairly high-standing plain west front, with eroded main doorway & 3 lancets partly gone; early C13

Fountains abbey: unornamented intact front (plus part of galilee porch) reinforced by side view of west range; mid & late C12, 1484

Frithelstock priory: intact plain front with 3 long lancets & doorway; mid C13

Hulne friary: plain gabled west front with lancet & vesica above; mid C13

Kirkstall abbey: austere & intact front displaying great west doorway

Lindisfarne priory: high-standing front apart from demolished north west tower; mid C12

Llanthony priory: largely intact front flanked by 2 towers each standing to full height, south west tower part of hotel; C12, early C13

Malling abbey: high-standing portion of front consisting of 5 stages incorporating much wall arcading, stump of tower looms overhead; mainly mid C12, also C14

Malmesbury abbey: almost half of front on south side survives to full height of 4 tiers, displays blank arcading with some overlapping; mid C12

Mount Grace charterhouse: largely intact front, standing to above great west window; early C15

Netley abbey: largely intact to above great west window including north & south aisle ends; mid C13

Newstead Augustinian priory: exceptionally well preserved intact front ornamented with large blank windows in stone with geometrical motifs; late C13

Stamford St. Leonard's priory: intact small front, with 3 semicircular headed arches below, 7 intermediate panelled arches, & vesica in roof gable; late C12

Strata Florida abbey: severely reduced front with intact great doorway, latter possesses 5 shafted jambs with continuous roll mouldings; c.1200

Tintern abbey: almost intact front characterised by great window still containing much tracery; early C14

Tynemouth priory: lower part of front only, displaying great doorway of 5 orders with shafts gone; C13

Valle Crucis abbey: front intact except for side-aisle projections, 3 lancet windows contained within great blank semicircular arch, with intact rose window above; late C13

Whitby abbey: front reduced by demolition & erosion to west doorway & high-standing end wall of north nave aisle; C14

York St. Mary's abbey: front reduced by demolition to high-standing north end & west door jambs; later C13

♦♦♦♦♦♦♦♦♦♦♦♦♦♦♦♦

Section 6:

SCREENS

6/1   HIGH ALTAR SCREENS

Christchurch priory: intact high screen (Jesse screen) with two flanking doorways, condition good but most statues missing; c.1350

Durham cathedral-priory: intact high screen (Neville screen) of openwork type with two flanking doorways, condition good but statues missing; 1373-1380

Malvern priory: intact low screen of double type with two flanking doorways, condition good; c.1450-c.1500, restored 1884

Milton abbey: high screen with two flanking doorways, condition good but statues missing; late C15, 1789

St. Albans abbey: high screen with two flanking doorways, condition good; 1484, statues replaced 1884-90

Selby abbey: intact low screen in good condition with no flanking doorways, on 3 sides of sanctuary of high altar; c.1320, restoration including new reredos placed in front of screen 1909

Southwark priory: intact high screen with 2 flanking doorways, condition good; 1520, statues replaced 1905

Waltham abbey: intact stone screen built up at Dissolution to form east wall of present church, possesses 2 blocked lateral doorways with segmental heads visible externally, similar in design to a rood screen; C14

Westminster abbey: intact low screen with 2 flanking doorways, condition good; 1420, west side of screen restored 1867

Winchester cathedral priory: intact high screen with 2 flanking doorways, condition good; late C15, restoration & statues replaced 1885-99

Wymondham abbey: intact high stone screen with 2 flanking doorways (now blocked) forming east wall of octagonal tower & backing of parochial high altar & modern Comper screen; c.1390/1400

6/2   REREDOSES

Bristol abbey: 1 intact stone reredos in Eastern lady chapel, comprising 3 large ogeed arches; early C14, c.1526
2. remnant of stone reredos at east end of north choir aisle; C15

Canterbury cathedral-priory: intact stone reredos in chapel of Our Lady of Undercroft, finely worked Perpendicular screen embodying long panelling below & openwork above, silver image of Mary gone; c.1400

Christchurch priory: intact stone reredos of lady chapel altar, devoid of figures; C15

Dorchester abbey: intact timber painted reredos of altar in People's chapel of south west nave aisle; C14

Ely cathedral-priory: part-dismantled & mutilated reredos of lady chapel altar, combination of wall & window stonework where the stained glass has been destroyed; 1321-1353

Gloucester abbey: 1. mutilated stone reredos in lady chapel, now decorated with modern embroidery; late C15

2. mutilated stone reredos in chapel of St. Edmund & St. Edward, minus figures; C15

3. intact stone reredos in chapel of St. Andrew, with restored figures; C15, C19

4. restored stone reredos in chapel of St. John Baptist; early C16, 1964

5. stone reredos in chapel of the Salutation of Mary, some mutilation; C15

Hexham priory: 1. intact timber canopied reredos on north side of sanctuary of choir displaying paintings of bishops of Hexham; late C15

2. intact timber painted reredos of altar of Leschman chantry, portraying Apostles, Resurrection & Instruments of Passion; C15

Little Dunmow priory: mutilated stone reredos attached to east wall of lady chapel, consisting of series of arched panels of varying heights & sizes; mid C14

Norwich cathedral-priory: 1. intact reredos with Adoration painting by Martin Schwartz in Jesus chapel; dated 1480 on frame but may be later

2. intact painted 5-panelled timber retable in chapel of St. Luke, given by Bishop Despenser; c.1381, restored 1958

3. intact painted retable of 5 parts in modern lady chapel, from redundant church; c.1430/40

Romsey abbey: intact timber painted reredos in modern chapel of St. Lawrence, formerly of high altar; c.1525

Thetford priory: intact & restored retable now at parish church of Thornham Parva St. Mary, timber panelling 12 ft. long depicting Crucifixion scene with saints on gilt background; c.1330, late C20

Westminster abbey: 1. damaged timber panel-painted retable (11 ft. x 3 ft.) in south ambulatory of choir, possibly former reredos or retable of high altar; 1241+ (See also entry under Paintings)

2. intact tabernacled reredos of altar of bridge chantry chapel of Henry V, with 6 of 7 niches occupied by original statues; 1437+

3. intact 2 niches of reredos of altar of chapel of St. Michael; C14/C15

4. set of intact reredoses against east walls of 5 of sub-chapels of Henry VII's chapel, largely still containing original statues in niches; 1504+

Winchester cathedral-priory: 1. intact stone reredos of altar in Guardian Angels' chapel, seven tall niches above & blank panelling below; C15

2. intact stone reredos in south east chapel (Langton chantry), seven low arches; c.1500

Worcester cathedral-priory: mutilated stone reredos of altar of chantry of Prince Arthur, with central figure of Christ & 2 flanking figures per side; 1504+

Worksop priory: intact & restored reredos of high altar relocated against north wall of north transept, 6 trefoiled & shafted arches under pointed gables; C13, relocated 1935

6/3 PULPITA

Amesbury priory: intact timber screen served as pulpitum at entrance to choir, with 5-light bays & original door; C15

Blyth priory: intact high stone pulpitum built up to roof after Dissolution, central doorway blocked & restored Doom painting on west facade; C14/C15(?), painting c.1400, restored 1987

Bungay priory: present lower part of east wall of post-Dissolution church pulpitum of nuns' choir; C14/C15

Canterbury cathedral-priory: intact stone pulpitum on west side of quire, central doorway, possesses six medieval figures of kings; 1304-5, c.1400

Carlisle cathedral-priory: intact timber pulpitum on west side of quire, with single asymmetrical (north) doorway & Victorian canopy; c.1450, C19

Chester abbey: incomplete stone pulpitum, now forms north & south quire backing; C14

Chirbury priory: intact timber pulpitum now forming east screen of Mongomery church of St. Nicholas, possibly reduced slightly in order to fit chancel; early C15

Christchurch priory: intact stone pulpitum, central doorway, base original & top modern, twentytwo medieval niches empty; c.1360, C19

Edington priory: intact timber pulpitum, central doorway & panelled; late C14/early C15

Ewenny priory: intact timber screen served as pulpitum with central doorway & upper openwork; C14

Hexham priory: intact timber pulpitum, central doorway, altered to east, panelled with restored paintings (See entries on Paintings); late C15, 1865

Ingham friary: intact lower half of stone pupitum with embattled top, plus piers of central archway standing to 7 ft.; C14/C15

Jervaulx abbey: almost intact timber open screen in Aysgarth parish church, vaulted & coved in 9 arched bays, with middle bay as doorway; c.1506

Malmesbury abbey: intact stone pulpitum, built up to roof after Dissolution, blocked central doorway; early C16

Milton abbey: intact stone pulpitum, considerably restored with ancient materials, central doorway; early C14, pDp

Mottisfont priory: lower portion of stone pulpitum survives in post-Dissolution mansion, central doorway intact; c.1521-36

Norwich cathedral-priory: intact stone pulpitum, central doorway, mostly original though some modern restoration; c.1470, much of carving 1833

Pamber priory: intact single wall of stone pulpitum with central doorway, built up to top of west crossing arch; possibly C13, C15/C16

Rochester cathedral-priory: intact stone & timber pulpitum but much altered, central doorway, modern statuary & carving on west facade; c.1227, c.1320, 1888

Smithfield St. Bartholomew's priory: intact stone pulpitum, central doorway now leads to vestry; c.1230, C17

Valle Crucis abbey: surviving ruined south side of stone pulpitum, displays 4 steps of winding stair to now vanished loft; C13

Westminster abbey: intact stone pulpitum, central doorway, much restored & ornamented though some medieval plain stonework; C13(?), c.1728, 1833

Weybourne priory: intact stone pulpitum, built up probably after Dissolution, ogee-arched doorway; C14

Yarmouth priory: stone pulpitum re-erected in main vestry, possesses 3 depressed 2-centred arches with blank tracery in spandrels; C15/C16

Binham priory: intact stone screen built up to roof at Dissolution, 2 doorways blocked; late C12

Blyth priory: intact timber screen devoid of loft across central nave aisle one bay west of pulpitum, consisting of 5 bays with cinquefoiled lights; C15

Bolton priory: intact stone screen built up to roof at Dissolution, 2 doorways blocked; of uncertain date

Boxgrove priory: intact stone screen built up to roof at Dissolution, 2 doorways blocked; probably of late C12 date

Canterbury cathedral-priory: ironwork screen broken into 2 parts to protect west & south doorways; Imp

Croyland abbey: high-standing stone screen almost complete, 2 doorways; c.1400

Davington priory: intact stone screen built up to roof at Dissolution to form east wall of church, 2 doorways; probably of c.1300 date

Dunstable priory: intact stone screen built up to roof at Dissolution with 2 blocked doorways of dissimilar size, converted from former pulpitum with blocked central doorway; C13/C14

Dunster priory: intact timber screen, probably reduced in width where it presently occupies east archway of south transept; early C15

Ewenny priory: intact stone screen stands to original height of 8½ ft., 2 doorways; C13

Great Bricett priory: intact timber screen heavily restored & now at west end of church, with 3 bays on each side of wide doorway; C15(?), C19

Little Malvern priory: intact & restored section of timber screen (i.e. minus one doorway) now located between 'chancel' & 'nave' of surviving church, timber rood beam rests on top of screen; C15

Minster-in-Sheppey priory: intact stone screen built up to gable at Dissolution, with three niches on west side & 2 lateral doorways (south blocked); C13, C14/C15

Newark priory: high-standing ruined stone screen; unknown date

Rumburgh cell: intact timber screen between nave & choir with central processional way, accompanied by stairway in north wall of nave; C15

St. Albans abbey: intact stone screen standing to original height, 2 doorways, 7 empty canopied niches on west face; c.1350

Totnes priory: stone screen from which its loft has been removed spanning three aisles, 3 doorways (equivalent to fence screen); c.1459

Tynemouth priory: high-standing ruined stone screen, 2 doorways; c.1195

6/5   FENCE SCREENS

Blyth priory: 1. intact timber screen with vaulting across south nave aisle, consisting of 5 bays with cinquefoiled lights; C15
2. timber screen reduced to fit part of south side of Bay 2 of central nave aisle, consisting of 3+ bays; C15

Dunstable priory: intact timber screen of 5 bays across central aisle of nave, one doorway; C15

Dunster priory: intact timber screen across 3 aisles of nave, 3 doorways; 1500

Freiston priory: 1. intact timber screen in north nave aisle in line with position of former rood screen, each bay divided into 2 cinquefoiled sub-lights; C15
2. intact timber screen in south nave aisle also in line with former rood screen, with big trefoiled ogee arches; C15

6/4 Tynemouth priory, rood screen to west

Lapley priory: intact heavily restored timber screen dividing choir from east side of crossing, mainly single light divisions; C15, C19
Minster-in-Sheppey priory: timber screen with cinquefoiled lights, central doorway retains intact doors; late C14
Pilton priory: intact timber screen across present chancel & south chancel chapel (possibly rood screen of lay part of church), devoid of vaulting; 1508

Rumburgh cell: intact timber screen dividing nave from choir with upper part restored, 4 bays on either side of wider archway; C15

Usk priory: intact timber screen across 2 aisles of nave, 2 doorways; C15

Westminster abbey: intact finely worked grille with doors & doorways at east end of chapel of St. Edward; 1431

6/6   OTHER SCREENS

Binham priory: timber screen (originally parclose?) cut to half height now in nave, displays pictures of saints behind post-Dissolution black-letter texts; C15

Brecon priory: intact timber parclose screen on south side of chapel of St Keyne, 6 bays each with paired lights; early C16

Bristol abbey: intact timber screen dividing Newton chapel from south transept to west, 3 bays; late C14/early C15

Bristol Carmelite friary: intact stone screen relocated to Bristol cathedral, stands between choir aisles & sanctuary of high altar; c.1500

Canterbury cathedral-priory: 1. intact 3-sided stone screen (not the pulpitum) enclosing quire, erected by Prior Eastry; 1304-5

2. intact stone screen enclosing crypt chapel of Our Lady Undercroft on 2 sides, delicate openwork; c.1400

3. intact stone screen at entrance to lady chapel (now Dean's chapel), 5 bays with lofty gables; 1448+

4. intact stone screen at entrance to chapel of St. Andrew, apart from doorway divided into 2-light bays; c.1300

5. intact double stone screen at entrance to chapel of St. Anselm, incorporating Archbishop Meopham's canopied monument; 1333+

6. intact double wood & iron screen at entrance to chapel of St. Edward Confessor, apart from doorway divided into 3-light bays; 1439

Carlisle cathedral-priory: 1. intact timber screen (Gondibour screen) enclosing chapel of St. Catherine on 2 sides, linenfold panelling & Gothic Flamboyant work; c.1500

2. intact timber screen (Salkeld screen) on north side of presbytery, early Renaissance detail; c.1541

Christchurch priory: intact stone screen between south choir aisle & Draper chantry chapel; displays openwork on each side of central doorway; early C16

Croyland abbey: timber screen with missing detail, probably moved from former lady chapel & now used as chancel screen; c.1413, C19

Dunster priory: two intact timber screens, each between choir & north & south choir chapels respectively; C15

Easby abbey: part of timber screen in Wensley parish church behind Scrope family pew, inscribed with names & heraldry of Scropes; c.1510

Ely cathedral-priory: 1. intact timber screen at entrance to chapel of St. Edmund in north transept, thin fenestration; late C14/early C15

2. intact stone screen at entrance to Bishop Alcock's chantry chapel at east end of north choir aisle, profusely ornamented; 1488+

3. intact stone screen at entrance to Bishop West's chantry chapel at east end of south choir aisle, well ornamented; 1525-33

Freiston priory: intact timber screen now at west end of north nave aisle of Fishtoft church, with wide ogee arches; C15

Gloucester abbey: 1. two intact double stone screens on north & south sides of presbytery respectively immediately east of quire stalls, each occupying single archway; 1337+

2. intact stone screen fronting 2 arches upwards on south side of presbytery immediately west of sedilia; 1337+

3. intact high stone screen above 2 stone-cage chapels in north presbytery arcade; 1337+

4. intact stone screen enclosing vestry to rear of high altar; 1337+

5. intact stone screen at entrance to lady chapel & below great window; c.1500

6. intact stone screen between upper part of bridge & lady chapel; late C15

7. two intact stone screens between transepts & north & south choir aisles respectively; 1337+

8. intact stone screen of veranda type stationed against north wall of north transept, not in original position & now providing entrance to new treasury; c.1230-40

9. intact stone screen enclosing southern part of north transept, openwork now partly filled; C15(?)

10. intact timber screen enclosing chapel of St. John Baptist on north side of south transept; early C16

11. intact stone screen enclosing chapel of Salutation of Mary at east end of south nave aisle; c.1457

12. two intact stone screens at entrances to chapel of St. Edmund & St. Edward & chapel of St. Stephen (off ambulatories) respectively ; C15

13. two intact stone screens with galleries at entrances to small chapels on north & south sides respectively of lady chapel; late C15/early C16

Hatfield Broad Oak priory: intact timber screen of north chapel, simple traceried one-light divisions, said to have been part of buttery screen in refectory; C15

Hatfield Peverel priory: part of traceried timber screen in east bay of north arcade; C15

Hexham priory: 1. intact & largely original timber screen surrounding chantry chapel of Prior Ogle between presbytery & south choir aisle, dismantled & recently restored; c.1410, C19/C20

2. intact & largely original screen with stone base & timber upperwork enclosing on two sides chantry chapel of Prior Leschman between sanctuary & north choir aisle, Flamboyant detail; c.1490

3. remnants of oak parclose screen in east aisle of south transept; C15

King's Lynn priory: 1. set of intact timber screens in 6 sections, 3 on each side of presbytery; late C14

2. intact timber screen on south side of sanctuary of high altar, with shallow canopied arches displaying pseudo-vaulting; C15

Malmesbury abbey: 1. intact stone screen between south nave aisle & chapel of St. Aldhelm, has cinquefoiled lights; C15

2. intact similar screen on corresponding north side of church; C15

Malvern priory: 1. intact tiled screen along north side of sanctuary occupying space of Bays 2 & 3 of choir; c.1450-1500

2. intact tiled screen along south side of sanctuary occupying space of Bay 3; c.1450-1500

Norwich cathedral-priory: 1. intact stone screen in ambulatory arcade on either side of reliquary niche, with interlaced semicircular blind arcading; early C12

2. intact stone screen between south transept & south choir aisle, possesses original doors; c.1501, restored mid C19

3. part of stone screen against north side of pulpitum & formerly at entrance to Jesus chapel; C15/C16

Pershore abbey: part of timber screen at junction of north transept & north choir aisle, may be remnant of abbey rood screen; dated 1435

Peterborough abbey: 1. set of 3 intact timber screens on east side of south transept at entrances to chapels (ss. Oswald, Benedict & Kyneburgha et al.); C15/C16

2. set of 4 intact timber screens dividing off eastern aisle from remainder of north transept, probably not all *in situ*; C15

Pilton priory: intact parclose screen of 3 bays, dividing west side of chancel from south chancel chapel (Raleigh chapel); early C16

Polesworth abbey: intact but reduced small timber screen of 7 bays at entrance to tower vestry but not *in situ*, has ogee headed lights & plain panels below; C14

Rochester cathedral-priory: 1. intact stone screen in 3 sections (one cut through for doorway) standing on low wall between south nave aisle & lady chapel; C15/C16

2. intact timber screens on 2 sides of vestry in south choir aisle, with short & long panels & original paintwork; C14

St. Albans abbey: 1. two intact low stone screens on either side of sanctuary; late C15

2. intact iron screen or grille protecting Gloucester chantry, composed of 14 x 3 rectangular panels; late C13

Sherborne abbey: ancient base & restored upperwork of stone screen at east end of south choir aisle; C15, c.1921

Smithfield St. Bartholomew's priory: intact but damaged stone strainer screen of 2 bays occupying north crossing archway, also formerly providing backing to quire stalls; C15

Swine priory: 1. intact timber screen in north choir aisle on west side of Hilton chantry chapel, displays much Renaissance detail; dated 1531

2. intact timber half-screen at entrance to modern chancel (possibly reduced former rood screen), panelled with linenfold carving & openwork double doors; c.1530+

Tewkesbury abbey: 1. intact stone screen occupying 2 archways to rear of high altar, upper part pierced with quatrefoils etc; C14

2. intact timber screen behind modern seating on north side of quire; C14

3. intact stone screen at entrance to north ambulatory chapel of St. Margaret, tomb of Sir Guy de Brien set into screen; C14

4. intact stone screen at entrance to chapel of St. James from north choir aisle, openwork above & blank arcading below; C14

5. partly intact stone screen in 'chancel' arch of now St. Nicholas chapel, resembling window; C14

Totnes priory: two intact stone parclose screens, each standing on either side of present chancel & joined to main east-west screen; c.1459

Waltham abbey: intact timber screen of 3 bays across north nave aisle separating off easterly 2 bays of aisle, earlier side bays & later door; C14, door C15

Westminster abbey: 1. intact timber screen at entrance to chapel of St. Edmund from south choir ambulatory, 8 bays & somewhat plain; C15

2. intact stone screen at entrance to chapel of St. Nicholas from south choir ambulatory, 5 bays with doorway in middle bay; c.1386/1420

3. heavy stone screen cut into by later tomb of Lord Bourchier at entrance to chapel of St. Paul from north choir ambulatory, highly gilded; early C15

4. intact high stone screen between Jesus (Islip) chapel & north choir ambulatory, panelled in 3 bays & 2 stages; c.1532

5. intact stone screen on east side of chapel of St. John Evangelist, unpierced but panelled & niched at upper level; late C15

6. intact stone panel on west side of chapel of St. John Evangelist, in 3 stages & 3 bays but doorway in middle blocked by Franklin monument; C15

7. part-surviving stone screen of 2 bays under south west tower enclosing modern chapel of St. George; c.1532

8. intact metal grill in lady chapel enclosing inner chapel & tomb of Henry VII & Elizabeth of York; early C16

9. intact 2 stone reduced screens enclosing northern & southern sub-chapels respectively in Henry VII's chapel; early C16

Winchester cathedral-priory: 1. two intact stone screens enclosing presbytery on north & south sides with each screen divided into 3 sections, display early Renaissance influences; dated 1525

2. intact stone screen at entrance to Silkstede chapel in south transept, in 4 bays with timber door; C14/C15

3. intact timber screen at entrance to lady chapel, in 7 bays & surmounted by gallery; early C16, restored C19

4. intact timber screen at entrance to Langton chapel on south side of lady chapel; c.1500

5. intact tall & elaborate stone screen at entrance to Venerable chapel in south transept; C15/C16

6. intact wrought-iron grille with repeating volutes at entrance to south choir aisle from south transept; C13

7. intact timber screen at entrance to Guardian Angels chapel, of 8 bays with doorway occupying 2 middle bays; C15

8. intact timber screen of 6 divisions at rear of choir stalls, occupying space of Bay 1 on south side of nave; probably C15

Worcester cathedral-priory: 1. relocated intact stone screen at entrance to north choir transept (chapel of St. George), 7 bays with 3-light divisions; 4 bays C15, 3 bays 1936

2. intact stone screen at entrance to Jesus chapel north of nave, in 2 bays with niches minus their statues; C16

◆◆◆◆◆◆◆◆◆◆◆◆◆◆◆◆

Section 7:
OTHER FITTINGS, FIXTURES & FURNISHINGS 1

7/1 STONE ALTARS

Arundel priory: [4 altars are said to survive; unknown date]

Bardney abbey: mensa comprises high altar of parish church, formerly of shrine of St. Oswald; unknown date

Binham priory: 1. intact stone altar at east end of south choir aisle, 5 consecration crosses evident; unknown date
2. largely intact mensa & base of high altar; unknown date
3. part of base of altar only in north choir chapel (lady chapel); unknown date

Bolton priory: altar mensa re-erected in church, possesses 5 crosses & sunk square for housing reliquary; unknown consecration date, re-erected 1985

Boxgrove priory: 1. altar mensa in chapel of St. John; unknown date
2. altar mensa in chapel of St. Catherine, recovered from churchyard; unknown date

Bridlington priory: [altar mensa laid in floor of present sanctuary, possesses 5 consecration crosses; unknown date]

Brinkburn priory: intact stone mensa in north transept, displays consecration crosses; unknown date

Bury St. Edmunds abbey: almost intact altar in former crypt chapel of St. Robert; probably c.1090+

Byland abbey: bases of 5 chapel stone altars in line at east end of choir; probably late C12

Canterbury St. Augustine's abbey: 1. almost intact stone altar in presbytery crypt chapel of St. Richard of Chichester; unknown date

2. restored stone altar in presbytery crypt axial chapel of St. Mary & The Angels; dedicated 1325, 1937

3. intact stone altar in presbytery crypt chapel of St. Thomas Apostle, with cutout top for placement of relic holder; unknown date

Castle Acre priory: bases of altars in nave & choir chapels; unknown dates

Christchurch priory: lady chapel mensa of Purbeck marble, 11 ft. long; probably C15

Croyland abbey: intact altar in parvise chapel; C15(?)

Dore abbey: high altar mensa with 5 crosses restored to church after Dissolution, 12 ft. long; consecration unknown date, restoration 1633

Dunster priory: altar in north sacristry; C13(?)

Easby abbey: 1. intact altar in infirmarer's chapel; C15(?)

2. intact mensa in north nave chapel, apparently devoid of consecration marks; early C14(?)

Ewenny priory: intact mensa of high altar, with 3 observable consecration crosses; C12/C13

Fountains abbey: intact bases of 9 altars in The Chapel of The Nine Altars; C13

Furness abbey: intact bases of 3 altars in north transept chapels; unknown date

Garway preceptory: stone altar with 4 consecration crosses; unknown date

Gloucester abbey: 1. restored altar in chapel of St. Edmund & St. Edward; unknown date

2. altar(?) in small chapel on lady chapel bridge; C15(?)

3. altar in choir triforium chamber; unknown date

4. altar in south east crypt chapel, no discernible consecration marks; C12/C13

Hexham priory: stone altar in Prior Leschman's chantry, with 5 consecration crosses; unknown date

Jervaulx abbey: 1. intact & weathered altar in north chapel of north transept, displays consecration crosses & relic niche; unknown date

2. base of altar in south chapel of south transept; unknown date

3. mutilated altar in abbot's ruined chapel; unknown date

Mattersey priory: two altars in former chapter-house; C13(?)

Neath abbey: 3 partly intact altars in former transept chapels; c.1300

Norwich cathedral-priory: 1. altar mensa of Jesus chapel, with no dedication crosses; C12

2. altar mensa of St. Andrew's chapel, with 5 dedication crosses; unknown date

Nun Monkton: altar mensa let into floor below wooden altar of modern chancel, displays 5 consecration crosses; unknown date

Ovingham cell: altar mensa lies on floor behind present altar; unknown date

Peterborough abbey: intact altar mensa in chapel of St. Benedict, one consecration cross visible; unknown date

Rievaulx abbey: 1. incomplete high altar in original location, c.1152/1200

2. intact small stone altar of chapel in Bay 4 of north nave aisle; unknown date

3. other less intact altars of similar size to above in Bays 2 & 3 of north & south nave aisles; unknown dates

4. bases of 5 chapel stone altars in line at east end of choir; probably late C12

Salley abbey: 1. altar with bevelled top in north chapel of north transept; C13(?)

2. altar base in south chapel of south transept; unknown date

Temple Bruer preceptory: base of stone altar lies against east wall of tower; C13(?)

Tewkesbury abbey: high altar mensa of Purbeck marble longest in country now 13ft. 6in.; consecrated 1239, restored to present position 1879

Thetford Cluniac priory: altar bases in various conditions in infirmary chapel, nave, choir & south transept; unknown dates

Thurgarton priory: high altar mensa recovered in good condition from nearby well, displays 5 consecration marks; probably C13, restoration c.1846

Valle Crucis abbey: bases of 4 altars survive in east chapels of north & south transepts; C13(?)

Wenlock priory: intact altar in infirmary chapel; unknown date

Westminster abbey: 1. intact altar in chapel of the Pyx, with circular recess for relic; mid C13

2. intact tiled platform of altar in chapel of St. Benedict; unknown date

3. intact platform & base of altar of demolished infirmary chapel of St. Katherine; unknown date

York Holy Trinity priory: [medieval altar slab, details unavailable; unknown date]

Abergavenny priory: circular stone bowl with cable moulding, on modern base; C12

Aldeby priory: intact decorated stone font with octagonal bowl & 8 engaged shafts attached to angles of stem; C15

Alkborough cell: plain cylindrical stone bowl on modern base; C12

Alvingham priory: later medieval bowl set on Norman base, lead lined bowl; C12, C13/C14

Amesbury priory: square Purbeck marble font on square base, latter with 3 arched panels per side; bowl C12, base C15

Arundel priory: intact octagonal stone font with rectangular panelling on bowl & stem; C15

Atherstone friary: intact octagonal stone font with trefoil panels; C15

Beaulieu abbey: intact but knocked about octagonal font, with blank arcading on sides of bowl & stem; C13/C14

Binham priory: intact octagonal stone Seven Sacraments font; c.1490

Blackmore priory: intact plain font of Purbeck marble; with octagonal bowl, stem & base; C13

Blakeney friary: intact stone font of traditional East Anglian design, octagonal with 4 Evangelists & their symbols; C15

Blanchland abbey: intact big plain round stone font; probably C12/C13

Bourne abbey: intact octagonal stone font, inscribed with name of Jesus; C15

Boxgrove priory: intact octagonal stone font with shields inside quatrefoils; late C15

Brecon priory: intact circular stone font carved in shallow relief, with some interlace work; c.1130/50

Breedon priory: intact octagonal stone font panelled with shields & tracery; C15

Bridlington priory: intact but heavily restored round font of Frosterley marble on square & octagonal base, modern canopy; C14, C19, canopy 1955

7/2 Blakeney friary, font

Blanchland abbey: intact big plain round stone font; probably C12/C13

Bourne abbey: intact octagonal stone font, inscribed with name of Jesus; C15

Boxgrove priory: intact octagonal stone font with shields inside quatrefoils; late C15

Brecon priory: intact circular stone font carved in shallow relief, with some interlace work; c.1130/50

Breedon priory: intact octagonal stone font panelled with shields & tracery; C15

Bridlington priory: intact but heavily restored round font of Frosterley marble on square & octagonal base, modern canopy; C14, C19, canopy 1955

Brinkburn priory: intact round stone font, wineglass shaped; probably early C13

Bristol abbey: intact small octagonal & otherwise plain font, now in north transept; C13/C14

Bromfield priory: intact round font of plain appearance; C12(?)

Bungay priory: ancient stone bowl (Anglo-Saxon or Norman); C11(?)

Burton-on-Trent abbey: intact octagonal bowl, with arches & tracery patterns; C15

Cardigan cell: intact octagonal stone font, ornamented with floral motifs inside quatrefoiled panels; C14/C15

Chepstow priory: 1. intact stone font on less ancient shaft; C12
2. intact octagonal stone font, recovered from churchyard & now disused; C15

Christchurch priory: intact but weathered 4-sided font of Purbeck marble, roundels & quatrefoils on sides depict Biblical scenes; C12

Church Preen cell: intact plain square stone font in porch; C12(?)

Clare friary: intact but maltreated octagonal stone font in modern church, with wide & shallow bowl; early C14

Clerkenwell priory: intact octagonal font from site of Hogshaw commandery (Bucks.), on renewed quatrefoiled base; unknown date

Cranborne cell: intact octagonal stone font of Purbeck marble with 2 blank pointed arches per face on bowl & supported on 8 outer shafts; C13

Croyland abbey: 1. intact octagonal panelled stone font; C15

2. Norman immersion font inserted into pier; early C12

Dale abbey: intact octagonal stone font with shields on cardinal sides, retrieved from garden; C15

Deeping St. James priory: intact circular font of Caen stone ornamented with intersecting blank arches; C12

Deerhurst priory: intact cylindrical stone font, possibly oldest with ornament in country; C9

Dorchester abbey: intact tub shaped lead font moulded with figures of apostles in relief; c.1120

Dunstable priory: intact heavily restored stone tub font with tapered lower portion & no base, has interlace work around the bowl & rope carving around the bottom; c.1180, later C19, 1985

Dunster priory: 1. intact octagonal stone font with embellished quatrefoils; C15

2. intact but worn old round font bowl; unknown date

Easebourne priory: intact square stone font of Purbeck marble with blind arcading; late C12

Edington priory: intact octagonal stone font with modern bowl, medieval stem & dated Jacobean timber cover; C14, 1626, late C19

Elstow abbey: intact octagonal stone font with quatrefoiled panels on bowl; C15

Ewenny priory: ancient round stone bowl on modern stem; C11/C12

Frieston priory: intact octagonal stone panelled font, with original timber font cover; C15

Goring priory: cylindrical stone bowl recovered from exterior of church with modern base; C12, C20

Great Bricett priory: intact square stone font with inscribed arches i.e. blind interwoven & straight arcading on alternate faces; late C12

Haughmond abbey: damaged plain octagonal stone font, now in chapter-house; C14/C15

Hayling priory: intact square bowl of Purbeck marble (antedating present building) with blank arches per side, standing on 4 corner shafts with central drain & square base; bowl C12, stem & base C13

Hexham priory: circular stone bowl of Roman origin on C13 base

Heynings priory: intact octagonal stone font, with blank ogeed trefoiled arches on faces; C14

Hurley priory: intact octagonal tapered stone font, panelled with trefoils; C15

Ingham friary: intact octagonal arcaded bowl of Purbeck marble, stem & base modern; C13

Lancaster priory: battered octagonal stone font (or possibly stoup) in north choir chapel, with round bowl interior; unknown date

Lenton priory: intact square ornamented stone font in Holy Trinity church, recovered from local garden; mid C12

Leominster priory: intact polygonal stone font, restored after use as garden bowl; C13/C14

Little Dunmow priory: bowl & stem of stone font medieval, base modern; C14

Little Malvern priory: intact stone plain octagonal font, with stem & base broader than bowl; C13/C14

Little Maplestead commandery: intact square stone font with chamfered angles & crude Romanesque carvings; c.1080

Llanbadarn-fawr cell: intact octagonal stone font now restored, with incised plain arches round the bowl; C13

Llangennith cell: intact square stone font with scalloped pattern on underside of bowl; C12(?)

Llanllugan priory: intact circular plain stone font with modern octagonal stem; c.1200

Malvern priory: circular stone bowl on modern base, with plain & tapering shape; C12

Maxstoke priory: intact circular stone font at Stoneleigh parish church, arcaded with figures of Apostles; late C11 or C12

Milton abbey: intact octagonal font of Purbeck marble, with 2 pointed trefoiled blank arches on each side, in parish church of St. James at Milton Abbas; C13

Minster-in-Sheppey priory: intact octagonal stone font with concave faces, otherwise plain; C15

Monkland cell: intact tapered tub standing on square base, almost devoid of decoration; C11/C12

Monkton priory: intact modern round bowl supported on 8 ancient shafts & ancient square base; C13, C19

Morville cell: intact tub-shaped font, with medallions carved in shallow relief; C12

Norwich cathedral-priory: intact Seven Sacraments font from redundant church now in chapel of St. Luke; c.1480

Nun Monkton priory: intact plain circular stone bowl on broad round stem & polygonal base; probably c.1200

Ovingham cell: intact round flat cylindrical bowl on 4 round shafts with central round stone drain, all devoid of decoration; C11/C12

Owston abbey: intact octagonal bowl & stem, with variety of carved motifs e.g. St. Andrew's cross on faces of bowl; C14

Pamber priory: 1. intact round bowl, plain & crude with knobs on; C11/C12

2. intact octagonal font, with quatrefoils & fleurons on faces of bowl; C14

Penmon priory: intact square stone font apparently fashioned from base of Celtic cross, adorned with key pattern; C11/C12

Pershore abbey: intact circular stone font carved in shallow relief with modern base, formerly used as cattle trough & garden ornament; mid C12, 1921

Peterborough abbey: round stone bowl of Alwalton marble elaborately carved with floral designs on modern shafts & base, recovered from garden; C13, C19

Pilton priory: intact plain octagonal font & timber cover with 8 pinnacles; C15

Polesworth abbey: large plain octagonal bowl with plain ogee headed panels, on modern stem & base; C14/C15

Portchester priory: circular stone font with upper floral work & lower intersecting arcading, all on modern octagonal base; C12, 1888

Redlingfield priory: intact octagonal stone font with well ornamented panels on bowl & stem; C15

Royston priory: intact plain octagonal stone bowl on octagonal & niched stem; bowl C13, stem C15

Rumburgh cell: intact octagonal bowl ornamented with quatrefoils, on octagonal stem & base; C14/C15

St. Clear's cell: intact circular bowl & stem on square base, of plain design; C12/C13

St. Germans priory: badly preserved square Purbeck marble font, stands on 4 corner shafts; c.1200

Selby abbey: intact plain round stone font with magnificent timber cover; font C12, cover C15

Sele friary: intact plain stone font with octagonal bowl, stem & base; C13/C14

Sherborne abbey: composite stone font in chapel of St. Mary le Bow, with earlier bowl & later base/stem; bowl C13/C14, base/stem C15

Shipley preceptory: intact font with octagonal bowl & stem in form of capital; C13

Shrewsbury abbey: stone font believed to have been made from Roman capital or upturned base; unknown date

Smithfield St. Bartholomew's priory: intact octagonal stone font of plain design; early C15

Stogursey priory: intact tub shaped stone font decorated with 4 heads; C11/C12

Stow abbey: intact octagonal stone bowl on 9 round stems (including drainage pipe), with non-Christian carving symbols e.g. green man; C13

Temple Guiting preceptory: intact stone octagonal font, with fleurons round bowl & attached circular shafts down fat pedestal; C15

Tewkesbury abbey: old stem under modern bowl; stem late C13, bowl C19

Totnes priory: intact octagonal stone font with richly cusped quatrefoiled panels; mid C15

Usk priory: stone square bowl with chamfered angles & circular stem on later base; late C12

Waltham abbey: intact octagonal plain font of Purbeck marble; C12/C13

Wilmington priory: intact square font with hollow chamfered corners, supported on central shaft with 4 angle-shafts; C14

Winchester cathedral-priory: intact square black marble font from Tournai; C12

Wymondham abbey: intact octagonal stone font, highly decorated with emblems on panels; C15

York Holy Trinity priory: intact but worn bowl of font, plain octagonal; unknown date

7/3 LECTERNS

Boxley abbey: intact timber desk shaped lectern in Detling parish church, reputedly from abbey; mid C14

Byland abbey: largely intact stone base of chapter-house lectern in site museum; early C13

Evesham abbey: intact stone lectern, dug up from site of abbey, now in use in church at Norton; c.1190

Finchale priory: intact stone base with central hole for lectern in presbytery of choir; probably C13

Gloucester abbey: intact stone desk opposite tomb of Edward II; C14

Hexham priory: intact timber lectern in choir may have come from refectory, has paintings of Our Lord, BVM & 12 Apostles; C15

King's Lynn priory: intact brass double eagle lectern; c.1500

Newstead Augustinian priory: intact brass eagle lectern, in use at Southwell Minster; c.1510

Norwich cathedral-priory: intact Flemish brass pelican lectern; C15, added figures 1845

Pershore abbey: intact stone lectern in Crowle parish church, reputedly from abbey; c.1200

Peterborough abbey: intact brass eagle lectern, given by Abbot William Ramsey; 1471/1496

Ramsey abbey: intact timber desk shaped lectern, in use in parish church; c.1450

Wenlock priory: intact marble lectern, excavated on site & kept in adjacent house; C13

7/4   PULPITS

Arundel priory: [intact stone pulpit with rich canopy; late C14, early C19]

Cranborne cell: intact timber pulpit, with rich tracery in blank arches; mid C15

Elstow abbey: intact timber pulpit with tracery panels; C15

Milton abbey: intact pulpit with narrow niches crowned by crocketed ogee gables, now in parish church of Winterborne Whitechurch; C15

Pilton priory: intact stone pulpit, panelled with trefoiled heads; late C15/early C16, sounding-board C17

Totnes priory: intact octagonal stone pulpit, with trefoiled panels; mid C15

Westminster abbey: intact timber pulpit and canopy with linenfold carving in nave, removed here from Henry VII's chapel; c.1507

Winchester cathedral-priory: intact timber choir pulpit of Prior Silkestede, restored with new work; c.1500, C19

♦♦♦♦♦♦♦♦♦♦♦♦♦♦♦♦

Section 8:
OTHER FITTINGS, FIXTURES & FURNISHINGS 2

8/1   **PISCINAS & AUMBRIES**

Abergavenny priory: 1. intact piscina with cinquefoiled arch in south choir (Herbert) chapel; C15
2. intact plain rectangular aumbry in north wall of north choir (Lewis) chapel; unknown date
Aconbury priory: intact piscina with trefoiled arch in south wall (Bay 2) of church; c.1260+
Alberbury priory: intact double piscina in south wall of chapel of St. Stephen; C13
Aldeby priory: intact fluted piscina under trefoiled recess, part of sedilia group (See entry under Sedilia); late C14
Amesbury priory: 1. intact very big double piscina in south wall of Jesus chapel, with simple pointed arch & hoodmould with floral stops; C13
2. intact small squarish aumbry in north wall of Jesus chapel with metal door; probably C13
3. intact piscina with mutilated bowl in south wall of south nave aisle, fitted with shelf & has thick hood & some ornament; early C15
4. intact rebated aumbry outside north wall of choir; C13
Bamburgh cell: 1. intact piscina in south wall of choir forming part of sedilia group (See entry under Sedilia); C13
2. intact piscina in north wall of choir, with large bowl & continuous mouldings under pointed head; C13/C14

3. intact aumbry further west on north side of choir, with trefoiled head & fitted with doors; C13

4. intact aumbry further west than above aumbry on north side of choir, tall rectangular & rebated; probably C13

5. intact aumbry in wall on south side of choir, rectangular & rebated & partly hidden by timber stall backs; probably C13

6. intact big aumbry in north wall of north transept, rebated & long; C13/C14

7. intact piscina in south wall of south transept, semicircular shaped niche & fluted bowl; C13

8. intact aumbry in south wall of south transept west of above, wide rectangular & rebated; C13/C14

9. piscina in south wall of crypt, no details available; unknown date

Bayham abbey: 1. largely intact piscina in south wall of inner chapel to east of new south transept, with trefoiled head & shelf but bowl mutilated; C13

2. partly intact rectangular piscina in south wall of aisle between old & new south transepts, niche with canted edges but bowl broken; C13/C14

3. intact piscina in south wall of inner chapel of old south transept, with semicircular arched niche & protruding bowl; C13

4. intact small aumbry in north wall of old south transept, almost square niche which widens within; C13/C14

5. intact aumbry (or piscina?) in south wall of north nave aisle chapel with trefoiled niche & post-Dissolution added memorial inscription; C13, C19

Binham priory: intact piscina in west side of stone rood screen to south of nave altar, on left side of niche with trefoiled top; late C13

Bishopsgate St. Helens priory: 1. intact 2 piscinas in east wall of south transept at low level marking raised floor serving former 2 chapels, with square embattled tops & cinquefoiled niches fitted with shelves; late C14

2. intact piscina(?) niche in exterior of west wall of south transept, with triangular head; unknown date

Blakeney friary: 1. intact piscina on south side of lady chapel of south nave aisle, with 4-centred arch fronted by modern metal grill; C15

2. intact piscina on south side of chapel of north nave aisle, with simple 2-centred arch; C15, or earlier if moved from another location

3. intact aumbries on either side of deep arched recess in east wall of choir; C13

Blanchland abbey: 1. intact piscina with trefoiled arch in south wall of inner chapel east of north transept, converted into strong-box; C13, pDp

2. upper portion of double piscina in south wall of nave near west end; C13

3. intact piscina in outer side of west wall of tower, serving former chapel; c.1300

Blyth priory: 1. intact but roughly treated aumbry in south wall of south nave aisle (Bay 3), devoid of rebate & wide rectangular; c.1300

2. intact piscina in plain wide rectangular niche in south wall of south nave aisle (Bay 6), small plain round basin in stone credence shelf; c.1300

Bolton priory: 1. piscina with semicircular arch in south wall of north transept near crossing, projecting bowl gone; late C12

2. piscina with semicircular arch in north wall of north nave aisle, front part of projecting bowl chopped off; late C12

3. intact piscina with semicircular arch within rectangular stone frame in south wall of nave main aisle, bowl does not project; late C12

Bourne abbey: 1. intact small piscina in south wall of chapel of south transept, with bowl projecting from ogeed niche; C14

2. intact square aumbry in south wall of nave, with canted sides & top; C13(?)

Boxgrove priory: 1. intact small arched piscina on west side of stone rood screen; probably late C12

2. intact arched piscina with projecting bowl & aumbry in chapel of St. John, both next to each other on south side; C13

3. intact big piscina in chapel of St. Catherine in east wall on south side, with projecting bowl below square niche; C13

4. intact aumbry in north wall of chapel of St. Catherine, with pointed arch; C13

5. intact piscina in east wall south side of high altar, with projecting bowl & simple pointed arch of niche; C13

6. intact pillar piscina in chapel of St. Blaise, with octagonal stem; C12

Brecon friary: 1. intact double piscina in choir under 2 trefoiled arches, similar to sedilia next to it (See entry under Sedilia); mid C13

2. intact double piscina with trefoiled head in present ante-chapel, probably moved from nave; mid C13

3. intact double sedilia with 2 trefoiled arches in chapel north of walking place; mid C13

Brecon priory: 1. intact triple piscina in choir, under 3 trefoiled arches & similar to sedilia next to it, possibly restored from earlier date (See entry under Sedilia); mid C13

2. intact piscina in south wall of chapel of St. Lawrence, with plain pointed arch & engaged shafting at sides, possibly relocated from elsewhere; early C13

Breedon priory: intact squarish aumbry hidden behind wainscoting of south wall of south choir aisle; probably C13

Brewood St. Leonard's priory: intact aumbry in north wall of choir; probably late C12/early C13

Bridlington priory: intact pillar piscina attached to west pier of north side of Bay 1 of church, well carved with coats-of-arms etc.; C15

Brinkburn priory: intact combined piscina & aumbry in choir; C13

Bristol abbey: 1. intact piscina in Elder Lady Chapel, part of sedilia group (See entry under Sedilia); c.1215

2. intact piscina (minus bowl) in south wall of Newton chapel, has simple arch with continuous mouldings; C14

3. intact piscina in south wall of Berkeley chapel, has crocketed gable over trefoiled arch; C14

4. intact identical piscina to above in Berkeley chapel between 2 altars; C14

5. intact elaborate triple aumbry in south wall of Berkeley chapel, possesses 3 trefoiled arches & carved heads in spandrels; C14

6. intact rectangular aumbry in north wall of Berkeley chapel, now has new door; C14

7. intact double aumbry in wall at base of nightstairs, with 2 trefoiled arches; C14

8. intact piscina in westerly bay of sacristy; C15

Bromfield priory: intact pillar piscina attached to pier at south east corner of north nave aisle, stands on square column with triple rolls on each face; C13

Buckland abbey: 1. intact big aumbry in north side of choir (now domestic chapel), niche within moulded 2-centred arch; C14/C15

2. reconstituted piscina on south side of choir, with head on each side of 2-centred arch; unknown date

Bungay priory: 1. intact piscina in south wall of south nave aisle chapel, with 2 drain holes, over niche are carved griffins & mitred head; C15

2. defaced large piscina at east end of north nave aisle chapel, ornamented with coats-of-arms; C15

3. intact tall rectangular aumbry (or locker) within interior of north wall of nuns' choir at upper storey level, rebated; unknown date

Byland abbey: stone drainer of triple piscina in south wall of south transept, bowls are shovel shaped; probably C13

Caldey cell: intact piscina in south wall of choir, with simple trefoiled head; C13

Cambridge St. Radegund's priory: intact double piscina in south wall of choir, with intersecting arches & dogtooth moulding; mid C13

Canterbury cathedral-priory: 1. intact piscina on south side of chapel of St. Martin, with trefoiled niche & wide 3-lobed bowl; C13

2. intact piscina on south side of chapel of St. Stephen, with trefoiled niche & wide 3-lobed bowl; C13

3. intact piscina on south side of chapel of St. Andrew, projecting bowl & with cinquefoiled arch in rectangular frame; C15

4. intact low aumbry in south wall of chapel of St. Anselm, rectangular with rebated top; unknown date

5. intact piscina in south wall of chapel of St. John Evangelist, with trefoiled niche & new base fitted in place of bowl; C13, C19

6. intact long rectangular aumbry in north wall of chapel of St. John Evangelist, fitted with door; probably C13

7. intact piscina in south wall of chapel of St. Gregory, with trefoiled niche & wide 3-lobed bowl; C13

8. intact piscina & matching aumbry on either side of altar, piscina with projecting bowl & both with cinquefoiled niche in rectangular frame; C15

9. intact non-rebated square aumbry in south wall of All Saints chapel; C15

10. intact piscina on south side of crypt chapel of St. Nicholas, niche with semicircular head & fitted with new base; C12

11. intact piscina on south side of crypt chapel of St. Mary Magdalene, square niche with fluted bowl; C13

12. intact 2 aumbries on north side of crypt chapel of St. Mary Magdalene, one with semicircular head & other almost square; C12/C13

13. intact piscina on south side of crypt chapel of St. Gabriel, niche with semicircular head & fitted with new base; C12

14. intact aumbry on south side of crypt chapel of St. Gabriel (to right of above piscina), with semicircular head; C12

15. intact aumbry on north side of crypt chapel of St. Gabriel, with semicircular head & fitted with curious rear shelf at bottom; C12

16. intact piscina on south side of crypt chapel of St. Audoen (Huguenot church), 2-centred arch of niche incorporating inner cinquefoil; C15

17. intact piscina on south side of crypt chapel of St. Paulinus (Hugeonot church), as above piscina but with new base instead of bowl; C15

Canterbury St. Augustine's abbey: square or rectangular aumbry with missing top in 'north' wall of presbytery crypt chapel of St. Thomas Apostle; c.1073+

Cardigan cell: intact piscina in south wall of choir, niche embellished with crocketed & pinnacled arch; C14

Carisbrooke priory: 1. intact large piscina in south wall of present lady chapel, with trefoiled arch & modern replacement shelf for bowl shelf; C13

2. intact square aumbry in north wall of present lady chapel, fitted with modern wooden door; unknown date

Carlisle cathedral-priory: 1. intact square aumbry in south wall at east end of south choir aisle, fits within one of several blank wall-arches; C13

2. intact ogeed trefoiled piscina in east wall of retrochoir, has big fluted bowl; early C14

3. intact big square aumbry in north wall of north choir aisle chapel, under blank cinquefoiled arch decorated with dogtooth; C13

Cartmel priory: 1. intact plain piscina in south wall of north choir aisle chapel, with trefoiled head; early C13

2. intact piscina in south wall of south choir chapel, has ogeed niche with flanking shafts & pinnacled tops; C14

Castle Acre priory: small piscina in south wall of prior's chapel within plain pointed arch, lobed bowl cut away in front; earlier C14

Catesby priory: [intact piscina built into new parish church at Lower Catesby, with crocketed & pinnacled head; c.1300]

Chester abbey: 1. intact double piscina in north choir aisle (modern chapel of St. Werburgh); mid C13

2. intact piscina in chapel east of north transept, with trefoiled head & stiff-leaf capitals; mid C13

3. half piscina in east wall of north transept similar to above piscina, remainder destroyed in late medieval period; mid C13

4. intact double piscina in south wall of lady chapel composite with sedilia, divided by 2 lights & now gilded; late C13, restored C19 (See entry under Sedilia)

5. intact aumbry with door & arched top in north wall of lady chapel; late C13

6. intact but mutilated piscina in south wall of south chapel of south transept (chapel of St. Nicholas), with ogeed & vaulted head, composite with sedile (See entry under Sedilia); later C14

7. intact double piscina in chapel of St. Erasmus: mid C13

8. intact 2 aumbries (one long & other short) on north side of sanctuary of high altar, with ogeed tops & finialed gables; C14/C15

Chetwode cell: intact aumbry in north wall of choir, with triangular chamfered niche; C13

Chichester friary: 1. aumbry with 2-centred head & attached shafts in south wall of choir & west of sedilia; late C13

2. aumbry & piscina(?) in triple niche of east wall of choir, with hollow chamfers on jambs & arches; late C13

Chirbury priory: 1. intact piscina at east end of south nave aisle in south wall, with small round basin in simple 2-centred arched niche; early C13

2. intact arched aumbry to west of above piscina, rebated & with shelf; early C13

Christchurch priory: 1. intact well ornamented piscina in St. Michael's loft; unknown date

2. intact small piscina in wall of south nave aisle (Bay 5), consisting only of small round bowl projecting from wall; C13(?)

3. intact aumbry in north wall of chapel of St. Stephen, square with door; unknown date

4. intact 2 similar recesses in south wall of south choir aisle with 4-centred arches, may have been piscinas combined with credence shelves; C15

5. intact piscina in south wall of Draper chantry chapel, with canopied head & internal plinths for small statues; 1529

6. intact similar piscina to above in south wall of chapel at east end of north choir aisle: early C16

7. intact big rectangular aumbry in north wall of above chapel, not rebated; early C16

8. intact small piscina in south east pier of central nave aisle (i.e. at base of former rood screen), with rebate & pointed arch; C13(?)

9. intact piscina in north east chapel of Montacute chantry, with 2-centred arch & carved head protruding from front of basin; 1280

10. intact aumbry in west wall of north transept, with 2-centred arch; 1280

Church Preen cell: intact piscina in south wall of choir, with trefoiled niche & curious drain apparently in lieu of bowl; C13

Clare friary: intact & weathered piscina with credence shelf in nave south wall, remnant of multi-cusped arch overhead; C14

Cleeve abbey: 1. intact piscina in south wall of sacristy, with arched recess & circular drain; early C13

2. intact 2 aumbries in west end of sacristy, with pointed heads; early C13

3. intact aumbry at west end of south wall of sacristry; early C13

Creake abbey: intact & well preserved piscina in outer north choir chapel, trefoiled head & hoodmould; C13

Croxden abbey: intact aumbry & credence shelf with plain pointed arch above in south chapel of south transept; C13

Cymmer abbey: 1. piscina in south wall of choir with plain pointed arch, base gone; early C13

2. intact square rebated aumbry in south wall of extended north nave chapel; early C13

Davington priory: intact piscina in east wall of north nave aisle chapel, niche with simple 2-centred arch containing plain round bowl; C13

Deeping St. James priory: 1. intact double piscina in choir, with double arch & central round shaft; mid C13

2. intact piscina in east wall of inner chapel of south nave aisle, basin of 7 foils within 2-centred arched niche; late C13

3. intact big aumbry in north wall of inner chapel of south nave aisle, with rebated 2-centred arch, late C13

4. intact piscina in south wall of outer chapel of south nave aisle within ogeed trefoil arch, with big basin & credence shelf; C14

5. intact big square rebated aumbry, in south wall of outer chapel of south nave aisle & west of above piscina; C14

Deerhurst priory: intact ancient piscina possibly of Anglo-Saxon origin, in square headed niche at east end of south nave aisle; C10/C11(?)

Denbigh friary: 1. weathered piscina with pointed arch to east of sedilia in choir, remnants of basin & drain; late C13

2. incomplete piscina in south wall of nave, possesses ogeed arch; C14

Dinmore commandery: intact piscina in south wall of church at east end, niche with ogeed arch & bowl projecting forward in triple moulded platform; C14

Dorchester abbey: 1. intact double piscina in new presbytery, part of sedilia ensemble (See entry under Sedilia); C14

2. intact piscina in south wall of People's chapel, trefoiled head inside hoodmould consisting of pointed arch; late C13

3. intact squarish aumbry in wall on north side of People's chapel; probably late C13

4. 2 aumbries north & south of central nave aisle; unknown dates

5. reduced piscina in south wall of lady chapel opposite shrine of St. Birinus; unknown date

6. intact double piscina in south wall of modern Requiem chapel, with engaged shafts under canopied & pinnacled head; c.1320

7. intact rectangular aumbry with door in east wall north side of above chapel; c.1320

8. intact aumbry in east wall north side of lady chapel altar, rectangular & with door; c.1320

9. intact piscina on south side of altar of chapel of St. Birinus, with broken trefoiled arch inside plain pointed arch with hoodmould; 1225/93

10. intact 3 square aumbries in north wall of above chapel, all with doors; unknown date

11. intact big double piscina in south wall of old presbytery, under pointed canopy with damaged lateral pinnacles; late C13

12. intact piscina or aumbry in north wall of chapel of St. Birinus west of doorway, with deep niche behind simple pointed arch; C13

Dore abbey: 1. intact double piscina in south wall of Hoskyns chapel, with projecting bowls under prominent trefoil & hood; C13

2. intact trefoiled aumbry on west side of above, tall & rebated; C13

3. intact small credence niche between above piscina & aumbry niches, with plain pointed arch; C13

4. intact large aumbry with door in south wall of south transept, with dogtooth along 4 sides; early C13

5. intact large trefoiled aumbry in east end of north wall of north choir aisle, fitted with 2 pairs of grooves for shelving; C13

6. intact 2 aumbries in south wall of south choir aisle, rebated with 4-centred heads; C14/C15

Dover Augustinian priory: 1. intact piscina in south wall of choir, niche with simple 2-centred arch & containing small round bowl; C13

2. intact 2 rectangular aumbries in north wall of choir set one below other, fitted with doors; C13

3. almost intact double piscina in cill below south window of nave chapel, forming part of sedilia composite (See entry under Sedilia below); C13

Dunstable priory: intact rood screen piscina on south side of south doorway, arched niche with spandrels filled with floral pattern; C13/C14

Dunster priory: 1. intact double piscina on south side of choir, with each plain round bowl under its own pointed arch; C13

2. intact plain square small aumbry in south wall of south transept chapel, not rebated; unknown date

Durham cathedral-priory: 1. intact small aumbry in east wall near north altar of Galilee chapel, rectangular & rebated; unknown date

2. intact larger aumbry like above at south end of east wall of Galilee chapel near tomb of Venerable Bede; unknown date

3. intact aumbry in south wall of nave west of east processional doorway, rectangular & rebated; unknown date

4. intact big aumbry in east wall of middle bay of south transept (chapel of Durham Light Infantry), fitted with original(?) door; unknown date

5. 2 large aumbries on either side of central altar of Chapel of Nine Altars, both fitted with doors; unknown date

6. intact similar aumbry to above in north wall of Chapel of Nine Altars, also with door; unknown date

7. intact twin aumbries (i.e. 4 in all) in north & south walls of presbytery west of sedilia, with original ironwork doors; unknown date

8. intact 2 rectangular aumbries of slightly dissimilar size but next to each other in north wall of Gregory chapel, have doors with original ironwork; unknown date

Edington priory: 1. mutilated piscina within long trefoiled niche in south wall of south nave aisle, projecting bowl cut off to level of wall; C14

2. mutilated piscina in small rectangular niche immediately east of above; earlier C14

3. mutilated piscina forming part of sedilia group (See entry under Sedilia); C14

4. intact small rectangular aumbry in north wall of sanctuary of high altar; unknown date

5. intact piscina in east wall of north transept (lady chapel), has niche with trefoiled top & wide projecting bowl; C14

6. intact credence shelf forming part of statue niche north of & next to above piscina; C14

Egglestone abbey: 1. intact piscina in south wall of choir with narrow rear shelf & heavy hoodmould, bowl placed asymmetrically to left in stone base; C13

2. intact piscina with shouldered head in east wall of choir, bowl placed asymmetrically to left in stone base; C13

3. intact aumbry in south wall of choir at east end, oblong & fitted with small shelf in recess each side; C13

4. intact aumbry in east wall of choir at north end, also oblong with shelf in recess each side; C13

Elstow abbey: intact piscina in south wall of south nave aisle, niche with trefoiled top under heavy hoodmold & 6-foiled bowl; c.1200

Ely cathedral-priory: intact rectangular aumbry in south wall of chapel of St. Catherine; unknown date

Ewenny priory: 1. intact double piscina in choir, under plain semicircular arch; late C12

2. intact big aumbry in north wall of choir, with semicircular head & rebated; C12

3. piscina intact minus basin in south wall of former north transept inner chapel, has simple trefoiled head; early C13

Finchale priory: 1. moderately preserved double piscina, with pointed twin arches, in south wall of choir; C13

2. intact aumbry in north wall of choir, rebated & displays chasing for shelf; C13

3. intact piscina (minus bowl) or aumbry in east wall of south transept, with ogeed arch; C14

4. aumbry at south end of east wall of south transept, partly blocked to make way for nightstairs; early C13

Fountains abbey: 3 intact aumbries in east wall of Chapel of The Nine Altars, other 6 blocked; C13

8/2 Furness abbey, choir sedilia

Furness abbey: 1. incomplete but unusually elaborate piscina with remnants of lateral towel recesses in choir, part of sedilia group (See entry under Sedilia); C15
2. intact 2 aumbries in south wall of choir to east & west of sedilia group respectively; late C15
3. incomplete piscina in sacristy on south side of choir, with big projecting bowl; late C15
4. intact rebated aumbry in north wall of south transept chapel; late C15
5. incomplete piscina in south wall of south chapel of north transept, fluted stem with projecting bowl half gone; late C15
6. intact piscina in south wall of infirmary chapel; c.1300
Garway preceptory: intact piscina in south choir chapel, with shelf & trefoiled head; C14

Glastonbury abbey: 1. intact large piscina with pointed arch in south wall of south chapel of north transept (former chapel of St. Thomas Martyr); C13

2. intact square rebated aumbry on north side of north choir aisle; C13

Gloucester abbey: 1. intact pillar-piscina in sanctuary of high altar east of sedilia but not part of latter, has canted panelled sides; C16

2. intact canted pillar-piscina in sanctuary of lady chapel east of sedilia but not part of latter, has cinquefoiled wall panel behind it; c.1500

3. intact canted piscina with small projecting bowl, attached to stone screen on south side of chapel of Salutation of Mary; c.1457

4. intact canted pillar-piscina attached to panelled south wall of chapel of St. Stephen, has fluted basin; C15

5. intact canted pillar-piscina attached to stone screen on south side of small chapel north of lady chapel; late C15/early C16

6. intact canted pillar-piscina attached to wall-panelling south of altar of chapel of St. Edmund & St. Edward; late C15

7. intact canted pillar-piscina attached to wall south of altar of chapel of St. Paul, is accompanied by 2 small plinths for niches; late C15

8. intact double piscina in crypt chapel below chapel of St. Stephen, has trefoiled head & shelf; C13

9. damaged piscina on south side of crypt chapel below chapel of St. Paul, has trefoiled arch but bowl(s) gone; C13

Gloucester Dominican friary: intact(?) cinquefoil headed piscina in south wall of south nave aisle; C14/C15

Gloucester St. Oswald's priory: weathered but otherwise intact double piscina in north aisle, trefoiled head; C13

Goring priory: damaged piscina in south wall at east end of north nave aisle, ogeed niche has credence shelf; early C14

Great Bricett priory: 1. intact piscina in south wall of choir now possibly relocated, cinquefoiled niche with crocketed & finialed gable & restored pain base; C14/C15

2. intact piscina for rood screen altar south side of nave, with ogeed trefoiled head & damaged bowl; early C14

Hamble priory: 1. intact double piscina in south wall of choir, has cinquefoiled head under hoodmould ending in plain stops; C15(?)

2. intact aumbry next to above with pointed arch; C13

3. intact aumbry in north wall of choir, with segmental arch; C13

Hatfield Broad Oak priory: 1. intact piscina in 4 centred niche in south wall of chapel at east end of south nave aisle, elaborate square bowl with 4 drainer holes; C15

2. intact rectangular aumbry in east wall of same chapel, fitted with modern wooden door; C15(?)

Hayling priory: 1. intact double piscina in south wall of choir in twin trefoiled niches, with unusual halfmoon shaped bowls; early C13

2. intact piscina in south wall of south transept chapel, small round bowl in trefoiled niche; C13

Hexham priory: 1. intact piscina on south side of outer east chapel of south transept, asymmetrically placed bowl under semicircular arch; c.1200

2. intact big square aumbry west of above piscina, not rebated; c.1200

3. partly intact piscina in south wall of south choir aisle, niche with trefoiled arch but bowl partly missing; C13

4. intact aumbry in Prior Leschman's chantry, no details available; unknown date

Hinton charterhouse: [intact trefoil headed piscina in north wall of chapter-house, with stiff-leaf in small spandrels; C13]

Hulne friary: 1. small intact piscina with pointed head in sacristry south of choir; mid C13

2. aumbry or recess in above sacristry, with bowl, shelf & flue for making communion bread; mid C13

Ingham friary: intact piscina accompanying sedilia (See entry under Sedilia); C15, also C19

Jarrow priory: Anglo-Saxon aumbry in south wall of choir, niche with semicircular arch & additional shelf; C10(?)

Jervaulx abbey: intact rectangular aumbry in west wall of south transept, rebated; C12/C13

Kidwelly cell: 1. intact piscina in south wall of choir containing credence shelf, with ogeed & multifoiled head; c.1320

2. intact piscina in south wall of south transept (lady chapel), with ogeed trefoiled head & credence shelf; c.1320

3. intact 2 small aumbries in east & west walls of south porch; c.1320

4. mutilated piscina in vestry north of choir; unknown date

Kirkstall abbey: intact piscinas & aumbries in choir & transeptal chapels with semicircular heads & simple mouldings; later C12

Lacock abbey: 1. intact piscina in south chapel immediately north of former church, has shouldered head & shelf; late C13

2. intact 2 square aumbries in south wall of sacristy, fitted with rebates for doors; C13

Lancaster priory: largely intact piscina in south wall of south choir chapel, niche with 4-centred head; 1420+

Lanercost priory: 1. intact aumbry in east wall of choir with segmental head, rebated & slotted for shelf; C13

2. intact piscina sited diagonally between east & south walls of lady chapel, with semicircular niche & pedestal; C13

3. intact big aumbry in north wall of outer chapel of north transept, oblong shaped & rebated; C13

Lapley priory: intact piscina in east wall of choir, niche with trefoiled head, round bowl partly removed; late C13

Latton priory: piscina minus drain & basin in east wall of north transept, has niche with shafted jambs & trefoiled head; C13/C14

Leominster priory: 1. intact trefoiled piscina at east end of outer south nave aisle east chapel probably moved from elsewhere in church, has heavy hoodmould with 3 figure-stops; C13

2. intact rectangular aumbry with metal door in east wall of present central nave aisle; unknown date

Leonard Stanley priory: 1. intact double piscina to south of high altar, under single trefoiled arch; C13

2. intact piscina in south wall of south transept, with trefoiled head; C13

3. intact rectangular aumbry immediately to east of high altar piscina; C13(?)

4. intact large aumbry on north side of choir, with ornamented segmental head & rebated; C12

Lindisfarne priory: 1. intact trefoil headed piscina in south wall of choir extension, bowl gone; c.1200+

2. intact aumbry with square head in north wall of choir extension, high in wall & not rebated; c.1200+

3. intact aumbry further west in north wall of choir, wide & not rebated; C12

Little Dunmow priory: piscina in south wall of lady chapel, trefoiled niche combined with engaged shaft to floor, front of foiled bowl shorn off; mid C14

Little Malvern priory: intact small aumbry (former piscina?) in south wall of choir, almost square niche with small mouldings along edges; C14

Llangennith cell: 1. intact piscina in south wall of choir, with plain square niche & plain round bowl; C13

2. over same piscina is small square aumbry with modern brass door; unknown date

London charterhouse: [aumbry in east wall of chapterhouse behind panelling, no details available; unknown date]

Malvern priory: 1. intact piscina standing on engaged panelled shaft on south side of chapel of south choir aisle; probably mid C15

2. intact similar piscina on south side of chapel of north choir aisle, but has recessed ogeed trefoiled arch at rear; probably mid C15

Margam abbey: 1. intact piscina in south wall of former outer chapel of south transept, with square niche & projecting fluted bowl; C13

2. broken square aumbry west of above, of similar appearance; C13

Milton abbey: 1. intact piscina in choir, accompanying sedilia (See entry under Sedilia); C14

2. intact squarish aumbry on west side of pulpitum at north end; C14

3. intact piscina in south wall of south transept, with ogeed arch & fluted bowl; C14

Minster-in-Sheppey priory: 1. piscina with trefoiled head (niche intact but bowl broken), at south end of rood screen on east side of present St. Sexburgha's chapel; C13
2. intact small piscina with trefoiled head at east end of south wall of south nave aisle (now area of chancel); C13

Monk Bretton priory: 1. intact stone base of piscina containing basin in south wall of south chapel of south transept; late C12
2. similar remnants of piscinas south of high altar of choir & in south wall of north chapel of north transept respectively; late C12
3. intact big aumbry in south wall of south transept, with square head; late C12
4. intact rectangular aumbry in north wall of chapter-house; early C13

Monkland cell: intact round piscina basin in stone window sill on south side of nave, served altar south of screen between nave & choir; later C13
(N.B. Combined piscina & double sedilia of chancel designed in late C13 style are Victorian insertion.)

Monks Kirby priory: 1. intact relocated piscina in south wall of choir, with trefoiled head matching design of nearby but not contiguous sedilia; late C13
2. intact 2 aumbries in north wall of choir, with 4-centred arches & rebates, one larger than the other; C15
3. intact but damaged piscina in east wall of south choir chapel, with trefoiled head under outer ogeed arch; mid C14

Monkton priory: 1. intact piscina in south wall of choir, has niche with ogeed trefoil & 8-foiled basin; early C14

(N.B. Triple sedilia to west of above appear to be modern insertion or replacement.)

2. intact piscina in south wall of north choir chapel, with simple arched niche & small round basin; C13

Monkwearmouth cell: intact trefoiled piscina in south wall of choir; C13

Neath abbey: 1. intact square aumbry in south wall of former outer chapel of south transept, with filleted half roll along sides; c.1300

2. lower half of square niche & bowl of piscina next to above aumbry, with similar moulding along sides; c.1300

Netley abbey: 1. quite well preserved trefoiled double piscina in south wall of south choir aisle, with segmentally headed aumbry next to it; mid C13

2. equivalent aumbry in north wall of north choir aisle; mid C13

3. mutilated trefoiled piscina in south wall of south east chapel of south transept; mid C13

4. intact aumbry in inner side of west wall of south transept, with chamfered margin; C13

5. intact trefoiled long piscina with square & rebated aumbry in south wall of sacristy; mid C13

6. intact aumbry in reredorter undercroft, rebated with segmental top; C13

Norwich cathedral-priory: 1. 2 intact niches in south wall of chapel of St. Andrew, with pointed heads, left is credence niche & right is piscina; C13

2. intact aumbry in north wall of chapel of St. Andrew, rectangular with fitted door; unknown date

3. intact piscina in south wall of Jesus chapel, cinquefoiled head in square frame; C15

4. intact piscina in south wall of Bauchon chapel, niche with trefoiled head under pointed & pinnacled gable; C14/C15

5. intact piscina or credence niche in chapel of St. Catherine of Alexandra, with round top; C12

Nun Monkton priory: aumbry in south wall of nave towards west end, possibly serviced former altar, fitted with modern door of brass & glass; probably C13

(N.B. Piscina & triple sedilia in chancel area appear to be modern insertions.)

Ovingham cell: intact piscina in south wall of choir with simple pointed arch, adapted as modern aumbry with door; C13

Owston abbey: 1. largely intact small piscina in east wall of nave at south end, shallow niche with 2-centred arch & front of bowl gone; C13

2. mutilated recess possibly aumbry or piscina in east wall of north nave aisle south of present doorway, retains some carved ornamentation on south side; unknown date

Oxford St. Frideswide's priory: 1. intact piscina on south side of south choir aisle (Military chapel), with thick ogee surround decorated with fleurons; C14/C15

2. intact plain piscina with trefoiled head on south side of high altar; C13

3. intact plain piscina (or aumbry) in south wall of chapel of St. Lucy, with segmental top; unknown date

4. intact piscina (or aumbry) with trefoiled head in east wall of lady chapel, has shelf & wooden base; C13

5. intact small square shaped piscina in east wall of Latin chapel, has canted rear interior; unknown date

Pamber priory: 1. intact shafted piscina with trefoiled head in south wall of choir, with traces of paintwork; C13

2. intact square aumbry in north wall of choir; C13

Penmon priory: intact pillar piscina located now in nave, with square tapered bowl; c.1150

Pershore abbey: 1. intact piscina in chapel of St. Michael & All Angels, with plain pointed arch & projecting bowl; C13

2. intact small square-shaped aumbry in chapel of St. Michael & All Angels; probably C13

3. intact piscina reduced to shelf on south side of chapel at east end of north choir aisle, with plain pointed arch; C13

4. intact large aumbry with doors on north side of chapel at east end of north choir aisle; unknown date

5. intact 2 trefoiled niches in east wall of chapel at east end of north choir aisle & chapel in north east transept respectively, may have been credence shelves or statue recesses; C13

6. intact aumbry in original location on now external east wall of south transept (next to relocated sedilia), placed within crocketed & finialed surround; C13

Peterborough abbey: 1. intact double piscina in north choir aisle, south choir aisle & chapel of St. Sprite respectively, with 2 trefoiled arches divided by central shaft & shallow credence shelf; C13

2. 2 large intact rectangular aumbries on north side of former chapel in south choir aisle, with rebated sides; C13

3. intact aumbry on south side of chapel of St. Kyneburgha, with sides lined with modern timber; unknown date

Pilton priory: 1. intact piscina on south side of chancel with cinquefoiled ogeed head, foiled bowl may have been cut back; C15

2. cut back piscina on south side of south chancel chapel (Raleigh chapel) converted into modern aumbry, niche with ogeed head; C14/C15

Polesworth abbey: 1. intact small piscina in south wall of nave (Bay 3), with squarish bowl; C13/C14

2. intact aumbry in south wall of nave (Bay 1 below modern pulpit), square & rebated; C13/C14

Portchester priory: [piscina of unknown condition relocated in east wall of reduced choir; C12]

Redlingfield priory: intact large piscina for rood screen altar on south side of nave, niche with ogeed trefoil; early C14

Rievaulx abbey: intact but weathered piscina in south wall of south nave aisle, with multifoiled head under ogeed arch & projecting bowl; C14

Roche abbey: 1. mutilated aumbry & piscina in south wall of choir near position of high altar, combined in 2 square niches divided by common wall; late C12

2. almost intact piscina in south chapel of north transept, with round arch; c.1200

Rochester cathedral-priory: 1. intact wide rectangular aumbry in east wall of Jesus chapel, rebated; unknown date

2. intact shafted piscina in Jesus chapel; mid C13

3. intact piscina in crypt chapel of St. Ithamar, small trefoiled niche on south side; C13

4. intact small piscina on south side of south bay of crypt Holy Trinity chapel, with semicircular headed niche; C13

5. intact small piscina on north side of north bay of crypt Holy Trinity chapel, with niche almost triangular shaped; C13

Romsey abbey: 1. intact piscina in south wall of chapel of St. Anne, consisting of small projecting square basin; mid C12

2. intact square aumbry with door in north wall of above chapel; mid C12

3. intact piscina in south wall of chapel of St. George, with segmental head & converted to locker; probably mid C12

4. intact aumbry in north wall of above chapel, with round head & door; mid C12

5. intact piscina in south east wall of north transept, consisting of 5-sided projecting bowl; C12

Rothley Temple preceptory: intact double piscina in choir, shafted niche with trefoiled head & plain round basins; c.1280

Royston priory: intact stone drainer for single piscina built into modern niche on south side of present chancel; bowl has 8 foils; unknown medieval date, 1891

Rumburgh cell: intact small plain niche in south wall of choir with semicircular head, possibly piscina or credence niche; C13(?)

Ruthin priory: intact piscina in south wall of central (i.e. north) nave aisle, with trefoiled head; early C14

St. Albans abbey: 1. intact triple arched double piscina & shelf in south wall of chapel of Our Lady of Four Tapers; C13

2. intact rectangular rebated aumbry with door within outer wall arch forming part of same composition as above double piscina composition; C13

3. intact aumbry in east wall south end of chapel of Our Lady of Four Tapers, has rebated trefoiled niche; C13

4. intact square aumbry apparently inserted at later date within east stall of sedilia in lady chapel (See entry below under Sedilia); C14(?)

5. intact large aumbry with segmental head immediately to east of above sedilia in lady chapel; C15

6. intact pair of similar aumbries on either side of altar, each has rebated trefoiled niche placed within wall arcading; early C14

7. intact aumbry in west wall of chapel of Transfiguration, with 4-centred arched niche inside square label & frame, with grooves for missing shelf; C15

8. intact aumbry in south wall of south choir aisle at west end, has trefoiled niche & hoodmould; C13

9. intact small square aumbry on north side of archway between south transept & south choir aisle, rebated & fitted with modern metal doors; unknown date

10. intact plain rectangular aumbry in north wall of south choir aisle at west end, not rebated but with canted top; unknown date

St. Anthony-in-Roseland cell: 1. intact aumbry with trefoiled head at south end of east wall of south transept, may have been piscina with bowl replaced by stone shelf; C13

2. intact aumbry with plain trefoiled head at south end of east wall of north transept, may also have been piscina with bowl replaced by stone shelf; C13

St. Bees priory: intact piscina in east wall of north transept (near altar of St. Bega), with deep & projecting round bowl under simple pointed arch; early C13

St. Clear's cell: intact piscina in south wall of choir, trefoiled niche with bowl now replaced by modern shelf; late C13/early C14

St. Germans priory: 1. intact piscina in east wall of south nave aisle chapel, shallow bowl & niche with ogeed top; early C14

2. intact square aumbry also in east wall of same chapel, fitted with modern metal door; early C14

3. intact piscina in south wall of south nave aisle (midway along), niche under trefoiled ogeed head & bowl of shamrock shape; C15

Salley abbey: stone drainer of triple piscina in north nave aisle; C13

Selby abbey: intact small piscina in sacristy (War Memorial Chapel); C14(?)

Sele friary: intact rectangular aumbry in north wall of choir with shallow 4-centred head, now fitted with inner & outer doors; C15, C19/C20

Sherborne abbey: 1. intact piscina in south wall of chapel of Bishop Roger; C13(?)

2. intact piscina in south wall of chapel of St. Katherine, with trefoiled head; C13

3. intact piscina in south wall of chapel of Holy Sepulchre, with ogeed head & credence shelf but drain now blocked; C14

4. intact piscina in chapel of St. Mary le Bow, with pinnacled arch & big fluted bowl; C15

Shipley preceptory: 1. intact piscina in south wall of choir, square niche fitted with shelf; C12

2. intact 2 aumbries on either sides of high altar, north fitted with door & south has segmental head; unknown date

3. intact aumbry in wall on north side of choir, has segmental shaped top & fitted with grille; unknown date

Shrewsbury abbey: pillar piscina in north aisle; C12

Snaith cell: intact piscina in south wall of choir near east end, with niche & round bowl under plain 3-centred arch; early C14

Southwark priory: 1. intact piscina in east wall of Harvard chapel, projecting fluted bowl & niche with simple 2-centred arch; C13

2. rectangular aumbry partly bricked up in north wall of north transept, with partly obscured decorative trefoil overhead; C13

3. intact piscina in east wall of chapel of St. Andrew, with trefoiled niche & small projecting bowl; C13

Stogursey priory: 1. intact trefoiled piscina in south wall of south choir aisle chapel, converted to aumbry with door; C13

2. intact piscina in east wall (south end) of north choir aisle chapel, trefoiled niche under pointed arch; C13

(N.B. Combined piscina & triple sedilia, & aumbry in choir appear to be Neo-Norman insertions of 1865.)

Stow abbey: intact small niche with flat base on east side of nave north doorway, has 2-centred arch & chamfered margin, may have been piscina or more likely receptacle for holy water bowl; unknown date

Sudbury St. Bartholomew's cell: [intact double piscina in small church; C13]

Sutton-at-Hone St. John's Jerusalem commandery: intact plain double piscina in choir; C13

Swine priory: 1. intact aumbry in south wall choir at east end, fitted with new door of metal & timber surround; unknown date

2. intact long rectangular aumbry in north wall of south choir chapel, fitted with timber surround; unknown date

Temple Balsall preceptory: intact but severely restored piscina in south wall of choir; unusual design with triangular shaped niche; late C13, 1849

Temple Bruer preceptory: intact piscina under 2-centred arch in south wall of tower, in architectural combination with adjacent sedile; C13

Temple Ewell preceptory: intact aumbry in north wall of choir, trefoil shaped niche with inner locker fitted with modern door; C13

Temple Guiting preceptory: 1. intact but damaged piscina in east wall of north chapel, with ballflower round pointed arch; early C14

2. intact aumbry in north wall of north chapel, with trefoiled top & rebate for missing door; early C14

Temple preceptory: 1. intact double piscina of Purbeck marble on south side of south choir aisle, twin arches with trefoiled heads; C13

2. intact rebated aumbry with trefoiled head in each of north & south walls of choir aisles, raised in accordance with former floor level of choir; C13

3. piscina & aumbry in choir undercroft, no details available; c.1170

Tewkesbury abbey: 1.   5 piscinas of same design in apsidal chapels, in varying states of intactness, with trefoiled heads under pointed arches & with credence shelves; C14

2. partly blocked piscina in west wall of south transept, with simple pointed arch; C13

3. largely intact piscina or sink in west wall of chapel of St. Margaret; C14

4. intact rectangular aumbry in each of chapels of St. Faith, St. Edmund & St. Margaret; C14

Thornton abbey: intact piscina in south wall of south transept, trefoil arch; C13

Tintern abbey: intact large aumbry in south wall of sacristy, with segmental head; C13

Torre abbey: intact but weathered piscina in chapel of south transept, with semicircular top; probably c.1200

Totnes priory: 1. intact piscina in south wall of parochial chancel, with protruding drainer shelf & bowl with foils at front only; mid C15

2. piscina with front of niche surround shorn off in south wall of chapel of St. Leonard, has shallow foiled bowl with 4 drainage holes; mid C15

3. intact wide aumbry/wall niche in north wall of chapel of St. Leonard, with moulded 4-centred arch; C15

Tynemouth priory: 1. intact big piscina with pointed trefoiled head in south wall of presbytery; C13

2. intact dainty piscina with ogeed pointed arch in south wall of Percy chapel; mid C15

3. 2 intact aumbries in east wall of presbytery on either side of doorway; C13

4. intact & almost square aumbry on east side of piscina in south wall of presbytery, rebated; C13

5. 2 intact aumbries in east wall of Percy chapel on either side of tomb-altar; mid C15

Upholland priory: 1. intact double piscina in south wall of south choir chapel, ogeed trefoiled niche containing small plain round basins; early C14

2. intact rectangular rebated aumbry in north wall of north choir chapel; early C14

Valle Crucis abbey: 1. double aumbry in choir, with two semicircular headed recesses for communion vessels; probably C13

2. intact double piscina in south chapel of south transept, trefoil arch; C13

3. two small aumbries & corbel-piscina in south chapel of north transept; C13

4. intact square aumbry in south wall of south transept to left of doorway into sacristy; unknown date

Walsingham priory: piscina with broken bowl in wall on south side of north choir aisle, niche has segmental arch ornamented with fleurons; C14

Waltham abbey: piscina with intact lower part & bowl but missing upper part at east end of south wall of lady chapel; probably c.1320

Wenlock priory: intact piscina in south wall of south transeptal chapel, with trefoiled head; C13

Westminster abbey: 1. intact columnar piscina in chapel of Pyx; C13

2. mutilated (double?) piscina with shelf in east wall of chapel of St. Andrew, niche with twin trefoiled heads but bowls gone; C13

3. intact twin rectangular aumbries in north wall of chapel of St. John Baptist, rebated & with roll mouldings; C13

4. identical twin aumbries in south wall of chapel of St. Nicholas; C13

5. intact piscina in south wall of chapel of St. Faith, niche with trefoiled head & projecting bowl; C13

6. set of intact rebated aumbries in bridge chantry chapel of Henry V, sited below reredos on either side for storing relics etc.; 1437+

Weybourne priory: 1. intact piscina south side of parochial (now present) high altar, with trefoiled arch under ogeed top; early C14

2. intact piscina on south side of east end of south nave aisle (now main aisle of parish church), with cinquefoiled head; C15

3. intact aumbry in upstairs room of porch, pointed arch & rebated; unknown date

Whalley abbey: 1. intact triangular piscina in south wall of Peter of Chester's chapel; C13

2. intact rectangular aumbry in north wall of same chapel; C13

Whitby abbey: 1. 2 intact square & rebated aumbries in east wall of presbytery, on either side of position of former high altar; probably C13

2. intact weathered piscina on south side of north choir aisle chapel, possesses trefoiled head; C13

3. intact long rectangular rebated aumbry in north wall of north chapel of north transept; probably C13

Wilmington priory: 2 intact aumbries in east wall on either side of high altar; unknown date

Winchester cathedral-priory: 1. intact aumbry in north wall of Venerable chapel, square with wooden door; unknown date

2. intact piscina in south wall of lady chapel, has 4-centred arch & is fitted for shelf in upper area; C15

3. intact big aumbry in north wall of Guardian Angels chapel, possesses stepped arch & is rebated; probably C15

Worcester cathedral-priory: 1. intact piscina in east wall of St. George's chapel, with trefoiled head; C13

2. intact aumbry in north wall of St. George's chapel, with pointed head; C13

3. intact aumbry in north wall of chapel at east end of north choir aisle, rectangular & rebated; C13

4. intact piscina in south wall of lady chapel, trefoiled; C13

5. intact aumbry in north wall of lady chapel, rectangular & rebated; C13

6. intact piscina in south wall of chapel at east end of south cloir aisle, trefoiled; C13

7. intact piscina in south wall of chapel of south choir transept, trefoiled; C13

8. intact aumbry in east wall of chapel of south choir transept, pointed arch & rebated; C13

9. intact piscina on south side of St. John's chapel, cinquefoiled head; C14

Worksop priory: 1. intact double piscina in lady chapel, with 2 orders of shafting under 2-centred arch; mid C13

2. intact piscina with partly mutilated fluted bowl at east end of south nave aisle marking parochial altar of St. Leonard; 1300

3. intact pillar piscina in chapel of St. Cuthbert, possesses rectangular shaped basin; C13

Wymondham abbey: 1. intact piscina with broken bowl in south wall of north nave aisle chapel, niche has pointed arch below square head; c.1440-45

2. intact aumbry to west of above piscina with modern door; c.1440-45

3. intact square aumbry on north side of north nave aisle chapel, with moulded top but not rebated; c.1440-45

Yarmouth priory: 1. intact aumbry in north wall of north choir aisle/chapel, large & square with rebate for door; C14/C15

2. intact pair of cinquefoiled niches with outer plain pointed arches in south wall of south nave aisle, one with foiled piscina bowl & other with flat base; C15

3. intact larger aumbry niche immediately to west of above, with plain pointed arch but no cinquefoil; C15

4. intact 2 aumbries in same wall further west, one with triangular head & other with tall rectangular shape; unknown date

8/2 SEDILIA

Aldeby priory: intact double sedilia combined with piscina, under cinquefoiled arches; late C14

Bamburgh cell: intact triple sedilia combined with piscina, with trefoiled heads & dividing shafts; C13

Binham priory: intact triple sedilia combined with priest's door, used to facilitate nave altar; late C13

Blakeney friary: 1. intact triple sedilia south side of choir, with trefoiled arches & plain dividing shafts (no sign of accompanying piscina unless hidden behind modern altar screen); C13

2. intact window sedile in lady chapel within south nave aisle; C15

Blanchland abbey: extensively restored triple sedilia on south side of choir; C13, C19

Bolton priory: mutilated quadruple sedilia in south wall of choir with intact projecting canted seats having trefoiled panels on their fronts, 3 seat backs survive but canopies gone; late C13/early C14

Brecon friary: intact quadruple sedilia in choir next to double piscina, under trefoiled heads; mid C13

Brecon priory: intact triple sedilia in choir next to triple piscina, with trefoiled arches & possibly restored from earlier date; mid C13

Bristol abbey: 1. intact triple sedilia under trefoiled arches in Elder Lady Chapel, with piscina in fourth arch; c.1215

2. intact & reconstructed quadruple sedilia on south side of Eastern Lady Chapel, with 4 trefoiled arches sub-cusped & sub-foiled; C14, mainly C19

Buckland abbey: reassembled 2 (of 3 or more) canopied stalls on south side of choir (now domestic chapel), with mini-vaulting; C14/C15, 1917

Buildwas abbey: largely intact triple sedilia with 3 pointed arches & dog-tooth mouldings, shafting gone; early C13

Calder abbey weathered triple sedilia in ensemble with doorway to west, with trefoiled arches; c.1300

Cambridge St. Radegund's priory: intact double sedilia in choir, with stepped seats & extended series of similar canopied stalls to west; mid C13 (See also under Thrones, Chairs & Other Seats)

Cartmel priory: 1. double sedilia in presbytery of choir, disfigured by insertion of tomb; C13

2. intact double sedilia in south choir chapel, with nodding ogeed heads; mid C14

Castle Acre priory: intact single sedile in south wall of prior's chapel, with ornate stone pinnacled canopy; late C14/early C15

Catesby priory: [intact triple sedilia built into new parish church of Lower Catesby, with 3 richly crocketed & pinnacled canopied arches; c.1300]

Chester abbey: 1. intact quadruple sedilia on south side of high altar, with ogeed heads & elaborate canopies; late C14, C19

2. intact double gilded sedilia matching accompanying piscina in lady chapel (See entry under Piscinas & Aumbries); late C13, restored C19

3. intact sedile in chapel of St. Erasmus, with cinquefoiled top & continuous moulding; C15

4. mutilated sedile in south wall of chapel of St. Nicholas at south end of south transept, with vaulted top, accompanying piscina (See entry under Piscinas & Aumbries); later C14

Chetwode cell: intact quadruple sedilia with one stall converted into doorway, with stiff-leaf foliage & dogtooth work; c.1240

Chichester friary: intact triple sedilia in choir, trefoil headed canopies supported on nearly detached circular shafts; late C13

Church Preen cell: intact window sedile on south side of choir, below lancet; C13

Clare friary: weathered sedilia in south wall of former choir with sharply pointed arches, originally triple but cut into by tomb & now double; mid C14

Cymmer abbey: weathered & robbed triple sedilia in south wall of choir, with pointed arch surviving; early C13

Deeping St. James priory: intact sedilia in south wall of choir forming series of 6 arches, placed below 6 semicircular heads; C12

Denbigh friary: weathered & robbed triple sedilia in south wall of choir, with arches of stalls gone; late C13

Dorchester abbey: 1. intact triple sedilia in new presbytery of choir, incorporating windowing at rear; C14
2. intact plain sedile below window in south wall of People's chapel; late C13

Dover Augustinian priory: 1. intact 2-seater sedile in south wall of choir, single arch with dogtooth & detached round shaft per side; C13
2. intact 2-arched composite in south wall of nave chapel, housing 2-seater sedile in west arch & double piscina in east arch; C13

Dunster priory: intact triple sedilia on south side of choir, plain pointed arches with round caps on 2 twin central shafts; C13

Durham cathedral-priory: intact quadruple sedilia on both sides of high altar, stylistically part of Neville screen; 1380

Edington priory: mutilated triple sedilia with accompanying piscina in south wall of sanctuary of high altar, seats intact but upperwork gone except for west sedile which retains mini-vaulting; C14

Ely cathedral-priory: 6-seater sedilia arranged in 3 paired sittings located on each side of raised sanctuary of lady chapel, worked into overall wall pattern of chapel; 1321-53

Finchale priory: mutilated double sedilia (originally 4 before insertion of window) in south wall of choir, with pointed arches; C13

Furness abbey: intact but weathered quadruple sedilia in choir, with elaborate canopies (See also entry under Piscinas & Aumbries); C15

Gloucester abbey: 1. intact elaborately canopied quadruple sedilia in choir, recently restored; C16, C19

2. intact triple sedilia in lady chapel, recently restored; c.1500, C19

3. intact wide window sedile (3 seater) in chapel of St. Stephen; late C15(?)

Hexham priory: intact timber quintuple sedilia in choir, vaulted canopies & small figures of angels; C15

Hulne friary: incomplete triple sedilia with pointed arches, in south wall of former choir; c.1300

Ingham friary: intact triple sedilia on south side of sanctuary with accompanying piscina, under 4 cinquefoiled arches; C15, also C19

Kidwelly cell: intact triple sedilia in choir, plain with pointed arches over seats (possesses no architectural relationship with piscina to east); C14

Kirkstall abbey: sedilia south of high altar under round arch , flanked by shafts with scalloped capitals; C12

Lapley priory: intact triple sedilia in south wall of choir west of piscina, with 3 simple arches divided by triple shafts; late C13/early C14

Leominster priory: intact triple sedilia on south side of outer south nave aisle, with shafted trefoiled heads adorned with ballflower & plain triangular gables overhead; C14

Little Malvern priory: intact sedile west of aumbry under south window of choir, in form of wide undecorated bench seat; C14

Malvern priory: intact sedile on north (*sic*) side of chapel of south choir aisle, has plain pointed arch & may originally have been doorway; unknown date

Milton abbey: intact stepped triple sedilia in presbytery open at rear to south choir aisle, moved from former Middleton chantry in south transept; C15

Minster-in-Sheppey priory: intact double sedilia at east end of south wall of present north nave aisle (chapel of St. Sexburgha); late C13

Monk Bretton priory: remnant of bench sedile in south wall of choir west of piscina; late C12

Monks Kirby priory: intact relocated triple sedilia in south wall of choir, with trefoiled heads matching nearby but not contiguous piscina; late C13

Nun Monkton: (See entry under Piscinas & Aumbries above)

Ovingham cell: intact double sedilia in south wall of choir much restored, trefoiled pointed arches; C13

Pershore abbey: intact weathered triple sedilia now located on external side of east wall of south transept, possesses crocketed & finialed gables; late C13

Rochester cathedral-priory: intact triple sedilia in presbytery of choir, display later Decorated style; late C14

St. Albans abbey: intact triple sedilia in lady chapel with pointed gables over stalls, east stall converted to housing aumbry; early C14

Selby abbey: intact ornate quadruple sedilia in choir, similar to sedilia at Durham; late C14

Shipley preceptory: intact sedile in south wall of choir, plain rectangular & under window; unknown date

Smithfield St. Bartholomew's priory: intact & largely reconstructed window type triple sedilia in south wall of lady chapel; C14, 1895-98

Swine priory: intact sedile in form of stone bench in frame of window at east end of south wall of choir; unknown date

Temple Balsall: intact triple sedilia heavily restored; C13/C14, C19

Temple Bruer preceptory: intact arched sedile in south east corner of tower, in architectural combination with adjacent piscina: C13

Temple Ewell preceptory: intact sedile (room for 2) in south wall of choir, consisting of big arched niche with canted moulding; C13, restored 1874

Tewkesbury abbey: mutilated triple sedilia (with signs of fourth) in choir, with gabled canopies now truncated; C14

Tintern abbey: intact benches of triple sedilia survive under window in south wall of south choir aisle, upperwork gone; late C13

Totnes priory: intact plain bench sedilia on south side of parochial chancel, under south window & with seats arranged for 2 above & one below; C15

Tynemouth priory: intact double sedilia in south wall of presbytery, with pointed trefoiled heads & central shaft; C13

Waltham abbey: intact 3 plain stepped stone seats in south wall of lady chapel below 3-light window; c.1320

Westminster abbey: 1. intact timber quadruple sedilia in sanctuary of choir, rest on tomb of Sebert reputed founder of abbey; erected 1308

2. intact large recess on south side of chapel of St. Benedict & probably a sedile, modified to accommodate monument of Dean Goodman; mid C13

Weybourne priory: intact triple window sedilia, probably in combination with adjacent piscina; early C14

Worcester cathedral-priory: intact quadruple sedilia in sanctuary of high altar fronting chantry of Prince Arthur & employing chantry wall as backing; 1504+

Worksop priory: intact sedile in south wall of lady chapel similar to adjacent piscina (See entry under Piscinas & Aumbries above); mid C13

Wymondham abbey: intact triple sedilia (alternatively thought to be monument of Abbot Ferrers) on south side of present high altar, constructed of terracotta in emerging neo-Classical style; c.1525

◆◆◆◆◆◆◆◆◆◆◆◆◆◆◆◆

Section 9:
OTHER FITTINGS, FIXTURES & FURNISHINGS 3

9/1   STALLS, CANOPIES & MISERICORDS

N.B. All items in this list are intact unless stated otherwise.

Abergavenny priory: 1. set of 23 stalls in quire with 16 original misericords, rear stalls backed by continuous part-surviving canopy; 1380, 1493/1516, 1998
2. single stall (Royal stall) east of quire 12 south stalls, possesses tall pierced canopy; c.1501
3. single stall east of quire 11 north stalls, possesses tall pierced canopy; c.1501, restored recently
Binham priory: 2 stalls with original identical misericords, now located in modern chancel; probably C15
Bishopsgate St. Helens priory: 13 stalls of set of 15 in nuns' choir with grotesque arm-rests & no misericords, modernised with supplementary work; C15, C19
Blakeney friary: 4 return stalls & 8 misericords, latter displaying mainly shields; C14
Brecon friary: 6 stalls with misericords in antechapel; c.1400, repaired 1664
Bristol abbey: set of 28 stalls in quire with misericords, rear stalls backed by horizontal coved cornice; c.1520, restored 1899
Carlisle cathedral-priory: set of 46 stalls in quire with misericords, rear stalls backed by individual tabernacle work; 1399-1413, 1433+

Cartmel priory: set of 26 stalls in quire with 25 original misericords, rear stalls recanopied when choir was reroofed 80 years after Dissolution; late C14, restoration 1620

Chester abbey: set of 48 stalls in quire with 43 original misericords, backed by elaborate tabernacle work & fronted by desks with carved ends; c.1385, restoration 1868-76

Chirbury priory: 12 stalls with 9 original misericords now in chancel of Montgomery parish church of St. Nicholas; early C15

Christchurch priory: set of 58 stalls in quire with 40 original misericords, modern continuous concave topped canopy; earliest stall dated 1210, others 1350 & 1515, canopy 1820

Clare friary: [set of 10 stalls in parish church of Belchamp St. Paul, traditionally believed to have come from friary, their misericords have carvings of plain vaulting & motifs; C15]

Dorchester abbey: stalls with poppyheads in quire, given by Abbot Beauforest whose crozier is carved on deskend; early C16

Easby abbey: set of 16 stalls with 12 original misericords in Richmond parish church, canopies supported by detached shafts; c.1515

Ely cathedral-priory: set of 84 canopied stalls in quire with 65 original misericords; c.1341/2

Farewell priory: set of 10 stalls arranged in groups of 2s & 3s with 10 misericords, some with elaborate carvings; C15/C16

Gloucester abbey: set of 58 stalls in quire with 46 original misericords, rear stalls backed by individual canopies; c.1370

Hexham priory: set of 38 stalls in quire with 32 original misericords, now minus canopies; c.1425

Ingham friary: set of 10 stalls per side in quire devoid of misericords, fronted with poppyheaded desks & back-panelling; C15

Jervaulx abbey: timber reading desk in Aysgarth parish church, now incorporating two elaborately carved bench ends probably from stalls; c.1506

King's Lynn priory: set of 16 stalls in quire with 16 original misericords, fronted by old desks carved with coats-of-arms & floral designs; 1370-77

Lancaster priory: set of 14 gabled stalls in quire with 12 original misericords; C14/C15

Little Malvern priory: set of 10 stalls shorn of their misericords, repositioned in present building; C14/C15

Malton priory: 8 original misericords in present chancel; late C15/early C16

Malvern priory: set of 36 stalls in front & rear tiers with 22 original misericords; c.1480

Milton abbey: two stalls with canopies & paintings on backs, also 12 original misericords; possibly 1498

Norwich cathedral-priory: set of 64 stalls in quire with double canopies & 61 original misericords; several periods i.e. c.1420, c.1480, 1515

Oxford St. Frideswide's priory: two sets of stalls in Latin chapel & 2 original misericords, relocated from quire; C14, c.1520

Peterborough abbey: 3 misericords of former stalls in south west chapel, incorporated into modern stall design; C14

Rochester cathedral-priory: fragmentary rear stallwork in quire, benches incorporate trefoiled arches on octagonal shafts; c.1227

St. Germans priory: one quire stall with its misericord, not *in situ*; late C14

Sherborne abbey: original elbow rests & misericords serving 10 renewed stalls with modern continuous canopy, present set probably reduced in number; 1436+, C19

Swine priory: set of 8 stalls with original misericords placed in modern chancel, carvings on misericords mostly of human heads; c.1500

Tewkesbury abbey: 16 original misericords placed in 24 modern quire stalls, also 3 other misericords in nave; C14

Thurgarton priory: 3 quire stalls with original misericords in form of triple seat now at west end of church, also another original misericord on window shelf; C15

Westminster abbey: set of original & later (east bay) stalls with tabernacled canopies in Henry VII's chapel with 40 original misericords; c.1520, 1725

Whalley abbey: 22 stalls with original misericords & high tabernacled canopies in parish church chancel; c.1430

Winchester cathedral-priory: set of 68 stalls in quire with 66 original misericords, stall backs & gabled canopies display geometrical tracery; c.1308 by William Lyngwode

Woodspring priory: [5 stalls complete with misericords in Worle church, with initials of Prior Richard Spryng; 1491/1525]

Worcester cathedral-priory: 37 original misericords in modern quire stalls; c.1379

Worcester St. Wulstan's hospital: 2 fine stall ends in Commandery, probably from former chapel, one featuring dog & the other a lion; C15

N.B. This list excludes collation seats which are identified in Section 11.

Bamburgh cell: intact stone bench adjacent to shrine of St. Aidan; unknown date
Binham priory: 11 original timber benches with well preserved poppyhead bench ends carved with figures; C15
Blakeney friary: intact stone benches under nave north & south windows; C15
Bolton priory: some intact stone benches in chapter-house, with quatrefoiled fronts; C13/C14
Bristol abbey: intact set of stone common benches & individual shallow alcoves round walls of vestibule & chapter-house; C12
Byland abbey: 1. largely surviving tiered stone benches along 4 sides of chapter-house; late C12
2. largely intact set of 35 stone canopied seats for lay-brothers along east side of cloister lane; late C12
Cambridge St. Radegund's priory: intact long stone plain wall bench on north side of choir, opposite sedilia on south side & occupying 5+ bays; mid C13
Canterbury cathedral-priory: 1. St. Augustine's chair (Ethelbert's chair) standing in Corona, Purbeck marble; C13 or earlier
2. intact prior's stone canopied seat against interior of east wall of chapter-house; C14
3. intact set of 2 tiers of stone benches around sides & east end of chapter-house; C14
4. intact 2 small stone elbow seats outside east processional dooway for use of overseers of cloister; c.1490

5. intact stone seat on south side of entrance to pulpitum, fitted with arm rests; unknown date

6. intact plain stone benches around walls of cloister-walks; unknown date

Christchurch priory: stone seat for prior in porch of church; C13

Cleeve abbey: [large chair said to have been abbot's throne now in library of Dunster castle, , made of ash & believed to be early example of wood turning, ; C15]

Dale abbey: [some benches & bench ends with poppyheads in Radbourn church; Imp]

Deerhurst priory: intact 8 pews in west end of south nave aisle of church, with traceried & buttressed end-panels; C15

Dunster priory: intact stone benches along each side of south porch, decorated on fronts with quatrefoils; C15

Durham cathedral-priory: stone episcopal throne mounted in choir, presented by Bishop Hatfield; mid C14

Easby abbey: some stone benches along sides of chapter-house; early C13

Ely cathedral-priory: intact series of stone seats against walls of lady chapel, with nodding ogee canopies; c.1322+

Evesham abbey: timber abbot's chair, now placed in almonry; C14/C15

Finchale priory: many intact stone benches, including prior's seat, around walls of chapter-house; probably C13

Fountains abbey: 1. 3-tiered stone benches in chapter-house; unknown date

2. intact stones benches along north & south sides of Chapel of The Nine Altars; C13

3. intact stone benches along outer walls of choir; C13

Furness abbey: 1. intact stone benches line walls of infirmary chapel; C14

2 intact stone benches line walls of cemetery gatehouse; early C14

Glastonbury abbey: some intact stone benches along walls of north & south choir aisles, also along south & west nave walls; C13

Gloucester abbey: 1. intact stone benches attached to walls of nave & south transept, possess fronts with trefoiled panels; C14

2. other stone benches attached to various walls e.gs lady chapel, cloister walks; C14/c.1500

Hexham priory: 1.stone bishop's seat (Frith Stool, Wilfrid's Throne) in choir; late C7

2. plain bench ends with poppyheads in north transept; C15(?)

3. intact stone benches against wall in east cloister walk; C13

Jarrow priory: 1. timber Venerable Bede's chair, plain design; probably C14

2. 4 timber desks with bench ends displaying elaborate tracery patterns; late C15

Jervaulx abbey: stone benches round 4 walls of chapter-house; early C13

Kyme priory: intact stone bench along each side of interior of south porch; C14(?)

Lacock abbey: 1. original stone window seat in warming house; unknown date

2. intact stone benches round cloister-walks; probably C15

Little Dunmow priory: timber prior's chair (so-called Flitch Chair), probably originally end one of row of stalls made into single chair; C13, C15

Milton abbey: intact stone benches along walls of choir aisles; early C14

Neath abbey: intact but battered stone bench along west side of north transept; c.1300

Norton abbey: intact stone benches ranged along each side of outer parlour; C12

Norwich cathedral-priory: stone bishop's throne in choir, composite job; C8, c.1105, restored 1959

Ovingham cell: intact low stone benches on north & south sides of choir; probably C13

Peterborough abbey: [reputed timber abbot's chair, subsequently in Connington parish church; late C14, heavily restored c.1840]

Portchester priory: 3 stone seats within arcaded recesses; C12

Rievaulx abbey: 1. largely intact tiered stone benches around horseshoe shaped chapter-house interior; mid C12, C15
2. intact stone benching along sides of inner parlour; mid C12

Sherborne abbey: intact stone benches in choir ambulatory & lady chapel; C13

Stogursey priory: 31 timber bench ends of Quantock type, displaying green man & pelican etc.; c.1524

Stow abbey: 1. 6 timber benches with carved ends displaying blank tracery; C14(?)
2. continuous runs of stone benches round south east & north walls of choir, located below semicircular wall arcading with zigzag round the tops; C12

Temple Bruer preceptory: intact set of 7 stone stalls placed against south & west walls of tower, each stall with overhead arch mounted on round shafts & similar in design to neighbouring sedile; C13

Tintern abbey: intact stone benches survive on 3 sides of cloister & in choir & nave of church; probably C13

Tynemouth priory: intact stone benches along both sides of Percy chapel; c.1450

Waltham abbey: intact stone bench on south side of lady chapel situated west of stepped seats of sedilia; c.1320

Westminster abbey: 1. timber Coronation chair stands in chapel of St. Edward Confessor; c.1308

2. intact set of 5 stone seats under trefoiled arches on east side of chapter-house for abbot & senior obedientaries; mid C13

3. stone wall benches around interior of chapter-house in form of triple tiered steps; mid C13

4. intact stone benches on either side of inner & outer vestibules; mid C13

5. intact stone benches around 4 sides of cloister; unknown date

6. some stone benches on east & west sides of south transept; probably 1245-55

Weybourne priory: a few surviving nave timber benches with original poppyheads; C15/C16

Winchester cathedral-priory: 1. intact chair used by Mary Tudor for her marriage to Philip of Spain; 1554

2. [intact timber bench used by infirm monks; unknown date]

9/3   PAVEMENTS & TILING

N.B. All items in this list are intact unless stated otherwise.

Beaulieu abbey: display of square floor tiles in west range undercroft; illustrating several designs such as circles, fleur-de-lys, triangles etc.; late C13/early C14

Binham priory: some areas of plain small floor tiles especially in eastern parts, some set diagonally, colours yellow, black, terracotta; unknown date

Bishopsgate St. Helens priory: area of tiles in boarded over trench marking old floor level of south transept chapels, nicely patterned forming diagonal squares; C14/C15

Bradwell priory: [area of floor tiles, made at Little Brickhill; C14]

Buildwas abbey: large array of encaustic floor tiling in chapter-house of varied sizes & patterns; probably Imp

Byland abbey: considerable portions of encaustic floor tiling almost intact in chapels of south transept, laid in geometrical patterns; after 1177

Canterbury cathedral-priory: nearly intact mosaic pavement (Opus Alexandrinum) in front of site of Becket's shrine in Trinity chapel, complex geometrical pattern executed in marble; c.1220

Castle Acre priory: 1. some small square tiles in north choir chapel laid squarely, various colours but patterns badly worn; C14

2. area of medium sized tiles laid diagonally in south choir chapel, various colours; C14

3. some small square tiles in chapter-house, laid diagonally; C14

4. 2 small areas of large plain tiles in cloister-walks, laid diagonally; C14/C15

5. variety of tiles of different sizes in prior's chapel; C14/C15

Chirbury priory: small area (say 6 ft. x 4 ft.) relaid in south nave aisle, composite patterns from groups of tiles; C14, relaid 1906

Christchurch priory: portions of encaustic floor tiling in north transept; probably c.1300

Cleeve abbey: portions of encaustic tiling in former north-south refectory & south nave aisle, displaying coats-of-arms & geometrical shapes etc.; C13

Coventry cathedral-priory: several sets of encaustic tiles with composite patterns displayed in visitors' centre; c.1360

Croxden abbey: 2 or more minor areas of small square ceramic tiles of varying colours in church; probably C13

Dale abbey: loose tiles in varying condition, now kept in chapter-house museum; unknown date(s)

Dore abbey: tiles on either side of high altar, many bearing arms of benefactors; C13

Dudley priory: encaustic tiles in choir & south choir chapel, some with arms of Somery (two lions *passant*); c.1400

Easby abbey: portions of flagged pavement of nave & transepts, displaying incised circle for processional stations; unknown date

Ewenny priory: rectangular area of large tiles in crossing immediately to east of rood screen & elsewhere, displaying a variety of patterns; C13/C14

Fountains abbey: 1. tesselated tile work at high altar, probably relaid; C13, C18

2. area of small square plain tiles in nave near east processional doorway; C13

3. several small areas of tiles in transepts & transept chapels, some tesselated with various colours; C13

4. some plain tiles set diagonally in south end of infirmary hall; C13

Furness abbey: 1.considerable run of stone slabbing in nave, especially in north nave aisle; late C12(?)

2. tiled floor set diagonally in south chapel of north transept; unknown date

Glastonbury abbey: areas of small square encaustic tiles in former north transept, displaying coats-of-arms, quadrant patterns & floral rounds etc.; C13

Gloucester abbey: 1. considerable portion of encaustic tiled pavement in sanctuary of chapel of Salutation of Mary; c.1457

2. encaustic tiles of sanctuary floor of lady chapel, heraldic designs; C15

3. encaustic tiles of floor of chapel of St. Edmund & St. Edward; C15

4. encaustic tiles of floor of chapel of St. Stephen; C15

Hailes abbey: some excellent examples of tiles in museum, displaying naturalistic & other designs & patterns as well as tiles shapes; late C13, C14

Lacock abbey: display of ceramic tiles in chapter-house, e.g. mythical creatures, geometrical shapes etc.; late C13

Lapley priory: area of tiles in sanctuary of high altar near sedilia, small size with some geometrical patterning; C14/C15

Little Malvern priory: encaustic tiles of sanctuary floor, from same kiln as those at Malvern priory; C15

Malvern priory: considerable number of encaustic wall tiles (usually rectangular) & floor tiles (usually square) in choir; C15 including a few tiles dated 1456

Milton abbey: some encaustic floor tiles in south transept, including at least one from Malvern dated 1456

Monk Bretton priory: areas of small rectangular flagstones exist in various parts of church; Imp

Monmouth priory: sets of tiles displayed on south wall of nave, many different patterns such as mythical creatures

& coats-of-arms; C14 & C15, rediscovered 1732 & again 1882

Muchelney abbey: variety of encaustic tiles from former lady chapel, reset in sanctuary of parish church; various centuries including C13

Netley abbey: area of reset tiling round altar in sacristy, some tiles highly patterned; C13(?)

Norton abbey: considerable portions of floor tiles mainly of choir, in geometrical patterns; c.1312, also C15

Norwich cathedral-priory: area of small plain coloured square tiles in north choir aisle east of reliquary vaulting;C14(?)

Pershore abbey: floor tiles in chapel of St. Michael & All Saints, removed from former north transept; C15, relocated 1862

Rievaulx abbey: 1. large area of tiles at west end of nave with many cracked, they are large & plain in design & colour; C13

2. other smaller areas of tiles in other parts of church, e.gs south transept & near nave altars; C13/C14

Roche abbey: several areas of stone slabbing in western part of nave; probably late C12/early C13

Rochester cathedral-priory: some patches of tiles apparently *in situ* in north east transept; unknown date

Romsey abbey: floor tiling in chapel east of north transept (chapel of St. George), displays knights in armour; C14

St. Albans abbey: area of ceramic floor tiling on east side of north transept within east archway, reset tiles with jumbled pattern; C13/C14

Salley abbey: areas of tiles in transept chapels, diagonal patterns of tiles of various sizes & shapes; C13

Sherborne abbey: areas of tiles relaid in chapel of St. Mary le Bow & ambulatory; C13

Strata Florida abbey: some areas of tiles especially in transept chapels; C14

Tewkesbury abbey: one or two small areas of relaid brightly patterned tiling, e.g. in small recess of south transept; C15/C15

Thetford Cluniac priory: 1. 2 largish areas of medium sized square tiles in choir, mostly terracottas & set diagonally; unknown date

2. area of medium sized square tiles with some set diagonally, mostly plain but some colours also; unknown date

3. area of small square tiles in infirmary chapel near altar, several colours & patterns such as coats-of-arms, quatrefoils, lettering, quadrants; C14/C15

Titchfield abbey: some good areas of floor tiling in cloister, with displays of chequerboard & birds in quatrefoils etc.; late 13/early C14

Tynemouth priory: 1. some large stone slabs set diagonally at entrance & sides of chapter-house; unknown date

2. area of large plain square tiles at north end of warming house; unknown date

Ulverscroft priory: good number of encaustic tiles, with variety of designs especially heraldic; mainly C14

Wenlock priory: a good run of tiles on library floor with geometric patterns, heads & flowers; unknown date(s)

9/3 Titchfield abbey, pavement of ceramic tiles

Westminster abbey: 1. encaustic tiled pavement in chapter-house; 1259

2. much patched encaustic tiled floor in Pyx Chamber; 1291

3. complete mosaic pavement of sanctuary (Cosmati work), composed of Italian porphyry, jasper & marble in patterns of circles & squares (to assist in formation of religious processions); dated 1268

4. similar but less complex patterned pavement to 3. above in feretory of Edward the Confessor; c.1267

5. many floor tiles in chapel of St. Faith; mid C13

6. many tiles on floor of Muniment Room over east cloister-walk; C14

7. altar platform of chapel of St. Benedict dressed with small patterned tiling; C13

Wigmore abbey: several small well coloured tiles on display in abbot's chamber, patterns include fish, lion, fleur-de-lys & quadrant shapes; C14

Winchester cathedral-priory: 1. large number of encaustic tiles in retrochoir, claimed to be largest number & oldest in country: C13
2. encaustic tiles relaid in north choir aisle; unknown date

9/4   STAINED GLASS

N.B. All items in this list are intact unless stated otherwise.

Blanchland abbey: some small pieces of glass in choir, especially showing likenesses of white canons; C15
Bolton priory: 3 aisle windows retain glass, including 2 heads of king & one of queen; C14
Bristol abbey: east window (Jesse Window) of Eastern Lady Chapel retains some original glass, notably seated Virgin; C14
Canterbury cathedral-priory: 1. 8 of 12 original windows of ambulatory of Trinity chapel show miracles of St. Thomas Becket; 1220+
2. several window panels of Corona display chief events from Good Friday to Pentecost foreshadowed by Old Testament events; C13
3. 84 window panels distributed among clerestorey of choir, Trinity chapel, south transept & west window of nave, show genealogy of Christ & His Mother; late C12
4. remains of 'Theological' series in two windows of north choir aisle displaying Old & New Testament coupling sequences; c.1200
5. rose window of north east transept shows the Old Dispensation represented by Moses etc.; late C12
6. upper tracery lights in nave west window display arms of Richard II & his wives; c.1399

7. window in north transept shows Edward IV & Queen Elizabeth Woodville with their children; 1482

8. east window of Dean's chapel displays small armorial panels; mid C15

9. window of chapel of St. Edward Confessor displays 3 surviving figures of St. Christopher, St. Edward & St. Catherine; C15

Carlisle cathedral-priory: two thirds of tracery lights of great east window, represents Doom or Last Judgment; c.1380, 1856, 1982

Cartmel priory: 1. central panels of great east window of choir retain original stained glass displaying Blessed Virgin Mary holding Jesus, St. John Baptist & an archbishop etc.; C15

2. several panels of Jesse window at east end of south choir chapel; C14

3. small pieces of stained glass in south porch displaying musician & angel etc.; C14

Chetwode cell: 3 lancets in south wall of chancel display early royal arms & figures including St. John Baptist & St. Nicholas; c.1260, C14

Dale abbey: [stained glass windows (e.g. stories from Invention of Holy Cross & St. Robert of Knaresborough etc.) used to glaze the cloister arcades, now in Morley church (most in north chancel chapel); dated 1482]

Deerhurst priory: west window of south nave aisle shows St. Catherine & St. Alphege in separate panels; c.1300-40, & c.1450 respectively

Dorchester abbey: 1. largely intact Jesse window on north side of sanctuary shows family tree of Christ; c.1340

2. great east window of choir contains reassembled glass; c.1340

3. 4 small panels behind sedilia & piscina show scenes from life of St. Birinus; C12

Durham cathedral-priory: 1. many fragments of glass mostly reassembled in various windows; dates range from C14 to C16

2. roundel of Virgin & Child in east window of gatehouse chapel; C15

Edington priory: 1. almost intact east window of north transept shows Crucifixion; C14

2. west window of north transept displays angels with part of organ & lute; C14

3. some panels of nave clerestorey (north side) display figures e.g. St. William of York; late C14

Gloucester abbey: 1. great east window of choir (Crecy window) shows Coronation of Virgin; c.1350, restored c.1862 & 1914

2. east window of lady chapel contains disorderly arrangement of glass on subject of Blessed Virgin; C14, C15, modern

Great Bricett priory: stained glass portraying Four Evangelists, originally in east window of choir & now in south side of nave; c.1330

Jarrow priory: circular window on south side of choir, not *in situ*, claimed to be oldest stained glass in Europe; c.681

Little Malvern priory: east window of choir displays partially intact representation of royal family of Edward IV; c.1480

Llanllugan priory: 3 lights of east window with Crucifixion, king & prioress; c.1453, assembled 1891

Malvern priory: 1. great east window of choir retains partial array of original glass, subjects include Passion & Resurrection scenes; c.1450

2. windows of choir clerestorey (north side) display scenes of foundation of priory; mid/later C15

3. windows of choir clerestorey (south side) display Crucifixion scenes etc.; mid/later C15

4. windows of south choir aisle show remnants of Old Testament stories; mid/later C15

5. windows of north choir aisle show mainly fragmentary scenes; mid/later C15

6. one window of north nave aisle includes all surviving glass of 5 windows on this side, mainly New Testament scenes; mid/later C15

7. great west window of nave displays various saints & is believed to be gift of Richard duke of Gloucester (later Richard III) & his wife Anne; 1474/1485

8. window of north transept displays Coronation of Virgin, given by Henry VII; 1501

Norwich cathedral-priory: window (Erpingham window) in north choir aisle containing collection of fragmentary medieval glass; C15

Oxford St. Frideswide's priory: 1. 3 windows of Latin chapel display various figures mainly saints; mid C14

2. tracery lights of east window of chapel of St. Lucy show several subjects particularly Martyrdom of Thomas Becket; 1320

3. north & south windows of chapter-house display collection of mainly heraldic glass; C15 & C16

Sherborne abbey: many fragments including whole bearded figures set in windows of chapel of St. Katherine, formerly of choir clerestoreys; mostly C15

Temple Guiting preceptory: 3 long panels of glass in south window of nave, displaying BVM, St. Mary Magdalene & St. James the Less; C15

Tewkesbury abbey: set of 7 windows of choir clerestorey contain glass almost intact, principal lights filled with full length religious & English historical figures; 1340/44

Westminster abbey: 1. 6 medallions now in Jerusalem Chamber display mainly New Testament scenes, in quatrefoils & vesicas; mid C13

2. another medallion of similar type to above in Muniment Room, in form of roundel; mid C13

3. 3 east windows of apse clerestorey contain glass assembled by Wren, show figures including St. Edward Confessor; C15 & other periods

4. single figures in aisle windows under south west & north west towers, not *in situ*; C15 & c.1400 respectively

5. coats-of-arms in windows of chapel of St. Edmund; c.1270

Winchester cathedral-priory: 1. glass in clerestorey windows displaying canopied figures; C15, C16

2. many other fragments of glass rearranged in a number of windows in church; period represented C13 to C16

Worcester St. Wulstan's hospital: stained glass in Commandery, featuring birds, wheatear, flower etc.; late C15

Wroxall priory: much glass in north nave aisle & some in east window; C14, C15

N.B. All items in this list are intact unless stated otherwise.

Blyth priory: painting on west side of former west crossing arch of painting of Last Judgment (Doom); unknown original date, rediscovered 1885, restoration 1987
Bradwell priory: [series of wall paintings including subject-matter on purpose of chapel; c.1370, restored 1967-84]
Canterbury cathedral-priory: 1. painting of St. Paul & the Viper in Malta, to left of apse of chapel of St. Anselm; C12
2. series of paintings (e.g. Naming of St. John Baptist) in crypt chapel of St. Gabriel; c.1130
3. painting of St. Eustace giving episodes of his life, in north choir aisle; late C15
4. extensive vault of chapel of Our Lady Undercroft painted to depict the heavens; c.1450
Carlisle cathedral-priory: paintings on stall backs of Apostles etc.; 1484/1507
Chetwode cell: paintings in niche east of north choir chapel, featuring stylized leaves & tendrils; C13
Christchurch priory: paintings of red & white roses & white carnations on ceiling of Berkeley chantry; c.1486
Cranborne cell: wall paintings of St. Christopher etc. above south nave arcade; early C14
Dale abbey: wall paintings of Annunciation, Visitation & Nativity on north wall of infirmary chapel (now All Saints church); late C13
Dorchester abbey: (See entry under Reredoses)
Durham cathedral-priory: 1. wall paintings of king & bishop in galilee; c.1175/85

2. wall paintings especially of Nativity & Resurrection recently exposed in prior's chapel (east range); C15, rediscovered 1974

Ely cathedral-priory: wall paintings in chapel of St. Edmund displaying scenes from his life & martyrdom; C13/C14, conserved & cleaned 1992

Hexham priory: 1. paintings of Annunciation & Visitation respectively on panels above north & south doors of pulpitum; late C15

2. paintings of bishops of Hexham & Lindisfarne on west dado of pulpitum; late C15

3. paintings on 4 projecting central panels on upper east side of pulpitum of St. John Evangelist, St. Oswald, St. Ethelreda & St. Andrew; late C15

4. paintings of 7 Hexham bishops who became saints on canopied reredos on north side of sanctuary; C15

5. paintings of Dance of Death on 4 panels in choir; C15

6. paintings of Christ, BVM & Twelve Apostles on traceried panels of lectern; C15

7. paintings of Resurrection & Instruments of Passion on timber reredos in Leschman chantry; C15

8. paintings in north choir aisle of 9 pictures of Passion; C15

9. painting in 3 parts under tester of Ogle chantry of Our Lord rising from tomb flanked by BVM & St. John; C15

Horsham St. Faith's priory: painting of Crucifixion & other scenes on inner east wall of refectory, also other paintings; mid C13, C15

Lacock abbey: partly preserved fresco on wall of lavatorium, shows scene of bishop blessing nun & displays name of Abbess Agnes Frary below; c.1429-45

Milton abbey: 1. paintings on return stall backs of Queen Egwyma & King Athelstan; C15, restored C19

2. 12 seven ft. panels of Apostles on painted plinths (now in parish church of Hilton), believed to be from former screen; c.1500

Norwich cathedral-priory: paintings on vault above reliquary arch displaying pictures of saints & apostles round central figure of Christ; C13, C14

Peterborough abbey: painted timber ceilings of nave & transepts, consisting of lozenge shaped compartments filled with figures of saints & kings etc.; c.1220

Rochester cathedral-priory: 1. well preserved painting of Wheel of Fortune on north side of choir; C13

2. less well preserved frescoes of Crucifixion & St. Andrew in south choir aisle; C13

3. Venetian painting of St. Sebastian & St. Roch within Bishop Lowe's monument in chapel of St. John Baptist; c.1500

Romsey abbey: 1. (See entry under Reredoses)

2. wall painting south side of north arch in retrochoir, depicts scenes from life possibly of St. Nicholas; C13

3. painting on wood of priest at prayer in retrochoir, origin unknown; late C15/early C16

St. Albans abbey: 1. paintings on south sides of Norman north arcade piers displaying pictures of saints including St. Christopher & St. Thomas of Canterbury; late C13, C14

2. partly preserved paintings on west sides of Norman north arcade piers displaying mainly New Testament scenes; c.1215-1275

3. various wall paintings (some not complete) in eastern parts of church, especially figure of St. William of York in north east corner of feretory; c.1330, C15

4. wall painting of scene displaying Doubting Thomas on east side of north transept; C15

5. painting of seated figure of King Offa in north choir aisle; probably early C15

6. painting of Christ in Majesty on east side of east crossing arch, flanked by saints in niches; mid C13

7. painting over 6. above of Eagle & Lamb (badge of Abbot Wheathampstead) & shields; C15

8. original paintings on timber vault over choir; C13, repainted C15, repaired & repainted 1930+

9. paintings on coffered panels of ceiling of nave over quire, sacred monograms & coats-of-arms, also 2 with Coronation of Virgin; C15, restored early C20

10.some original paintings on panelled flat ceiling of crossing, displaying Tudor roses & shields; early C16

Shulbrede priory: [faded set of frescoes on walls of prior's apartment, featuring animals in dialogue about Nativity; mid C16]

Stow abbey: remnant of painting of St. Thomas Becket on east wall of north transept over altar, late C12/early C13

Waltham abbey: Doom painting on east wall of lady chapel; C15, discovered 1876

Westminster abbey: 1. large panelled portrait in nave against south west tower of Richard II, in full regalia & seated on throne; c.1385-90

2. wall painting of St. Faith in her chapel; c.1270

3. 2 large wall paintings on south wall of south transept show St. Christopher & Incredulity of St. Thomas; c.1295

4. series of damaged wall paintings in chapter-house, show New Testament scenes such as Last Judgment & Apocalypse; late C14-early C15

5. damaged panel paintings at rear of sedilia in sanctuary of high altar; c.1308 (See also entry under Sedilia)

6. series of paintings, some damaged, on former reredos or retable of high altar, displaying theme of Christ as Creator of World; 1241+ (See. entry under Reredoses)

Winchester cathedral: 1. largely preserved wall & vault paintings in chapel of Holy Sepulchre, displaying many NT scenes etc. ; c.1230

2. vault paintings in Guardian Angels' chapel display angels in roundels on vault; c.1240

3. vault paintings in Langton chantry chapel; unknown date

4. wall paintings of scenes of Our Lady in lady chapel, coloured in browns & greys; early C16

Worcester cathedral-priory: deteriorated painting of Christ in Majesty on east wall of refectory; c.1220/30

Worcester St. Wulstan's hospital: wall paintings in upstairs room of Commandery, of religious subjects (e.gs Martyrdom of St. Erasmus, Crucifixion, Saints); early C16

9/6   STATUARY & SCULPTURE

N.B. 1. These entries do not normally include references to work on tombs.

2.   All items in this list are intact unless stated otherwise.

Abergavenny priory: incomplete representation in timber of genealogy of Christ from Jesse; C15

Barking abbey: weatherworn & defaced stone Holy Rood in upper storey chapel of gatehouse, object of medieval pilgrimage; C12

Breedon priory: 1. series of Anglo-Saxon carvings comprising 63 ft. of interior wall friezes, displaying narrow vine scrolls; C8

2. series of 'inhabited vine scrolls', wider than above & full of mythical beasts, birds & human figures; C8

3. series of panelled figures of BVM & other saints; C8

4. figure of Breedon Angel; c.800

5.small collection of free-standing cross fragments; C9/C10

Bridlington priory: exquisite figure of woman's head carved on nave springer (The Smiling Lady); late C13

Bristol abbey: Saxon stone coffin-lid displaying Harrowing of Hell, may have come from Shobden; c.1000/1050, rediscovered 1831

Caldey cell: 6 ft. high Caldey Stone, with Ogham & Latin inscriptions; early C6

Canterbury cathedral-priory: 1. rich series of carved Romanesque capitals in crypt of church, displaying much bestial work; 1096-c.1100

2. 6 original statues in good condition of kings on pulpitum; early C15

Carlisle cathedral-priory: 1. alabaster panel of Crucifixion in chapel of St. Catherine, Nottingham school; C14/C15

2. set of 14 carved stone capitals in choir, including Labours of the Months; mid C14

Cleeve abbey: 1. figure of BVM with Child in half-relief in panel on front face of inner gatehouse; C15/C16

2. Crucifixion figure in high relief on rear face of inner gatehouse; C15/C16

Croyland abbey: part surviving array of large figures in niches or on panels of ruined west front of church; C13, C15

Deerhurst priory: stone carving of Deerhurst Angel on exterior side of apse arch, displays Byzantine influence; C10

Dore abbey: some nave roof bosses survive, e.g. displaying Coronation of Virgin with Christ etc.; late C13/early C14

Durham cathedral-priory: 1. statue of St. Cuthbert in shrine area, holding head of St. Oswald; early C14

2. collection of various pre-Conquest stone carvings in dormitory; c.1000

Elstow abbey: weathered tympanum over north doorway of nave, displaying Our Lord in attitude of blessing with St. Peter & St. John; C11

Ely cathedral-priory: incomplete collection of sculpture work in lady chapel, based on Life & Miracles of Virgin; c.1322+

Forde abbey: stone figures of St. Catherine & Queen Margaret in alcove of great hall, originally located at west door of conventual church; C13/C14

Hailes abbey: 6 great bosses from chapter-house in good condition in museum, one displaying Christ wrestling with Satan; C13

Haughmond abbey: 1. figures of St. Paul & St. Peter carved on shafts of west processional doorway; C14

2. figures of 8 saints carved on shafts of entrances to chapter-house; C14

Hexham priory: 1. rough stone carving of St. Christopher at entrance to Prior Leschman's chantry; unknown date

2. series of crude stone carvings on north face of Prior Leschman's chantry of mainly grotesque & bizarre figures; C15

Kidwelly cell: alabaster effigy of Madonna & Infant Saviour in choir; C14

Kirkham priory: part surviving array of religious figures under small canopies with seated figure of Christ in central vesica, on front facade of ruined gatehouse; late C13

Kyme priory: 1. worn stone statue of Coronation of Virgin within ogeed niche over south porch entrance; C14

2. Anglo-Saxon sculptural fragments built into interior of north wall behind chancel panelling; C7/C8

Lanercost priory: statue of St. Mary Magdalene in gable niche of west front of church; C13

Lastingham abbey: pieces of Anglo-Saxon crosses of several dates associated with pre-Norman monastery; late C8-C11

Malmesbury abbey: orders of arch of inner doorway of south porch display important carvings in semi-relief of many biblical scenes & figures; c.1170

Milton abbey: statue of St. James the Great (of Compostella), bearded & wearing brimmed hat; C15

Norton abbey: free standing large statue of St. Christopher with Infant Jesus in outer parlour, not *in situ*; C14

Norwich cathedral-priory: 1. nearly 400 bosses of cloister-walk vaulting, displaying many biblical & other scenes; C14/C15

2. 47 bosses of lierne vault of choir, displaying mainly miracles of Virgin; C15

3. effigy now believed to be of St. Felix, attached to wall of ambulatory; unknown date but very early

Pershore abbey: 41 bosses enrich choir vault, carved in naturalistic style & are all different with green men etc.; c.1288+

Peterborough abbey: Hedda or Monks' Stone at east end of choir apse, 12 figures on 2 faces; C9

Rochester cathedral-priory: 1. well preserved elaborate sculpture & detail on chapter-room doorway, showing great scholars & teachers of the church; c.1350
2. well preserved sculptured tympanum depicting Our Lord in Glory over great west door of nave; late C12
Romsey abbey: 1. weather worn crucifix (Romsey Rood) attached to outer side of west wall of south transept; early C11(?)
2. low-relief stone carving of Crucifixion scene in chapel of St. Anne at east end of south choir aisle; c.960
St. Bees priory: large dragon over gateway west of nave; C11/C12
Sandford preceptory: [alabaster relief of Assumption of Virgin surrounded by angels, with traces of red colouring; C15]
Sherborne abbey: wooden statue of St. James in chapel of Holy Sepulchre, Spanish; C15
Thorney abbey: complete set of 9 statues of Anglo-Saxon saints etc. in high niches of west front; c.1400
Thornton abbey: part surviving array of large & small religious figures in niches on front facade of great gatehouse; c.1380
Wenlock priory: 2 panels of lavatorium including one of Christ on Lake; late C12
Westminster abbey: 1. large figures of Gabriel & Virgin Mary in Annunciation scene at inner exit from chapter-house; c.1253
2. niche figures in reredos of altar of bridge chantry chapel of Henry V, including patron saints of England & France etc.;1440-48+
3. series of niche figures mostly of saints, undamaged in sub-chapels of Henry VII's chapel; 1504+

4. series of 76 smaller figures of saints etc. than above at triforium level of central aisle of Henry VII's chapel; 1504+

Winchester cathedral-priory: 1. headless stone statue executed in English style near entrance to Langton Chantry chapel, possibly representing Ecclesia or Synagogue; c.1230

2. small demi-figure of Winchester Madonna, placed near bishop's throne; c.1500

3. dignified representation of head of God in library; unknown date

Worcester cathedral-priory: 1. preserved but chipped effigy of King John on tomb, facial likeness believed to be based on fact; c.1230

2. tryptych in Dean's chapel featuring Nottingham alabaster figure of Madonna & Child; c.1470

York St. Mary's abbey: collection of carved stone figures (notably Moses & St. John Evangelist) & other sculpture including bosses; mostly late C12

◆◆◆◆◆◆◆◆◆◆◆◆◆◆◆◆

Section 10:
CHANTRIES, SHRINES & TOMBS

10/1   CHANTRIES & CHANTRY CHAPELS

Bamburgh cell: chantry of Thomas de Bamburgh: occupying north transept known as Fowberry Porch, with bequest continuing today; 1333+

Bath cathedral-priory: chantry of Prior William Bird: intact stone-cage chapel in south arcade of choir; early C16

Boxgrove priory: chantry of Thomas lord De La Warr: intact stone-cage chapel on south side of choir; mid C16

Brecon priory: intact Havard chantry: chapel to north of choir & east of north transept; early C14

Bristol abbey: 1. chantry of Thomas lord Berkeley: intact antechapel/sacristry & chapel projecting southwards from choir; early C14

2. Newton chantry: intact chapel to east of south transept, contains chantry tomb-chest probably of grandson (died c.1500) of Sir Richard Newton, tomb decorated with lozenges; mid C14

Canterbury cathedral-priory: 1. chantry of Edward Black Prince: intact double apsidal chapel now Huguenot church (inner chapel of St. Audoen & outer chapel of St. Paulinus) in crypt below south east transept, with semicircular apses; c.1095, refurbished 1363

2. chantry of Henry IV: intact small chapel of St. Edward Confessor north of north choir ambulatory; c.1435

3. chantry of Archbishop William Wareham: chapel destroyed but adjacent tomb survives in north transept; 1507

4. chantry of Joan lady Mohun: mutilated tomb within still existing earlier crypt chapel of Our Lady Undercroft; c.1396

Carlisle cathedral-priory: chantry of John de Capella: intact timber screened chapel dedicated to St. Catherine to east of south transept; C13, screens c.1500

Christchurch priory: 1. chantry of Margaret countess of Salisbury: intact stone-cage chapel on north side of choir; built 1529

2. chantry of Prior John Draper: intact screened chapel (& now vestry) within east end of south choir aisle ; 1529

3. Berkeley chantry: intact stone-cage chapel on north side of choir; c.1486

4. chantry of Robert Harys: intact stone-cage chapel on south side of choir; 1525

5. chantry of Lady Alice West: intact wall-tomb on south side of lady chapel; c.1395+

6. chantry of Thomas Lord West: intact wall-tomb on north side of lady chapel; c.1406

7. Montacute chantry: intact double chapel on east side of north transept; 1280

Durham cathedral-priory: 1. chantry of Bishop Thomas Hatfield: intact 2-storeyed structure in choir consisting of small chapel & tomb with bishop's throne overhead; 1362+

2. Neville family chantry: tombs & slight indications of destroyed screened chapel between 2 bays of south nave arcade; 1417

Edington priory: intact free-standing stone-cage chantry of Sir Ralph Cheney (probably) under arch of south nave arcade; c.1401

Ely cathedral-priory: 1. chantry of Bishop John Alcock: intact stone screened chapel within east end of north choir aisle; 1488+

2. chantry of Bishop Nicholas West: intact stone screened chapel within east end of south choir aisle; 1525-33

3. chantry of Bishop Hugh Northwold: intact chapel of St. Edmund in north transept may have been location of chantry, tomb in north choir aisle; c.1254

4. chantry of Bishop Redman: intact canopied tomb on north side of presbytery; early C16

Gloucester abbey: 1. chantry of Abbot William Parker: intact stone-cage chapel on north side of choir; c.1535

2. chantry of Abbot Thomas Seabroke: intact screened chapel of Salutation of Mary occupying space under Bay 1 arch of south nave arcade; c.1457

3. chantry believed to be of Abbot John Browne: intact timber screened chapel of St. John Baptist between south crossing piers; c.1514

Hexham priory: 1. chantry of Prior Rowland Leschman: intact stone and timber screened chapel between sanctuary & north choir aisle; c.1490

2. chantry of Prior Robert Ogle: intact re-erected & restored timber screened chapel between presbytery & south choir aisle; c.1410, C19/C20

Malvern priory: chantry of unknown person : intact 2-bay open arched sunken chapel below Knotsford tomb to south of sanctuary; C15

Milton abbey: chantry of Abbot William Middleton: architectural vestiges in south transept; c.1481+

Norwich cathedral-priory: 1. chantry of Bishop James Goldwell: intact canopied chapel on south side of choir; c.1490

2. chantry of Bishop Richard Nykke or Nix: vaulted chapel now minus screens in Bays 7 & 8 of south nave aisle; c.1530

3. chantry of Sir James Hobart: intact tomb on north side of nave; 1506+

4. chantry of Prior Bozoun; low recess under arcade of south choir aisle; early C16

Pilton priory: chantry of Sir William de Raleghe: intact chapel on south side of parochial chancel; 1320

Rochester cathedral-priory: 1. chantry of Bishop Hamo de Hythe: no surviving chapel but intact arched wall-tomb to north of choir; c.1352

2. chantry of Bishop John de Sheppey: no surviving chapel but intact canopied & effigied tomb in north choir aisle; c.1360

St. Albans abbey: 1. chantry of Humphrey duke of Gloucester: intact 2-storeyed open arched chapel to south of shrine of St. Alban; c.1444

2. chantry of Abbot Thomas Ramryge: intact stone-cage chapel on north side of sanctuary; c.1519

3. chantry of Abbot William Wallingford: intact chapel with wide arch closed by ironwork on south side of sanctuary; 1471/1483

4. chantry of Abbot Wheathampstead: intact framed doorway flanked by 2 traceried niches in south wall of south choir aisle (opposite Humphrey chantry) leads to destroyed chantry chapel; c.1420

Selby abbey: chantry of Archbishop Lathom: intact chapel (now vestry) on east side of north transept; 1476

Snaith cell: chantry founded by Revd. Henry Snayth: intact chantry chapel of St. James (now Boynton chapel) comprising transept north of 'crossing'; 1380

Southwark priory: chantry of John Gower: chapel destroyed but intact canopied wall-tomb survives in north nave aisle; c.1408

Swine priory: Hilton chantry: intact chapel within east end of north choir aisle, divided by oak screen from remainder of aisle & now mortuary chapel; 1531

Tewkesbury abbey: 1. chantry of Robert fitzHamon: intact stone-cage chapel on north side of presbytery; c.1395

2. chantry of Edward lord Despenser: intact stone-cage chapel of St. Mary & Holy Trinity on south side of presbytery; 1390/1400

3. chantry of Richard Beauchamp earl of Worcester: intact stone-cage Warwick chapel on north side of presbytery; 1422

Tynemouth priory: chantry of Henry Percy earl of Northumberland: intact chapel built to east of ruined choir; c.1450

Westminster abbey: 1. chantry of Henry VII: intact small screened inner chapel containing tomb of king & his wife Elizabeth of York, in turn constructed within new lady chapel to east of ambulatory of choir (See also entry under Lady Chapels); 1502-18

2. chantry of Margaret countess of Richmond; intact sub-chapel comprising south aisle of Henry VII's chapel; 1505

3. chantry of Abbot Islip: intact Jesus double chapel divided into upper & lower sections (upper section now Nurses' chapel), located immediately to east of chapel of St. John Evangelist to north of north choir ambulatory; 1245/55, 1523+

4. chantry of Aymer de Valance: intact tomb on north side of sanctuary of high altar & chantry in intact chapel of Our

Lady of the Pew (See also entry under Other Chapels); chapel c.1370-75, chantry foundation 1377

5. chantry of Sir Thomas Vaughan: intact chantry tomb in chapel of St. John Baptist (See entry under Apsidal Chapels); 1483+

6. chantry of Geoffrey Chaucer: intact tomb moved to south transept in Elizabethan period; 1400+

7. chantry of Cardinal Simon Langton: intact altar tomb on north side of chapel of St. Benedict (See entry under Other Chapels); 1376

8. chantry of Henry V: intact bridge chapel over east ambulatory of choir, below chapel is intact table tomb (with restored effigy) marking king's burial place; 1422+

Winchester cathedral-priory: 1. chantry of Bishop Adam de Orleton: intact chapel of Guardian Angels flanking lady chapel to north; C13, appropriated & remodelled by bishop c.1345

2. chantry of Bishop William Edington: intact stone-cage chapel in south nave arcade; c.1366

3. chantry of Bishop William Wykeham: intact stone-cage chapel in south nave arcade; c.1400

4. chantry of Cardinal Henry Beaufort: intact stone-cage chapel on south side of retrochoir; c.1430

5. chantry of Bishop William Wayneflete: intact stone-cage chapel on north side of retrochoir; c.1480

6. chantry of Bishop Thomas Langton: intact timber screened chapel flanking lady chapel to south; C13, remodelled c.1498

7. chantry of Bishop Richard Fox: intact stone-cage chapel on south side of St. Swithun's shrine; c.1518

8. chantry of Prior Thomas Silkstede: intact stone screened chapel within middle bay of east aisle of south transept; late C11, c.1520

9. chantry of Bishop Stephen Gardner: intact stone-cage chapel on north side of location of St. Swithun's shrine; c.1540

Worcester cathedral-priory: chantry of Prince Arthur son & heir of Henry VII: intact stone-cage chapel between sanctuary and south choir aisle; died 1502, chantry 1504+

10/2   SHRINES

Bamburgh cell: floor slab marking shrine of St. Aiden; unknown date

Bicester priory: [part of shrine of St. Eadburgha relocated to parish church of Stanton Harcourt; 1294-1317]

Bodmin priory: (See entry under Other Rare, Special or Unusual Items of Interest)

Chester abbey: reconstructed & incomplete shrine of St. Werburgh behind high altar; C14

Dorchester abbey: new shrine incorporating fragments of rib vaulting of the old shrine of St. Birinus; C14, 1964

Durham cathedral-priory: 1. intact plain tomb chest of Venerable Bede; 1370+

2. floor slab marking shrine of St. Cuthbert; unknown date

Ely cathedral-priory: carved fragments of stone may have been part of shrine of St. Etheldreda, site marked by stone in presbytery; C14(?)

Finchale priory: open stone coffin (minus coffin slab) of St. Godric in choir of conventual church; died 1170

Folkestone priory: [lead casket containing relics of St. Eanswythe buried in masonry of chancel north wall of parish (priory?) church; died C7]

Hailes abbey: stone foundations of platform of shrine of Holy Blood, located to east of position of high altar; later C13

Norwich cathedral-priory: 1. intact reliquary arch & spiral stair leading to former reliquary chapel, upper stage converted into modern treasury; c.1424, 1972

2. intact recess for holy relics on west side of eastern ambulatory, with round arch & equipped with flue to disseminate 'vapours' to bishop's throne above; C12

Oxford St. Frideswide's priory: reconstructed shrine of St. Frideswide; late C13, 1889-90

Peterborough abbey: stone wall shrine of St. Tibba with empty niches, in New Building; C15, modern

Rievaulx abbey: ruined shrine of St. William set into west wall of chapter-house; C13

Rochester cathedral-priory: plain stone slab in westernmost of 3 recesses in north wall of north choir transept marks shrine location of St. William of Perth; probably C13

St. Albans abbey: 1. reconstructed shrine of St. Alban in Saints' chapel immediately east of high altar; erected c.1302-8, restored 1872

2. reconstructed & incomplete shrine of St. Amphibalus in north choir aisle; C14

Shaftesbury abbey: lead box containing bones of St Edward, K. & M., recently reburied under modern shrine in Brookwood Cemetery; died 978, lead box probably C13

Shrewsbury abbey: re-erected portion of shrine of St. Winefride in nave; late C14

Snaith cell: remnant of stone shrine of St. Etheldreda in south wall of guild chapel of Holy Trinity; C14/C15

Westminster abbey: intact shrine of St. Edward, king & confessor, with marian timber superstructure; mid C13, 1557
Winchester cathedral-priory: intact raised platform east of high altar screen on which shrine of St. Swithun stood; probably C13

10/3 FOUNDERS' TOMBS & BURIAL PLACES

Blakeney friary: 1. intact founder's tomb in north wall of choir, converted into easter sepulchre with modern canopy; C13, C19
2. grave & brass of John Calthorpe, benefactor & later founder (i.e. benefactor); c.1503
Bridlington priory: founder's stone of Tournai marble, said to have covered grave of Walter de Gant; c. 1113+
Canterbury St. Augustine's abbey: site of grave of St. Augustine marked on north side of nave under former arcade; died 605
Dore abbey: mutilated effigy of Robert FitzHarold under arch on south side of presbytery; C12
Ewenny priory: tomb of Maurice de Londres, including readable inscription; late C12
Gloucester abbey: monument of Osric reputed C7 founder of original monastery; early C16

10/2 St. Albans abbey, reconstructed shrine of St. Amphibalus in north choir aisle

Ingham friary: 1. tomb of Sir Oliver de Ingham in founder's position on north side of choir (probably responsible for rebuilding choir); c.1343
2. remnant of brass memorial on south side of choir to Sir Miles & Lady Joan de Stapleton (co-founders of actual friary); died 1364
3. intact tomb of Sir Roger (also co-founder of priory) & Lady Margaret de Boys in south nave aisle; mid C14
Lacock abbey: tombstone with iron railings of Ela, abbess & countess of Salisbury, moved from original position to cloister; old stone, inscription probably pDp

Lewes priory: William de Warenne & Gundreda his wife reburied in chapel in Southover (now) parish church; both died c.1085, reburied 1847

London charterhouse: [grave & tomb of Sir Walter Manny, marked by inscribed slab in grass of Chapel Court; c.1352]

Norwich cathedral-priory: grave of Herbert de Losinga in middle of presbytery, marked by black slab of post-Dissolution date; died 1119, slab repositioned 1682

Quarr abbey: grave of Baldwin de Redvers earl of Exeter on north side of choir; foundation year 1131/32

Reading abbey: Henry I (Beauclerc) buried in choir, modern plaque marks spot; c.1136

Smithfield St. Bartholomew's priory: tomb chest of Rahere, under elaborate gabled canopy; mainly 1405

Tewkesbury abbey: tomb of Robert fitzHamon (See also entry under Chantries); c.1395

Westminster abbey: 1. burial place of K. Edward the Confessor; mid C13 (See also entry under Shrines)

2. tomb of Sebert, king of East Saxons & reputed original founder of abbey, south side of sanctuary below sedilia; unknown date of tomb

10/4 TOMBS & BURIAL PLACES OF PROMINENT PEOPLE
(not listed previously)

Bury St. Edmunds abbey: Mary Tudor Queen of France reinterred in sanctuary of St. Mary's church near abbey, site covered by original slab; died 1533

Canterbury cathedral-priory: 1. intact alabaster double tomb of Henry IV & his second wife Joan of Navarre in north arcade of Trinity chapel (near his chantry chapel); died 1413 & 1437 respectively

2. intact Purbeck marble tomb chest of Edward Black Prince, including latten gilt effigy (not to be confused with his chantry in crypt); died 1376

Canterbury St. Augustine's abbey: sites of 4 graves of reburied Kentish & Wessex Anglo-Saxon kings in south transept; Edbald died 640, Lothaire died 685, Wihtred died 725, Mulus died 686

Clare friary: remnant of tomb of Lionel Duke of Clarence (son of Edward III) & Elizabeth his wife in wall south side of choir, tomb also attributed to Joan of Acre daughter of Edward I also buried here; Joan died 1307, Elizabeth died 1363, Lionel died 1368

Cwmhyr abbey: Llewelyn the Last said to have been interred in front of the high altar, location marked by modern tablet in turf; died 1282

Glastonbury abbey: King Arthur's alleged burial site marked by modern rectangle of plain stone in choir; died c.516, reburial 1278

Gloucester abbey: 1. Edward II buried on north side of sanctuary below magnificent canopied & effigied tomb; died 1327, , effigy etc. c.1330

2. Duke Robert Courthose of Normandy buried in presbytery, timber effigy; died 1134, effigy C13

King's Langley friary: [tomb of Edmund of Langley Duke of York & son of Edward III transferred to All Saints parish church; died 1402, tomb 1393/98]

Leicester abbey: according to tradition Cardinal Wolsey is buried in the conventual church, a modern slab marks the place; died 1530

Malmesbury abbey: an empty effigied table tomb marks the burial place of Athelstan, king of England; died 939, tomb C15

Peterborough abbey: burial place of Queen Catherine of Aragon marked by black marble slab in north choir aisle; died 1536, slab 1895

Sherborne abbey: 2 coffins at east end of north choir aisle, removed from behind high altar, said to have contained bones of King Ethelbald & King Ethelbert; died mid C9

Tewkesbury abbey: 1. burial vault of George Duke of Clarence (brother of Edward IV) in ambulatory at east end of presbytery; died 1478

2. burial place under crossing of Edward Prince of Wales (son of Henry VI), marked by modern memorial brass; killed 1471

Thetford Cluniac priory: tomb of Henry Fitzroy Duke of Richmond & natural son of Henry VIII removed to Framlingham parish church; died 1536

Waltham abbey: Harold II believed to have been buried before the high altar of the minster church, a modern slab marks the place; died 1066

Westminster abbey: 1. Richard II & his wife Anne of Bohemia interred below canopied effigied table tomb in chapel of St. Edward Confessor; died 1400 & 1394 respectively

2. Edward III interred below big and sumptuous canopied 2-storeyed effigied tomb in chapel of St Edward Confessor; died 1377

3. Philippa of Hainault wife of Edward III interred below much reduced tomb in chapel of St. Edward Confessor; died 1369

4. Eleanor of Castile wife of Edward I interred below effigied tomb chest of Purbeck marble in chapel of St. Edward Confessor, with elaborate iron grille; died 1290

5. Henry III interred below big canopied 2-storeyed tomb in chapel of St. Edward Confessor; died 1272

6. Edward I (Longshanks) interred below large canopied plain black tomb in chapel of St. Edward Confessor; died 1307

7. Catherine of Valois wife of Henry V interred at foot of altar of that king's chantry chapel; died 1437

8. Anne of Warwick wife of Richard III interred at entrance to chapel of St. Edward Confessor; died 1485

9. Edward VI interred in nave of Henry VII's chapel under nave altar; died 1553

10. bones alleged to be those of Edward V & his brother Duke of York placed in coffer at east end of north aisle (Elizabeth I's sub-chapel) of Henry VII's chapel; both died c.1483

11. Mary I interred in north aisle (Elizabeth I's sub-chapel) of Henry VII's chapel in vault with Elizabeth I, Latin inscription on base of tomb placed by order of James I; died 1558

Winchester cathedral-priory: 1. William II (Rufus) buried in the crossing under a black marble slab on a simple plinth; died 1100

2. bones of Egbert, first king of England, reposited in gilded mortuary chest on top of screen of north choir aisle; died 839

3. bones of Ethelwulf, second king, similarly reposited; died 858

4. bones of Canute, Danish king of England, similarly reposited; 1035

5. bones of Emma of Normandy wife of Canute, similarly reposited; died 1052

Worcester cathedral-priory: King John interred in the choir before the high altar, effigied tomb marks site;   died 1216, effigy 1232, tomb chest c.1529

10/5   MONKS' CEMETERY GRAVESTONES

Furness abbey: 18 gravestones in varying conditions located to east & north east of choir; unknown dates

Lindisfarne priory: 4 intact but worn gravestones located to south east of choir; unknown dates

Strata Florida abbey: set of about 12 graves covered with flat slabs of slate, located in angle between choir & south transept; unknown dates

10/6 HAGIOSCOPES, LYCHNOSCOPES, WATCHING LOFTS & WINDOWS

Bamburgh cell: 1. intact large hagioscope on south side of entrance to choir, filled with Decorated tracery; C14

2. intact lychnoscope on north side of choir, with cinquefoiled head; C15

Bishopsgate St. Helens priory: nuns' hagioscope concealed within lower part of easter sepulchre in north wall of nuns' choir; 1525, repaired C17/C18

Bolton priory: watching alcove or window in wall reached by mural stairway; mid C13

Brecon friary: 2 intact hagioscopes in south wall of choir; probably c.1250+

Breedon priory: intact hagioscope at upper storey level in north wall of north choir aisle; C13/C14

Canterbury cathedral-priory: 1. intact windowed watching chamber for Becket's shrine over chapel of St. Anselm; c. 1220

2. intact vaulted watching chamber (Wax Chamber) for Becket's tomb in Ernulf's crypt, c.1184

Deeping St. James priory: intact but blocked lychnoscope on south side of nave south wall; unknown date

Deerhurst priory: intact triangular squint in east wall of west tower, repeated in north & south walls of nave; C10(?)

Dinmore commandery: intact but blocked hagioscope high in north wall of church, possibly for inmates of infirmary to view high altar; C14

Dover Augustinian priory: intact hagioscope within external wall on south side of west doorway of nave, with semicircular head & now glassed; C12/C13

Ewenny priory: intact hagioscope between former north transept & choir; unknown date

Gloucester abbey: 1. intact lady chapel bridge & 'Whispering Gallery'; c.1470+

2. intact hagioscope on east side of crypt chapel below high altar; unknown date

Hurley priory: intact but blocked lychnoscope window on south side of conventual church, with ogeed head; early C14

Kidwelly cell: anchorite cell with grill for overlooking sanctuary, reached by mural stairway on north side of choir; C14

Lacock abbey: intact abbess's hagioscope for observing nuns in cloister, on winding stair in south west corner of cloister; unknown date possibly C13

Little Malvern priory: 2 intact hagioscopes (blocked at outer ends) in choir, one on each side for viewing high altar from side chapels; C14

London charterhouse: intact hagioscope in south wall of treasury for looking into former church; unknown date

Malmesbury abbey: intact watching loft & windows; probably lmp

Monkton priory: intact but blocked hagioscope in upper part of north wall of choir, directed towards high altar; unknown date

Oxford St. Frideswide's priory: intact loft with stone base & timber upper stage; C15

Peterborough abbey: stairway to former watching tower in chapel of St. Oswald; unknown date

Pilton priory: 1. intact but externally blocked lychnoscope in west wall of central aisle of present nave; unknown date

2. [lychnoscope reportedly at east end of church behind monument; unknown date]

Portchester priory: [squint window in north wall of nave, of indeterminate purpose; unknown date]

Rumburgh cell: watching window on north side of choir; possibly C16

St. Albans abbey: intact 2-storeyed timber loft; c.1480

Smithfield St. Bartholomew's priory: Prior Bolton's watching chamber with oriel window; c.1517

Swine priory: intact hagioscope in wall between choir & present priests' vestry, giving view of high altar; unknown date

Temple preceptory: intact small upper chamber (Penitential Cell) on north side of arch dividing nave from choir, possesses squint of high altar; C12(?)

Totnes priory: intact hagioscope at angle in wall between chapel of St. George & area of high altar; probably C15

Walsingham priory: 2 hagioscopes (one now blocked) in east wall of east range undercroft, fitted with rebates for doors; probably late C13

Westminster abbey: 1. intact Henry V's chantry chapel served as watching chamber; C15

2. intact timber Abbot's Pew, projecting from south wall of south nave aisle; early C16

Weybourne priory: curious cutting (now blocked) in east wall of upper chamber of porch, probably hagioscope; unknown date

Worcester cathedral-priory: intact sacrist's oriel watching window; C14

Wymondham abbey: intact 2 hagioscopes over south arcade of nave, formerly permitting monks to observe parochial central aisle of nave; unknown date

◆◆◆◆◆◆◆◆◆◆◆◆◆◆◆

Section 11:

CLOISTERS

11/1   **CLOISTERS-WALKS**

Aylesford friary: intact 2 walks (south & west) each of 5 bays, now part of house of refounded monastery; C15, pDp

Bisham abbey: [one cloister-walk, part of private house; probably C14]

Bridlington priory: re-erected & restored 2 short sections of cloister double arcading, one of 3 arches & one of 2 arches; later C12

Bristol abbey: one intact (east) walk survives; late C15/early C16

Bristol Dominican friary: intact 2 walks, part of city register office; probably originated mid-late C13

Cambridge St. Radegund's priory: intact 4 walks much altered with post-Dissolution windows, now part of Jesus College; late C15, C18

Canterbury cathedral-priory: intact 4 walks, lavishly adorned with 800+ coats-of-arms recently repainted; 1390-1411

Carlisle cathedral-priory: intact 2 bays of south walk only, serving as porch to refectory; C15, C19

Chester abbey: intact 4 walks; mainly 1525-30, with restoration by Scott 1911-13

Chicksands priory: intact portions of north & south walks, part of private mansion now airforce base; late C15

Clare friary: intact 2 small timbered cloister-walks on south side of west range, probably connected small kitchen to west range: C15/C16

Cleeve abbey: incomplete portions of west walk only; C13, C16

Combe abbey: intact 7 bays of west arcade & 3 bays of north arcade, incorporated into post-Dissolution mansion; C15

Coventry Carmelite friary: intact east walk & end portions of north & south walks, converted into house; C15, c.1506

Croxden abbey: reconstructed 3 arches (½, 1, 1, ½) in museum, with trefoiled tops & no caps; C13

Davington priory: intact west walk, part of post-Dissolution mansion; C12/C13 & later

Delapre abbey: much reconstructed 4 cloister-walks occupy medieval locations, with north walk retaining original walling on both sides; C12/C13, pDp

Dunwich Franciscan friary: high-standing ruined south walk integrated within remnant of former refectory; C14

Durham cathedral-priory: intact 4 walks; 1390-1418, tracery c.1773, timber ceilings 1828

Ely cathedral-priory: largely intact north walk & blocked arcading of east walk; c.1510, C19, 1994

Forde abbey: intact north walk, part of post-Dissolution mansion; late C15/early C16

Gloucester abbey: intact 4 walks with walls panelled throughout; 1373-1412

Hailes abbey: 3 arches only of west walk, probably reassembled; C15

Hereford friary: high-standing ruined west cloister-walk, adapted as part of post-Dissolution house; c.1400

Hitchin friary: [intact portions of west walk (2 arches & part of upper storey) & north walk (4 arches) built into post-Dissolution house; C15]

Ingham friary: high-standing ruined south walk, displaying 4 blocked arches of arcade; C15

Lacock abbey: intact three walks (north, south & east), part of post-Dissolution mansion; mainly C15 but some C14 work in south walk

Malling abbey: length of original arcading in south walk, part of present Anglican nunnery; C13

Milton abbey: intact set of 5 4-light windows with panel tracery & gargoyled buttresses probably from destroyed cloister, reconstructed in north aisle of parish church of Hilton; C15/C16

Muchelney abbey: intact 6 double storeyed bays of south walk, retained as part of former post-Dissolution farmhouse; C16

Newminster abbey: reconstructed sections of cloister arcades; late C12

Newstead Augustinian priory: intact 4 walks but with leanto roof removed & replaced by upper storey, all now part of post-Dissolution mansion; late C14/early C15

Norwich cathedral-priory: intact 4 walks, unusually double storeyed; C12, 1297-1430

Norwich Dominican friary: intact & much modified 3 mostly double storeyed walks (east, west & south); C14, C15

Oxford St. Frideswide's priory: intact east walk & most of north & south walks, incorporated into Christchurch college; 1499, late C19

Rievaulx abbey: some reconstructed arcading in north west corner of cloister; late C12

Smithfield St. Bartholomew's priory: intact east walk, used as post-Dissolution stables & now restored; C15, C19
Ware friary: intact south walk & three bays of west walk, now part of council property; C15, C18
Westminster abbey: intact 4 walks; c.1250, C14
Worcester cathedral-priory: intact 4 walks; C12, C14, C15
Yarmouth friary: intact 2 bays of west walk, probably saved as part of post-Dissolution house; C14

11/2 PROCESSIONAL DOORWAYS BETWEEN CLOISTER & CHURCH

N.B. The location (south or north) of the cloister in relation to the conventual church is given in the Directory.

Aconbury priory: 2 small intact blocked doorways in south wall of nave (Bays 1 & 3), with triangular heads & single chamfered continuous moulding; c.1260+
Alberbury priory: [intact east doorway blocked with 2-light window, with 2-centred arch & one order (shafts gone); C13]
Amesbury priory: intact doorway with pointed arch (now blocked) in west wall of north transept, apparently only route to cloister from church; C13
Bath cathedral-priory: intact west doorway now leading into modern vestry, with 4-centred head; late C15
Bayham abbey: 1. largely intact west doorway, plain with 2-centred arch & one order of engaged shafts; early C13
2. intact doorway from east cloister-walk to old south transept, with series of continuous mouldings; C14

Beaulieu abbey: 1. weathered east doorway, with pointed arch of 3 orders less shafting; C13

2. weathered west doorway, with pointed arch of 2 orders less shafting; C13

Bishopsgate St. Helens priory: intact large plain doorway now at bottom of stairway within church, with 2-centred arch & continuous mouldings; C13

Blackmore priory: intact but blocked east doorway, with 2-centred arch & outer trefoiled surround; C13

Blyth priory: east doorway with 2-centred arch but otherwise stripped of mouldings, now possesses inserted modern square headed doorway; unknown date

Bolton priory: 1. intact east doorway with plain pointed arch, cloister-walk arcading continued over front of doorway; mid C13

2. intact west doorway with pointed arch identical to above, cloister-walk arcading also continued over front of doorway; mid C13

3. intact but weathered doorway from east cloister-walk to south transept, more elaborate than east doorway; C14

Boxgrove priory: intact blocked east doorway, 2-centred arch with continuous mouldings; C13

Brecon friary: intact blocked west doorway, with pointed head; mid C13/C14

Brecon priory: intact small east doorway, with pointed arch & continuous mouldings; C14/C15

Breedon priory: intact but blocked east doorway on north side of choir at west end, with pointed head; C13/C14

Brewood St. Leonard's priory: intact & well preserved west doorway of one order, with interesting decoration around semicircular top; late C12

Bridlington priory: 1. almost intact east doorway, with pointed arch of 8 orders; c.1300

2. intact west doorway, identical to above; c.1300

Brinkburn priory: 1. intact east doorway with semicircular arch, one order; late C12

2. intact west doorway with semicircular arch, 2 orders; late C12

Canterbury cathedral-priory: 1. intact east doorway with label, between east cloister-walk & north transept (Martyrdom), inserted within older doorway & flanked by elbow seats; c.1490

2. intact west doorway with label opening into former cellarer's range, with segmental head & continuous mouldings; c.1490

Carlisle cathedral-priory: blocked east doorway cut off flush with outer side of wall, has semicircular arch but no other architectural detail; early/mid C12

Cartmel priory: 1. intact east doorway (south side) of 3 orders, with detached shafts & highly decorated round arch; c.1190

2. intact & pitted west doorway (Cromwell's Door) (south side), pointed arch of plain appearance & with continuous mouldings; C13

3. intact east doorway (north side) of 2 orders, with stiff-leaf & dogtooth mouldings; c.1210

Chester abbey: 1. intact east doorway of 3 orders with detached shafts under capitals with acanthus leaves; C11/C12

2. intact west doorway with 4-centred head; late C15/early C16

Christchurch priory: 1. intact but over restored east or Prior's Door, rich with semicircular head & one order of round detached shafts; c.1200

2. intact west or Canons' Door, pointed arch with 2 continuous chamfers divided by quirk; C13

Church Gresley priory: blocked low west doorway visible from interior only, unknown date

Church Preen cell: intact east doorway with pointed head (not to be confused with blocked doorway with shouldered arch in choir); C13

Clare friary: intact but weathered east doorway, 2-pointed, with continuous wave moulding; early C14

Cranborne cell: intact but blocked west doorway, with 2 centred arch & concave chamfer moulding; C13/C14

Creake abbey: intact west doorway, with pointed arch & continuous mouldings, said to have been reversed; c.1300

Croxden abbey: weathered & robbed east doorway, with pointed arch of 4 orders; mid C13

Davington priory: intact tall west(?) doorway in Bay 3, with plain semicircular head; C12

Deeping St. James priory: 1. intact but blocked east doorway (Prior's Door) on north side of east end of nave, curious ogeed arch composed of 2 mouchettes: C14

2. intact but blocked west doorway near tower, with plain chamfered 2-centred arch; probably C14

Deerhurst priory: 1. intact east doorway with semicircular head & hoodmould, blocked & converted into small window; C8(?)

2. blocked west doorway with semicircular head; C15

Denbigh friary: intact east doorway somewhat weathered, with 4-centred head & chamfered(?) edge; C15

Dorchester abbey: 1. intact but blocked small east doorway appearing to have been replacement for larger doorway, with 2-centred arch with continuous mouldings; C14

2. intact blocked doorway at right angles to above in north transept, has semicircular arch & one order of round shafts with stiff-leaf on caps; c.1200

Dudley priory: intact west doorway, with 2-centred arch & continuous moulding; C13

Dunster priory: intact east doorway round corner in north transept facing west; with continuous moulding on angle of jambs; C14/C15

Durham cathedral-priory: 1. intact well ornamented east doorway, with semicircular head & 3 orders of shafting; late C12

2. intact west doorway, with semicircular head & 3 orders of shafting, with minimal decoration; early C12

3. intact but blocked small doorway with semicircular head in west wall of south transept, of 2 orders & with minimal decoration; early C12

Easebourne priory: intact single doorway almost halfway along north cloister-walk (There never was a west doorway), with 2-centred arch; C13

Edington priory: intact east doorway with 4-centred arch, has a continuous casement moulding displaying fleurons; C15

Egglestone abbey: intact small west doorway, with semicircular head & continuous bevelled moulding; c.1200

Elstow abbey: intact & apparently restored west doorway, with 4-centred arch below spandrelled label; C15, C19(?)

Ely cathedral-priory: 1. intact east doorway (Monks' door), with semicircular arch of 2 orders; mid C12

2. intact west doorway (Prior's door), highly decorated with tympanum & one order; mid C12

Ewenny priory: 1. intact east doorway, with semicircular arch of one order & outward facing zigzag moulding; mid C12

2. intact west doorway similar to east doorway, reset in garden; mid C12

3. intact doorway in west wall of south transept, with semicircular arch of one order & plain roll moulding; mid C12

Finchale priory: intact original tall plain east doorway, with pointed arch dying at shoulders; early C13

Fountains abbey: intact but weathered small & plain east doorway, with semicircular head & one order of engaged shafting; late C12

Freiston priory: intact east doorway in good condition, with plain semicircular head & one order of detached round shafting; C12

Furness abbey: intact east small doorway set within larger doorway of similar design, both have semicircular arch & continuous mouldings of roll & recessed concave; C12

Glastonbury abbey: intact right half of west doorway, with semicircular arch & 2 orders: C12

Gloucester abbey: 1. intact east doorway, with high pointed arch & early Perp. panelling; 1373-1412

2. intact lower & plainer west doorway, also with pointed arch & early Perp. panelling; 1373-1412

Goring priory: intact but blocked west doorway only visible from inside church, has semicircular head; C12

Great Bricett priory: intact west doorway in Bay 4 of nave, with 4-centred arch (internal); C15/C16

Hailes abbey: worn & damaged 2-centred east doorway of one order, of which most detail has gone; C13

Hamble priory: intact east doorway, with unadorned semicircular archway; C12

Haughmond abbey: intact west doorway of 2 orders originally leading into church, with later figures of St.. Peter & St. Paul inserted between angles of shafts; late C12, C14

Hexham priory: 1. intact west doorway with pointed arch & continuous mouldings; C15

2. intact but blocked doorway in west wall of south transept leading into east cloister walk, 2-centred & of one order with shafting gone; C13

Hulne friary: intact east doorway, simple arch with pointed top; mid C13

Hurley priory: intact & blocked west doorway, 2-stepped with semicircular arch; C12

Ingham friary: 1. intact blocked east doorway, possesses basket arch & single chamfer down sides; C15/C16

2. intact blocked west doorway, with 2-centred arch & continuous mouldings including recessed flat chamfer; C14

Jarrow priory: intact but blocked tall doorway on south side of central tower possibly served as processional doorway, has semicircular head & chamfered continuous moulding; early C11

Jervaulx abbey: intact west doorway with semicircular head, ornamented with nailhead & has 2 orders with some shafting missing; late C12

Kirkstall abbey: 1. weathered east doorway, semicircular arch with 3 orders less shafting; C12

2. weathered west doorway, semicircular arch with 2 orders less shafting; C12

Lacock abbey: 1. intact large east doorway, with 2-centred pointed arch of one order & detached round shafting; C13

2. intact much restored smaller west doorway replacement for earlier partly visible one, 4-centred arch with continuous flat chamfer moulding; C15, C19

Lanercost priory: 1. intact 2-centred headed east doorway (blocked), 2 orders with plain caps; c.1200

2. intact west doorway (blocked), semicircular arch of one order with waterleaf caps; c.1190

3. intact doorway from south transept to cloister, semicircular arch of one order with waterleaf caps; c.1190

Latton priory: blocked east doorway of unknown condition; C14(?)

Leonard Stanley: 1. intact & blocked identical east & west doorways, with semicircular arches & one order of engaged shafting; C12

2. intact doorway in west wall of south transept, has 4-centred arch & label with coats-of-arms in spandrels; C15/C16

Letheringham priory: intact west doorway blocked & apparently turned inside out, has one order with cushion caps & zigzag round the semicircular head; C12

Lilleshall abbey: intact east doorway, semicircular arch of 2 main orders, & with zigzag & cable mouldings; late C12

Little Malvern priory: intact east doorway with pointed arch & continuous concave mouldings; C15

Malmesbury abbey: 1. intact east doorway set inside former Norman doorway, 4-centred arch with ornate cusped head (damaged); early C15

2. intact west doorway in Bay 6, plain arch with basket top & continuous moulding; C15

Malton priory: intact but weathered east doorway in 2 orders, semicircular arch with waterleaf on one cap; late C12

Malvern priory: 1. intact & weathered east doorway (now blocked with stone), semicircular arch of 2 engaged orders; C12

2. intact & weathered west doorway with timber door, possesses 4-centred arch; C15

3. intact smaller doorway (blocked with stone) next to west doorway, has similar design; C15

Margam abbey: intact east doorway, with pointed 2-centred arch & continuous mouldings; C13

Milton abbey: intact doorway leading off Bay 7 of choir on north side of church, chief ornamentation of 2 orders on inner side of church; early C14

Monk Bretton priory: ruined east doorway of one order, with semicircular arch devoid of mouldings; late C12

Neath abbey: ruined east doorway of which top is stripped of stone, jambs have 3 main filleted rolls & hollows; c.1300

Netley abbey: mutilated & eroded wide 2-centred east doorway, arch deeply cut with small rolls & with 2 orders though all shafts have gone; C13

Newstead Augustinian priory: 1. blocked east doorway survives below springing of arch, outer shafting largely gone; late C12/ early C13

2. blocked west doorway survives also below springing of arch, small caps display early stiff-leaf; late C12/early C13

Norwich cathedral-priory: 1. intact east doorway (Prior's), 4 orders with carved seated Christ & other figures on arch; early C15

2. intact less imposing west doorway, series of continuous mouldings & empty small niches etc.; early C15

Norwich Dominican friary: intact north east doorway to nave (Bay 2); c.1345

Nun Monkton priory: 1. intact east doorway, semicircular arch of 3 orders, with zigzag mouldings; C12
2. intact west plain doorway, with semicircular arch comprising continuous triple chamfer mouldings; C12
(See also entry under Collation Seats below)
Owston abbey: west doorway blocked externally but visible & intact internally, with tall semicircular plain arch, possibly retained as cupboard; C12
Oxford St. Frideswide's priory: 1. intact but blocked recessed east doorway, has panelled jambs & broad arch ornamented with pendants; late C15
2. intact but blocked similar west doorway; late C15
3.   intact central 4-centred doorway between above doorways, also recessed deeply with small engaged shafts & nominal caps; early C16
Pershore abbey: intact & weathered east doorway with pointed & deep cut arch, on each side are 3 major & 3 minor engaged shafts; C13
Peterborough abbey: 1. intact east doorway (Canons' Door), with semicircular arch of 4 orders & cushion capitals; early C12
2. intact west doorway (Bishop's Door), pointed arch of 4 orders & dogtooth mouldings; C13
Pilton priory: 1. intact east doorway on north side of tower, shouldered arch; C14
2. intact west doorway on north side of original nave (now north nave aisle), plain pointed arch with continuous moulding; C14/C15
Polesworth abbey: 1. intact but weathered blocked east doorway with plain semicircular arch, with suggestion of being one order; C12
2. intact small plain west doorway with square head; unknown date

Portchester priory: 1. two blocked overlapping east doorways; C12(?)

2. intact west doorway now leading into new annexe; C12(?)

Ranton priory: intact small west doorway in remnant of nave south wall, plain semicircular arch with continuous roll moulding & prominent hood; C12

Reading friary: intact small west doorway in nave north wall, with 2-centred head & 2 chamfers; early C14

Redlingfield priory: intact doorway blocked with brick half way along nave, has 2-centred arch with continuous chamfered moulding; C13/C14

Rochester cathedral-priory: 1. heavily restored east doorway to chapter room from cloister, has 2-centred arch with continuous simple mouldings & is blocked with window inserted; early C14

2. intact west doorway to south choir aisle from cloister, has 2-centred arch & is of one order; C13

Romsey abbey: 1. intact east doorway (Abbess's Door), with semicircular arch of 2 orders & cable mouldings etc.; late C12

2. intact west doorway, with pointed arch of one order; early C13

Rumburgh cell: intact east doorway on north side of choir, with internal 2-centred arch & external square head; C13(?)

St. Albans: intact east doorway with small vaulted lobby, has elaborate decoration on inner side consisting of label & niches etc.; late C14

Selby abbey: 1. intact east doorway with 2-centred arch & continuous mouldings; C14

2. intact west doorway identical to above, but more weathered; C14

Sherborne abbey: intact east *inner* doorway & lobby with outer doorway blocked, big ogeed arch with pinnacle; C15

Shrewsbury abbey: 1. intact east doorway, with moulded pointed arch of 3 orders; C14/C15 but may be C19

2. intact west doorway, plain semicircular arch of one order & with hoodmould; mid C12

Smithfield St. Bartholomew's priory: intact east doorway, plain semicircular arch of one order; c.1150

Southwark priory: 1. east doorway intact less head, has 3 orders with detached round shafts & waterleaf caps; C12

2. west doorway with mouldings only visible from inside church, with semicircular arch & continuous chamfer; unknown date

Stow abbey: intact doorway midway along nave north wall, possibly processional doorway, one order of shafting with semicircular head displaying 2 bands of zigzag; late C11

Tewkesbury abbey: 1. intact east doorway less imagery, with 4-centred archway & rich panelling overhead; late C15

2. no west doorway in normal position, but further west is blocked doorway with segmental head; C15

Thetford St. Sepulchre's priory: intact small west doorway of plain appearance, with triangular internal arch; probably C14

Tintern abbey: 1. almost intact east doorway, with cusped & pointed arch, continuous outer moulding; late C13

2. no normal west doorway but intact doorway from west walk to west range & another intact doorway (less facing stones) from west range into north west corner of nave; C14

Trentham priory: intact restored west doorway, with plain triangular chamfered head; C15, 1844

Tynemouth priory: blocked & mutilated west doorway with pointed(?) arch, leading from outer parlour to nave of church; C13

Valle Crucis abbey: weathered but intact east doorway, pointed arch of 3 orders & capitals with stiff-leaf foliage & engaged shafts; early C13

Wenlock priory: weathered & largely intact west doorway, pointed & ornamented arch of 2 orders with stiff-leaf foliage but shafting gone; early C13

Westminster abbey: 1. intact east doorway, acute 2-centred well ornamented arch of 2 orders of Purbeck shafts & rosettes; mid C13

2. intact west doorway with pointed arch, placed within outer arch with segmental head, spandrels decorated with 4 circles; late C14

Winchester cathedral-priory: 1. intact but blocked ornate east doorway, 2-centred arch with label & coats-of-arms in spandrels; late C14

2. intact but blocked west doorway in Bay 9, with 4-centred arch & roll & concave continuous mouldings; late C14

Woodspring priory: intact 4-centred west doorway, with post-Dissolution doorway inserted; C15, pDp

Worcester cathedral-priory: 1. intact east doorway, pointed   arch   of   one   order   with   keel   mouldings; c.1290/1300

2. intact west doorway, with 4-centred arch & 2 main orders of nominal caps & engaged shafts; C15

Worksop priory: 1. intact east doorway now blocked, with plain semicircular arch of 3 orders; late C12

2. intact west doorway, with semicircular arch decorated with zigzag & dogtooth mouldings, 2 major & 2 minor orders; late C12

3. intact doorway from east cloister-walk to north transept, heavily restored & of one order; late C12

Yarmouth priory: 1. intact large doorway in west wall of south transept, 3 principal orders with detached shafting & stiff-leaf caps; C13

2. intact doorway in south wall of south choir aisle, has square label over 2 centred arch; C15

Yedingham priory: [1. intact blocked east doorway, with 2-centred arch & 2 orders with stiff-leaf; late C12

2. intact west doorway with single chamfered segmental arch to north; late C12(?)]

11/3   BOOK CUPBOARDS

N.B. Normally located on east cloister-walk side of west wall of south (or north) transept.

Bayham abbey: 2 round-headed rebated recesses in south wall of old south transept; early C13

Beaulieu abbey: 1. intact small pointed arched recess to east of east processional doorway in west wall of south transept, later used as lamp niche; early C13

2. intact bookcase consisting of large recess in wall to south of lamp niche, vaulted interior but some of ribbing gone; early C13

Boxgrove priory: intact but blocked big recess, with semicircular top; C12

Bridlington priory: intact wide 2-centred arched recess immediately to west of east processional doorway; c.1300

Brinkburn priory: intact double recess, with square tops; c.1200

Chester abbey: intact round headed recess in west cloister-walk near west processional doorway; C11/C12

Coverham abbey: intact recess in west side of west wall of south transept; C13+

Fountains abbey: intact but now blocked plain big recess in west side of west wall of south transept, with semicircular arch; C12

Furness abbey: intact doorway with plain semicircular arch originally leading to slype, later blocked & probably converted to cupboard; C12

Hailes abbey: 3 well preserved arched recesses (out of 5) in north walk of cloister built into church wall, probably used for books; mid C13

Kirkstall abbey: intact round headed recess in west wall of south transept; C12

Lacock abbey: 2 recesses with trefoiled heads (one altered to doorway & now blocked) at north end of east cloister-walk; C13

Lanercost priory: intact cupboard in west wall of south transept, with curious ill adapted segmental head; c.1190

Lilleshall abbey: intact double recess with common semicircular arch; C12

Margam abbey: intact blank arched recess next to east processional doorway, 2-centred arch has continuous mouldings & ogeed tracery remnant within head; early C14

Monk Bretton priory: recess with semicircular top at north end of east cloister-walk, its rear now open to south transept; late C12

11/3 Lilleshall abbey, book
cupboards

Norwich cathedral-priory: 1. 3 intact large recesses close to east processional doorway, with finialed & crocketed ogee-gabled heads; late C14/early C15
2. 2 lockers in east wall of bay 4 of east walk, with pointed tops & fitted doors; unknown date
Pershore abbey: intact small rebated locker immediately to right of east processional doorway in west wall of south transept; unknown date
Rievaulx abbey: plain recess; C12

Romsey abbey: intact small square locker, rebated for door; C12

Tintern abbey: 2 intact round headed recesses, one blocked; C12(?)

Whalley abbey: 3 alcoves or recesses in west wall of south transept; early C14

Worcester cathedral-priory: 2 rectangular recesses in wall between east slype & chapter-house; probably C12

11/4   STOUPS

Alkborough cell: intact free-standing stone stoup of approximately cubic shape, recovered after being thrown out of church; unknown date

Binham priory: intact stoup at foot of eighth pier on north side of nave, big bowl within plain arched niche; unknown date

Blakeney friary: intact stoup in north porch on west side, niche with triangular head & bowl in projecting shelf; C15

Blyth priory: intact large free standing stone vessel, with 4 knobs on sides; with asymmetrical plughole, may have served as stoup; unknown date

Bolton priory: mutilated stoup on east side of east processional doorway with decorated bowl; probably mid C13

Bourne abbey: 2 holy water stoups of similar appearance, one by west door & other outside south porch, with broken bowls & below ogeed hoods; C15

Boxgrove priory: intact oblong shaped stoup in entrance porch of church; C13/C14

Breedon priory: intact small stoup with niche on east inner side of south doorway of south transept (porch); probably c.1300

Bromfield priory: stoup with broken bowl in intact squarish niche with roll moulding, inside inner north doorway; C13

Bungay priory: 1. large stoup with broken bowl outside porch on west side, fitted into angle of wall, accompanied by remnant of twin stoup on opposite side of doorway; C14/C15

2. stoup with sliced off bowl in east side of wall exterior by doorway leading to north side of nave, plain niche with canted margins; C14/C15

Cambridge St. Radegund's priory: intact stoup inside north door of nave on east side, possesses mini-vault & accommodates removable bowl within projecting shelf; C15

Cardigan cell: 1. intact triangular niche for removable stoup inside nave on east side of now blocked north doorway; C14

2. intact rectangular shaped stone basin, free-standing; unknown date

Chirbury priory: intact large free-standing stoup serving as font, has prominent angle knobs; C14/C15

Clare friary: largely intact stoup in west wall of east range near east processional doorway, its niche possesses pointed arch; C13

Cranborne cell: intact stoup niche on south side of west doorway of tower, possesses trefoiled head & may have been moved; C13/C14

Croyland abbey: Norman font built into south east pier of north west tower for use as stoup; C12, C15

Davington priory: intact stoup niche in west face of third pier from east near north doorway, wide & shallow shape with 2-centred arch; C12/C13

Dinmore commandery: intact stoup within church near north doorway, niche with ogeed arch & intact bowl projecting forwards on ornamental cap; C14

Elstow abbey: mutilated stoup inside nave north doorway on east side, with shallow ogeed niche moulded with double quarter rolls; early C14

Hatfield Broad Oak priory: intact pair of identical stoups on either side of front wall of south porch, each with half moon shaped bowl in 4 centred niche; C15

Hatfield Peverel priory: stoup on east inner side of nave north doorway, niche with 7-foiled arch but bowl destroyed; C15

Kidwelly cell: small stoup in east wall of south porch; C14

Kyme priory: intact stoup except for missing front of bowl, located in porch to east of inner doorway, bowl stands on pedestal attached to rear wall; C14

Lanercost priory: small intact stoup in west wall of south transept near east processional doorway, with round head; c.1200

Malling abbey: intact stoup outside south doorway of gatehouse chapel, has overhead label; C15

Minster-in-Sheppey priory: intact stoup niche within south wall of church to east of main doorway, plain 2-centred arch; C13

Monkton priory: 1. intact stoup niche in wall on inside of porch inner doorway, possesses segmental arch; probably C13/C14

2. intact but worn portable stone stoup, circular interior inside squarish exterior; unknown date

Pilton priory: 1 intact stoup in outside of south wall of porch, with pinnacled decoration; C14/C15

2. recess of stoup inside south doorway of nave on east side, partly hidden by panelling & with bevelled top; unknown date

Rumburgh cell: intact stoup inside south doorway of nave on east side, with deep niche under plain semicircular head & shallow unspoilt basin; C13

St. Albans abbey: intact stoup within north west corner of north nave aisle, niche displays ogeed head & pinnacled gable; early C14 (if not C19)

St. Germans priory: intact stoup niche within south nave aisle at west end of south wall, shouldered niche under 2-centred plain arch without basin; C15

Southwark priory: worn stoup to east of east processional doorway, niche with ogeed arch; C14

Totnes priory: intact stoup in internal angle between north & east walls of south porch, has bowl with ornamented front panels; C15

Yedingham priory: [intact stoup on north side of west processional doorway, with stiff-leaf & trefoiled canopy; late C12]

11/5   CARRELS

Chester abbey: 5 carrel-bays at south end of west cloister-walk; c.1525-37, restored 1911-13

Durham cathedral-priory: carrel positions marked off in north cloister-walk by peg-marks; unknown date

Gloucester abbey: 20 carrels along south cloister-walk; early C15

Westminster abbey: continuous stone wall bench along north side of north cloister-walk, provided explicitly for study; mid C13

11/6 COLLATION SEATS

Cleeve abbey: shallow recess halfway along north cloister-walk, with trefoiled head & coved back; C13

Hexham priory: wide recess with 4-centred arch (alternatively a carrel); late C13

Nun Monkton priory: intact narrow & tall blind recess in outer side of south wall of nave between processional doorways, with semicircular head & continuous mouldings consisting of 2 plain steps; C12

Strata Florida abbey: low remnant of alcove displayed in south wall of north cloister-walk; C15

Tintern abbey: almost complete arched alcove seat halfway along south side of south cloister-walk; C13

Westminster abbey: intact abbot's bench in first bay of east cloister-walk, marked by absence of wall-shafts; mid C13

11/7 LAVATORIA

Aylesford friary: intact wall-type lavatorium at west end of south wall of south cloister-walk, has wide 4-centred arch with trough replaced with flat slabs of stone; C14/C15

Blanchland abbey: partly intact wall-type lavatorium at south end of west cloister-walk, with single wide depressed arch; late C13

Bushmead priory: wall-type lavatorium with trefoiled arch converted into post-Dissolution doorway; C13

Canterbury cathedral-priory: intact 2 traceried bays in west end of arcade of north cloister-walk, troughs & windows gone; C15

Chester abbey: almost intact wall-type lavatorium west end of north cloister-walk, 3 arches displaying multi-shafting; C13

Clare friary: partly intact wall-type lavatorium at west end of north cloister-walk, one high arch & part of second arch; early C14

Cleeve abbey: mutilated wall-type lavatorium halfway along south cloister-walk, single recess with broad segmental head; C13

Davington priory: partly intact big wall-type trefoil headed lavatorium in south west corner of cloister; unknown date

Dover Benedictine priory: robbed lavatorium in north wall of north cloister-walk occupying Bays 4 & 5 from east, consisting of 3 equal sized 2-centred arches; C13

Durham cathedral-priory: big Teesdale marble basin of destroyed lavatorium in cloister-garth; 1432-33

Forde abbey: surviving arches of wall-type lavatorium in north cloister-walk; C13

Fountains abbey: 1. partly intact wall-type lavatorium placed on both sides of refectory doorway; c.1200
2. large stone bowl located in cloister-garth, probably not in original place; unknown date

Gloucester abbey: largely intact wall-type lavatorium at west end of north cloister-walk on garth side, 4 double bays with miniature fan traceried vaulting; early C15

Gloucester Dominican friary: remnant of lavatorium in north wall of south range at west end of cloister-walk, displays 6 trefoil-headed arches; late C13

Hailes abbey: weathered & mutilated wall-type lavatorium under wide segmental arch, soffit retains blind tracery; C13

Haughmond abbey: partly intact wall-type lavatorium at south end of west cloister-walk, in two high blank arches; C12

Hexham priory: weathered wall-type lavatorium at south end of west cloister-walk, elaborate composition of 7 gabled blank arches; c.1300

Horsham St. Faith's priory: wall-type lavatorium at west end of north cloister-walk, converted into doorway; probably C12

Kirkham priory: partly intact wall-type lavatorium at south end of west cloister-walk, recessed in 2 bays; late C13

Kirkstall abbey: partly intact wall-type lavatorium divided into compartments by trefoiled arches & shafting; C13

Lacock abbey: largely intact but partly blocked wall-type lavatorium at west end of north cloister-walk, divided into 2 sections; C13, C15

Lanercost priory: part destroyed wall-type lavatorium towards west end of south cloister-walk, with dogtooth moulding on 4 reduced arches; C13

Langley abbey: part destroyed wall-type lavatorium at south end of west cloister-walk, with 2 high arches & intermediate vesica arch; late C13

Michelham priory: largely intact wall-type lavatorium consisting of 2 arched & shafted bays; C13

Mount Grace charterhouse: intact small wall-type lavatorium under 4-centred arch, still equipped with stone trough; early C15

Netley abbey: weathered & mutilated wall-type lavatorium divided into 4 compartments by shafting & shallow arches; C13

Newcastle Dominican friary: almost intact wall-type lavatorium under plain trefoiled arch; late C13

Newstead Augustinian priory: wide wall-type lavatorium survives minus top of arch; C13, has plain chamfer moulding & hoodmould; C13

Norwich cathedral-priory: almost intact large wall lavatorium at south end of west range occupying 2 bays, with 3 niches per bay; C14

Peterborough abbey: mutilated wall-type lavatorium in south cloister-walk, richly panelled in 5 bays; C15

Rievaulx abbey: mutilated arcaded wall-type lavatorium flanking both sides of entrance to refectory; late C12

Rochester cathedral-priory: partly intact wall-type lavatorium on south side of south cloister-walk, partly hidden behind modern wall in double arched vaulted recess; c.1200

Sherborne abbey: free-standing lavatorium (Conduit) now standing in town square, hexagonal with buttressed angles; C16

Shulbrede priory: partly intact wall-type lavatorium in south cloister-walk, 3 trefoiled arches; mid C13

Syningthwaite priory: [2 simple low arches to right of main refectory doorway; unknown date]

Valle Crucis abbey: walled rectangular basin in south east corner of cloister-garth probably came from free-standing lavatorium; C13/C14

Wenlock priory: part-dismantled free standing octagonal lavatorium in cloister-garth; C12

Westminster abbey: largely intact wall-type lavatorium at south end of west cloister-walk, single segmentally headed recess under pointed arch containing central quatrefoil; C13

Whalley abbey: largely intact wall-type lavatorium, under great segmental arch; C14

Worcester cathedral-priory: intact wall-type lavatorium at south end of west cloister-walk, in 2 bays with troughs extant; C14

◆◆◆◆◆◆◆◆◆◆◆◆◆◆◆◆

Section 12:
DORMITORY RANGES 1

N.B. East range unless stated otherwise.

12/1   WHOLE RANGES

Abergavenny priory: intact north part of range, now part of new Priory Centre; C13, restored late C20

Anglesey priory: largely intact range, adapted as core of mansion; mid C13 & post Dissolution

Battle abbey: high-standing ruin (except for demolished chapter-house & inner parlour), probably used as farm building after Dissolution; C13

Beeleigh abbey: largely intact range, adapted as core of mansion; early C13

Bristol abbey: largely intact range, redeveloped as cathedral accommodation; C12, upper storey pDp

Bristol Dominican friary: intact dormitory in north range, orientated east west; mid C13

Burnham abbey: [partly intact range; C13, 1913-15, 1951-52]

Calder abbey: high-standing ruined range, with part of undercroft covered to south by post-Dissolution mansion; C13

Caldey cell: intact range, contiguous with Prior's Tower to north; C13

Castle Acre priory: largely high-standing ruin, robbed of architectural detail especially median undercroft piers; mid C12

Chicksands priory:　range intact but considerably adapted as part of post-Dissolution mansion; C13, C15, C19

Cleeve abbey:　intact range except for reredorter; early C13

Coventry Carmelite friary:　almost intact range; C14

Creake abbey:　intact building (Abbey Farmhouse) difficult to interpret, but retaining some definite medieval features; C13(?), C15, C19

Deerhurst priory:　intact shell of range, modified as private house (Priory Farm); C11, C14, C15/C16 & pDp

Durham cathedral-priory:　intact west range, used as cathedral accommodation; early C12

Easebourne priory:　intact but considerably adapted range as part of post-Dissolution house; late C13, C17, C18

Forde abbey:　almost intact range; C12, C13, C15

Furness abbey:　high-standing ruined range, most of vaulting gone ; mid C13

Ixworth priory:　[intact east range with good undercroft, less chapter-house, adapted as post-Dissolution house; c.1230, C17, C18]

Jervaulx abbey:　much of ruined range stands to full height, south wall displays 9 long lancets of dormitory; early C13

King's Lynn priory:　intact building in Church Street (Nos. 17-18) now domestic, probably originally part of east range but difficult to interpret; C14, c.1470, C18

Kirkstall abbey:　high-standing ruined range; late C12, C13

Lacock abbey:　intact range, modified as part of mansion; mid C13

Littlemore priory: [intact rectangular building with small gabled block to north (Minchery Farm), believed to be part of east range; late C15, remodelled c.1600, C17]

Missenden abbey: medieval walls of range survive within remodelled mansion , now adult education centre; C15, c.1600, c.1800, c.1810, 1988

Newcastle-upon-Tyne Dominican friary: partly intact range considerably altered, devoid of slype & sacristry at north end; C13+

Newstead Augustinian priory: largely intact range now part of mansion, lower storey vaulted; mid C13

Norwich Dominican friary: partly intact & altered range, used as granary & nonconformist chapel after Dissolution, chapter-house gone; C14, C19

Oxford Durham college: intact range containing Old Library; 1417-21, 1602

12/1 Valle Crucis abbey, east range to east

Oxford St. Frideswide's priory: intact range drastically modified, in use as cathedral accommodation (Priory House); C12, C13

Valle Crucis abbey: almost intact range, used as farm buildings after Dissolution; early C13, late C14/early C15

Westminster abbey: intact range, variety of post-Dissolution uses; mid C11, C12, mid C13, C19, C20

Whalley abbey: much of range stands quite high, but vaulting gone; earlier C14

Worcester cathedral-priory: partly intact range; c.1120, C14

12/2 SUB-DORTERS OF EAST RANGES SURVIVING ON OWN OR UNDER POST-DISSOLUTION WORK

Buildwas abbey: most of south end (nearer church) survives; later C12

Chester abbey: range intact at ground floor level (upper floor scheduled for rebuilding); C13

Coggeshall abbey: part of undercroft vaulting survives under post-Dissolution building; c.1180, early C13

Neath abbey: intact south end of sub-dorter & part of reredorter form undercroft of post-Dissolution house raised above it; C13

Norwich Dominican friary: intact 4x4 vaulted sub-dorter of former house of Friars Penitential, now coffee bar; 1258/1267, c.1300

St. Osyth abbey: intact section of sub-dorter below post-Dissolution building, with rough groin vaulting; early C13

Stoneleigh abbey: [partly intact sub-dorter, forms part of post-Dissolution mansion; late C13/early C14]

Walsingham priory: partly intact vaulted sub-dorter, said to have been warming-house, of 2 aisles & 3 bays; late C13

12/3   ENTRANCES TO CHAPTER-HOUSES & VESTIBULES

Bayham abbey: intact triple arches of equal size between vestibule & chapter-house, 2-centred plain chamfered tops & twin round piers; mid C13

Beaulieu abbey: intact but weathered 3 arches of roughly equal size to chapter-house, with pointed tops & detached shafts under small caps; early C13

Beeleigh abbey: [intact wide archway divided by trumeau to chapter-house, with flanking 2-light windows in top of which are quatrefoils; earlier C13]

Birkenhead priory: intact plain doorway to chapter-house with 2 small plain flanking windows, all with semicircular heads; C12

Boxgrove priory: intact but weathered doorway to chapter-house flanked by 2 windows of roughly equal size, all possess semicircular tops & each window is divided into 2 sub-lights; early C12

Bristol abbey: intact 3 arches to chapter-house with middle doorway larger than flanking windows, semicircular heads ornamented with cable mouldings; mid C12

Buildwas abbey: intact weathered 3-ordered large doorway to chapter-house flanked by much smaller equally plain windows, all have semicircular arches & scalloped caps over jamb-shafts (some missing); mid C12

Burnham abbey: [intact single doorway to chapter-house, has detached shafts & moulded caps; C13]

Calder abbey: intact triple opening to chapter-house, of 3 pointed archways, north with Y-tracery leading to small rib vaulted library, south window now devoid of tracery; late C13

Cambridge St. Radegund's priory: intact triple opening of central doorway & 2 large flanking windows to former chapter-house, all pointed, elaborate composition with shafts & stiff-leaf caps; c.1230

Canterbury cathedral-priory: intact 3 arches to chapter-house superimposed on earlier walling, rather plain 2-centred arched doorway with fleuron decoration, side windows with trefoiled tops & quatrefoiled shafts; 1304-05

Carlisle cathedral-priory: 1. intact entrance to former vestibule from former east cloister-walk, consisting of trumeau with twin arches within super-arch; mid/late C13
2. intact single archway to chapter-house from vestibule, with acute 2-centred head & deep cut mouldings; mid/late C13

Chester abbey: 1. intact 3 arches to vestibule from cloister-walk, side arches divided into glazed sub-lights with trefoils over; C13, restored early C20
2. intact similar 3 arches from vestibule to chapter-house, with unglazed windows; C13

Clare friary: intact 2 lateral windows with continuous mouldings & central modern doorway with square head; early C14, probably C19

Cleeve abbey: intact large pointed doorway to chapter-house with 2 continuous chamfered orders, flanked by 2 small pointed unglazed windows each divided into 2 sub-lights; early C13

Cockersand abbey: intact weathered semicircular headed single doorway to chapter-house, now mostly walled up & with smaller doorway inserted, with nook-shafts each side of which only caps remain; c.1200

Combe abbey: intact 3 arches of red sandstone to former chapter-house, with semicircular tops & zigzag mouldings; late C12

Coventry Carmelite friary: intact doorway to vestibule, with obtuse head divided into 3 lights; C14/C15

Croxden abbey: intact & weathered 3 arches of 2 & 3 orders devoid of shafting to former chapter-house, stiff-leaf capitals below pointed & multimoulded arches; early C13

Durham cathedral-priory: intact central doorway to chapter-house flanked by 2 windows all with semicircular head, arches enriched with zigzag & windows have twin openings; c.1133/1141

Easebourne priory: intact tripartite entrance to chapter-house of 3 pointed arches, with short piers & detached Purbeck shafts; c. 1260

Evesham abbey: intact pointed doorway now standing on its own, of sumptuous design with 2 orders containing little statues in canopied niches; c.1285+

Finchale priory: intact though weathered or mutilated set of 3 pointed archways of which central doorway is largest, latter has one order of colonnettes & windows single chamfers only; late C13

Fountains abbey: intact 3 stately archways of equal height to chapter-house, all 3 have 5 orders of colonnettes with waterleaf caps & all appear to be doorways; c.1170

Furness abbey: 1. intact but weathered doorway of 4 orders to small vestibule flanked by 2 library room doorways, all of similar proportions & with semicircular head; late C12

2. intact inner doorway between vestibule & chapter-house, with acutely pointed arch & fine multi-shafting; c.1230

Gloucester abbey: intact doorway to chapter-house with semicircular arch, flanked to north by smaller window also with semicircular top & to south by library doorway; c.1100, C14

Hailes abbey: intact & weathered triple arches to chapter-house, of equal size & with pointed tops, much detail now missing; mid C13

Hardham priory: [intact 3 arches to chapter-house, of equal height with 2-light side-windows having quatrefoils above, arches are pointed with dogtooth mouldings & rest on delicate detached shafts; c.1250]

Haughmond abbey: largely intact 3 arches to chapter-house, with semicircular heads & 3 orders of shafts; late C12, early C14

Hexham priory: 1. intact central restored doorway & 2 original flanking windows to vestibule, latter are sharply pointed with one order; C13
2. intact central dooway & 2 flanking windows to former chapter-house, sharply pointed doorway with continuous roll mouldings & windows of 2 orders also sharply pointed; C13

Hinton charterhouse: [intact pointed doorway to chapter-house, with fine mouldings & stiff-leaf stops to hoodmould; C13]

Jervaulx abbey: intact 2 windows (central doorway gone), each semicircular & fronted by 2 orders with shafts gone; c.1200

Kirkstall abbey: intact 2 large doorways to vestibule, both of same size & flanked by 2 small arches on each side all with semicircular tops, inner small arches are windows & outer ones are blanks; later C12

Lacock abbey: intact triple archways at entrance to chapter-house, flanking windows are smaller than doorway & have Y-tracery; late C13, altered C15

Langley abbey: intact chapter-house doorway with plain pointed arch & trefoil head, 2 small flanking windows are minus much of their facings; early C13

Margam abbey: 1.intact triple archways to vestibule, 2-centred heads with dogtooth on central arch; c.1200/20
2. intact simple doorway & flanking windows with pointed arches to chapter-house from vestibule, with 2 continuous chamfers; c.1200/20

Netley abbey: largely intact 3 arches to chapter-house of equal height & approximately same size, central doorway separated from flanking windows by composite columns; early C13

Newcastle-upon-Tyne Dominican friary: intact doorway with pointed arch to vestibule, flanked by 2 small windows each divided into 2 sub-lights; late C13/early C14

Newstead Augustinian priory: intact doorway to chapter-house flanked by 2 smaller windows, doorway with semicircular head & flanking windows with pointed arches, all have detached round shafts; earlier C13

Norwich cathedral-priory: intact identical 3 arches to chapter-house, each having 2 main lights with ogeed heads & with cinquefoiled light above; early C14

Oxford St. Frideswide's priory: intact chapter-house doorway with 2 continuous mouldings of zigzag & 2 orders, this & 2 small plain flanking windows have semicircular arches; C12, C19

Pill priory: intact wide arched entrance from vestibule to chapter-house; late C12/early C13

Reading abbey: ruined triple entrance, semicircular arched doorway & flanking windows robbed of architectural detail; C12

Rochester cathedral-priory: intact decayed 3 round archways to former vestibule, of equal height of which 2 outer are now blocked, arches decorated with zigzag & overhead are 3 windows; early C12

Smithfield St. Bartholomew's priory: intact blocked doorway & 2 blocked flanking windows, all with 2-centred arches & continuous mouldings; C15

Stoneleigh abbey: [intact 3-ordered doorway doorway to chapter-house, with roll mouldings in its arch & waterleaf caps over shafts; c.1200(?)]

Torre abbey: intact & worn doorway to chapter-house with 3 ordered semicircular arch, flanked by 2 small windows also with semicircular arches; c.1200

Valle Crucis abbey: intact single & central doorway to chapter-house with no flanking windows except for screened library recess to left, with plain pointed arch & continuous mouldings; C14

Wenlock priory: intact but weathered doorway & flanking 2 windows of equal proportions leading to now ruined chapter-house, heads are all semicircular & are covered with various geometrical motifs; c.1150

Westminster abbey: 1. intact arched twin entrances to vestibule under common super-arch, latter is of 2 orders & has 3 statues over twin arches; mid C13

2. intact trefoiled twin entrances to chapter-house under common super-arch, with modern figure of Christ over twin arches; mid C13, C19

Whalley abbey: 1. intact doorway to vestibule with continuous mouldings covered with fleurons, flanked by small nook-shafted windows each divided into 2 lights; earlier C14

2. intact doorway from vestibule to now destroyed chapter-house, has segmental head on vestibule side & pointed arch on chapter-house side; mid C14

Winchester cathedral-priory: intact arcade of 5 archways fronting former chapter-house, with central doorway larger than flanking 2 per side, all having semicircular tops, round piers & big caps of 2 scallops each; 1079+

Worcester cathedral-priory: intact single doorway to chapter-house, with no flanking windows, panelled surround & soffit; C15

York St. Mary's abbey: reconstructed rich triple entrance to chapter-house from vestibule in Transitional style of mixtures, with round doorway & pointed arched windows; c.1190+

12/4   CHAPTER-HOUSES

Anglesey priory: intact chapter-house though devoid of vaulting, now living room of mansion; C13

Beeleigh abbey: [intact chapter-house used as chapel of private house, with vaulting in 8 units; early C13]

Birkenhead priory: intact chapter-house, now church; C12

Bristol abbey: intact & in use as cathedral chapter-house; C12, C19

Buildwas abbey: intact chapter-house; later C12

Burnham abbey: [intact chapter-house, now in use as chapel of Anglican nunnery; C13, extended 1951-52]

Calder abbey: high-standing ruined chapter-house, with one bay of vaulting intact; late C13

Canterbury cathedral-priory: intact large chapter-house, still in use by present cathedral; C11, C14, C15

Castle Acre priory: high-standing ruined chapter-house, nearly all robbed of architectural detail; mid C12

Chester abbey: intact & in use as cathedral chapter-house; C13

Cleeve abbey: intact chapter-house except for east side, became farm building after Dissolution; early C13

Cockersand abbey: intact chapter-house, now mausoleum; C13

Durham cathedral-priory: intact & now chapter-house of cathedral; early C12, extensively rebuilt C19

Easby abbey: high-standing ruined chapter-house, minus vaulting & west wall; early C13

Easebourne priory: intact but altered chapter-house, now part of post-Dissolution house; late C13

Forde abbey: intact chapter-house, now domestic chapel of private house; C12, C13, C15

Fountains abbey: high-standing ruined chapter-house; later C12

Furness abbey: high-standing ruined chapter-house; c.1230-40

Gloucester abbey: intact chapter-house now serving as chapter-house of cathedral: C11, C12, C15

Hardham priory: [high-standing ruined chapter-house, 3 finely detailed arches at west end & 3 lancets at east end; earlier C13]

Haughmond abbey: intact chapter-house, used as domestic hall after Dissolution; C12

Hinton charterhouse: [intact chapter-house, retained as domestic accommodation after Dissolution; C13]

Hulne friary: high-standing ruined chapter-house, oblong shaped; later C13

Jervaulx abbey: moderately ruined oblong chapter-house, with re-assembled piers; early C13

Kirkstall abbey: intact chapter-house, used as farm building after Dissolution; C13

Lacock abbey: intact chapter-house, part of private mansion after Dissolution; mid C13

Langley abbey: moderately ruined chapter-house displaying considerable detail in west & south walls, vaulting gone; C13

London charterhouse: intact chapter-house, converted into post-Dissolution chapel with additional north aisles; C14, c.1500, 1612-14, 1824, 1841

Malling abbey: [intact chapter-house, restored & reroofed; C13, pDp]

Margam abbey: high-standing ruin of 12 sides & central vault shaft, used as coalhouse after Dissolution; c.1200/20

Netley abbey: high-standing ruined chapter house, oblong shaped & vaulting gone; C13

Newstead Augustinian priory: intact chapter-house, used as domestic chapel after Dissolution; mid C13

Oxford St. Frideswide's priory: intact & now used as cathedral chapter-house; C12, C13, 1881

Pill priory: intact chapter-house with barrel vault & thick walls, now living accommodation of private house; C12/C13

Reading abbey: high-standing ruined chapter-house; probably C12

Stoneleigh abbey: [chapter-house intact except for vaulting, now part of post-Dissolution mansion; C12]

Thetford St. George's priory: partly intact chapter-house especially west wall, with quadripartite vault; c.1160, 1990-91

Thornton abbey: high-standing ruined part of chapter-house, displays blank Geometric tracery in 2 walls; 1282/c.1308

Valle Crucis abbey: intact chapter-house, served as farm building after Dissolution; late C14/early C15

Wenlock priory: high-standing ruined chapter-house open to sky, with extensive wall arcading on north & south sides; C12

Westminster abbey: intact octagonal chapter-house used for storage after Dissolution, possesses undercroft; mid C13

Worcester cathedral-priory: intact & in use as cathedral chapter-house, unusual circular interior; c.1120, windows C14

12/5   VESTIBULES OF CHAPTER-HOUSES

Anglesey priory: partly intact vestibule leading to modified chapter-house, part of domestic accommodation after Dissolution; C13

Bristol abbey: intact vestibule leading to intact chapter-house; C12

Chester abbey: intact vestibule leading to intact chapter-house; C13

Coventry Carmelite friary: intact vestibule, leading to site of destroyed chapter-house, used as domestic accommodation after Dissolution; C14

Furness abbey: intact small vestibule leading to ruined chapter-house, vaulted & with 6 trefoil headed blind arches at sides; c.1230-40

Hexham priory: intact vestibule leading to site of destroyed chapter-house & in modern use as shop, devoid of original vaulting but with richly panelled walls; C13, C20

Kirkstall abbey: intact vestibule leading to intact chapter-house; C12

London charterhouse: intact vestibule leading to intact chapter-house, has tierceron vault below Chapel Tower; C14, dated 1512

Margam abbey: almost intact vestibule leading to ruined roofless chapter-house; c.1200/20

Newcastle-upon-Tyne Dominican friary: intact vestibule leading to destroyed chapter-house, used by trades' community in post-Dissolution period; C13

Westminster abbey: intact outer & inner vestibules leading to intact chapter-house; mid C13

Whalley abbey: high-standing ruined vestibule open to sky;C14

York St. Mary's abbey: partly reconstructed vestibule leading to ruined chapter-house; late C12

12/6 SACRISTRIES (VESTRIES) & BOOKSTORES (LIBRARIES)

NB These are all in east range unless stated otherwise.

Beaulieu abbey: intact west part of library/sacristy, with intact vaulting minus ribbing, now forms modern vestibule to Montagu family burial plot; C13

Boxgrove priory: intact sacristy, north of north choir aisle & not in east range; C14/C15

Bristol abbey: intact sacristy south of choir, leading to Berkeley chapel; C14

Buildwas abbey: intact bookstore & sacristry vaulted in 2 & later 3 bays, between north transept & chapter-house; C12

Burnham abbey: [intact sacristry, between chapter-house & former church; C13, C16]

Calder abbey: intact small library north west of chapter-house, possesses rib vault & fronted by archway with Y-tracery; C13

Cleeve abbey: 1. intact sacristry next to south transept, barrel vaulted; early C13

2. intact bookstore between sacristry & chapter-house, barrel vaulted; early C13

Croxden abbey: intact book room with tunnel vault between south transept & chapter-house, has ruined sacristry to east; mid C13

Dunster priory: small sacristry north of choir; C13

Fountains abbey: intact bookstore & sacristry (later slype), next to south transept, part tunnel & part rib vaulted; c.1170, C13

Furness abbey: 2 intact barrel vaulted small library rooms on either side of vestibule of chapter-house; c.1230-40

Gloucester abbey: intact library over slype to north of north transept; became schoolroom after Dissolution; C14, C15/C16

Hinton charterhouse: [1. intact tunnel vaulted sacristry, next to chapter-house; C13

2. intact library above chapter-house, vaulted in 2 bays; C13]

Hulne friary: high-standing ruined sacristry south of choir, not part of east range; late C13

Kidwelly cell: intact sacristry north of choir, also used as anchorite cell; C14

Kirkstall abbey: intact tunnel vaulted bookstore & sacristry between south transept & chapter-house, bookstore adapted as rustic summer-house; C12, 1800

Lacock abbey: intact sacristry occupies western half of vaulted room between former choir & existing chapter-house; mid C13

Lilleshall abbey: intact sacristry between south transept & east slype, barrel vaulted; late C12

Netley abbey: intact quadripartite vaulted bookstore & sacristry in 3 bays, between south transept & chapter-house; mid C13

Peterborough abbey: intact sacristry in 3 vaulted bays west of south transept; late C12

Rochester cathedral-priory: intact timber screened sacristry in south choir aisle (See entry under Other Screens); C14

Selby abbey: intact sacristry south of choir in 2 bays (now War Memorial Chapel), double storeyed with scriptorium over; c.1280-c.1340, refurnished 1955

Snaith cell: intact sacristry or vestry north of choir; mid/late C14

Stoneleigh abbey: [intact sacristry between south transept & chapter-house; C12/C13]

Tewkesbury abbey: intact 2-storeyed sacristry east of south transept & occupying chevet chapel; early C14

Tintern abbey: part-surviving bookstore & sacristry between north transept & chapter-house, with finely carved doorway; C13, C14

Valle Crucis abbey: 1. intact barrel vaulted sacristry between south transept & chapter-house; early C13
2. intact bookstore immediately west of chapter-house, fronted by screen; C14

Wenlock priory: intact library of 3 bays on west side of south transept; C13

Westminster abbey: intact revestry between south transept & chapter-house, with chapel of St. Faith at east end; mid C13

Winchester cathedral-priory: intact library over south end of south transept & slype of east range, refounded as Bishop Morley's library after Dissolution; c.1150, C17

Worcester cathedral-priory: intact library over south nave aisle; C15

12/7   SLYPES & INNER PARLOURS OF EAST RANGES

Anglesey priory: [largely intact slype between chapter-house & warming house; C13]

Battle abbey: intact slype between novices' room & common room south of chapter-house; C13

Beeleigh abbey: [intact inner parlour between chapter-house & warming house; earlier C13]

Bristol abbey: intact slype next to chapter-house on south side, has segmental arches at ends; C12

Buildwas abbey: intact slype/inner parlour on north side of chapter-house, ribbed 2-bay vault; C12

Burnham abbey: [intact inner parlour combined with warming house on north side of chapter-house; C13]

Calder abbey: slype devoid of vaulting yet otherwise intact, between chapter-house & undercroft of east range; C13

Canterbury cathedral-priory: intact slype (Dark Entry) between chapter-house & former warming house (sub-dorter & now part of library), groin vaulted; late C11

Chester abbey: intact slype on north side of chapter-house; C13

Cleeve abbey: 1. intact inner parlour on south side of chapter-house; mid C13

2. intact slype on south side of inner parlour; mid C13

Coventry Carmelite friary: intact inner parlour to left (north) of chapter-house vestibule; C14

Croxden abbey: intact slype on south side of inner parlour, pointed ribbed vault of 4 bays rising from shoulder high corbels; mid C13

Durham cathedral-priory: intact slype/inner parlour on south side of south transept; early C12

Fountains abbey: 1. intact inner parlour on south side of chapter-house, with rib vaulting; c.1170

2. ruined slype on south side of inner parlour, occupies first bay of dormitory undercroft; c.1170

Furness abbey: 1. high-standing ruined inner parlour on south side of chapter-house; C13

2. high-standing ruined slype on south side of inner parlour, occupies first bay of dormitory undercroft; C13

Gloucester abbey: intact tunnel vaulted slype between north transept & chapter-house, later lengthened & adapted as vestry with library over, now cathedral treasury; C12, C14

Hexham priory: intact rib vaulted slype occupying south bay of south transept; early C13

Ixworth priory: [1. intact slype at north end of range & immediately south of destroyed chapter-house, converted into domestic chapel after Dissolution; c.1230

2. intact inner parlour at south end of range, with 2 double bays; c.1230]

Kirkstall abbey: 1. intact inner parlour on south side of chapter-house, rib vaulted in 2 bays; C12, C15

2. intact tunnel vaulted slype at south end of east range; C12

Lacock abbey: intact slype on north side of chapter-house (Infirmary Passage), pointed tunnel vault; C13

Lilleshall abbey: intact slype between sacristry & former chapter-house, vaulted in 2 ribbed bays; C12

Llanthony priory: intact vaulted slype/inner parlour between south transept & former chapter-house; C13

Newstead Augustinian priory: intact 2-bay inner parlour between south side of south transept & chapter-house, now devoid of vaulting & blocked, formerly used as Lord Byron's plunge pool; C13

Oxford St. Frideswide's priory: intact slype between chapter-house & south transept, tunnel vaulted; C12, doorway late C15

Pill priory: intact barrel vaulted slype between former south transept & extant chapter-house, now divided into 2 parts by modern panelling; late C12/early C13

Reading abbey: roofless slype between south transept & chapter-house, with semicircular doorway from cloister; C12

Rievaulx abbey: ruined inner parlour of 3 bays, standing up to springing of former vault; late C12

St. Albans abbey: intact slype on south side of south transept, recently in use as cathedral shop; C12, reconstructed later C19

Sherborne abbey: intact slype & 2 other small vaulted rooms on north side of north transept; C12, C13

Stoneleigh abbey: [1. intact tunnel vaulted room (inner parlour?) on south side of chapter-house; c.1200
2. intact tunnel vaulted passage with doorway to east (providing access to former infirmary?); c.1200]

Thornton abbey: almost intact narrow inner parlour between south transept & chapter-house, vaulted & with arcaded seating; late C13

Ulverscroft priory: [intact inner parlour under prior's lodging; C13]

Valle Crucis abbey: intact slype on south side of chapter-house, in 2 rib vaulted bays; late C14/early C15

Waverley abbey: intact barrel vaulted inner parlour on south side of chapter-house; c.1200

Westminster abbey: 1. intact slype & inner parlour occupying 2 bays of east range undercroft between warming house & chapel of the Pyx, now part of museum area; mid C11

2. intact slype towards south end of east range leading from Dark Cloister to former infirmary; mid C11

Winchester cathedral-priory: intact slype between south transept & former chapter-house, library overhead; late C11/early C12

Worcester cathedral-priory: intact vaulted slype/inner parlour between south transept & chapter-house, now cathedral refectory; c.1100

◆◆◆◆◆◆◆◆◆◆◆◆◆◆◆

Section 13:
DORMITORY RANGES 2

13/1   DORMITORIES

N.B. All are on the east side of the cloister unless stated otherwise.

Anglesey priory: [largely intact dormitory, modified as part of post-Dissolution mansion; C13, pDp]
Battle abbey: high-standing ruined dormitory on split level site, with substantial intact undercrofts; C13
Beeleigh abbey: [intact dormitory, now library of private mansion; early C13]
Calder abbey: high-standing ruined dormitory; C13
Caldey cell: intact dormitory; C13
Cleeve abbey: intact dormitory over warming room or common room, post-Dissolution farm use; mid C13
Coventry Carmelite friary: intact dormitory, part of post-Dissolution town-house; C14
Durham cathedral-priory: intact dormitory (west range), now cathedral library & exhibition area; 1398-1404
Easby abbey: high-standing ruined dormitory (west range); early C13
Easebourne priory: intact but altered dormitory, part of post-Dissolution house; C14, C15, pDp
Forde abbey: intact dormitory, divided into small bedrooms in post-Dissolution mansion; C13, pDp
Furness abbey: high-standing ruined dormitory, minus vaulting below; C13

Gloucester Dominican friary: partly intact dormitory (north end), converted into part of post-Dissolution house; mid C13, C15, c.1540

Ixworth priory: [intact dormitory adapted as upper storey accommodation of post-Dissolution house; c.1230, C17, C18]

Jervaulx abbey: high-standing ruined large portion of dormitory south of chapter-house; c.1200

Kirkstall abbey: portion of high-standing ruined dormitory; later C12, C13

Lacock abbey: intact dormitory, divided into gallery & bedrooms of post-Dissolution mansion; mid C13, pDp

Newcastle-upon-Tyne Dominican friary: intact but adapted after Dissolution as part of accommodation for trades' communities; C13+

Newstead Augustinian priory: intact dormitory, divided into bedrooms of post-Dissolution mansion; mid C13, pDp

Norwich Dominican friary: intact & altered dormitory, adapted as granary & then place of worship after Dissolution; C14, C19

Penmon priory: high-standing ruined dormitory (third storey of south range); C13

Valle Crucis abbey: intact dormitory, part of post-Dissolution farmhouse; C14/C15

Westminster abbey: intact dormitory, part reconstructed as library & part as school hall; C12, C19, C20

13/2   TREASURIES

Birkenhead priory: intact treasury or scriptorium over chapter-house; c.1375

Bristol abbey: intact small treasury over Newton chapel; c.1330+

Canterbury cathedral-priory: intact treasury north of chapel of St. Andrew, with octopartite rib vault; c.1150, late C13, pDp

Durham cathedral-priory: intact treasury (Spendement) in northern bay at west end of undercroft of west range, possesses medieval iron grille;

Fountains abbey: intact chamber near daystairs at junction of east & south ranges; C12/C13(?)

Kirkstall abbey: intact chamber at north end of dormitory near nightstairs; late C12(?)

London charterhouse: [intact chamber in Chapel Tower above vestibule; C14, 1613]

Thornton abbey: chamber on ground floor behind inner parlour, entered by spiral stair from above; late C13/early C14

Westminster abbey: 1. chamber occupied first 2 bays of sub-dorter, also served as chapel of Pyx; C11, late C13/early C14

2. intact undercroft of chapter-house; mid C13

3. intact Muniment Room (perhaps originally royal pew) over east cloister-walk; late C14

13/3   NIGHTSTAIRS

Beaulieu abbey: largely intact stone stairs built into thickness of west wall of south transept; C13

Bishopsgate St. Helens priory: intact narrow staircase in thickness of north wall of church, now blocked behind small 4-centred doorway; C15

Brecon priory: intact stone spiral stairway in south west corner of south transept; mid C13

Bristol abbey: intact stone stairs built into thickness of south wall of south transept, rise from east to west; probably late C12

Buildwas abbey: partly surviving stone stairs in north west corner of north transept; probably late C12

Chester abbey: intact spiral stairs in north east angle of north transept; C12

Christchurch priory: intact doorway & a few steps leading down in east end of south wall of south transept; unknown date

Dudley priory: partly surviving winding stair in north east corner of north transept, consisting of 10 intact stone steps; later C12

Durham cathedral-priory: intact winding stair in south west corner of south transept (original nightstairs before dormitory was moved from east to west range); early C12

Ewenny priory: intact spiral stairs in south west corner of south transept; C12

Finchale priory: base of stone nightstairs along south wall of south transept; C13

Fountains abbey intact lay-brothers' stone stairs at north end of west range leading to nave; mid C12

Furness abbey: almost intact set of stone stairs at south west corner of south transept; late C12/early C13

Haverfordwest priory: largely intact stone stairs concealed within thickness of west wall of south transept; C13

Hexham priory: intact stone stairs on south side of south transept; early C13

Jervaulx abbey: 1. remnant of flight of stairs in south transept; later C12

2. intact lower portion of lay brothers' stone stairs at north end of west range leading to nave; later C12

Kirkstall abbey intact stone stairs on south side of south transept; C12

Lacock abbey: intact stone stairs built into thickness of west wall of sacristry, lowest steps visible below blocked doorway; early C13

Lindisfarne priory: intact lower portion of winding stairway in south west corner of south transept, 8 steps survive; C12

Neath abbey: base of stone stairs with intact handrail in south transept; c.1300

Pershore abbey: intact winding stairway in south west corner of south transept leading to blocked dormitory doorway in south wall of transept; probably C12

Rufford abbey: intact lay-brothers' stone stairs at west end of now-vanished nave; C13

Salley abbey largely intact stone stairs in south transept; late C12/early C13

Strata Florida abbey   start of lay brothers' spiral staircase at north end of west range; late C12/early C13

Tewkesbury abbey: intact spiral stairs in south east angle of south transept; C12

Tintern abbey: intact stone stairs in north transept, largely reconstructed; originally c.1270+

Westminster abbey: intact bridge over revestry on south side of transept, leading from dormitory to nightstairs' doorway (now blocked) behind present Argyll monument in transept; unknown date

Basingwerk abbey: partly surviving stairs rise in south east corner of cloister; C13

Beaulieu abbey: partly surviving stairway (7 intact steps) at south east corner of cloister; C13

Bristol abbey: intact original doorway & modern stairway halfway along east range; unknown date

Byland abbey: 1. largely intact 2 stair flights at south east corner of cloister, partly reconstructed; late C12/early C13

2. intact lowest 8 steps of daystairs of lay-brothers at south end of cloister-lane; late C12

Caldey cell: intact stone stairs in west wall of east range rise to dormitory; C13

Chester abbey: intact stone stairs rise from north end of east cloister-walk; C13

Cleeve abbey: intact stone stairs rise from south end of east cloister-walk; late C15

Fountains abbey: 1. intact stone stairs in south east angle of cloister; late C12

2. largely intact lay-brothers' stone stairs midway along outer side of west range; mid C12

Hailes abbey: start of stone daystairs (8 steps) in angle between east & south ranges; mid C13

Jervaulx abbey: some stone lower stairs facing south in south east angle of cloister; c.1200

Kirkstall abbey: 1. ruined daystair remnant in east range; C12

2. ruined later daystair remnant in south east corner of cloister; C13

Leiston abbey: largely intact stone stairs in south east angle of cloister, overlaid with modern stairs; C14

Neath abbey: solid start of ruined daystairs in south east corner of cloister; mid C13

Rochester cathedral-priory: considerably ruined stone stairway rises from middle of east cloister-walk; C12

Valle Crucis abbey: intact stone stairs rise from south end of east cloister-walk; C14/C15

Westminster abbey: intact set of stone stairs rise from south end of east cloister-walk to upper storey of east range (library end); late C11/early C12

13/5   COMBINED NIGHT- & DAYSTAIRS

Beaulieu abbey: intact lay-brothers' stone stairs midway along east side of west range, with 2 flights of steps; C13

Castle Acre priory: almost intact stone stairs on south side of chapter-house; late C12

Easby abbey: largely intact stone stairs rise from south end of west walk to dormitory in west range; doorway C12, stairs early C13

Jervaulx abbey: lower section of lay-brothers' stone stairs at north end of west range; late C12

Thetford Cluniac priory: intact 4 or 5 steps leading to solid platform within east range immediately south of chapter-house; C12

13/6   REREDORTERS

N.B. All are joined to east range unless stated otherwise.

Beeleigh abbey: mostly intact reredorter, adapted as part of post-Dissolution house; C13, C16

Burnham abbey: intact(?) reredorter at end of north placed east range; C13

Castle Acre priory: part of high-standing ruin displays basic arrangement well; mid C12

Clare friary: largely intact reredorter joins east end of infirmary & survives as part of modern church; late C13

13/6 Clare friary, reredorter and infirmary to south west

Coggeshall abbey shell of (now?) detached reredorter stands, converted into barn; c.1200

Easby abbey: high-standing ruined reredorter in outer west range of 3 storeys; early C13

Flaxley abbey: [partly intact reredorter, adapted as part of post-Dissolution house; C12]

Forde abbey: north 3 bays of east range, including undercroft, represent part of reredorter; C13, pDp

Fountains abbey:　high-standing ruined lay-brothers' reredorter leading off west range; C12

Jervaulx abbey:　partly high-standing ruined reredorter with drainage channel below; early C13(?)

Kirkham priory:　partly high-standing ruined reredorter with drainage channel; late C13

Kirkstall abbey:　intact reredorter of lay brothers originally leading off west range, adapted & altered as farm building & now cafeteria; C12, pDp

Lacock abbey　intact reredorter, adapted within fabric of post-Dissolution mansion; C13, C14

Leominster priory:　partly intact reredorter (or infirmary) adapted within fabric of post-Dissolution house; C15, pDp

Lewes priory:　high-standing ruined reredorter, probably used as farm buildings after Dissolution; C13

Malmesbury abbey:　[intact & adapted lower stages of reredorter within Abbey House (latter built immediately after Dissolution) to north east of church; C14/C15]

Margam abbey:　intact 3 bays of undercroft (or bridge to undercroft) connected at right angles to former east range; c.1210

Muchelney abbey:　intact reredorter, served as farm granary after Dissolution; C13(?)

Neath abbey:　intact lower parts of reredorter survive under post-Dissolution house; C13

Netley abbey:　high-standing ruined reredorter, with intact vaulted lower storey (possibly infirmary), outhouse of post-Dissolution mansion; C13

Pill priory: intact barrel vaulted undercroft south of east range within Priory Inn (possibly part of infirmary); C12

Salley abbey: reredorter (of lay-brothers) off west range, survives within post-Dissolution cottage; C12/C13, pDp

Whalley abbey: high-standing ruined reredorter, still connected to east range by bridge; C14

Worcester cathedral-priory: considerable portions of ruined reredorter to west of west range & below ruined dormitory; c.1110/20, remodelled c.1375

13/7 GREAT DRAINS

Brinkburn priory: stone lined mill race served as great drain

Castle Acre priory: passage to sites of kitchen & reredorter

Croxden abbey: sections survive with ashlar sides & roofs; C13

Fountains abbey: River Skell serves as great drain

Furness abbey: stream continues to flow along stone walled drain

Hailes abbey: intact deep drain of series of stone walled tunnels & open sections, still carrying stream; C13

Haughmond abbey: course of stone lined drain down hillside, fed by spring from above

Kirkham priory: great drain lined with stone; probably late C13

Monk Bretton priory: well-tooled stone lined great drain; probably C13

Neath abbey: much of drainage system survives under ruined post-Dissolution house at south end of former east range; mid C13

Netley abbey: fast stream continues to flow beneath reredorter/infirmary block; C13

Roche abbey: stream continues to flow along great drain

Salley abbey: surviving good specimen lined with stone & roofed in sections

Shap abbey: largely surviving outflow channels from reredorter into River Lowther, with tooled ashlar revetments etc.; later C13

Tintern abbey: considerable well-tooled portions of drainage system visible throughout claustral area; probably mainly early C13

Whalley abbey: bed of drain though now dry & silted up, illustrates how water was diverted off river

13/8 WATER CONDUIT-HOUSES & CISTERNS

Alnwick abbey: intact small building to north west (White Well); C14

Beaulieu abbey: intact conduit head (Monk's Well) near Hilltop House, consisting of small building vaulted inside ; C13

Canterbury cathedral-priory: 1. intact water tower north of church (Prior Wibert's water tower); c.1151
2. intact(?) conduit house behind Canterbury Sports Hall off Brymore Road, square shaped & made of flint with brick top; unknown date probably C12

Chester abbey: intact fresh water stone lined cistern in cloister garth; unknown date

Dinmore commandery: intact well-head covering spring 550 yards to west of Manor House; C14

Edington priory: [intact small stone-vaulted cell over spring in hollow south west of church; C14/C15]

Fountains abbey: [intact well-house (Robin Hood's well); 1160+]

Gloucester abbey: intact cistern in cloister-garth; unknown date

Grantham friary: intact building, system probably existing before post- Dissolution reconstruction; dated 1597

Haughmond abbey: intact stone building on hillside above precinct; C14

Lincoln Carmelite friary: intact building, reconstructed at time of Dissolution; unknown earlier date, 1539

London charterhouse: [intact store cistern or conduit-house within precinct & near gatehouse; C14/C15, pDp]

Monkton Farleigh priory: intact building; C14, rebuilt 1784

Mount Grace charterhouse: 1. intact building (north east spring-house), reconstructed; late C14/early C15
[2.   intact   building   (south   east   spring-house), reconstructed; late C14/early C15
3. another   spring-house (St. John's well) south east of precinct; unknown date]

Penmon priory: intact well house (Wishing Well House); unknown date

St. Germans priory: [intact spring house (Dupath Well) at Callington; c.1500]

Valle Crucis abbey: intact small conduit-house to west of precinct; C14(?)

Wymondley priory: [intact conduit head, medieval stone patched with later brick; C14/C15, brickwork C16]

13/9   WARMING HOUSES

Anglesey priory: [intact vaulted warming house (east range) now dining room of post-Dissolution mansion; C13]

Battle abbey: intact vaulted undercroft at south end of east range (also identified as novices' room); C13

Beeleigh abbey: [intact warming house (east range), now sitting room of post-Dissolution house; C13]

Burnham abbey: [largely intact warming house combined with inner parlour (east range), now part of accommodation of modern nunnery; C13, 1913-15]

Byland abbey: partly intact warming house (south range), with large fireplace in west wall; late C12

Caldey cell: intact warming house (east range) below dormitory, used as scullery of Victorian house; C13

Chester abbey: intact warming house (east range), recently song school of cathedral; C13

Cleeve abbey: intact warming house or common room (east range), survives in undercroft as part of farm buildings after Dissolution; C13

Coventry Carmelite friary: intact warming house (east range), part of post-Dissolution house; C14

Croxden abbey: east & south walls (south range) stand almost to maximum height; C13

Durham cathedral-priory: intact warming house in south end of west range undercroft, now cafeteria of cathedral; C13

Easby abbey: part of high-standing ruined west range building; C13

Easebourne priory: [intact but altered warming house (east range), now part of post-Dissolution house; C14 & later]

Fountains abbey: intact warming house (south range) with high chimney but open to south, probably used as farm building after Dissolution; c.1190

Ixworth priory: [intact warming house (east range) in 4 double bays, domestic use in post-Dissolution house; c.1230]

Lacock abbey: intact warming house (east range), domestic use in post-Dissolution mansion; C13

Netley abbey: high-standing ruined warming house (south range), partly rebuilt (i.e. south wall) as accommodation for post-Dissolution mansion now gone; early C13 & later

Newcastle-upon-Tyne Dominican friary: intact but adapted warming house (east range), accommodation for trades' company after Dissolution; C13+

Newstead Augustinian priory: intact vaulted warming house (east range), adapted as domestic rooms of post-Dissolution mansion; C13

Penmon priory: high-standing ruined warming house in basement of building at south east corner of cloister & contiguous with south range; early C16

Tintern abbey: almost intact warming house (north range); early C13

Walsingham priory: (See entry under Sub-Dorters of East Ranges Surviving on Own)

Westminster abbey: intact warming house in sub-dorter of east range (now museum), occupying 3 bays immediately north of passage to former infirmary; mid C11

◆◆◆◆◆◆◆◆◆◆◆◆◆◆◆

Section 14:
REFECTORY RANGES

14/1   WHOLE RANGES

Birkenhead priory: almost intact north range, recently restored as conference centre etc.; C14, modern

Boston friary: intact north(?) range, now arts centre; C13

Chester abbey: almost intact north range; C12, C13/C14

Chicksands priory: intact south range considerably altered, now part of private mansion; C13,C15

Cleeve abbey: intact south range, used as farm buildings after Dissolution; C15

Durham cathedral-priory: intact south range, part used as library after Dissolution; C11/C12, 1366-70

Easby abbey: high-standing ruined south range with undercroft of which vaulting has gone; early C13, c.1300

Flanesford priory: [intact south range though considerably altered after Dissolution as part of private house; C14]

Forde abbey: intact north range, considerably altered after Dissolution as part of private mansion; C13, C15, pDp

Fountains abbey: high-standing ruined south range; late C12

Gloucester Dominican friary: largely intact south range (with lower storey used for storage & upper storey as scriptorium or library with 10+ carrels per side), part of industrial premises after Dissolution; C13, pDp

Horsham St. Faith's priory: intact north range, adapted as part of post-Dissolution farmhouse; C12, mid C13, C15

King's Lynn priory: intact south range converted into post-Dissolution cottages; C14, C15, 1974-75

Lacock abbey: intact north range, adapted as part of post-Dissolution mansion; C13, C16

Leiston abbey: high-standing ruined south range probably used as farm building after Dissolution; C14

Michelham priory: intact south range, adapted as part of post-Dissolution house; C13

Newcastle-upon-Tyne Dominican friary: intact south range, remodelled by trades' companies after Dissolution; C13+, 1739, 1843

Newstead Augustinian priory: intact 2-storeyed south range, adapted as part of post-Dissolution mansion; C13, modern

Oxford Gloucester college: intact south range of students' lodgings; C15

Oxford St. Frideswide's priory: intact south range, considerably adapted as part of Christ Church after Dissolution; C13, c.1490

Penmon priory: high-standing ruined south range of 3 storeys, with dormitory in third storey; C13

Rievaulx abbey: high-standing ruined 'south' range; C13

Torre abbey: intact south range, considerably adapted as part of post-Dissolution mansion; core probably C13

Totnes priory: intact north range, converted & extended into town's guildhall after Dissolution; C12, C15, pDp

Vale Royal abbey: intact south range, adapted as part of post-Dissolution mansion; late C14/early C15, C16+

Ware friary: intact south range, used as part of private house after Dissolution & recently as council offices; C15, C18

Worcester cathedral-priory: intact south range; C11, C14

14/2 SUB-FRATERS SURVIVING ON OWN OR UNDER POST-DISSOLUTION WORK

Brinkburn priory: south range undercroft (part), late Georgian house above; unknown date
Calder abbey: south range undercroft, late Georgian house overhead; C14, c.1770
Lanercost priory: south range intact undercroft, upper storey demolished; late C12
Malton priory: [south range undercroft (part), outbuilding of post-Dissolution house; C13]
St. Olave's (Herringfleet) priory: north range intact undercroft, post-Dissolution barn above; late C13/early C14

14/3 MAIN DOORWAYS TO REFECTORY FROM CLOISTER-WALK

Beaulieu abbey: intact doorway of Transitional appearance, with almost semicircular head but detached shafting, door & ironwork said to be original; early C13
Birkenhead priory: intact & weathered small doorway at west end of south wall of refectory, has arched head with continuous mouldings; C14
Bristol abbey: intact small doorway from halfway along south cloister-walk to refectory, 4-centred with casement moulding; C15

Canterbury cathedral-priory: doorway halfway along north walk leads now to garden, has luxuriant capitals with stiff-leaf foliage & complex multiple shafting; 1226-36

Carlisle cathedral-priory: intact doorway with shallow outer & 2-centred inner arch, probably heavily restored; C14/C15, C19

Chester abbey: 1. intact but worn main doorway from north cloister-walk to refectory, with semicircular head & wavy inner moulding, 3-ordered shafting & caps with stiff-leaf; c.1200 or earlier

2. intact & worn secondary doorway from north cloister-walk to kitchen area, smaller & plainer with semicircular head & one order; late C12

Cleeve abbey: intact doorway with pointed arch at west end of refectory, possesses 2 orders of which outer is richly moulded; early C13

Dover Benedictine priory: robbed 2 doorways from north cloister-walk in Bays 1 & 7 from east, with semicircular heads; C12(?)

Easby abbey: intact doorway with finely moulded 2-centred arch of 2 orders; C13

Finchale priory: intact prominent doorway with pointed archway at west end of south cloister-walk, has 2 orders of colonnettes; early C14

Fountains abbey: intact luxuriant doorway with semicircular arch, has 4 main orders of colonnettes & deeply cut mouldings on the arch; c.1180/1210

Gloucester abbey: intact doorway at west end of north cloister-walk blocked with window, with 2 orders of colonnettes & richly moulded pointed arch; c.1246+, C19

Hailes abbey: weathered original doorway with 2-centred top & series of major & minor orders, with inserted later smaller doorway; C13, C15

Kirkham priory: almost intact & relocated doorway of 3 orders, lavishly ornamented semicircular head with cross-banding; late C12

Kirkstall abbey: intact large plain doorway, possesses round shafts of one order below moulded caps; later C12

Merevale abbey: intact but weathered doorway minus shafting, with 2-centred pointed arch deeply moulded & 3(?) orders; C13

Michelham priory: intact & blocked large doorway with pointed top immediately to west of lavatorium in north wall of refectory, has 2 hollow chamfers dying into imposts; later C13

Newstead Augustinian priory: blocked doorway less its arch, mainly one order of detached round shafts & inverted bell caps; C13

Norwich cathedral-priory: intact doorway at west end of south cloister-walk, arch has 5 engaged shafts per side & prominent hoodmould; C15

Notley abbey: [intact doorway to former refectory, has stiff-leaf cap over detached shafts; C13]

Oxford St. Frideswide's priory: intact doorway to refectory halfway along south cloister-walk, has 4-centred arch with square label & shallow spandrels; late C15/early C16

Penmon priory: intact blocked doorway possibly inserted within former doorway, with 2-centred head & continuous chamfered mouldings; C13

Peterborough abbey: intact well ornamented doorway at west end of former south cloister-walk, has 2-centred arch of 4 orders with detached shafts; C13

Prittlewell priory: intact restored 2-order doorway at west end of south cloister-walk, displaying Transitional features such as pointed arch with zigzag; c.1180

Rievaulx abbey: intact doorway reconstructed in early medieval period, with outer semicircular head & inner trefoiled head; late C12, early C13

Rochester cathedral-priory: intact decayed doorway of Merstham stone & Purbeck marble with trefoiled arch at west end of south cloister-walk; of 4 orders but some shafting has gone; c.1200

Walsingham priory: intact 2-centred doorway at west end of refectory, with inner & outer continuous mouldings divided by one-ordered nominal cap each side; C14/C15

Westminster abbey: intact doorway at west end of south cloister-walk, top arched & cinquefoiled with cusps & sub-cusps; mid C14

Worcester cathedral-priory: intact acute pointed doorway towards west end of south walk, series of deep cut rolls & continuous mouldings with fleurons round hoodmould; mid C14

Yarmouth priory: intact acute pointed doorway on north side of refectory towards west end; lateC13/early C14

14/4   REFECTORIES

N.B. These are located in the south range unless stated otherwise.

Aylesford friary: intact but modified refectory on upper floor, now sitting room & library; C15, pDp

Basingwerk abbey: high-standing ruined refectory, main axis north-south; later C13

Beaulieu abbey: intact refectory with north-south axis, now parish church; C13, C19

Birkenhead priory: intact north range refectory over undercroft, now conference centre; C14, modern

Blanchland abbey: intact refectory converted into row of cottages; probably c.1300, pDp

Boston friary: intact refectory on upper storey, part of arts centre; C13, modern

Bradenstoke priory: [intact north range refectory removed to & reconstructed at St. Donat's castle; c.1320]

Bradsole St. Radegund's abbey: intact refectory on upper storey, adapted as major part of post-Dissolution farmhouse; C13, modern

14/4 Carlisle cathedral-priory, refectory to north west

Bristol abbey: intact though much altered refectory with undercroft, now part of cathedral school; C12/C13, C15/C16, C19

Bushmead priory: intact north range refectory, partitioned into domestic accommodation after Dissolution; C13

Calder abbey: much of refectory embedded within post-Dissolution mansion, together with more of range; C14, pDp

Cambridge St. Radegund's priory   intact north range refectory on upper floor, now college hall; C15, C18

Canterbury Dominican friary: intact west range refectory on upper storey, now school accommodation; C13

Carlisle cathedral-priory: intact refectory on upper storey, now cathedral library; C14, C15

Chester abbey: intact north range refectory, now cathedral cafeteria; C12, late C13/early C14

Cleeve abbey: intact east-west refectory on upper storey, used as farm building after Dissolution; C15

Denney abbey: intact north range refectory, used as barn after Dissolution; C14

Dover Benedictine priory: intact north range refectory, now school hall; C12

Durham cathedral-priory: intact refectory on upper storey, used as library after Dissolution; C11/C12, 1366-70

Easby abbey: high-standing ruined refectory on upper storey, displaying geometric tracery in east window; c.1300

Easebourne priory: [intact & much altered refectory on 2 floors, first barn after Dissolution & then house & now church premises; late C13, C17 & later]

Exeter St. Nicholas' priory: [intact north range refectory on upper storey, adapted as part of private house after Dissolution; C12/C13, modern]

Finchale priory: high-standing ruined refectory on upper storey, with intact vaulted undercroft below; early C14

Flanesford priory: intact refectory on upper storey, adapted as part of post-Dissolution house; C14

Forde abbey: intact north range refectory with north-south axis, divided horizontally & now part of post-Dissolution mansion with library on upper floor; C13, C15, 1890

Fountains abbey: high-standing ruined refectory on north-south axis; c.1200

Gloucester abbey: [intact misericord on upper storey to west of little cloister, adapted as part of school building after Dissolution; C13, C15(?), modern]

Halesowen abbey: high-standing ruined south wall of refectory, with lancet windows; C13

Hardham priory: [intact refectory walls now comprising farmhouse, with groin vaulted 6-bay undercroft,; C13, modern]

Hinton charterhouse: [intact refectory on upper storey in north location, now barn; c.1300]

Horsham St. Faith's priory: intact north range refectory in 4 bays adapted as part of post-Dissolution farmhouse; C12, mid C13, C15, pDp

Hurley priory: intact north range refectory, adapted as part of post-Dissolution house; C11/C12, late C13, C16+

King's Lynn priory intact refectory, drastically divided into small houses after Dissolution; C14, C15, pDp

Kirkham priory: high-standing ruined refectory in 2 storeys with intact & beautiful doorway from cloister; vaulting gone; late C13

Kirkstall abbey: mostly high-standing ruined refectory with north-south axis; late C12, C15

Lacock abbey: intact north range refectory on upper storey, divided into gallery & small rooms after Dissolution as part of mansion; C13, C16

Leiston abbey: high-standing ruined refectory lacking architectural detail; C14

Merevale abbey: high-standing ruined refectory with most of walls in place including main doorway & reading pulpit; C13

Michelham priory: intact refectory, divided into rooms as part of post-Dissolution mansion; C13, modern

Monk Bretton priory: ruined part of south wall stands to above windows; late C13

Newcastle-upon-Tyne Dominican friary: intact refectory probably located in lower storey (with extant room for library above), adapted as part of accommodation of trades' companies after Dissolution; C13+, 1739, 1843

Newstead Augustinian priory: intact refectory on upper storey, now drawing room of post-Dissolution mansion; core C13, pDp

Norwich cathedral-priory: substantial portion of ruined refectory, especially north wall standing to full height displaying 23 shafted windows; C12

Norwich Dominican friary: intact refectory on upper storey of west range, considerably adapted as granary & school building after Dissolution; C14, C19

Oxford St. Frideswide's priory intact refectory, divided into college rooms after Dissolution; C13, c.1490, modern

Penmon priory: high-standing ruined refectory on middle storey of three, with dormitory on top & undercroft below; C13

Prittlewell priory: intact refectory, incorporated into private house after Dissolution; C12, C15, C20

Rievaulx abbey: high-standing ruined refectory on upper storey of 'south' range; C13

Romsey abbey: refectory largely intact within post-Dissolution house; unknown date

St. Anthony-in-Roseland cell: refectory within post-Dissolution mansion (Place House), contiguous with north transept & north side of nave; unknown medieval date, 1840

St. Germans priory: [intact refectory, now hall of post-Dissolution mansion; C13(?), pDp]

St. Michael's Mount priory: intact refectory now dining hall (Chevy Chase Room) of post-Dissolution mansion, south of church but not in normal location; C12, C15, C19

Shulbrede priory: [intact refectory, divided horizontally within post-Dissolution farmhouse; mid C13, pDp]

Sibton abbey: high-standing ruined refectory, displaying some original windows; c.1200

Syningthwaite priory: [partly intact refectory built into post-Dissolution farmhouse, displays richly carved Norman doorway; late C12, C19]

Temple Balsall preceptory: intact refectory in detached west range, divided into rooms of post-Dissolution cottages; C13, C15, modern

Tintern abbey: walls of north refectory stand quite high especially on east side where much of windowing is intact; early C13

Torre abbey: intact refectory on upper storey with groin vaulted undercroft below, considerably adapted within south range as part of mansion; C13(?), modern

Totnes priory: intact north range refectory, adapted to form part of post-Dissolution guildhall; C12, C15, pDp

Tupholme abbey: high-standing ruined stretch of south wall of refectory; late C12-mid C13

Vale Royal abbey: intact refectory on upper floor divided into smaller room ante-Dissolution, & post-Dissolution as part of wing of new mansion; lateC14/early C15, c.1480, pDp

Walsingham priory: high-standing ruined refectory, south & west walls chiefly surviving; late C13

Ware friary: intact refectory on upper floor, now divided by partitions into modern rooms; C15, pDp

Worcester cathedral-priory: intact refectory over undercroft, now used as school hall; C11, mid C14

Yarmouth priory: intact refectory, recently in use as school hall; late C13/early C14, C19

14/5　　READING PULPITS

Aylesford friary: intact pulpit projection in south wall, with inner arch & steps; C15

Basingwerk abbey: substantial remains of pulpit; mid C13

Beaulieu abbey: intact pulpit, restored; C13, C19

Canterbury Dominican friary: recess of pulpit intact; C13

Carlisle cathedral-priory: intact pulpit; C15

Chester abbey: intact pulpit; late C13/early C14

Clare friary: projection in wall for reader's pulpit; probably early C14

Cleeve abbey: intact doorway & some steps; C16

Easby abbey: high-standing ruined pulpit bay, still in fine condition; c.1300

Forde abbey: recess of pulpit intact: C13(?)

Fountains abbey: substantial remains of stairs & gallery, with locker for books at base of stairs; c.1200

Horsham St. Faith's priory: substantial remains on 'wrong' (i.e. claustral) side of refectory; C13/C14

Merevale abbey: weathered doorway & stairway, nevertheless in good condition; C13

Oxford St. Frideswide's priory: substantial remnant of pulpit though much altered after Dissolution, interior rib vault; C13, c.1613, C18

Penmon priory: intact window seat for reader in south east corner of middle floor refectory; C13

Rievaulx abbey: substantial remains in west wall; C13

Shrewsbury abbey: intact pulpit with domed roof & open panels, now free standing; early C14

Tintern abbey: intact entrance archway with mini-vault & some steps; early C13

Tupholme abbey: substantial remains of doorway, window & seat; early C13

Walsingham priory: substantial remains of stairway & pulpit wall; late C13

Worcester cathedral-priory: intact stairway & bay of pulpit; mid C14

14/6   KITCHENS

Aylesford friary: intact kitchen in angle between south & west ranges, displays wide stone fireplace; C15

Blanchland abbey: intact kitchen of west range, now forming part of ground floor accommodation at south end of hotel, 2 heavy fireplaces; C13

Durham cathedral-priory: intact main kitchen in south range extension, used as dean's kitchen till 1940; 1366-70

Exeter St. Nicholas' priory: intact main kitchen in north west corner between north & west ranges, part of domestic property after Dissolution; C13

Forde abbey: intact main kitchen in extension of north range, in use in post-Dissolution mansion; C15, C17

Glastonbury abbey: intact abbot's kitchen now detached, used as Quaker meeting house after Dissolution; C14

Haughmond abbey: ruined main kitchen with remnants of 3 fireplaces & chimney breasts; C14, C15

Jervaulx abbey: considerable portions of abbot's meat kitchen to east of east range, with 2 large fireplaces; C13, C15

Lacock abbey: intact main kitchen in west range; C13

Muchelney abbey: intact kitchen in abbot's house in angle between south & west ranges, part of farmhouse after Dissolution; pre C16

Penmon priory: high-standing ruined kitchen on upper storey of building in south east corner of cloister (warming house below); early C16

Sherborne abbey: [intact abbot's kitchen embedded & adapted within west range, now part of school accommodation; probably C15/C16]

Thame abbey: [intact but altered part of south(?) range, adapted as kitchens of post-Dissolution mansion; C13/C14, late C16]

Vale Royal abbey: intact kitchen at junction of west & south ranges, divided into 2 storeys after Dissolution; C14/C15, pDp

Westminster abbey: intact abbot's kitchen west of west range, incorporated into school accommodation; C14

Whalley abbey: high-standing ruined detached abbot's kitchen; late C15/early C16

14/7 SLYPES OF SOUTH & NORTH RANGES

Bristol abbey: intact slype at east end of south range; C12, C14

Cleeve abbey: intact slype at east end of south range; C13/C15

Durham cathedral-priory: intact slype at east end of south range; late C11

Gloucester abbey: intact slype (Dark Cloister) at east end of demolished north range; C13

Horsham St. Faith's priory: intact barrel vaulted slype at east end of north range; probably C12

Humberston abbey: intact passage at east end of former south range, has thick walls & barrel vault, apparently converted into icehouse; C12/C13

Lacock abbey: intact slype at east end of north range sometimes called the parlour, has plain ribbed vault; C13

Newstead Augustinian priory: intact slype (Dark Entry) at east end of south range; C12/C13

Norwich cathedral-priory: intact slype (Dark Entry) now Song School at east end of demolished south range, barrel vaulted; C12

Peterborough abbey: high-standing ruined slype (Hostry Passage) at east end of demolished south range; c.1330

St. Osyth abbey: intact slype at east end of north range converted into post-Dissolution chapel, double aisled & 3 bays with 2 slender Purbeck shafts; early C13

Tintern abbey: partly intact slype in north range of 2 bays east of warming-house, with rib-vaulting & tunnel vaulting; early C13

Waltham abbey: intact slype (Dark Entry) at east end of demolished north range; late C12

Westminster abbey: intact slype (Dark Cloister) at east end of demolished south range; C11, C14

Worcester cathedral-priory: intact slype to east of south range; C12

14/8   SERVING HATCHES

Basingwerk abbey: intact serving hatch at cloister end of west wall of refectory; later C13

Bushmead priory: small serving hatch (now blocked) in north wall near west end; c.1250

Canterbury cathedral-priory: intact hatch (rota) in west wall of west walk of cloister for distribution of refreshment from cellarer's range; unknown date

Carlisle cathedral-priory: 2 intact hatches in west wall, led to destroyed kitchen; C14/C15

Easby abbey: 2 hatches in south wall of vestibule of refectory; c.1300

Fountains abbey: intact doorway from kitchen to refectory, used to contain circular turnstile; unknown date

Haughmond abbey: hatch between kitchen & refectory; C12/C13

Horsham St. Faith's priory: hatch at west end of former refectory, next to former kitchen (now small sitting room); unknown date

Jervaulx abbey: 1. intact hatch in east wall of abbot's meat kitchen, rebated on east side; C15
2. intact hatch in west wall of abbot's meat kitchen, with tapered roof on both sides; C13

London charterhouse: [intact food hatch beside doorway of south west corner cell; late C14]

Mattersey priory: hatch in west wall of former refectory; C14/C15

Monk Bretton priory: intact hatch with segmental top in south wall of former refectory; late C13

Mount Grace charterhouse: intact many food hatches to individual cells, right-angled & rebated externally; early C15

Muchelney abbey: blocked hatches(?) in abbot's house between original kitchen & anteroom of refectory; unknown date

Netley abbey: 1. intact hatch between reredorter undercroft & dorter undercroft, has segmental head; late C13

2. intact hatch of similar type to above in wall of dorter undercroft connecting to unidentified former building to south; late C13

Rievaulx abbey: imperfect hatch between kitchen & refectory; c.1225

Tintern abbey: intact rectangular serving hatch with triangular head, in south end of west wall of refectory; early C13

Westminster abbey: [intact hatch on south side of former refectory from destroyed kitchen; unknown date but probably mid C11/C12]

Whalley abbey: intact hatch in west wall of abbot's kitchen; C15/C16

14/9 TOWEL, CUTLERY & OTHER CUPBOARD RECESSES

Aylesford friary: intact trefoiled recess at north end of prior's hall; unknown date

Battle abbey: intact locker in east wall of lowest undercroft (novices' room) of east range, has pointed head & is rebated; C13

Bayham abbey: 1. intact square plain niche in west wall of sacristy (south of new south transept), with canted edges & drain hole for sink at rear; C13/C14

2. intact wide rectangular locker in east wall of west range facing west cloister-walk; unknown date

Beaulieu abbey: intact tall rectangular locker in northernmost bay of west range undercroft, not rebated; C13

Canterbury St. Augustine's abbey: damaged locker at east end of north wall of north cloister-walk, with semicircular top & apron; C12

Castle Acre priory: 1. 3 intact square lockers in outer parlour, all rebated; probably mid C12

2. intact small triangular arched recess in east wall of undercroft below prior's solar, containing intact stone sink; earlier C14

3. intact locker in north wall of above undercroft, rebated & almost square; earlier C14

4. intact trefoiled & ogeed recess in west wall of prior's solar, containing intact rectangular stone sink & broken shelf at rear; earlier C14

Easby abbey: intact 2 small recesses (& evidence of others) at east end of refectory, probably for cutlery; c.1300

Finchale priory: intact rectangular locker in prior's lodging; probably C14

Fountains abbey: 1. towel recess in cloister outside warming house, with plain semicircular head; 1180/1210

2. 3 intact cutlery recesses in north wall of kitchen; 1180/1210

Gloucester abbey: towel recess in north cloister-walk, opposite lavatorium; unknown date

Hailes abbey: 1. 4 almost intact trefoil headed small cupboards on east side of main doorway of refectory, for cutlery etc.; C13

2. 2 intact deep lancet shaped cupboards on west side of main doorway of refectory, grooved for shelves & probably used for storing table linen; C13

Haughmond abbey: 2 intact cupboards in refectory, with semicircular heads; unknown date

Jervaulx abbey: intact 2 long & rebated cupboards with semicircular heads in east wall of warming house, possibly used for storing towels; C12/C13

Kirkstall abbey: 1. intact towel cupboard with semicircular head in outer side of west wall of south transept; C12

2. intact 2 square rebated cupboards or lockers in end wall of abbot's kitchen; C13

Lanercost priory: intact square cupboard in west range undercroft at south end next to fireplace; C13

Langley abbey: towel recess at south end of west cloister-walk; unknown date

Michelham priory: intact small arched towel recess immediately to east of lavatorium in north wall of refectory; later C13

Monk Bretton priory: intact cutlery cupboard in south wall of former refectory; late C13

Peterborough abbey: towel recess at south end of west cloister-walk; unknown date

Rochester cathedral-priory: towel recess near lavatorium; unknown date

Thetford Cluniac priory: recess or niche at ground floor level on north side of prior's lodging, with ogeed top; C14

Tintern abbey: 1. intact spoon locker & companion recess with drain for washing spoons & plates, in south east corner of refectory, double arched with trefoiled heads; early C13

2. intact utensil locker in wall in north west corner of kitchen, retains shelf but not its facing stone; probably C13

Walsingham priory: 2 recesses in east wall of east range undercroft, one on each side of entrance doorway, with crude pointed heads; late C13

Westminster abbey: 4 tall towel recesses at west end of south cloister-walk; mid C14

Whalley abbey: intact rebated locker in west wall of abbot's kitchen; C15/C16

♦♦♦♦♦♦♦♦♦♦♦♦♦♦♦

Section 15:
CELLAR RANGES

15/1   **WHOLE RANGES**

Aylesford friary: intact range plus inner gatehouse west wing, adapted as domestic accommodation after Dissolution; mainly C15, later C16, C17, C20

Battle abbey: intact range, adapted as domestic & later school accomodation after Dissolution; C13, C16, C19, C20

Beaulieu abbey: intact range, used as post-Dissolution storage facility; C13

Birkenhead priory: high-standing ruined range; mainly late C13

Blanchland abbey: intact range with undercroft at north end, converted with many alterations into post-Dissolution mansion & now Lord Crewe Arms hotel; C13, pDp

Brecon priory: intact range drastically remodelled as modern Canonry & vestries; late C13/early C14, C17, 1926-27

Buckfast abbey: old range incorporated into post-Dissolution new range, now part of modern Benedictine abbey; C14, C19

Caldey cell: intact gatehouse range, upper storey adapted as pigeon loft after Dissolution; C13

Cambridge St. Radegund's priory: intact range, adapted as part of college after Dissolution; c.1500

Castle Acre priory: partly intact & partly ruined range, retained as post-Dissolution house; C12, C14, C15

Chicksands priory: intact range adapted as part of mansion after Dissolution, whole undercroft of 7 bays intact; C13, C15, pDp

Clare friary: intact range, adapted as part of private house after Dissolution & now owned by religious community; C14, C16

Davington priory: almost intact range, adapted as private house after Dissolution; C12/C13, C17, C19

Durham cathedral-priory: intact range formerly used as monks' dormitory, now part of cathedral accommodation; C13, 1398-1404

Easby abbey: high-standing ruined west range of complex design, including accommodation for canons & guests as well as reredorter; early C13

Exeter Polsloe priory: intact range, used after Dissolution as farmhouse; C13

Exeter St. Nicholas' priory: intact range, used as house after Dissolution; C13, C15

Flaxley abbey: almost complete range, adapted as mansion after Dissolution; C12, C14, C18, C19

Forde abbey: part intact range, adapted as part of post-Dissolution mansion; early C16

Fountains abbey: high-standing ruined range; C12

Gloucester Dominican friary: intact range partly remodelled at north end after Dissolution, south end occupied by refectory; C13, C17/C19

Great Bricett priory: intact range of unknown condition, now Bricett Hall; of varied medieval & post-Dissolution dates

Hartland abbey: [intact range incorporated into post-Dissolution house, involving considerable alteration & addition; C14, C16, C18, C19]

Hexham priory: intact with rib vaulted chambers, rebuilt upper floor; late C11/early C12, C14, c.1790, 1819

Kersey priory: [intact range comprising hall of hospital (antidating the priory), now inside brick-fronted post-Dissolution farmhouse; early C13, C19]

Kington St. Michael's priory: [intact range, converted into farmhouse (Priory Farm) after Dissolution; C15, C17]

Kirkstall abbey: high-standing ruined north & east walls, vaulting gone; later C12

Lacock abbey: intact range, converted into part of post-Dissolution mansion; C13, C16

Lanercost priory: intact range, adapted as house after Dissolution; C13, C16

Langley abbey: intact but drastically modified range adapted as farm buildings after Dissolution, most of vaulting removed; C13, C14, C19

Little Malvern priory: intact range forming core of post-Dissolution mansion (Little Malvern Court); C13/C14, pDp

Llanthony priory: intact range including undercroft, converted after Dissolution into private house & now hotel; late C12/early C13, c.1800

Monks Horton priory: [intact range plus portion of west front of church contained within post-Dissolution house renewed recently; C12, C14, C16, 1913-14]

Neath abbey: high-standing ruined range, industrial use after Dissolution; c.1170-1220

Newcastle-upon-Tyne Dominican friary: intact range, used by trades' companies after Dissolution; C13 & later

Newstead Augustinian priory: intact range including undercroft, part of post-Dissolution mansion; C13, C19

Norwich Dominican friary: almost intact range with refectory above, adapted as granary & other usages after Dissolution; C14, C19

Penmon priory: intact range now house of 3 storeys (See entry below under Presidents' Lodgings & Guests' Accommodation); unknown date, pDp

Polesworth abbey: intact building in west range position now vicarage, contains some medieval remains especially arch-braced roof timbers of so-called refectory; C15, mainly C19

Poughley priory: [some of west range incorporated into post-Dissolution farmhouse; late C13, pDp]

Quarr abbey: [intact west range converted into post-Dissolution barn; C13, pDp]

Repton priory: intact range, now part of school; C12, c.1400, C16+

Rufford abbey: high-standing ruined range, converted after Dissolution into part of mansion & subsequently made derelict; C13, C17

Sherborne abbey: intact range, now school accommodation; C14, C15, 1850

Shulbrede priory: [intact range including undercroft, converted into farmhouse after Dissolution; c.1200, mid C13, mid C16]

Tintern abbey: high-standing ruined range; C13

Torre abbey: intact range, converted into part of mansion after Dissolution; C12, C15, C18

Vale Royal abbey: intact range considerably modified into part of post-Dissolution mansion; late C13/early C14, pDp

Ware friary: intact 3 southerly bays of range, made to form part of post-Dissolution house; C15, C18

Whalley abbey: intact range, now R.C. parish centre; C14

15/2 UNDERCROFTS OF WEST RANGES SURVIVING ON OWN OR UNDER POST-DISSOLUTION WORK

Bradenstoke priory: [intact part of undercroft stands bereft of upper storey, but with part of (non-church) tower at north end; C14]

Chester abbey: intact undercroft, now used as accommodation by cathedral; C12

Hickling priory: [undercroft survives devoid of vaulting & also 3 bays to north west in vaulted room, all part of post-Dissolution farm house; C13]

Langdon abbey: [undercroft survives (3 x 2 units of bay) devoid of vaulting over springing; c.1200]

Mottisfont priory: intact undercroft, partly hidden beneath post-Dissolution mansion; C13

Norton abbey: intact undercroft, formed part of now demolished post-Dissolution mansion; late C12

St. Osyth abbey: intact sections of undercroft, with single chamfered ribs; C13

Shap abbey: partly intact undercroft (2 bays), probably used for storage after Dissolution; C13, C14

Stone priory: [intact 4 bays of undercroft, beneath post-Dissolution town house; unknown date]

Syon abbey: [2 vaulted compartments (one of 3 bays & one of 2 bays), located contiguously with each other at south end of range below post-Dissolution Syon House; C15]

Thurgarton priory: [undercroft of unknown condition below post-Dissolution mansion (The Priory) on site of west range; unknown date]

Welbeck abbey: [intact 7 bays of undercroft, beneath part of post-Dissolution mansion; c.1250, C18]

West Acre priory: partly intact undercroft, retained as farm buildings; C12

15/3   SLYPES & OUTER PARLOURS OF WEST RANGES

Birkenhead priory: high-standing ruined parlour occupying lower of 2 storeys; C13, C14

Caldey cell: gate-hall of gatehouse served as outer parlour; C13

Castle Acre priory: intact parlour later forming part of prior's lodging; mid C12

Chester abbey: intact parlour (Abbot's Passage); c.1150

Clare friary: intact small clumsily vaulted lobby at south end of west range; C14

Elstow abbey: intact parlour now vestry of church, with vaulted roof supported on central pier; C13

Exeter Polsloe priory: intact parlour; probably c.1300

Exeter St. Nicholas' priory: intact parlour (known as Cloister Entry); C12, C13

Gloucester abbey: intact parlour next to church; C12

Guisborough priory: almost intact slype at south end of west range; late C13/early C14

Hexham priory: intact slype in middle of west range, with barrel ribbed vault; C14

Hickling priory: [parlour devoid of vaulting, at north end of   west range undercroft (See entry above under Undercrofts); C13]

Jervaulx abbey: parlour at north end of west range stands to full height, intact doorways with semicircular arches at each end, vaulting gone; later C12

Kirkham priory: high-standing ruined parlour with part of tower above; C13

Lanercost priory: intact parlour at north end of west range though somewhat altered; C13, pDp

Langdon abbey: [intact parlour at north end of range, tunnel vaulted; c.1200]

Langley abbey: intact vaulted parlour at north end of range, with central column; C13, C14

Llanthony priory: intact parlour now dining room of hotel, groin vaulted in 3 bays; early C13

Marham abbey: intact parlour of 2 bays, rib vaulted with roll & fillet mouldings; C14

Michelham priory: intact parlour with adjacent north-south slype at south end of truncated west range; C13

Mottisfont priory: intact parlour at north end of west range, within post-Dissolution mansion; late C12

Neath abbey: intact parlour at south west corner of west range; probably C14

Newstead Augustinian priory: intact parlour, incorporated into post-Dissolution mansion; C13, C19

Norton abbey: intact parlour except for vaulting, good wall arcading & stone seating; late C12

Norwich cathedral-priory: intact parlour, recently song school & shop of cathedral; C12, late C13

Repton priory: intact tunnel vaulted parlour between undercroft & former church; late C12

Rufford abbey: intact parlour midway along west range; c.1200

Sherborne abbey: intact parlour at south end of range; c.1000, C14, C15

West Acre priory: ruined parlour at north end of west range; C12

Westminster abbey: 1. intact parlour (Jericho Parlour); early C16

2. intact slype at south west corner of cloister; C12, C14

Worcester cathedral-priory: intact slype immediately south of nave; C12

Worksop priory: intact parlour at south end of former west range, now vestry of church; C12/C13

15/4 PRESIDENTS' LODGINGS & GUESTS' ACCOMMODATION

N.B. These are part of the west range unless stated otherwise.

Aylesford friary: 1. intact prior's hall; C15, later C16, C17, C20

2. intact guest-house (Pilgrims' Hall), originally detached; now joined to later buildings; late C13

Battle abbey: 1. intact abbot's lodging, now part of school accommodation; C13, C15, C19, C20

2. cellarage of guest-house (south of west range), 8 barrel vaults; C13

Beauvale charterhouse: intact prior's lodging in form of 3-storeyed tower house; C14/C15

Birkenhead priory: high-standing ruined prior's lodging & guesthall; mainly C13

Blanchland abbey: intact but considerably altered abbot's lodging & guest-house (including kitchen), converted after Dissolution into mansion & then hotel, big fireplace; C13, modern

15/4 Battle abbey, west range (abbot's lodging) to west

Boxgrove priory: high-standing ruined guest-house (detached), probably had domestic use after Dissolution; early C14

Bradenstoke priory: [intact guest-house (upper portion of west range?) removed to St. Donat's; C15]

Bradsole St. Radegund's abbey: intact guest-house (detached), converted into tithe barn after Dissolution; C15

Brecon friary: intact guest-house hall (now called Small School), south of former south range; C14/C15

Brecon priory: intact prior's lodging (now detached, possibly from east range) drastically remodelled after Dissolution & now deanery (Priory House); mid C13, early C16, pDp

Buckfast abbey: intact abbot's tower, incorporated into mainly modern range; C14, C19

Buckland abbey: (See entry under Service Buildings In Or Near Great Court)

Buildwas abbey: intact abbot's house (attached to north end of east range), converted & altered into post-Dissolution house; C13(?), modern

Caldey cell: 1. intact upper story of gatehouse west range served as guest-house; C13

2. intact Prior's Tower at north end of east range; possibly C12, C13

Cambridge St. Radegund's priory: intact prioress's lodging, now part of college accommodation; c.1500

Canterbury cathedral-priory: 1. intact guest-house (detached), now school house (Meister Omer's); c.1400

2. intact guest-house (detached), now archdeacon's house, incorporating upper part of gatehouse (Pentise Gate); c.1400

3. intact but much altered part of archbishop's palace (detached), comprising (mainly) 2-storeyed 3-bay range (detached) projecting to south; C13/C14

4. open undercroft of prior's chapel (less vault) occupying south walk of infirmary cloister, now below post-Dissolution brick Howley library; c.1260, C17

Canterbury Dominican friary: intact guesthall (detached), much modernised; C13, C14, pDp

Canterbury St. Augustine's abbey: partly intact undercroft of abbot's parlour & guesthall below modern library, contiguous with north end of west range; late C13

Carlisle cathedral-priory: intact prior's lodging (detached), now deanery of cathedral; c.1510

Carrow priory: intact prioress's lodging developed as post-Dissolution house, west of & parallel with west range; early C16, 1899-1909

Castle Acre priory: partly intact prior's house including chapel, core retained as post-Dissolution house; mid C12, C14, C15

Cerne abbey: intact guest-house (detached), retained as cottage after Dissolution; c.1460

Chester abbey: intact abbot's chapel (chapel of St. Anselm) at south end of west range over outer parlour; C12, early C17

Clare friary: intact prior's house adapted as post-Dissolution house, including cellarer's hall at ground floor level; C14, C16

Coggeshall abbey: abbot's lodging converted into post-Dissolution building (now harness room & stable), south of & contiguous with east range; early C13, pDp

Combermere abbey: intact though highly adapted abbot's hall, now evident as library on upper floor; C15

Coverham abbey: intact guest-house, adapted as private house after Dissolution; early C16

Croxton abbey: intact guest-house (detached), adapted as private house; C15/C16, pDp

Cymmer abbey: intact guest-house (detached), now farmhouse; unknown date

Dorchester abbey: intact guest-house (detached), converted into village school after Dissolution & now museum; C14, C15, pDp

Dover Benedictine priory: intact guest-house (detached), now school chapel; late C12, pDp

Dunster priory: intact prior's house, probably part of former range & adapted as private house after Dissolution; C15

Durham cathedral-priory: intact prior's lodging (part of east range), now deanery of cathedral; late C11, early C12, C13, C14, 1476

Easby abbey: high-standing ruined accommodation (guests' solar), part of outer west range; early C13

Ely cathedral-priory: 1..intact prior's house & guesthall (detached), considerably altered as post-Dissolution house in turn for bishop, dean, headmaster & now school boarding house; C12, C14, C15, pDp

2. intact prior's chapel (Prior Crauden's chapel) contiguous with prior's house; c.1325

3. intact guest-house (Storehouse) south extension of west range facing street called The Gallery, remodelled as school boarding house & library; C12, C14, 1964-65

4. intact great hall of monastery, now divided into rooms as part of bishop's residence; C13, C14, C19

5. intact Queen's hall of monastery, now divided into rooms as headmaster's residence; c.1330, C19

Exeter Polsloe priory: intact prioress's rooms & upper floor 3-bay guesthall, part of farmhouse after Dissolution; C13

Exeter St. Nicholas' priory: intact prior's lodging & guesthall, used as part of post-Dissolution townhouse; C13, C15

Finchale priory: high-standing ruined prior's house (detached), with vaulted undercroft; late C13, C15

Flaxley abbey: intact abbot's guesthall forming part of range, on upper floor above undercroft, adapted within post-Dissolution mansion; C12, C14, C18, C19

Forde abbey: intact abbot's house, adapted & altered as part of post-Dissolution mansion, contiguous with surviving part of west range; early C16

Fountains abbey: ruined high-standing 2 guest-houses (detached) near river bank; late C12, C13

Gloucester abbey: 1. intact original but much altered lodging of abbot, afterwards became prior's lodging, then deanery of cathedral & now Church House; C12, C13, C15, C19

2. intact Parliament Room, also once part of abbot's original lodging; C13, C15

Great Bricett priory: (For prior's house see entry above under Whole Ranges)

Hartland abbey: [intact abbot's chamber & adjoining hall forming north part of range; C14, C16]

Haughmond abbey: high-standing ruined abbot's lodging (detached), became post-Dissolution house now destroyed; C12, C15/C16

Ixworth priory: [intact timber framed building believed to be prior's lodging connected to south end of east range (now part of post-Dissolution house), late C15]

Kenilworth abbey: intact guest-house or almonry (detached), probably served as cottage after Dissolution; late C14

Kington St. Michael's priory: [intact lodging of prioress & guesthall, adapted as part of farmhouse (Priory Farm) after Dissolution; C15, C17]

Kirkstall abbey: high-standing ruined abbot's lodging (detached); C13

Lacock abbey: intact abbess' room & hall, adapted within range as part of post-Dissolution mansion; C13, C16

Lanercost priory: high-standing ruined prior's house (projecting south as pele tower from west range) & intact guest-house (west range proper), both adapted as private house after Dissolution; C13(?), C16, pDp

Leiston abbey: intact detached barnlike guest-house, thatched roof; C14/C15

Little Dunmow priory: intact timber framed building (Priory Place) within precinct area, probably guest-house; later C14

Little Malvern priory: intact prior's hall & ancillary small chambers over undercroft, adapted after Dissolution as part of private house (Little Malvern Court); C13/C14, pDp

Llanthony priory: intact prior's lodging & guest-house, adapted within range as part of private house & now hotel; late C12, pDp

Malling abbey: intact guest-house (detached), extended & now accommodation belonging to Anglican community of nuns; C15, early C20

Malmesbury abbey: intact portion of guest-house (detached), adapted as part of post-Dissolution house & now hotel (Old Bell); C13 & later

Michelham priory: intact prior's room in upper storey at south end of part-destroyed range, incorporated within post-Dissolution mansion; C13

Milton abbey: intact abbot's hall & porch retained within post-Dissolution mansion & now school, may have been part of a north range; c.1498

Mount Grace charterhouse: intact north guest-house (detached), retained as private house after Dissolution; C15

Muchelney abbey: intact abbot's house in angle between south & west ranges, retained as farmhouse after Dissolution; early C16

Netley abbey: high-standing ruined abbot's house (detached); C13

Newcastle-upon-Tyne Dominican friary: intact guesthall, retained after Dissolution within range as part of accommodation for trades' companies; C13 & later

Newstead Augustinian priory: intact prior's lodging including prior's oratory & guesthall, incorporated into post-Dissolution mansion, C13, C19

Norwich cathedral-priory: 1. prior's lodging (contiguous with site of east range), altered as core of now former deanery; c.1280

2. intact east porch (now detached) of Bishop Salmon's hall; c.1318+

3. intact undercroft of Bishop Turbe's hall, now chapel; C14

4. intact kitchen within undercroft of Bishop Losinga's 'keep'; C12, C14

Notley abbey: [intact abbot's lodging joined to drastically modified west range, incorporated into post Dissolution mansion; C13, C15, early C16]

Penmon priory: intact Prior's House, rebuilt & altered as post-Dissolution private house; unknown date, pDp

Peterborough abbey: 1. intact abbot's lodging (contiguous with site of west range), considerably altered after Dissolution to become bishop's palace; C13, C15/C16, C19

2. intact guest-house (detached), extensively rebuilt & remodelled as Archdeaconry House now deanery; late C12, late C13, C17, 1875-80

Pilton priory: intact prior's house or guest-house (Bull House) south west of church (not part of west range); house C15, solar C16

Pinley priory: [intact prioress's timber-framed house, projecting to west; c.1500]

Prittlewell priory: intact prior's lodging, adapted as part of private house after Dissolution; C14, C15, modern

Repton priory: 1. intact prior's original lodging including great hall, now considerably remodelled within range as school accommodation; C12(?), c.1400, C16

2. intact prior's new lodging (detached) incorporating Prior Overton's Tower, now core of headmaster's house of school, c.1437, Tower 1483

Robertsbridge abbey: [intact abbot's lodging (possibly detached) with vaulted undercroft & kingpost roof, considerably adapted after Dissolution as farmhouse; mid C13, pDp]

Sherborne abbey: 1. intact guesten hall on upper floor of west range proper, adapted as part of school buildings after Dissolution; C12, C14, C15

2. intact abbot's hall over undercroft of building attached to north end of west range, now school chapel; C12, C15, 1855

3. intact abbot's lodging including kitchen attached to north side of abbot's hall, considerably altered & adapted to modern use; C15 & later

Shulbrede priory: [intact prior's apartment on upper floor of range, part of farmhouse after Dissolution; c.1200, mid C13, mid C16, early C20]

Steventon priory: [intact guesthall(?) (detached?), now part of post-Dissolution house; C14-C16]

Tewkesbury abbey: intact abbot's lodging (detached), now vicarage; C15, early C16

Thame abbey: [intact abbot's lodging possibly extension of west range & including embattled tower, adapted as part of post-Dissolution mansion; early C16, also c.1530+]

Thetford Cluniac priory: high-standing ruined range (detached lodging of prior), formed post-Dissolution house & then cottages; late C14, C15

Torre abbey: intact abbot's lodging & guesthall, adapted & altered as part of post-Dissolution mansion; C12, C15, C18

Tynemouth priory: intact prior's chapel (east range) of 2 rib vaulted bays; early C13

Ulverscroft priory: [intact prior's lodging (east range), converted after Dissolution into private house; C13, pDp]

Ware friary: intact guest-house with undercroft connected to west range, converted into part of post-Dissolution mansion; C15, C18

Watton priory: intact prior's lodging (detached), adapted as post-Dissolution house; C15

Wenlock priory: intact prior's lodging, adapted as post-Dissolution house; c.1500

Westminster abbey: 1. intact abbot's lodging & guest-house (part detached), including hall, kitchen & Jerusalem Chamber, considerably adapted as school & office accommodation; C14, early C16

2. intact cellarer's block including guests' accommodation (detached); C14

3. intact prior's house (detached), converted into post-Dissolution house (Ashburnham House); C14, late C17

Whalley abbey: part intact & part ruined abbot's lodging (detached), surviving part converted into post-Dissolution mansion; early C16

Wigmore abbey: intact abbot's chamber & hall over undercroft (contiguous with west range), converted into post-Dissolution house; C14, C15, C16+ (See also entry under Other Rare, Special or Unusual Items of Interest)

Winchcombe abbey: 1. intact house (Abbey Old House) off Cowl Lane on site of west range & said to have been guest-house, with medieval stone roof & trusses; C16, early C19

2. intact Abbot's House in High Street, timber-framed & carrying arms of abbey; possibly C16

Winchester cathedral-priory: 1. intact prior's lodging (contiguous with east range & chiefly prior's hall & porch), now the deanery; C13, C15, C16

2. intact guesthall (detached) now known as the Pilgrims' Hall, has earliest known hammerbeam roof; mid C14

3. intact Strangers' Hall (detached, No. 10, The Dome) with substantial medieval remains, chiefly undercroft; C13, pDp

4. intact chapel of bishop's palace (Wolvesey Palace); C15

Worcester cathedral-priory: 1. intact bishop's palace (detached) mainly hall & chancel of chapel, largely rebuilt after Dissolution; C13, C18

2. high-standing ruined guest-house (detached) with roof preserved elsewhere, in use after Dissolution till C19 as Guesten Hall; c.1320

Worcester Franciscan friary: intact guest-house, adapted after Dissolution for domestic use; c.1480

York St. Mary's abbey: intact abbot's house (detached), converted after Dissolution into King's Manor & now part of university accommodation; C13, c.1480, C16

15/5 ACCOMMODATION FOR LAY-BROTHERS

Beaulieu abbey: intact west range; C13

Flaxley abbey: intact undercroft of west range, probably refectory & reredorter; late C12

Fountains abbey: high-standing ruined west range (including dormitory & refectory), reredorter, infirmary; all mostly C12

Kirkstall abbey: high-standing north & east walls of west range, reredorter; mid C12

Langley abbey: largely intact south end of west range converted into canons' dormitory & latterly granary; C13, C14, pDp

Neath abbey: undercroft of west range including lay-brothers' common room to north & refectory to south, vaulting gone; c.1170-1220 (See also entry under Whole Ranges)

Rufford abbey: high-standing ruined west range (including dormitory over & refectory under); C13, C17

Salley abbey: lay-brothers' undercroft of west range forms part of intact post-Dissolution cottage; late C12/early C13, pDp

Waverley abbey: largely intact south 4 bays of west range undercroft with some high-standing ruined portions above, collectively forming surviving portion of lay-brothers' quarters; C13

Whalley abbey: intact west range; C14

♦♦♦♦♦♦♦♦♦♦♦♦♦♦♦

Section 16:
LITTLE CLOISTERS & INFIRMARY BUILDINGS

16/1   **LITTLE CLOISTERS**

Bristol abbey: cloister garth now school playground, plus recognisable remnant of north cloister arcade; unknown date

Canterbury cathedral-priory: 4-sided pattern of cloister with two complete cloister-walks & garth walls on adjacent sides; C12, C13

Gloucester abbey: 4-sided pattern of cloister, cloister-walks with complete garth walls; C15

Rievaulx abbey: pattern of 4-sided cloister clearly visible, though none of arcading has survived; unknown date

Thetford Cluniac priory: 4-sided small cloister clearly visible with low walls, drain survives in centre of cobbled yard; C13

Tintern abbey: 4-sided pattern of cloister with remnants of surrounding buildings; probably late C13, C14

Walsingham friary: medium to high-standing ruined garth-walls stand on 4 sides with tracery in some windows; C15, C16

Wenlock priory: 4-sided pattern observable though not complete, with intact infirmary & prior's lodging on two adjacent sides; C13, c.1500

Westminster abbey: 4-sided pattern of cloister, together with ruins of infirmary hall & chapel; C12, C17

N.B. Medieval buildings contiguous with infirmary halls are included in this section.

Bilsington priory: [intact infirmary hall with undercroft, converted into part of post-Dissolution private house; mid C13, much restored 1906]

Bolton priory: intact portion possibly infirmary hall incorporated into post-Dissolution rectory; C15 & later, pDp

Brecon friary: intact large hall (Large Hall) with apsed east end, probably infirmary chapel & hall; C14/C15

Burnham abbey: [detached intact infirmary building much modified, with lancets & later brickwork; C13, C16]

Burton-on-Trent abbey: intact hall & chapel, adapted as part of The Abbey house now Abbey Inn; C13, C14, C19

Canterbury cathedral-priory: 1. medium to high-standing ruined hall & chapel; C12, C14
2. intact though heavily restored infirmary refectory (Table Hall, now cathedral song school); C14, pDp

Clare friary: intact hall & reredorter, now converted into church; late C13

Coggeshall abbey: part of undercroft of infirmary together with part of infirmary reredorter adjacent to river, contiguous with east range; early C13

Dale abbey: intact chapel & hall, chapel now parish church & hall adapted as house; C12, late C13, 1485

Ely cathedral-priory: 1. medium to high-standing ruined hall & chapel with part of site occupied by later buildings; C12
2. intact timber-framed house (Powcher's hall) north side of infirmary hall, used for monks' blood letting; C14/C15, early C16

3. intact house (Walsingham house) to east of Powcher's hall, including Painted Chamber, now school boarding house; c.1335

4. intact but much altered infirmary chapel, at one time the deanery & now cathedral chapter-house & offices; late C12, C14, pDp

5. intact house (Black Hostelry) to south of infirmary hall, with vaulted undercroft, former accommodation for visiting Benedictine monks; C13, pDp

6. intact & much remodelled cellarer's house (The Canonry) to south of infirmary hall, now school boarding house; C12, C16, C18

Furness abbey: intact chapel & buttery, probably served as storehouses after Dissolution; C14

Gloucester abbey: medium to high-standing ruined arched hall; C13

Halesowen abbey: intact infirmary building, adapted as barn after Dissolution; late C13

Haughmond abbey: high-standing ruined hall (or abbot's hall); early C14, also c.1500

Hulne friary: intact building of hall & chapel near gatehouse, converted into private house for keeper; later C13, C18

Jervaulx abbey: considerable portions of high-standing ruined infirmary & ancillary buildings; mid C13

Letheringham priory: intact & seemingly complete building to east of church, brick with original square headed windows; C16

Llanthony priory: intact chapel & hall, now parish church of St. David; 1175-1230

Peterborough abbey: 1. intact infirmarer's lodging including hall, converted after Dissolution as accommodation for cathedral; C13

2. ruined infirmary hall & chapel, enclosing modern houses; C13

St. Dogmael's abbey: high-standing ruined infirmary building except for one low wall, probably used as barn or stables after Dissolution; C14

Shrewsbury abbey: badly preserved & fragmentary building, converted after Dissolution to industrial uses & now Heritage Centre; C12

Tavistock abbey: intact misericord (infirmary refectory) not in usual location, adapted as Uniterian chapel; C15(?)

16/2 Woodspring priory, infirmary to north

Thetford St. George's priory: high-standing ruined infirmary hall & chapel; C15/C16

Wenlock priory: intact hall & chapel & infirmarer's lodging, adapted as private house after Dissolution, was contiguous with former east range; C13, c.1500

Westminster abbey: ruined infirmary hall of 3 aisles & 5 bays, displaying some intact arcading on south side; C12

Woodspring priory: intact hall, probably retained after Dissolution as stable or barn; early C15

Worcester cathedral-priory: intact portion of infirmary in form of undercroft, below reredorter to west of west range; c.1110/20

◆◆◆◆◆◆◆◆◆◆◆◆◆◆◆

Section 17:
MONASTIC PROPERTY MOSTLY OUTSIDE THE PRECINCT

17/1   MONASTIC BARNS & TITHE BARNS

Abbotsbury abbey: half intact & half ruined barn, continuing farm use of roofed portion; c.1400

Abergavenny priory: intact barn of old red sandstone, consists of 7 bays; C16 or earlier

Abingdon abbey: [intact barn, now local church (Christ Church); C13, C15/C16]

Aldeby priory: [intact barn ravaged by time, timber framed with double queenpost roof; early C16]

Alnesbourn cell: [intact barn of stone & brick; unknown date]

Bath cathedral-priory: [intact rectorial barn at Englishcombe, continuing farm use after Dissolution; C14]

Beaulieu abbey: 1. intact barn at Great Coxwell, continuing use after Dissolution; C13
2. ruined barn with high-standing gables at St. Leonard's; mid C13

Bermondsey abbey: [intact barn at Preston Plucknett, continuing farm use after Dissolution; c.1400]

Bisham abbey: [intact barn, converted to post-Dissolution house; unknown date]

Bolton priory: intact barn, continuing farm use after Dissolution; c.1300, C18

Boxley abbey: [intact barn, continuing farm use after Dissolution; c.1300, C16, C18]

Bradenstoke priory: [intact barn dismantled & taken to St. Donat's, 104 ft. long, used as theatre & conference centre; C14/C15]

Bradwell priory: [intact 5 bays of original 9-bay barn, with south porch & raised crucks; c.1320, C16]

Brecon priory: intact barn, probably retained after Dissolution for storage purposes; C15(?), C17

Bristol abbey: [intact barn at Ashleworth, continuing farm use after Dissolution; c.1481-1515]

Buckland abbey: intact barn, continuing farm use after Dissolution; early C15, 1772

Burnham abbey: [intact barn converted into modern house in Lake End Road, with arched braces & queen-strut trusses; unknown medieval date, converted 1922]

Canterbury cathedral-priory: [intact aisled barn at Brook, with low walls & high roof; c.1300]

Canterbury St. Augustine's abbey: [1. intact barn at Littlebourne, continuing farm use after Dissolution; early C14]

2. intact barn at Sturry, constructed of brick; early C16

Carlisle cathedral-priory: intact barn, now adapted as parish centre; C15

Cerne abbey: intact barn shortened in length, part adapted as house; mid C14, C18

Chertsey abbey: intact barn in fair condition, mixture of rubble stonework & Tudor brick; C15/C16(?)

Coggeshall abbey: [intact Grange Barn at Little Coggeshall, now display building; C13, c.1500, C20]

Dunster priory: intact barn, continuing farm use after Dissolution; C16

Easby abbey: half intact & half ruined, the surviving section adapted as cottage; unknown date

503

Ely cathedral-priory: (See entry under Service Buildings In or Near Great Court)

Evesham abbey: intact barn at Middle Littleton, continuing farm use after Dissolution, c.1260

Glastonbury abbey: [1. intact barn, now agricultural museum; c.1500

2. intact barn at Doulting, continuing farm use after Dissolution; C15

3. intact barn at Pilton, continuing farm use after Dissolution; late C14]

Gloucester abbey: [1. intact barn at Frocester Court, continuing farm use after Dissolution; c.1300, C16]

2. intact barn at Hartpury, with 11 bays & 2 gabled porches; late C14/early C15

Gloucester Lanthony priory: high-standing ruined barn; possibly C14

17/1 Hurley priory, monastic barn

Hailes abbey: remodelled barn of Farmcote grange; unknown date

Hood cell: [intact barn, with medieval doorway (2-centred arch) & 2-light cusped windows; C14, C15]

Hurley priory: intact barn converted into post-Dissolution house; C14

Kingswood abbey: [intact though rebuilt & mutilated barn (Calcot barn) at Newington Bagpath, continuing farm use after Dissolution; inscribed date 1300, 1729]

Lacock abbey: intact winged barn, used after Dissolution as market hall & subsequently for grain storage; C14

Leonard Stanley priory: intact barn to south west of conventual church (See also entry under Dovecotes); C14

Llantarnam abbey: high-standing ruined barn, probably in farm use after Dissolution; C14, C15

Malling abbey: intact barn, recently converted for use as chapel; C15

Michelham priory: intact barn, continuing farm use until recently & now museum; C16, C19

Redlingfield priory: intact barn south of church, currently in need of restoration; C14(?)

St. Osyth abbey: intact large barn near gatehouse, one side stone & other side timber framed; C16

Shaftesbury abbey: 1. intact barn at Barton Farm in Bradford-on-Avon, continuing farm use after Dissolution; C14

2. also intact granary at Bradford-on-Avon, continuing use after Dissolution; C14, C15

3. intact barn at Tisbury, continuing farm use after Dissolution; C15

[4. intact barn at Hinton St. Mary converted into modern theatre; C15, c.1900, 1929]

Sherborne abbey: [intact double barn at Wyke Farm nr. Bradford Abbas, with buttresses & raised crucks roof; C16 or earlier]

Takeley priory: [intact barn of Prior's Hall at Widdington, recently restored; C14, 1983]

Tarrant abbey: [intact barn of stone, with buttresses & hammerbeam trusses; unknown date(s)]

Taunton priory: [intact prior's barn, probable continuing farm use after Dissolution; C13]

Temple Cressing preceptory: 1. intact barn (Barley Barn), now display building; c.1200
2. intact barn (Wheat Barn), now display building; c.1260

Tewkesbury abbey: 1. intact small (almonry?) barn on west side of gatehouse, timber-framed & buttressed with 4 bays; C15/C16, pDp
[2. intact stone barn (Abbey Barton), heavily buttressed with brick upper floor & hipped roofs; Imp, brickwork C18
3. intact buttressed barn of 7 bays with stone roof at Stanway converted to now modern hall & theatre, possesses gabled porch; c.1370, 1927]

Thetford Cluniac priory: [group of intact & altered barns at Abbey Farm; C13 & later]

Titchfield abbey: intact barn with tiled hipped roof , walls of boarding & stone; C14/C15

Torre abbey: intact barn (Spanish Barn), continuing farm use after Dissolution & now municipal theatre; C13

West Acre priory: intact 2 barns with medieval walls, considerably renovated & altered since Dissolution; C16, C19

Winchcombe abbey: [intact barn at Enstone, continuing farm use after Dissolution; inscribed date of 1382 may have been of earlier building, more likely date C15]

Woodspring priory:　intact barn, continuing farm use after Dissolution; C15

17/2 MONASTIC MANOR HOUSES & GRANGES

Abingdon abbey:　[1. intact set of stone　buildings comprising grange (now manor house with chapel) at Charney Bassett much altered & rebuilt, continuing domestic use after Dissolution; late C13, C19
2. intact manor house (The Abbey) of Sutton Courtenay, continuous use as mansion after Dissolution, C14, early C19]
Axford 'priory':　[intact plain oblong chapel attached to house of Priory Farm, site may have been grange of unknown parent monastic house; C14, C15]
Bayham abbey:　[intact chapel at Otham (or Otterham) grange (& former abbey), used as barn after Dissolution; early C14]
Beaulieu abbey:　[intact farmhouse & ruined chapel of St. Leonard's grange (See also entry under Barns), continuing farm use after Dissolution; c.1300, C15]
Bermondsey abbey:　[intact & adapted house of grange of Preston Plucknett (See also entry under Barns), continuing domestic use after Dissolution; C15]
Bodmin priory:　[intact manor or grange house at Rialton & now farmhouse, with hall, porch, study & bedchamber; late C15]
Bristol abbey:　[1. intact manor house (Court House) at Ashleworth, continuing domestic use after Dissolution; c.1460, 1870
2. intact house of Ashleworth Manor, after Dissolution became vicarage; c.1460, C19, c.1904]

Buckfast abbey: intact set of farm buildings & gatehouse (Leigh Grange at Churchstow), continuing farm use after Dissolution; C15/C16, C17, restored 1984-86

Burnham abbey: [intact manor house (Huntercombe Manor), rambling house much modified with timber-framed hall as core; C14, later C17, C18, 1887]

Burton-on-Trent abbey: [derelict manor or grange house (Sinai Park) used as monks' holiday & convalescent home, black-&-white timbered building; c.1500]

Canterbury St. Augustine's abbey: [1. part intact & part ruined set of buildings comprising grange of Minster-in-Thanet; C12, C15, C19

2. intact hall & chapel plus ruins of other buildings of Salmestone grange, C13, c.1326]

Chester abbey: 1. high-standing ruined buildings of Ince manor, used as farm and domestic buildings after Dissolution; mainly C15

2. intact porch-tower of Saighton grange, continuing domestic use after Dissolution & now scholastic; c.1489

Cleeve abbey: [1. intact restored house of Chapel Cleeve grange, continuing domestic use after Dissolution; C14, C15, 1913]

2. intact townhouse of abbot at Dunster, now Luttrell Arms; c.1500, 1622-29

Earls Colne priory: intact half-timbered house in Lavenham known as The Priory, medieval great hall at heart of building, connected with wool trade; C15, c.1600

Flaxley abbey: [intact though much altered house of Dymock grange, continuing domestic use after Dissolution; C15, C18, 1896]

Fountains abbey: intact chapel with attached dwelling at Bewerley grange, continuing use as small church; early C16

Furness abbey: intact gate-tower or gatehouse of Hawkshead Old Hall; C15

Glastonbury abbey: [1. intact manor house at Ashbury, continuing domestic use after Dissolution; c.1488, 1697]

2. intact summer house of abbot at Meare, adapted for use as private house after Dissolution; c.1340 or earlier

[3. intact though much adapted & altered manor house at Pilton, continuing domestic use after Dissolution (See also entry under Barns); C14(?), C17, c.1800]

Gloucester abbey: [1. substantially intact & altered house (Frocester Court); hall C14, c.1554, C19

2. intact solar wing with fan vault at grange (Prinknash Park) now St. Peter's grange; c.1520-25]

Jervaulx abbey: [intact chapel of Thrintoft grange, now barn; unknown date]

Kingswood abbey: [1. intact but altered chapel of Estcourt grange at Tetbury, now kitchen; C14]

2. intact hall of grange, with solar over cellar & 2-bay roof (Bagstone Court Farm at Rangeworthy); C14, C17, early C19

Leicester abbey: [intact wing of manor house (Old Hall) at Ingarsby, continuing domestic use after Dissolution; late C15]

Lewes priory: 1. intact & altered hall & chapel (north range) & gatehouse of Swanborough grange, continuing domestic use after Dissolution; c.1200, C15

2. intact & restored chapel (ground floor) & great hall (upper floor) of Langney 'Priory' at Eastbourne; C12, C14

Neath abbey: [largely intact but part derelict (at time of writing) grange (Sker House), great hall on first floor; C15, C16]

Pershore abbey: intact house including chapel of Abbot's Grange at Broadway, continuing domestic use after Dissolution; C14

Seez abbey: [intact chapel of house of bailiff at Bailiffscourt (Atherington), became part of recreated house in recent years; late C13]

Shaftesbury abbey: 1. intact though much altered grange buildings comprising Barton Farm at Bradford-on-Avon (See also entry under Barns), continuing farm use after Dissolution; C15

2. intact set of buildings (Place Farm) including 2 gatehouses comprising Tisbury grange (See also under Barns), continuing farm & domestic use after Dissolution; C14, C15

Sheen charterhouse: [intact stone chapel (Champ's Chapel) & half-timbered house, both comprising grange; chapel C13, house lmp]

Sherborne abbey: [intact manor house (monks' rest-house) at Poyntington; C16]

Spalding priory: 1. high standing ruined chapel of prior's country house (Wykeham chapel); 1311

[2. intact brick rib vaulted chamber at Low Fulney, surviving from grange or cattle ranch; probably C15]

Strood preceptory: intact manor house (Temple Manor) with hall over undercroft; C13

Takeley priory: [intact house (Prior's Hall) at Widdington, possibly originating as pre-Conquest church or chapel; C11(?), C13, C15, pDp]

Tavistock abbey: substantially complete & intact set of buildings including gate-tower comprising abbot's country residence at Morwell; early C15+

Tewkesbury abbey: 1. intact gatehouse of grange at Llantwit Major, adapted as cottage after Dissolution; C13

2. intact hall, attached chapel & chamber block (Forthampton Court); early C15, pDp
Yedingham priory: [intact hall & traces of other buildings of Sinnington grange, hall used as barn after Dissolution; C12, C15]

17/3   COLLEGE PROPERTY

Augustinian abbeys (in collective ownership/control): 1. intact & reduced gatehouse of St. Mary's college (now Frewen hall belonging to Brasenose college, Oxford); 1435+, pDp
[2. intact cellar in south range of St. Mary's college (now Frewen hall), with column with scalloped capital & later vault; C12, 1435+]
Canterbury cathedral-priory (& others in collective ownership/control): intact set of students' lodgings at former Gloucester college (now part of Worcester college, Oxford) comprising 6 houses of south range; C15
Cistercian abbeys (in collective ownership/control): intact parts (i.e. Front quad) of former St. Bernard's college (now refounded as St. John's college, Oxford); 1437, early c16
Croyland abbey (& others in collective ownership/control): intact portions especially chapel & hall of Buckingham college (or Monks' Hostel), now First Court of Magdelene college, Cambridge; c.1430+, C18, 1876
Durham cathedral-priory: intact & remodelled east range of Durham college (now Old Library in Durham Quad of Trinity college, Oxford); 1417-21, C17

Battle abbey: [1. intact inn (The Star) at Alfriston, continuing use after Dissolution; c.1450 façade]
2. intact inn (Pilgrims' Rest) near abbey gatehouse, hall-house in continuing use after Dissolution; C15
Buckfast abbey: intact inn (Church Inn at Churchstow), continuing use after Dissolution; unknown date
Glastonbury abbey: intact inn (The George, now George & Pilgrims), continuing use after Dissolution; C15, C16
Gloucester abbey: [intact timber framed inn (New Inn) in city, continuing use after Dissolution; c.1450]
Grantham Templars: intact inn (The Angel, now Angel & Royal), continuing use after Dissolution; C15 facade
Hinton charterhouse: intact inn at Norton   St. Philip (The George), continuing use after Dissolution; C15
Tewkesbury abbey: [intact though much rebuilt inn (The Bell) near abbey church, continuing use after Dissolution; pDp, 1696]
Winchcombe abbey: intact inn (The George), now adapted as set of private residences; c.1525, 1991
Wymondham abbey: intact half-timbered inn originally called St. George and the Green Dragon (now the Green Dragon); Imp

17/5 COURTHOUSES & OTHER MISCELLANEOUS BUILDINGS

Abingdon abbey: intact business office (Checker & Checker Hall), now theatre etc.; C13, C15
Alnwick abbey: high-standing ruined lookout tower (Hefferlaw Tower); 1470-89

Bruton abbey: intact steward's house or courthouse, adapted as post-Dissolution townhouse; mid C15

Cirencester abbey: intact & immense 3-storeyed south porch of parish church, built by abbot for administrative purposes, became Town Hall after Dissolution; c.1490

Durham cathedral-priory: [intact pele tower (Prior Castell's Tower) in Farne Islands, oblong of rough masonry; c.1500]

Evesham abbey: intact original porch of Abbot Lichfield's Free School, main building extensively altered; 1513-24, alterations 1828-29

Fountains abbey: 1. ruined cellarer's office contiguous with west range; C12/C13

2. intact abbey mill; c.1147, C13, pDp, restored C20

Furness abbey: 1. high-standing ruined castle (Piel Castle); 1327+

2. intact pele castle at Dalton-in-Furness, used as courthouse & prison; C14

Glastonbury abbey: 1. high-standing ruined fisherman's house (Fish House), was roofed until recently & probably had storage use; early C14

2. intact Tribunal courthouse, retained as private house after Dissolution; c.1400, c.1500, C16

Hulne friary: intact great defensive tower within precinct; 1488

Leonard Stanley priory: intact small ancient church of St. Swithun standing on site of west range, may have served as guest accommodation by priory & was used as farm building after Dissolution; C11, C14, pDp

Monk Bretton priory: intact administrative building within precinct, probably used as storage barn after Dissolution; lateC13/early C14

Muchelney abbey: intact 2-storeyed priest's house near parish church, has great hall; C14/C15

Spalding priory: [intact small stone building (Prior's Oven) possibly lockup, principal room vaulted octagon; Imp]

Tewkesbury abbey: intact set of 23+ purpose-built cottages north of church, recently restored & in modern use; late C15, 1967-70

Thetford Cluniac priory: high-standing ruined tower house (Warren Lodge) possibly built for prior's gamekeeper, probably had storage use after Dissolution; C15

York Holy Trinity priory: [intact chantry house (later called Jacob's Well) in Trinity Lane off Micklegate, used for housing 2 chantry priests employed by convent; C15, restored 1991]

17/6 DOVECOTES

Abbotsbury abbey: 1. intact rectangular dovecote; C15 [2. intact small rectangular dovecote at Puncknowle; probably C13]

Alvecote priory: [intact dovecote; C13]

Bisham abbey: [intact circular dovecote; C14/C15]

Bruton abbey: intact tower-like dovecote with 4 gables; C16

Burnham abbey: [intact dovecote near Abbey House (Huntercombe Lane), thatched & brick; C16]

Dunster priory: intact circular dovecote with revolving central ladder; C13 or earlier

Evesham abbey: [1. intact dovecote at Middle Littleton; probably C14

2. intact circular dovecote at Kinwarton, with ogee arched doorway; C14

3. intact circular squat dovecote at Hillborough manor in Temple Grafton, 24 ft. diameter; unknown date]

Ewenny priory: intact rectangular tower in precinct wall converted into dovecote; C13(?), early C19

Garway preceptory: intact circular dovecote with inscribed date; 1326

Gloucester abbey: [intact rectangular dovecote at Frocester Court, part rebuilt; c.1300]

Godstow abbey: [intact circular dovecote at Daglingworth manor, with potence & ratproof string-course; unknown date]

Hayling priory: [intact double rectangular dovecote at Manor House, made of stone; C14]

Hinton charterhouse: [1. two intact dovecotes above chapter-house & library; C13

2. intact rectangular dovecote at Norton St. Philip, with Tudor detail; C15/C16]

Hurley priory: intact circular dovecote, buttressed; dated 1307

Leonard Stanley priory: intact dovecote mounted above wagon entrance of medieval barn; probably C14

Montacute priory: [intact rectangular shaped dovecote; unknown date]

Notley abbey: [intact square dovecote; perhaps C14]

Penmon priory: intact square shaped dovecote, with central stone column & projecting stone steps; C16 or earlier

Quenington commandery: intact circular dovecote with revolving central ladder; probably 1338

Shaftesbury abbey: [intact square shaped restored dovecote at Kelston, with 4 high gables; unknown date]

Sheen charterhouse: [intact rectangular dovecote at grange on Hayling island; C13/C14]

Slebech commandery: [intact circular dovecote at Rosemarket; C13(?)]

Stogursey priory: intact circular & thatched dovecote, probably reconstructed after Dissolution; C13, pDp

Tewkesbury abbey: intact circular dovecote at Llantwit Major grange, with flattened conical roof; C13

Witham charterhouse: intact rectangular dovecote with 2 storeys; C14, 1900

17/7   BRIDGES

Bury St. Edmunds abbey: intact bridge (Abbot's bridge), still functioning; early C13, C14

Coverham abbey: [intact bridge south of abbey site over River Cover, with one pointed arch; unknown date]

Croyland abbey: intact bridge (Trinity bridge or Three-Ways-To-Nowhere), now redundant; C14

Fountains abbey: 1. intact mill bridge over River Skell, 2 arches; C13

2. intact infirmary bridge; C12

3. intact bridge leading to east guest-house, 3 arches; C12

Furness abbey: [intact bridge (Bow Bridge) in Ennis Wood, 3 arches; unknown date]

Ramsey abbey: intact chapel bridge at St. Ives, continuing use after Dissolution; c.1426, 1716, 1736

Stoneleigh abbey: [intact bridge (Old Stare bridge), continuing use after Dissolution; late C13]

Waltham abbey: intact apron bridge in front of gatehouse; C14

Anglesey priory: [fishponds survive]
Barlings abbey: [several fishponds to south east of main precinct area, including at least one partly filled in]
Battle abbey: [fishponds in lower ground to south of abbey precinct]
Beaulieu abbey: abbey stewpond now church meadow pond
Beeston priory: [fishponds to north of site]
Bindon abbey: [long ponds likened to black canals beneath brown & melancholy trees]
Blanchland abbey: [3 shallow pits in trees to west of precinct above Stanhope road mark site of fishponds]
Bradsole St. Radegund's abbey: series of ponds across precinct site
Bushmead priory: [fishponds near river]
Butley priory: [some complete fishponds]
Caldey cell: fishpond to east of church
Chertsey abbey: 3 long fishponds to west of site
Croxton abbey: fishpond to west of site
Dinmore commandery: restored fishponds to the south of church; restored 1982
Edington priory: big fishpond to north of conventual church
Evesham abbey: remains of 3 fishponds due east of abbey site
Forde abbey fishponds converted into modern ornamental ponds
Fountains abbey: fishponds in East Applegarths alongside precinth wall

Furness abbey: site of retaining pool near abbey buildings, now used as football ground

Halesowen abbey: dry remnant of flight of 5 fishponds, & also other fishponds

Hurley priory: fishpond identifiable as marshy area near river

Kirkstead abbey (Lincs.): several large fishponds including row on Woodhall side of precinct

Kyme priory: [some fishponds & moats to south west of church]

Leonard Stanley priory: [fishpond to south of conventual church]

Little Malvern priory: 5 fishponds to south east below precinct

Louth Park abbey: one empty fishpond with island

Montacute priory: round fishpond located immediately to south of priory site

Morville cell: fishponds located to south west of church

Owston abbey: dry fishponds to north west of conventual church, in form of rectangular holding pens

Redlingfield priory: fishponds remain to west of site

St. Albans abbey: fishpond in valley to south of site, now developed as lake

St. Benet of Holme's abbey: 4 fishponds in form of pens near gatehouse

Shulebrede priory: [2 fishponds & moat]

Stixwould priory: [one fishpond survives on site]

Thornton abbey: [2 sets of fishponds, one to north west & other to south east of main precinct area, also dry moat fronting gatehouse]

Valle Crucis abbey: fishpond to east of conventual church, claimed to be only surviving one in Wales

Wendling abbey: [some reportedly fine fishponds]
Witham charterhouse: [2 small fishponds near Witham
Hall Farm by railway line]

♦♦♦♦♦♦♦♦♦♦♦♦♦♦♦♦

Section 18:
MISCELLANEOUS

18/1 OTHER RARE, SPECIAL OR UNUSUAL ITEMS OF INTEREST

Abergavenny priory: 1. timber effigy in excellent condition in north transept of cross-legged Sir John Hastings; c.1326 (notwithstanding style)
2. outstanding collection of medieval monuments; C13-C16
Abingdon abbey: chimney; C13
Aconbury priory: 2 windows with plate tracery on north side of building display exceptionally early cinquefoiled heads in their lights; c.1260+
Alkborough cell: intact turf maze near church, recently donated to village by Lady Dudding; C12(?)
Alvingham priory: conventual church & parish church in same churchyard
Atherstone friary: intact central octagonal tower; C14, 1782, 1849
Barlings abbey: [intact & fenced-in well; unknown date]
Beaulieu abbey: 1. intact lamp niche near east processional dooway; C13
2. west range alley for lay brothers; C13
3. abbot's timber bread cupboard; C14
Binham priory: partly ruined west front of nave displays earliest instance of bar tracery in England; 1226/1244
Bishopsgate St. Helens priory: unusual intact hagioscope or squint concealed behind easter sepulchre; 1525, repaired C17/C18

Blackmore priory: 1. almost intact cresset stone: unknown date

2. intact timber framed & timber clad west tower with broach spire, probably unique for conventual church; c.1480

3. piers of south nave arcade made of Tudor brick; early C16

Blakeney friary: 1. intact small tower, probably lighthouse; C15

2. easter sepulchre with Victorian canopy; unknown date

3. intact & original 7-light east window of choir, divided into lancets; C13

Blyth priory: intact 2 wall tombs of priors in outside wall of north nave aisle (i.e. north cloister-walk), with semicircular arches; C12

Bodmin priory: intact reliquary of St. Petroc i.e. casket of ivory displayed in south aisle of Bodmin parish church; C12

Bolton priory: intact west front of nave partly concealed by later west tower; C13

Bourne abbey: 2 holy water stoups of similar appearance, one by west door & other at entrance via south porch; C15

Brecon priory: 1. cresset stone; unknown date

2. intact 2 stone stairways to former rood screen on either side of nave; unknown date

Bridlington priory: stone alms box attached to west pier of Bay 1 on south side of church with attached bracket for small statue, has hinge & staple but no lid; C14/C15

Bristol abbey: 1. intact medieval candelabrum, said to be only one of its date in England, came from Bristol Temple church; 1460

2. intact banner stave cupboard in sacristy; C14

3. intact oven with chimney for baking communion bread; C14

4. intact series of 'star'recessed tombs along walls of church; C14, C15

Bury St. Edmunds abbey: 1. massive cathedral proportions of conventual church still evident

2. 5 early abbots resting places indicated in chapter-house by modern grave stones giving names & dates

Bushmead priory: intact rare timber roof frame, with crown posts & collar purlins; c.1250

Byland abbey: 1. west range alley displays 35 seat recesses for lay brothers; c.1170-1177

2. discernible area representing rare lay-brothers' cloister, has several arcade arches re-erected; probably late C12

Caldey cell: intact lampstead with chimney in south wall of choir; C13

Canterbury cathedral-priory: 1. intact hatch or rota for handing out refreshments, in east wall of former west range; unknown date

2. intact watertower for distributing water to precinct site; c.1160

3. intact earliest run of cloister-arcading alongside little cloister garth; C12

4. intact Norman porch at entrance to North Hall; c.1153+

Carlisle cathedral-priory: 1. intact great east window of choir, with flowing tracery & 9 main lights; early C14

2. orientation of crossing in relation to choir

Cartmel priory: 1. processional doorways on both side of nave; south c.1190, north c.1210

2. unique diagonal top stage to central tower; C15

Castle Acre priory: 2 recesses equipped with small stone sinks in prior's solar & undercroft below; earlier C14

Chester abbey: 1. carrels in west walk of cloister; 1525-30

2. water cistern in cloister-garth; unknown date

Chetwode cell: royal arms of Henry III claimed to be earliest representation of stained glass in England; c.1260

Christchurch priory: object of medieval pilgrimage (Miraculous Beam) protruding through window from south choir aisle into retrochoir; c.1094+

Clare friary: unusual 2 cloister-walks linking south kitchen with west range; C15/C16

Colchester St. Botolph's priory: except for facings, Roman brick used for constructing extant high-standing ruins of nave; 1093/1100, also mid C12

Coverham abbey: site unusually replete with carved stones & effigies etc.; C13+

Croxden abbey: stone pattern of 5-chapel chevet surviving at grass level; earlier C13

Deeping St. James priory: 1. unusually difficult small church to interpret in terms of architectural development

2. close set of 13 triforium arches with 2-centred pointed heads; C13

Deerhurst priory: Anglo-Saxon work of first order in conventual church; 804 or earlier, C10

Delapre abbey: intact 2 lantern recesses at ends of south wall of north cloister-walk; probably C13/C14

Dinmore commandery: intact original patriarchal (enclosed) cross of Hospitallers, on gable of east end of church; C14

Dorchester abbey: 1. restored preaching cross in churchyard south of church; C14, C19

2. intact oven for baking communion bread with flue in wall on north side of chapel of St. Birinus; C13

Dore abbey: 1. largely intact 5 chapels forming retrochoir at east end of presbytery; c.1180, early C13

2. intact original door in north wall of north choir aisle, fitted with iron scrollwork; c.1300

Dover Augustinian priory: 1. small cruciform church displays use of Roman materials in its work

2. high-standing ruined Roman pharos adapted as medieval detached bell tower; C2/C3(?), C13

Dover Benedictine priory: earliest intact instance of refectory now in use as school (dining) hall; C12

Dudley priory: normal west processional doorway, but *never* a corresponding east dooway

Dunstable priory: intact roodscreen & formerly pulpitum, now built up as east end of present church; C13/C14

Durham cathedral-priory: 1. intact Chapel of The Nine Altars attached to east end of choir; 1242+

2. intact gallilee chapel attached to west end of nave; c.1170-80

3. intact small prison (now sacristy) in east range; mid C12

4. intact prison below remnant of reredorter west of west range; unknown date

5. unusual layout of east & west cloister ranges with dormitory over west undercroft & prior's accommodation in east range; originating in C12

6. intact but altered & restored astronomical clock of Prior Castell in south transept; late C15, 1630, 1938

Earls Colne priory: 3 monuments of de Veres' family (Earls of Oxford) moved at Dissolution to St. Stephen's chapel at Bures; c.1300 & later

Easby abbey: 1. processional marker inscribed in nave floor, 12 inch diameter circle; unknown medieval date

2. large wooden box or reliquary in Wensley parish church; unknown date

Egglestone abbey: 1. unusual intact tracery in great east window of conventual church, 5 graduated lights divided by 4 plain vertical mullions; late C13

2. 14 ledger stones located in mainly nave & crossing area of church, some retain inscribed details

Elstow abbey: 1. intact detached bell tower to north of conventual church; C13, c.1500

2. memorial brass in good condition of Abbess Elizabeth Hervey; died 1527

Ely cathedral-priory: 1. intact central octagon & lantern; C14

2. intact stone vaulting of lady chapel, widest span in country; 1321-53

Esholt priory: [intact monument of last prioress in laundry of former hall (now part of Bradford sewage works); 1539+]

Ewenny priory: 1. rare example of fortified monastic precinct, with much of curtain wall, gatehouses & towers surviving; mainly C13

2. reset Norman west processional doorway of nave in east precinct wall; C12

Farewell priory: spring & well head still functioning north west of church

Finchale priory: 1. good example of reduced conventual church; early C13, mid C14

2. intact stone kitchen sink; probably Imp

Fountains abbey: 1. high-standing ruined Chapel of The Nine Altars attached to east end of choir; c.1210-40, 1483

2. display of coffin-lids of former abbots buried in chapter-house; mid C12/mid C14

3. metal staple for of fetter still attached to stone in remnant of prison cell; unknown date

4. intact lamp niche at north end of lay-brothers' dormitory by night-stairs; C12

5. intact high stone chimney of warming house; unknown date

6. intact archway from north transept to Abbot Huby's tower, possibly the highest arch in England; early C16

Freiston priory: intact north nave aisle constructed of brick of Tattershall type; C15

Furness abbey: 1. intact but weather-worn 18 grave slabs in monks' cemetery east of choir; unknown dates

2.   intact but weathered quadruple sedilia & piscina in choir, with elaborate canopies; C15

Garway preceptory: 1. lowermost courses of former round nave indicated in grass to north of present nave; later C12

2. curious enclosed passage connecting nave to west tower; pDp

Glastonbury abbey: 1. high-standing ruined lady chapel located to west of conventual church; 1184-86

2. intact abbot's kitchen; C14

3. intact reliquary of Crown of Thorns, now reportedly at Stanbrook abbey; unknown date

Gloucester abbey: 1. intact Crecy window at east end of conventual church, biggest medieval window in country, with Coronation of Virgin as subject; completed c.1350

2. intact great window at south end of south transept, believed to be earliest extant Perpendicular work in England; 1337+

3. intact wooden cope chest in south choir aisle; early C16

[4. intact Great Bell or Signum called Great Peter, only surviving medieval bourdon bell in England; c.1450]

Gloucester Dominican friary: 1. considerable lengths of early timber roofing in the conventual church & claustral buildings; C13

2. intact building believed to be library surviving as north end of west range; C13

Hailes abbey: stone pattern of 5-chapel chevet surviving at grass level; later C13

Hartland abbey: [intact tomb chest (possibly of Lady Muriel Dynham) from abbey now in parish church, of catacleuse stone & of elaborate design; Lady Muriel died 1369]

Hereford friary: intact & restored preaching cross; C14

Hexham priory: comprehensive collection of Roman tombstones; C1 onwards

Heynings priory: curious small nave reordered with north-south post-Dissolution arcade; reordering in C17

Hulne friary: 1. massive detached defensive tower constructed within precinct; 1488

2. intact & complete perimeter precinct wall around small friary site

3. unique gravestone in floor of church displaying Tau Cross; unknown date

Jarrow priory: 1. intact foundation stone inscribed with date; 685

2. fragments of Anglo-Saxon claustral buildings including V-headed doorway; early C11

Jervaulx abbey: 1. partly high-standing ruined misericord, standing next to site of refectory; C15

2. coffin lids or grave slabs of 9 abbots in floor of chapter-house; earlier medieval period

Kenilworth abbey: pig of lead bearing inscription of Henry VIII's Commissioners; c.1538

Kidwelly cell: 1. pseudocruciform design of church, with north west tower; c.1320

2. 4 mural staircases now hidden; c.1320

King's Lynn priory: intact memorial brasses, largest in England; mid C14

Kirkstall abbey: lay-brothers' lane on east side of west range; C12

Lacock abbey: 1. intact lampholder in warming house; unknown date

2. cauldron of bell metal in warming room, brought from Malines; c.1500

Lancaster priory: set of choir stalls displaying unusual Flamboyant style; C14/C15

Letheringham priory: a number of brasses & matrices in small church

Lilleshall abbey: 1. intact but robbed very large nave west doorway of Transitional style, with semicircular head & stiff-leaf caps; c.1200

2. intact 2 book lockers under common segmental head, decorated with saw tooth chevron ornament; late C12

Little Maplestead commandery: intact round or temple church; .1335

Llanllugan priory: intact representation of Cistercian prioress in east window of church; C15

Malmesbury abbey: orders of arch of inner doorway of south porch display important carvings in semi-relief of many biblical scenes & figures; c.1170

Malton priory: intact nave pier on north side unusually displaying panelling in 2 tiers, has rebus of Prior Roger Bolton; c.1500

8/1 Little Maplestead commandery, conventual church with round nave

Michelham priory: well in cloister garth; C13
Milton abbey: 1. layout of church similar to that of Oxbridge college chapel
2. unusual location of cloister on north side of north transept, indicated by vaulting remnants on wall; early C14
3. intact hanging oak tabernacle or pyx, 9 ft. high; C15
Monk Bretton priory: 1. intact detached administrative building; late C13
2. 13 coffin lids dispersed around church (but not in choir)
Monkton priory: intact earthenware monk's beer-jug; Imp
Morville cell: intact door on south side of nave of church, with ironwork decoration & crescent hinge derived from Danish influence; C12
Mount Grace charterhouse: 1. reconstructed house of brother; late C14/early C15, modern

2. water supply system with series of cisterns & channels; C15

Newstead Augustinian priory: rare example of 4 intact cloister-walks & arcading retained within post-Dissolution mansion; late C14/early C15

Norton abbey: 1. numerous stone coffins scattered around site; C12+

2. excavated tile kiln; C13+

Norwich cathedral-priory: intact recess for holy relics on west side of eastern ambulatory, below bishop's throne; C12

Owston abbey: fragment of wall tracery on exterior of buttress at west end of south wall of nave, probable corner remnant of interior of cloister walks; early C14

Oxford St. Frideswide's priory: foundation stone of Cardinal Wolsey's college at Ipswich reset in east wall of chapter-house; c.1528

Pamber priory: timber effigy of knight in good condition; probably early C14

Penmon priory: 1. holy well & remnant of cell of St. Seiriol north east of church; c.540

2. cloister area lies south of choir

3. 3-storeyed south range; C13

Pershore abbey: intact aumbry with gabled ornamental surround on now external side of east wall of south transept in former chapel of St. Edburgha (Was it a reliquary?); C13

Peterborough abbey: 1. timber ceiling of nave; c.1220

2. intact New Building to east of choir, with superb fan vaulting; 1496/1508

3. intact early recumbent effigies of abbots in semi-relief, made of black Alwalton marble; 1177+

Polesworth abbey: intact stone effigy of abbess; C12

Portchester priory: intact shoots of reredorter in Roman wall of castle; C12(?)

Repton priory: intact Prior Overton's Tower, ornate example of early domestic brick architecture; 1483

Rochester cathedral-priory: 1. largely intact west wall of east range of cloister in unusual location to south of choir; 1114-24

2. intact defensive tower of Gundulph on north side of church; late C11

3. intact richly ornamented doorway to chapter room, displaying naked body of Bishop Hamo de Hythe being taken to Heaven & other figures; c.1340

4. intact timber door (Gundulf Door), claimed to be oldest door in Great Britain, located in north east transept, c.1075

Ruthin priory: intact timber roofs of nave, with highly decorated panels; early C16

Rye Sack friary: only surviving intact house of this order of friars, comprising 2 separate buildings; late C13

St. Albans abbey: 1. much of central tower constructed of Roman brick; from early M1

2. intact original timber painted vault over choir; C13, repainted C15, repaired & repainted 1930+

3. intact memorial brass of outstanding quality of Abbot de la Mare; died 1396

St. Bees priory: 1. most of choir separated off by crosswall into school hall, leaving one bay for chancel of present parish church; c.1200

2. damaged cresset stone; unknown date

St. Benet of Holme's abbey: gatehouse converted into windmill; early C14, C18

St. Clear's cell: intact richly ornamented Norman arch at entrance to choir, consists of 2 orders plus rear stepped sub-arch; C12

St. Dogmael's abbey:　lectern slot in choir; unknown date

St. Osyth abbey:　intact façade of abbot's lodging (Bishop's Lodging); 1527

Sandford preceptory:　[bronze reliquary bearing relief of Christ in Majesty, now in Oxford Ashmolean Museum; C11]

Sherborne abbey:　whole conventual church remodelled & partly rebuilt in Perpendicular style; c.1425+

Smithfield St. Bartholomew's priory:　intact 'gatehouse' actually post-Dissolution construction based on south west doorway of nave of conventual church; C13, 1559, 1932

Snaith cell:　1. example of big pseudo-cruciform church; C12, C13, mainly C14 & C15

2. empty niche of St. Scytha, with lettering of name of saint overhead; unknown date

Southwark priory:　1. intact wooden effigy of knight, probably a Warenne, figure now restored & repainted; c.1280/1300

2. intact retrochoir of 4 aisles & 3 bays; C13, 1833

Stogursey priory:　iron sanctuary ring near crossing of church; unknown date

Strata Florida abbey:　1. several graves covered with slabs of stone in cemetery; unknown date

2. intact stone lined basin in choir, possibly used in *mandatum* rite; unknown date

Temple preceptory:　1. intact round nave; mainly C12

2. intact but restored set of Purbeck marble set of effigies of knights; C12 & C13, C20

Tewkesbury abbey:　1. intact door to sacristy, reinforced on inner side with strips of metal taken from armour gleaned from battlefield of Tewkesbury; c.1471+

2. intact great Norman west window of nave, with 6 concentric arches & later Perpendicular infill; early C12, renewed C17

[3. intact oak canopy of pyx; c.1400]

Thetford Cluniac priory: sites of tombs of Dukes of Norfolk in conventual church, some such tombs moved to Framlingham parish church;C15, C16 (See also entry under Tombs & Burial Places of Prominent People)

Thorney abbey: intact great refectory table of oak in kitchen of old vicarage; unknown date

Thornton abbey: largely intact barbican of gatehouse; C16

Tintern abbey: 1. surviving remnants of stone wall screens at bases of nave arcade piers, originally forming backing to lay-brothers' stalls; lateC12/early C13

2. intact small vaulted pantry between former refectory & warming house; early C13

Titchfield abbey: nave of conventual church converted into huge Tudor gatehouse (now ruined); 1232+, 1537-42

Tutbury priory: highly ornamented Norman nave west doorway, possesses 5 orders; c.1150

Tynemouth priory: two barbicans of gatehouse; c.1400

Upholland priory: unusual plan of church originally based on T-shape; early C14 & later

Usk priory: refectory table in use as high altar; unknown date

Valle Crucis abbey: 1. several stone slabs in monks' cemetery marking graves; dates unknown

2. a number of sculptured grave slabs on display in dormitory; dates range from 1237 to 1310

Walsingham priory: two holy wells (Tweyne Wells) located to east of site of conventual church, sides lined with ashlar; medieval date

Waltham abbey: Doom painting in lady chapel; C15

Westminster abbey: 1. intact timber gallery (Abbot's Pew) projecting from inner side of south wall of south nave aisle at west end; early C16

2. intact bridge chantry of Henry V over eastern end of choir; mid C15

3. unusual arrangement of east cloister-walk in relation to south transept; c.1250

4. intact bay of east range undercroft used as prison, located immediately south of passage to former infirmary from Dark Cloister; mid C11

5. largely intact Cosmati work ornamenting tomb of Henry III; late C13

6. intact chapel of St. Edward the Confessor (Chapel of the Kings) containing shrine in which body of saint is located, also unique ring of royal tombs under which are bodies of medieval kings & queens; 1245/55

7. internal dimensions of nave (height to width) far greater than in any other English medieval church & approach those of French churches; C13

Whalley abbey: 1. high-standing ruined bridge connecting dorter to reredorter; C14

2. intact though silted up drain through intact arches of reredorter; C14

St. Clear's cell: intact richly ornamented Norman arch at entrance to choir, consists of 2 orders plus rear stepped sub-arch; C12

Wigmore abbey: intact undercroft below abbot's lodging, displaying rare 6-bay timber arcade; C14/C15

Winchelsea friary: high-standing choir displaying apse at east end; early C14

Winchester cathedral-priory: 6 intact mortuary chests standing on top of lateral stone screens of choir, containing bones of pre-Conquest English kings; queens & bishops; early C16

Worcester cathedral-priory: 1. deteriorated painting of Christ in Majesty on east wall of refectory; c.1220/30

2. intact & chipped effigy of King John on tomb, facial likeness believed to be based on fact; c.1230

3. unusual layout of east & west cloister ranges with dormitory & reredorter on west side; originating in early C12

Wymondham abbey: 1. intact hammerbeam roof of nave; C15

2. high-standing roofless octagonal tower; c.1390/1400

Yarmouth priory: floor plan (narrow central aisles & wide side aisles) & general immense size of church; C12, C13, C19, but now mainly 1957-1961

18/2 OTHER BUILDINGS OR UNDERCROFTS WITHIN PRECINCTS OR ON OTHER SITES THAT DO NOT FIT THE NORMAL CLAUSTRAL ARRANGEMENT OR ARE DIFFICULT TO INTERPRET

Abbotsbury abbey: intact 2 small outbuildings to south east of parish church; C14 & pDp

Ansty commandery: intact rectangular building which may have been hospitium, now barn; early C16

Ashridge priory/college: [intact undercroft below Gothic-style mansion, with octagonal piers without caps & single chamfered ribs; C13]

Baswich priory: confused precinct site converted into farm buildings, reportedly parts of conventional church & 2 ranges; C13

Beverley Dominican friary: large intact rambling building, built partly of stone & partly of brick; unknown date

Brewood Benedictine priory: [intact T-shaped house of brick with mullioned & transomed windows; late C15/early C16]

Bruern abbey: [intact groin vaulted 3-bay chamber in Georgian cottage; unknown date]

Buckland abbey: [intact embattled building (Tower Cottage) standing to north of cloister area, may have been abbot's lodging & possibly connected to former east range; C15, pDp]

Cambridge Buckingham college (now part of Magdalene college):   intact chapel & hall (First Court); c.1430, C18, 1876

Cammeringham priory: [intact undercroft below rear range of post-Dissolution building (Manor House); unknown date]

Canterbury Franciscan friary: intact rectangular building straddling river Stour, may have been warden's lodging; C13

Chacombe priory: [intact house (The Priory) includes to north of east end a short building (The Chapel) of 2 storeys; late C13]

Clattercote priory: [intact quadripartite vaulted undercroft of 2 bays incorporated into post-Dissolution domestic building; C13/C14]

Clifford priory: [intact stone range forming part of Priory Farm, roof with cusped wind braces; C14]

Cogges priory: [intact building north of church (recently vicarage) incorporating pre-Dissolution sections; C13, C16, C19]

Coventry charterhouse: intact confused range of ashlar, with probable refectory on first floor; late C14/C15

Dinmore commandery: intact manor house exhibiting constructional work of several medieval & later periods, architectural relationship to conventual church nearby uncertain; C12 onwards, modern

Ecclesfield priory: intact building (including chapel with undercroft) forming core of post-Dissolution house (The Priory), 100 yds. north of parish church; c.1300, C16/C17, 1736

Gloucester Lanthony priory: intact half-timbered building, of domestic use; C15/C16

Grace Dieu priory: confused but quite high ruined set of monastic buildings, converted into post-Dissolution mansion & subsequently partly pulled down; mainly C15 & C16

Hinton charterhouse: [intact 3 storeyed & 4 gabled building, including vaulted chapel (ground floor), library & dovecot (middle floor) & another dovecot (top floor); C13]

Jervaulx abbey: intact rambling private house, believed to be gatehouse; late C12, C19

Kerswell cell: [intact farmhouse reportedly constructed on site of conventual church, displaying medieval fabric some *in situ* & some reset; C12, C17, C18]

King's Langley friary: [intact 2-storeyed building now incorporated into premises of private school, rectangular with crownpost roof; unknown date]

Kirklees priory: intact portion of building possibly gatehouse built into farmhouse, no visible archways or gate-hall; unknown date

London friary: [intact simple vaulted undercroft, beneath west side of Freshfields building (Whitefriars St.); probably C14]

Maiden Bradley priory: [intact L-shaped building of outer non-claustral ranges, with late medieval architectural features; C15/C16]

Meaux abbey: [intact cottage on site of abbey with medieval masonry & now museum, original purpose unknown; C13, pDp]

Moatenden friary: [intact small Tudor building of brick incorporated into post-Dissolution farm building; C15/C16]

Newstead Gilbertine priory: [intact vaulted chamber of 2 bays inside farmhouse, with central octagonal pier; C12/C13]

Norwich Carmelite friary: intact undercroft of unknown purpose 70 yds. north of gateway; flint & brick walls c.1300, sexpartite rib vaulting probably C15

Ovingham cell: intact building (Old Vicarage) south of conventual church, said to have been hostel for canons; C14 & later

Poling commandery: [intact single building (now Fairplace Farm) apparently representing original hall & contiguous small church; C13/C14, c.1830]

Ruthin priory: intact building (the Old Cloisters) immediately to north of conventual church & much modified since Dissolution, with original 5-bay vaulted undercroft, C14, pDp

Rye Sack friary: intact ecclesiastical-style building in Church Square, with Gothic windows: later C13

Salisbury friary: [rear (south) portion of intact post-Dissolution building (Windover House) retains small timber framed hall & 2-storeyed structure; C14, early C16, early C17]

Sele friary: vaulted undercroft of uncertain condition below house (The Priory) immediately north of church; unknown date

Shrewsbury friary: intact stone-fronted building near river converted into 3 cottages, diplays Perp. windows with some tracery; C15/C16

Snainton preceptory: [intact great hall hidden within post-Dissolution farmhouse; c.1288, C18]

Spalding priory: [intact brick range (Abbey Buildings) with stone dressings; C15]

Stonely priory: [intact small stone domestic building, with single chamfered doorway & 4-centred arch; c.1500]

Strood preceptory: intact stone & brick building, consisting of great hall above rib vaulted undercroft; c.1240, C17

Swaffham Bulbeck priory: [intact vaulted undercroft below post-Dissolution mansion (Abbey House), with one row of octagonal piers & 5 bays; late C13/early C14, house 1778]

Tarrant abbey: [intact farmhouse (Tarrant Abbey House), medieval part said to be guesthouse; C15]

Temple Balsall preceptory: intact set of domestic buildings, including parlour & great hall; C13, C15, pDp

Temple Combe preceptory: [intact barnlike long building, possibly refectory & kitchen; C13/C14, pDp]

Thetford St. George's priory: intact but considerably altered domestic building of nunnery, converted into farmhouse & now offices; lmp, early C17, 1990-91

Welnetham friary: [intact picturesque house (Chapel Hill Farm) displaying some medieval features such as angle buttress & flint walling; C15(?), pDp]

Wilmington priory: largely intact set of domestic buildings to south of church, including vaulted porch, prior's chapel & vaulted undercroft etc.; C13, C14

Wolston cell: [intact building (The Priory), displays variety of medieval architectural artefacts; C13, C15/ C16, pDp]

Worcester St. Wustan's hospital: intact half-timbered building of Commandery, mainly occupied by great hall; late C15

◆◆◆◆◆◆◆◆◆◆◆◆◆◆◆◆

Section 19:
MOST SURVIVING MONASTIC SITES CONSIDERED AS A WHOLE

19/1   BENEDICTINE ORDER

Two houses display the 4-sided claustral arrangement where many of the individual buildings round them are intact. They are:-

Durham cathedral-priory: intact conventual church, intact 4 cloister-walks, intact south range including sub-frater (i.e. intact refectory & intact kitchen leading off), east range almost completely intact (including partly rebuilt chapter-house etc.), intact west range (including sub-dorter and dormitory overhead), also intact gatehouse.
Chester abbey: intact conventual church, intact 4 cloister-walks, almost intact north range (i.e. intact refectory, but fragmentary kitchen), intact east range sub-dorter (including intact chapter-house & vestibule; upper storey dismantled), & intact west range sub-dorter (upper storey dismantled), also intact: main gatehouse (upper story partly rebuilt) & 2 small gateways.

Other Benedictine houses also display considerable remains, yet at the same time totally lack some of their former main buildings.   These houses & their chief surviving remains are:-

Birkenhead priory: high-standing west range, & now roofed & intact north range

Canterbury cathedral-priory: intact buildings including church, 4 cloister-walks, much of east range especially chapter-house, & various other (non-claustral) buildings; also high-standing ruined infirmary

Ely cathedral-priory: intact buildings including church, west range & its attached & closely associated buildings, & several gatehouses; also high-standing ruined infirmary with superimposed intact medieval houses

Finchale priory: almost all is ruined but much high-standing, especially church, refectory & prior's house

Gloucester abbey: intact buildings including church, 4 cloister-walks, much of east range especially chapter-house, infirmary cloister-walks, abbot's lodgings & gatehouses

Norwich cathedral-priory: intact buildings include church, 4 cloister-walks, prior's lodging & gatehouses,

Peterborough abbey: intact buildings including church, abbot's lodging & gatehouses; high-standing ruined infirmary

Westminster abbey: intact buildings including church, 4 cloister-walks, east range, extended part of west range & abbot's lodging

Worcester cathedral-priory: intact buildings including church, 4 cloister-walks, east range, refectory & gatehouse; also high-standing ruined guest-house

19/2 CISTERCIAN ORDER

All sites of this order are to a greater or lesser extent ruined. In two cases - Fountains and Kirkstall - much of the stone has been retain *in situ*, permitting a good visual impression of what houses of this order must have been like. But only Cleeve abbey displays some major buildings round the cloister which are intact:-

Cleeve abbey: intact east & south ranges, & part of west range, high-standing ruined gatehouse.

Fountains abbey: high-standing ruined conventual church (excluding crossing & arcades of choir), high-standing ruined south & east ranges (excluding largely destroyed chapter-house), intact undercroft of west range (upper storey roofless but otherwise intact), with most of other buildings in greater state of destruction.

Kirkstall abbey: high-standing ruined conventual church, high-standing ruined east range (including intact chapter-house) & south range, west range largely destroyed, intact gatehouse (converted to other use) & lay-brothers' reredorter, many other buildings may be identified but are in greater state of destruction.

Other Cistercian houses display considerable high-standing ruined remains, but with many key buildings totally vanished. These houses & their surviving remnants are:-

Furness abbey: east part of church & west tower, east range, part of infirmary & gatehouses

Netley abbey: walls of church, & east range & infirmary

Rievaulx: east part of church & refectory

Tintern abbey: church (except for part of nave) & warming-house area

Surviving sets of buildings of this order (& others) are all less extensive than those of the Benedictines & Cistercians. Three houses display considerable remains:-

Bristol abbey: intact conventual church (nave rebuilt in C19), intact east cloister-walk, east range (especially chapter-house), much of south range (absorbed into school buildings) & gatehouse; some buildings around little cloister survive in modified form

Carlisle cathedral-priory: intact conventual church (shorn of nave), intact double-storeyed refectory & intact gatehouse, detached prior's lodging

Penmon priory: small house retaining intact conventual cruciform church, intact south range (of 3 storeys) & west range (converted into house).

Other Augustinian houses displaying some remains:-

Haughmond abbey: intact chapter-house, significant ruins of infirmary/abbot's lodging, kitchen etc.

Lacock abbey: cloister-walks & 3 ranges converted into existing post-Dissolution mansion

Llanthony priory: intact west range (hotel) & infirmary (now parish church), high-standing ruin of much of conventual church

Newstead Augustinian priory: cloister-walks & 3 ranges converted into existing post-Dissolution mansion

Oxford St. Frideswide's priory: all surviving buildings intact including church, east & south ranges

19/4   OTHER CONTEMPLATIVE ORDERS

Of the *Cluniac* houses, only **Wenlock priory** & **Castle Acre priory** have something substantial to show. At Wenlock, besides some high-standing ruins of conventual church & chapter-house, are intact portions of infirmary buildings; at Castle Acre are intact portions of west range & ruined church. **Delapre abbey** was the house of Cluniac nuns. Although its medieval buildings have almost totally been replaced by post-Dissolution domestic structures, the original four-sided layout round the cloister is still evident.

The best *Premonstratensian* remains are to be seen at **Bayham abbey** & **Leiston abbey** (especially high-standing ruined portions of conventual churches), **Easby abbey** (high-standing ruined buildings round the cloister) & **Torre abbey** (intact south & west ranges, & intact gatehouse). A very reduced conventual church survives as parish church at **Blanchland abbey.**

The indigenous *Gilbertine* order displays little remains. At **Malton priory** is a reduced but intact conventual church but little else; at **Chicksands priory**, there are three intact sides of the cloister; & at **Mattersey priory**, some of buildings round the cloister stand fairly high.

The order of *Tiron* founded few houses in England or Wales. The only site to retain substantial buildings which are all intact is **Caldey cell** (conventual church, east & west ranges). **St. Dogmael's abbey** though destroyed, displays some high-standing remnants (especially the church & infirmary).

19/4 Mount Grace charterhouse, view across great
cloister garth to south west

To see a house of the *Carthusian* order, the site to visit is
that of **Mount Grace charterhouse** (high-standing ruins,
especially the conventual church; also a reconstructed
brother's house). The **London charterhouse** also
possesses some quite extensive remains but these are
largely mixed up with post-Dissolution work.

19/5 MENDICANT ORDERS

Layout of friaries was never standardised to the same
extent as houses of contemplative orders. Hence it is not
possible to identify a typical friary even if one exists. The
most complete house undoubtedly is the **Norwich.
Dominican friary** which displays an intact conventual

church (less tower), an intact east cloister-walk (with dormitory over), an intact west cloister-walk (with refectory over) & intact south cloister-walk (abutting the church). Also having much to show is the **Gloucester Dominican friary** (severely reduced & modified but intact conventual church, with intact south range & also parts of east & west ranges). A ruined site is evident at **Walsingham Franciscan friary** (high-standing ruins of arcading of little cloister, kitchen & guest-house)

Other mendicant houses less complete than these are :-

Bristol Dominican friary: intact portions of cloister ranges especially north range
Coventry Carmelite friary: intact portions of cloister ranges especially east range, also intact gatehouse
Gloucester Franciscan friary: ruined high-standing 2-aisled & 7-bay nave of conventual church
Newcastle-upon-Tyne Dominican friary: intact portions of cloister-ranges especially south & west)
Ware Franciscan friary: intact south range, part of west range & guest-house)

19/6   MILITARY ORDERS

Of the *Knights Templar* & the *Knights Hospitaller*, very little survives to give an indication of what their houses were like. Though one or two of their churches, and other single buildings are intact, the only site where more than this may be seen, is that of **Temple Balsall preceptory** (intact conventual church, hall & parlour). Another is the **Chibburn commandery** in Northumberland where though ruined, sufficient of the buildings has survived (chapel, living accommodation, small courtyard & surrounding moat) to indicated what a house of the Knights Hospitaller was like.

◆◆◆◆◆◆◆◆◆◆◆◆◆◆◆◆

Section 20
SUMMARY OF COMPOSITE
ADAPTATIONS AROUND THE CLOISTER

N.B. In many of the instances given below, only **part** of the particular fabric was adapted, the remainder usually having been destroyed. This has been noted accordingly

20/1 Three ranges of claustral area converted to various usages (with church surviving on fourth side)

Cambridge St. Radegund's priory - *into premises comprising Jesus college (university of Cambridge)*
church on south side of cloister
east range (part) intact
north range intact
west range intact

Chester abbey *into premises of newly created cathedral (diocese of Chester)*
church on south side of cloister
east range (undercroft) intact
north range (refectory) intact
west range (undercroft) intact

Delapre abbey - *altered drastically by successive rebuilds & modifications (now in care of Northampton borough council)*
church (some walls only) on north side of cloister
east range (part) intact
south range (part) intact
west range (part) intact

Durham cathedral-priory - *into premises of refounded cathedral (diocese of Durham)*

church on north side of cloister
east range (part) (plus extension) intact
south range intact
west range intact

Gloucester Dominican friary – *converted into manufactories (now in care of English Heritage)*
church (converted into private residence, Bell's Place) on north side of cloister
east range (small part at north end) intact
south range intact
west range (small part at north end) intact

Norwich cathedral-priory – *converted into premises of refounded cathedral (diocese of Norwich)*
church on north side of cloister
all ranges destroyed but...
4 two-storeyed cloister arcades intact

20/2 Three ranges of claustral area converted to various usages (church destroyed)

Birkenhead priory – *into private property (now in care of Wirral borough council)*
east range (chapter-house) intact
north range (recently restored) intact
west range high-standing ruin

Bristol Dominican friary - *into private residence & later, friends' meeting place known as Quaker Friars (now register office in care of city of Bristol corporation)*
east range intact
north range intact
south range (part) intact

Chicksands priory – *altered drastically & successively into private residence (now MOD property)*
east range (part) intact
west range (part) intact

south range (part) intact

Cleeve abbey – *into private residence & farm buildings (now in care of English Heritage)*
east range intact
south range intact
west range (part) intact

Forde abbey - *into private residence*
east range intact
north range intact
west range intact

Lacock abbey - *into private residence (now in care of National Trust)*
east range intact
north range intact
west range intact

Newcastle-upon-Tyne Dominican friary – *into manufactory used by trades guilds (in care of city of Newcastle corporation)*
east range (part) intact
south range intact
west range intact

Newstead Augustinian priory - *into private residence (now in care of city of Nottingham corporation)*
east range intact
south range intact
west range intact

20/3 Two ranges of claustral area [east range + south (or north) range] converted to various usages (with church surviving on fourth side)

Bristol abbey *into premises divided between newly created cathedral (diocese of Bristol) & school*
church on north side of cloister
east range intact

south range (now school premises) intact

Easebourne priory - *into private residence, but refectory now church property*
church on north side of cloister
east range (part) intact
south range (refectory) intact

King's Lynn priory – *divided into private residences*
church on north side of cloister
east range (part) intact
south range (with gatehouse) intact

Oxford St. Frideswide's priory - *into premises shared between newly created cathedral (diocese of Oxford) & Christ Church (college of university of Oxford)*
church on north side of cloister
east range (now cathedral premises) intact
south range (now college premises) intact

Worcester cathedral-priory - *into premises shared between refounded cathedral (diocese of Worcester) & school*
church on north side of cloister
east range (part) (cathedral premises) intact
south range (refectory now school premises) intact

20/4 Two ranges of claustral area [east range + south (or north) range] converted to various usages (church destroyed)

Calder abbey - *into private residence*
east range (part ruin & part intact undercroft) incorporated into house
south range – incorporated into house

20/5 Two ranges of claustral area [south (or north) range + west range] converted to various usages (with church surviving on fourth side)

Blanchland abbey - *into private residences*
church on north side of cloister
south range (now row of cottages) intact
west range (now hotel) intact

Lanercost priory - *into storage accommodation (now in care of English Heritage) & domestic accommodation (now in care of parish council)*
church on north side of cloister
south range (undercroft) intact
west range(part) intact

Penmon priory - *into private residences (south range now ruined, in care of CADW)*
church on north side of cloister
south range now ruined
west range (now private residence) intact

20/6 Two ranges of claustral area [south (or north) range + west range] converted to various usages (church destroyed)

Aylesford friary - *into private residence (now in care of modern religious community)*
south range (mainly refectory) intact
west range (plus extension) intact

Beaulieu abbey - *part into church (diocese of Winchester) & part into private storage accommodation)*
south range (refectory now church) intact
west range intact

Bradenstoke priory - *into private residence (mostly recently removed to & re-erected at St. Donat's castle, South Wales; part of west range undercroft staying on site)*
south(?) range (refectory) removed
west range part removed & part on site

Exeter St. Nicholas' priory - *into private residences & other uses (west range now in care of city of Exeter corporation)*
north range (part) intact
west range intact

Michelham priory – *into private residence (now in care of Sussex Archaeological Trust)*
south range intact
west range (part) intact

Prittlewell priory - *into private residence (now in care of Southend-on-Sea county borough council)*
south range (refectory) intact
west range (part) intact

Shulbrede priory - *into private residence*
south range (refectory) intact
west range intact

Torre abbey - *into private residence (now in care of Torbay county borough council)*
south range intact
west range intact

Vale Royal abbey *into private residence (now divided into apartments)*
south range (part) intact but considerably modified
west range intact but also considerably modified

Ware friary –*into private residence & now council offices (in care of Ware town council)*
south range intact
west range (part) intact

20/7 East & west ranges converted separately to various usages (with church surviving on fourth side)

Caldey cell – *into private domestic & storage accommodation (now in care of modern religious community)*
church on south side of cloister
east range (part) intact
west range (including gatehouse) intact

Norwich Dominican friary - *into storage facilities &, later a variety of other uses (now in care of city of Norwich corporation)*
church on south side of cloister
east range intact
west range intact

Westminster abbey - *into premises shared by collegiate establishment, Crown & school*
church on north side of cloister
east range intact
west range (part) plus extension intact

20/8 East & west ranges converted separately to various usages (church destroyed)

Battle abbey – *into private residence (now school) & storage facilities (now in care of English Heritage)*
east range (south end) now ruined
west range(school accommodation) plus extension intact

Neath abbey - *part into private residence & part into manufactory (whole site now in care of CADW)*
east range (part) into private residence now ruined
west range eventually into manufactory now ruined

St. Osyth abbey (parts) – *into private residence*
east range (undercroft at north end) intact

west range (small part at north end) plus extension of bishop's lodging intact

20/9 Single range only converted to various usages (with church surviving on fourth side)

Abergavenny priory - *probably into private residence (now part of Priory Centre)*
church on north side of cloister
east range (north end) intact

Brecon priory - *into private residence (now Canonry of recently founded cathedral of Swansea & Brecon)*
church on north side of cloister
west range remodelled & intact

Brinkburn priory - *into private residence (now in care of National Trust)*
church on north side of cloister
south range (mainly refectory) incorporated within mansion

Canterbury cathedral-priory – *into premises of refounded cathedral (diocese of Canterbury)*
church on south side of cloister
east range (chapter-house & part of undercroft) intact

Carlisle cathedral-priory - *into premises of refounded cathedral (diocese of Carlisle)*
church on north side of cloister
south range (refectory) intact

Davington priory – *into private residence*
church on north side of cloister
west range intact

Deerhurst priory – *into private residence*
church on north side of cloister
east range (shell of building) intact

Denney abbey – *into farm accommodation (now in care of English Heritage)*
church on south side of cloister
north range (refectory) intact as barn

Dunster priory – *into private residence*
church on south side of cloister
west range (part) intact

Ely cathedral-priory – *into premises divided between refounded cathedral (diocese of Ely) & school*
church on north side of cloister
west range (part) & extensions intact

Gloucester abbey - *into premises of newly created cathedral (diocese of Gloucester)*
church on south side of cloister
east range (chapter-house & part of undercroft) intact

Great Bricett priory – *into private residence*
church on south side of cloister
west range intact

Hexham priory – *into private residence (now council offices)*
church on north side of cloister
west range intact

Hurley priory - *into private residence*
church on south side of cloister
north range (refectory) intact

Little Malvern priory – *into private residence*
church on north side of cloister
west range intact

Malton priory - *into outbuilding of private residence*
church on north side of cloister
south range (undercroft) intact

Margam abbey - *into private residence & storage facilities (now in care of Margam Country Park)*
church on north side of cloister
east range (chapter-house & vestibule) now ruined

Mottisfont priory – *into private residence (now in care of National Trust)*
church (now part of house) on north side of cloister
west range (part of undercroft) intact

Polesworth abbey – *into private residence (& now vicarage)*
church on north side of cloister
west range (part) intact

Romsey abbey - *into private residence*
church on north side of cloister
south range (refectory) intact

St. Anthony-in-Roseland cell - *into part of private residence*
church on south side of cloister
east range (non-standard sited refectory) intact

20/9 St. Anthony-in-Roseland, view of Place House
to south, with steeple of conventual church
peeping over the top

St. Germans priory - *into part of private residence*
church on north side of cloister
south range (refectory) intact

Sherborne abbey – *into school accommodation*
church on south side of cloister
west range plus extension intact

Thurgarton priory – *into private residence*
church on north side of cloister
west range (undercroft) intact

Totnes priory - *into civic accommodation (in care of Totnes town council)*
church on north side of cloister
south range (refectory) intact as guildhall

Winchester cathedral-priory - *into premises of refounded cathedral (diocese of Winchester)*
church on north side of cloister
east range (extension of south end: prior's lodging) intact

◆◆◆◆◆◆◆◆◆◆◆◆◆◆◆◆

A Final Word from the Author

I am aware that the script may contain factual errors and omissions, although I hope not many. I should therefore be pleased to receive details of them so that if a revised edition is published, appropriate corrections may be made

♦♦♦♦♦♦♦♦♦♦♦♦♦♦♦♦

Notes

Notes

Notes

Notes

ISBN 1412026040

9 781412 026048